THE PARADOX OF PROFESSIONALISM

This book is ab[illegible] its central objective is to provide a de[illegible] between lawyers' commercial aims and public aspi[illegible] and comparative perspectives, it explores whether [illegible] to meaningfully contribute to systems of political acco[illegible] and distributional fairness. Its contributors – some of the world's [illegible] the legal profession – offer evidence that although justice is possible, it is never compl[illegible]ately, how much – and what type of – justice prevails depends on how lawyers respond to, and reshape, the political and economic conditions in which they practice. As the chapters demonstrate, the possibility of justice is diminished as lawyers pursue self-regulation in the service of power; it is enhanced when lawyers mobilize – in the political arena, workplace, and law school – to contest it.

Scott L. Cummings is a Professor of Law at the University of California, Los Angeles, where he is also the faculty coordinator of the Epstein Program in Public Interest Law and Policy. He specializes in the legal profession, law and social change, and economic development.

The Paradox of Professionalism

LAWYERS AND THE POSSIBILITY OF JUSTICE

Edited by

SCOTT L. CUMMINGS

University of California, Los Angeles, School of Law

CAMBRIDGE
UNIVERSITY PRESS

CAMBRIDGE UNIVERSITY PRESS
Cambridge, New York, Melbourne, Madrid, Cape Town,
Singapore, São Paulo, Delhi, Tokyo, Mexico City

Cambridge University Press
32 Avenue of the Americas, New York, NY 10013-2473, USA

www.cambridge.org
Information on this title: www.cambridge.org/9780521145992

First published 2011

Printed in the United States of America

A catalog record for this publication is available from the British Library.

Library of Congress Cataloging in Publication data
The paradox of professionalism : lawyers and the possibility of justice / edited
by Scott L. Cummings.
p. cm
Includes bibliographical references and index.
ISBN 978-0-521-19268-2 (hardback) – ISBN 978-0-521-14599-2 (paperback)
1. Lawyers – Congresses. 2. Sociological jurisprudence – Congresses.
3. Practice of law – Congresses. 4. Legal ethics – Congresses. I. Cummings,
Scott L., 1969– II. Title.
K117.P366 2011
173′.4–dc22 2010045749

ISBN 978-0-521-19268-2 Hardback
ISBN 978-0-521-14599-2 Paperback

Contents

Tables and Figures

TABLES

FIGURES

Contributors

Richard L. Abel, Michael J. Connell Professor of Law Emeritus, UCLA School of Law

Penelope Andrews, Associate Dean for Academic Affairs and Professor, CUNY School of Law

Scott L. Cummings, Professor of Law, UCLA School of Law

Marc Galanter, John and Rylla Professor of Law and South Asian Studies, University of Wisconsin Law School

Robert W. Gordon, Chancellor Kent Professor of Law and Legal History, Yale Law School

Terence C. Halliday, Research Professor, American Bar Foundation

John P. Heinz, Research Professor Emeritus, American Bar Foundation, and Owen L. Coon Professor Emeritus, Northwestern University School of Law

Carrie Hempel, Associate Dean of Clinical Education and Service Learning Programs, University of California, Irvine, School of Law

Philip Lewis, Associate Research Fellow, University of Oxford Centre for Socio-Legal Studies

Lynn Mather, Professor of Law and Political Science, University at Buffalo, State University of New York

Frank Munger, Professor of Law, New York Law School

John T. Nockleby, Professor of Law and Director of the Civil Justice Program, Loyola Law School

Anthony Paik, Assistant Professor, Department of Sociology, University of Iowa

Deborah L. Rhode, Ernest W. McFarland Professor of Law and Director, Center on the Legal Profession, Stanford Law School

Carroll Seron, Professor, Department of Criminology, Law and Society, University of California, Irvine

Ann Southworth, Professor of Law, University of California, Irvine, School of Law

Lucie E. White, Louis A. Horvitz Professor of Law, Harvard Law School

Preface and Acknowledgments

This book is a testament to the power of one person to make a difference. It grew out of a conference in September 2009 honoring the extraordinary legacy of Richard L. Abel, whose field-defining work on the legal profession has been a gift to all of us who care deeply about law as an instrument of justice. Abel's career has spanned – and helped define – the trajectory of contemporary sociolegal thought. He was a founding member of the law-and-society movement, editor of the *Law & Society Review*, and president of the Law and Society Association, which in 1989 bestowed on him its prestigious Harry J. Kalven Prize honoring the powerful impact of his overall body of scholarly work. He participated in the founding conference on Critical Legal Studies and helped organize the meeting on "Law and Racism: The Sounds of Silence," which contributed to the development of Critical Race Theory. His scholarly influence is broad, spanning the legal profession, disputing, law and social change, and torts. He is perhaps best known for fundamentally reshaping our understanding of the role of lawyers in society – focusing attention on their collective quest for power while also highlighting their individual struggles to redistribute it. It is this paradox at the heart of lawyers' "professional project" that is explored in this volume.

The 2009 conference also marked Abel's enormous influence on his community. It was organized to honor the occasion of his retirement from the UCLA School of Law, where he spent thirty-five years as brilliant scholar, beloved teacher, and esteemed colleague. He has touched a generation of students and mentored a legion of junior scholars – always with his characteristic warmth and generosity. Indeed, many of the conference participants spoke fondly of his influence. Perhaps his most enduring institutional legacy – and the one of which he is most proud – is the creation of the Program in Public Interest Law and Policy, which graduated its first class in 2000 and now counts nearly 300 graduates among its ranks.

While we have Abel's life work to thank for inspiring the conference, there are many others to thank for actually carrying it to fruition. The conference itself (and therefore this book) would not have been possible without the tremendous generosity of Michael Schill, who was Dean of the UCLA School of Law when it took place. His enthusiastic support was crucial in allowing us to bring together such a stellar lineup of world-class scholars. A special thanks also goes to the Epstein Program in Public Interest Law and Policy, whose directors, Cathy Mayorkas and Rochelle Adelman, contributed enormously to organizing the conference, and to Vice Dean Devon Carbado for his warm introductory remarks. I am grateful to my colleague Noah Zatz for prodding me to advance this project as part of a joint celebration of UCLA's two law and society giants, Rick Abel and Joel Handler. Last but not least, I am forever indebted to UCLA's Summer Rose, whose tireless efforts made the conference possible.

The contributors to this volume all participated in the conference, which also included other important scholars in the field of sociolegal studies and beyond, who I must thank for enriching the discussion. Robert Nelson, Director of the American Bar Foundation and Professor of Law and Sociology at Northwestern University, provided important insights on legal professionalism, while Bryant Garth, Dean of Southwestern Law School, offered a wonderfully nuanced international perspective. Gary Blasi, Professor of Law at UCLA, was the ideal facilitator for a discussion on "law and the power to change," and Kimberle Crenshaw, also from UCLA, was a brilliant interlocutor on our "law and social theory" panel. Others presented compelling papers: Professor Laura Gómez from the University of New Mexico School of Law spoke eloquently of law and racial inequality; Professor Christine Harrington from New York University gave a fascinating account of the politics of sociolegal theory; Professor Sally Engle Merry, also from NYU, discussed the role of indicators in global governance; and Professor Avrom Sherr traveled all the way from the University of London's Institute of Advanced Legal Studies to give an uproariously funny – and at the same time devastatingly serious – analysis of the reaction to Abel's work on the legal profession in England (which was published in a 2009 issue of the *International Journal of the Legal Profession*). Finally, I am deeply indebted to Marc Galanter and David Trubek, both towering figures in the law-and-society movement from Wisconsin Law School (and longtime friends of Abel), who gave absorbing, powerful, and moving speeches about Abel and his legacy.

This book is, in the end, a labor of love, dedicated to Rick Abel – my dear friend and mentor. Though your own professional project may remain unfinished, it lives on in all of us whom you have nurtured and inspired.

SLC
Los Angeles, California

1

Introduction

What Good Are Lawyers?

Scott L. Cummings

INTRODUCTION

What good are lawyers? It depends, of course, on whom you ask. Most Americans are ambivalent: When they are in need of help, they call a lawyer – and when they do, they are, more often than not, happy with the services that their lawyers provide.[1] Nonetheless, Americans generally hold lawyers as a group in low repute, suspecting that they are more concerned with collecting fees than serving the public good.[2]

This public cynicism reflects a fundamental paradox at the heart of the legal profession. The very notion that lawyers are members of a "profession" suggests a delicate balance of incentives and duties that pull in different directions. In the United States (as in most countries), lawyers are freely engaged in the commercial enterprise of rendering services for a fee. They are permitted – and indeed encouraged – to make money, often lots of it,[3] within the boundaries of broad rules, such as those limiting overly aggressive (or misleading) solicitation and advertising.[4] As professionals, they are accorded wide discretion to define their own standards for admission and rules of conduct in order to promote craft expertise and quality service. In exchange for this privilege, lawyers are expected to embrace a set of public values – a code of "professionalism" defined by a commitment to competence, independence, and public service – distinguishing them from "mere" commercial actors. They are asked, in short, to be "public citizens" with a special obligation to promote the "administration of justice."[5] This dual status – in the market, but above it; diligent servants of clients, but also special guardians of the "public interest" – raises our

[1] Leo J. Shapiro & Associates, Public Perceptions of Lawyers: Consumer Research Findings 19 (Am. Bar Ass'n 2002), *available at* http://www.abanet.org/litigation/lawyers/publicperceptions.pdf.

[2] *Id.* at 7.

[3] In 2009, the average profit per partner at the Am Law 100 firms was $1.26 million.

[4] *See* Model Rules of Prof'l Conduct R. 7.2, 7.3.

[5] Model Rules of Prof'l Conduct, Preamble: A Lawyer's Responsibilities.

expectations of lawyer conduct. And it inevitably causes disappointment when our expectations are not met.[6]

Over the past half-century, scholars have struggled with the fundamental professional paradox and the disappointment that it has produced. A core debate within this literature focuses on which facet of legal practice – the public-regarding or the self-interested, the political or the commercial – constitutes the central aim of the professional project.[7] Put simply, is the professional project a political one – defined by the protection and extension of fundamental rights and equality under law – or is it instead a commercial one – determined by lawyers' material interest in maximizing the return on their services? Do lawyers stand for justice? Or are they an impediment to its full realization?

The answers to these questions are more complex than such simple dichotomies suggest. What we know is that different lawyers, at different times, in different places stand for different projects. This is true both within countries and across them. No one would mistake the central project of contemporary American lawyers with that of their Pakistani counterparts, many of whom so prominently took to the streets and risked their lives in 2007 to protest General Musharraf's disregard for judicial independence. Professional projects, therefore, vary based on political and economic conditions, and change over time: It matters whether lawyers operate in a less developed authoritarian state or in a highly developed liberal democratic one, whether they are part of a political epoch powered by the struggle for new democratic possibilities or mired in affluent complacency. Projects, like the profession itself, are also internally differentiated. Whereas we may speak of a plurality of legal professions, we may also identify a plurality of competing projects – some oriented toward more money and power, others toward more equality and empowerment. This does not mean that there are no commonalities or structural trends. Nor does it suggest the absence of a central professional logic operating under certain conditions – such as an advanced capitalist economy conjoined with a liberal democratic state. To the contrary, our recognition of competing projects implies that there are winners and losers, and that we may ultimately tally score.

It may also be the case that the *same* lawyers simultaneously pursue different – and perhaps – competing projects. For instance, their actions may both enhance civil and political rights while undercutting economic and social ones; they may both promote access to justice through pro bono service while undermining it through practice restrictions. This duality also leaves open the possibility that individual lawyers may *believe* that they are advancing the cause of justice, when other observers would argue that they in fact are thwarting it. This disagreement could be a result of

6 *See* William H. Simon, The Practice of Justice: A Theory of Lawyers' Ethics 1 (1998).

7 Richard L. Abel, American Lawyers 20 (1989).

contested normative views – a liberal lawyer's project clashes with her conservative counterpart's. It could also be a product of false consciousness on the part of lawyers, whose subjective beliefs about the social value of their professional contributions could be falsified by objective measurement.

This book is about the role of lawyers in constructing a just society. Its central objective is to provide a deeper understanding of the relationship between lawyers' commercial aims and public aspirations. Toward this end, it presents original theoretical and empirical research by some of the world's leading scholars of the legal profession addressing the field's fundamental question: whether lawyers can transcend self-interest to meaningfully contribute to systems of political accountability, ethical advocacy, and distributional fairness. Drawing on interdisciplinary and comparative perspectives, the book's contributors offer evidence that although justice is possible, it is never complete. And in the ongoing struggle for justice, lawyers are complicated allies, often necessary – but never sufficient – for its achievement. As the essays demonstrate, lawyers take the most powerful stands for justice claims that are compatible with their collective interests, though episodically there are some who emerge as agents of transformative politics. Ultimately, how much – and what type of – justice prevails depends on how lawyers respond to, and reshape, the political and economic conditions in which they practice. The possibility of justice is diminished as lawyers pursue self-regulation in the service of power; it is enhanced when lawyers mobilize – in the political arena, workplace, and law school – to contest it.

PRACTICAL CONTEXT: PROFESSIONAL CRISIS AND THE POSSIBILITY OF JUSTICE

"You never want a serious crisis go to waste."[8] As political pundits know, crises are useful because they can convey messages – in simple, powerful terms – that expose underlying vulnerabilities, highlight the urgency of reform, and mobilize outrage to effectuate change. Reformers of the U.S. legal profession have long followed this piece of political wisdom.[9] Watergate helped spawn the American Bar Association (ABA) Model Rules of Professional Conduct and the modern system of professional ethics training in law school.[10] Enron brought significant changes to the professional rules governing when lawyers can break corporate client confidences.[11]

[8] *In Crisis, Opportunity for Obama*, Wall St. J., Nov. 21, 2008, at A2 (quoting Rahm Emanuel, White House Chief of Staff).

[9] Austin Sarat, *Enactments of Professionalism: A Study of Judges' and Lawyers' Accounts of Ethics and Civility in Litigation*, 67 Fordham L. Rev. 809 (1998–1999).

[10] *See* Carrie Hempel & Carroll Seron, *An Innovative Approach to Legal Education and the Founding of the University of California, Irvine School of Law* (in this volume).

[11] Model Rules of Prof'l Conduct R. 1.13.

The idea for this volume came at a moment of "crisis" for the legal profession in the United States and many other countries around the world caused by the global financial meltdown of 2008. Crisis talk, of course, is as old as the profession itself, so one should not overstate the peril of the current moment or rush to proclaim the end of old paradigms.[12] However, crises should serve a purpose and not be allowed to quietly recede in the rush to return to business as usual. In particular, they should be evaluated not just for what they demonstrate about how systems respond to extreme shock, but for what they reveal about the underlying distortions and contradictions that allowed pressure to build and the shock to have such destabilizing consequences. In this spirit, I describe the evolution of the U.S. model of dispensing "equal justice," not as a representative case, but a cautionary tale with important lessons about the impact of the professional project on the quantity and quality of legal services.

The 2008 recession posed a fundamental challenge to both the private and public interest sectors in the United States – and highlighted potential new synergies between them. The large law firm – the pinnacle of professional wealth and power – underwent a major restructuring characterized by partner terminations, salary reductions, and associate layoffs and deferrals. In the face of this upheaval, many large firms turned to temporary public interest placements as a way station for incoming or currently underemployed associates.[13] Large firms also increased their pro bono contributions, in part as a way to train underutilized associates. Yet, despite this short-term infusion of resources, legal aid and public interest organizations struggled to respond to low-income and underserved community needs, which were exacerbated by the recession. Public interest groups confronted their own deep staff and infrastructure cuts caused by a decline in law firm donations, foundation grants, and federal and state funding. At this moment of crisis, the contours – and vulnerabilities – of the U.S. public interest law system were thrown into sharp relief: Dependent on the monetary and volunteer resources of the private bar, nonprofit public interest groups rode their wave of support in good times and braced against their retrenchment in bad. How did this come to pass?

The seeds of this dilemma were sown in the previous decades by important changes in the structure of the American legal profession that expanded the role of the private sector in the delivery of public interest law services – both legal aid and

[12] Marc Galanter, *Lawyers in the Mist: The Golden Age of Legal Nostalgia*, 100 Dick L. Rev. 549 (1996).

[13] *See* Susan Dominus, *$80,000 for Year Off from Law? She'll Take It!*, N.Y. Times, Apr. 13, 2009, at A1; Jonathan D. Glater, *The Lawyer Squeeze: Layoffs and Closings in a Field Thought to Resist Downturns*, N.Y. Times, Nov. 12, 2008, at B1; Karen Sloan, *Trying to Make Deferrals into Something Positive*, Nat'l L.J., Apr. 13, 2009, at 6.

cause-oriented. One trend has been the relative growth in private practice. In the United States – as in many other countries around the world[14] – the number of lawyers has increased significantly since mid-century: more than fourfold, from 221,605 in 1951 to 1,066,328 in 2000,[15] and then to 1,180,386 in 2008.[16] This increase, which is more than double the rate of population growth, has rested on a fragile foundation. First, there has been an increase in entry to the profession. Law school enrollment – powered by the dramatic rise in the admission of women[17] – has grown from slightly more than 17,000 in 1951 to roughly 43,500 in 2000; by 2008, enrollment was just less than 50,000.[18] As student enrollment increased, so did tuition and, as a result, debt: increasing by 2005 to an average of over $50,000 for graduates of public law schools and nearly $80,000 for graduates of private ones.[19] Saddled with more debt after graduation, greater numbers entered private practice, which grew relative to the nonprofit and government sphere. And within private practice, the large firm, powered by its tournament model of growth,[20] expanded in relation to other private practice sites – from housing 7 percent of private sector lawyers in 1980 to 28 percent in 2000.[21]

During this time, law firms have become larger and more profitable. In the late 1950s, there were thirty-eight law firms with over fifty lawyers.[22] By 1990, over 600 firms had more than sixty lawyers and several had more than 1,000.[23] Not only did

[14] *See* Marc Galanter, *More Lawyers than People: The Global Multiplication of Legal Professionals* (in this volume).

[15] Clara N. Carson, The Lawyer Statistical Report: The U.S. Legal Profession in 2000 1 (2004). The success of supply control in the first half of the twentieth century artificially constrained the number of lawyers per capita; as this control eroded in the second half of the century, it helped unleash dramatic growth. *See* Abel, *supra* note 7, at 280 tbl. 22.

[16] Am. Bar Ass'n, Lawyer Demographics, *available at* http://new.abanet.org/marketresearch/PublicDocuments/Lawyer_Demographics.pdf.

[17] Carson, *supra* note 15, at 3.

[18] Bette H. Sikes, Clara N. Carson & Patricia Gorai, The 1971 Lawyer Statistical Report 20 (1972); Am. Bar Ass'n, Enrollment and Degrees Awarded, 1963–2008 Academic Years, *available at* http://www.abanet.org/legaled/statistics/charts/stats%20-%201.pdf. On the other end of the career cycle, more lawyers are living and working longer, leading to the growth of lawyers 65 or older. Leigh Jones, *Law Firm Retirement Policies Expected to Be Hot Issue at Annual ABA Meeting*, Nat'l L.J., Aug. 7, 2007 ("By some estimates, a full quarter of the country's 1 million attorneys – or 250,000 – will be at least 65 by 2011."); *see also* Marc Galanter, *"Old and in the Way": The Coming Demographic Transformation of the Legal Profession and Its Implications for the Provision of Legal Services*, 1999 Wis. L. Rev. 1081 (1999).

[19] Equal Justice Works, Financing the Future: Responses to the Rising Debt of Law Students 3 (2006).

[20] Marc Galanter & Thomas Palay, Tournament of Lawyers: The Transformation of the Big Law Firm (1994).

[21] Carson, *supra* note 15, at 8.

[22] *See* Galanter & Palay, *supra* note 20, at 46.

[23] *See* Carrie Menkel-Meadow, *Culture Clash in the Quality of Life in the Law: Changes in the Economics, Diversification and Organization of Lawyering*, 44 Case W. Res. L. Rev. 621, 629–30 (1994).

large firms grow in number, they also grew in size through mergers, satellite offices, and aggressive entry-level and lateral hiring.[24] In 1991, the average size of the Am Law 100 law firms was 375; by 2001, it was 621 and by 2008, 820.[25] As the big firms grew bigger, they also performed better, evident in increasing gross revenues and profits per partner.[26] Associate salaries also rose dramatically; in turn, billable hours increased.[27]

As large firms grew larger and more influential, they also came to play a greater role in the public interest law system. Indeed, one of the most significant trends over the past two decades has been the rise of pro bono activity, powered by the institutionalization of large-firm pro bono programs.[28] At the large-firm level, recent research on Am Law 200 firms shows that the total pro bono hours produced by such firms increased by nearly 80 percent between 1998 and 2005, while the per-lawyer average increased by five hours.[29] Between 2005 and 2008, total pro bono hours increased nearly 50 percent and the average hours per attorney grew by ten hours.[30] Among large firms, economic performance is positively correlated with pro bono service.[31] Firms that "do well" generally are better at "doing good."

The rise of pro bono has resulted from interlocking trends. First, law firm growth itself laid the groundwork for an institutionalized structure of pro bono activity. As firms grew bigger and more bureaucratic, it became harder to maintain decentralized systems with lawyer-initiated volunteer work, in part because of the difficulties it posed for tracking cases.[32] Such systems were ill-suited to prevent potential conflicts

24 *See* Milton C. Regan, Jr., *Law Firms, Competition Penalties, and the Values of Professionalism*, 13 GEO. J. LEGAL ETHICS 1, 9 (1999).

25 2009 Am Law 200 Data (on file with author); 2002 Am Law 200 Data (on file with author); 1992 Am Law 200 Data (on file with author).

26 Scott L. Cummings, *The Politics of Pro Bono*, 52 UCLA L. REV. 1, 37 (2004).

27 *Id.*

28 *See id.*

29 Steven A. Boutcher, *The Institutionalization of Pro Bono in Large Law Firms: Trends and Variation Across the AmLaw 200*, *in* PRIVATE LAWYERS AND THE PUBLIC INTEREST: THE EVOLVING ROLE OF PRO BONO IN THE LEGAL PROFESSION 145 & fig. 7.2 (Robert Granfield & Lynn Mather eds., 2009).

30 Total hours increased from 3,768,510 to 5,567,231; average hours grew from 38.25 to 48.77. The average hour-per-lawyer figure includes those firms that are in the ranking but did not report data and therefore are included as reporting 0 hours. If the average is taken based only on firms that reported data, the increase is 12 hours, from 40.48 in 2005 to 52.73 in 2008. *Compare* 2009 Am Law Pro Bono Survey (on file with author), *with* 2006 Am Law Pro Bono Survey (on file with author).

31 *See* Boutcher, *supra* note 29, at 149; *see also* Rebecca L. Sandefur, *Lawyers' Pro Bono Service and American-Style Civil Legal Assistance*, 41 LAW & SOC'Y REV. 79 (2007). For other discussions of the relationship between profitability and pro bono contributions, see Debra Burke et al., *Pro Bono Publico: Issues and Implications*, 26 LOY. U. CHI. L.J. 61, 82–83 (1994); Marc Galanter & Thomas Palay, *Public Service Implications of Evolving Law Firm Size and Structure*, *in* THE LAW FIRM AND THE PUBLIC GOOD 19, 44 tbl.2–3, 45 tbl.2–4, 46 (Robert A. Katzmann ed., 1995).

32 *See* Cynthia Fuchs Epstein, *Stricture and Structure: The Social and Cultural Context of Pro Bono Work in Wall Street Firms*, 70 FORDHAM L. REV. 1689, 1695 (2002) (suggesting that a "laissez faire" approach to pro bono activity works against substantial commitment).

of interest. As large firms became increasingly organized around departments, specialties, and functional roles, the institutionalization of formal, centralized pro bono programs seemed less of a leap.[33] Firm growth also created more revenue and "organizational slack," which could be used to subsidize additional unpaid work.[34] Finally, increases in size, particularly at the bottom of the firm pyramid, created new challenges for professional development. Large numbers of associates required opportunities for training and significant responsibility. Pro bono work was a way to provide them.

The rise of organized pro bono was also linked to a rise in demand. Although direct historical comparisons are not possible, the available data point to growth in both the number and size of public interest law groups over the movement's lifespan. In the mid-1970s, there were roughly 100 public interest law groups (excluding legal aid organizations) with approximately 6 attorneys per group;[35] in addition, there were over 850 legal aid offices with 3 attorneys per office.[36] According to Nielsen and Albiston's most recent figures, the number of public interest law organizations, including legal aid groups, has surpassed 1,000, and the average number of lawyers per group has nearly doubled since 1974, from 7 to 13.[37] Based on the early data, a rough estimate of the total size of the public interest bar in the mid-1970s was 3,600; in contrast, projecting from the 2004 data places the total figure at 13,000. During this period, the proportion of public interest lawyers in the total lawyer population has remained relatively constant at about 1 percent.

As the public interest law sector has developed, it has confronted economic challenges that have heightened the importance of private sector alliances. In Rhode's study of public interest law groups, almost all reported major challenges raising revenue, particularly for general operating expenses and litigation.[38] The strain on resources has created challenges in recruiting and retaining talented public interest lawyers whose salaries are low (at $38,500, average entry-level salaries of public interest lawyers are the lowest of any practice setting according to the *After the JD*

33 For a general overview of the transformation of large firms, see ROBERT L. NELSON, PARTNERS WITH POWER: THE SOCIAL TRANSFORMATION OF THE LARGE LAW FIRM 172–80 (1988).

34 Sandefur, *supra* note 31, at 93 (quoting RICHARD M. CYERT & JAMES G. MARCH, A BEHAVIORAL THEORY OF THE FIRM 37 [1963]).

35 NAN AARON, LIBERTY AND JUSTICE FOR ALL: PUBLIC INTEREST LAW IN THE 1980S AND BEYOND (1989) (reporting as of 1975).

36 EARL JOHNSON, JR., JUSTICE AND REFORM: THE FORMATIVE YEARS OF THE AMERICAN LEGAL SERVICES PROGRAM 188 (1978) (reporting as of 1972).

37 Laura Beth Nielsen & Catherine Albiston, *The Organization of Public Interest Practice: 1975–2004*, 84 N.C. L. REV. 1591 (2006).

38 Deborah L. Rhode, *Public Interest Law: The Movement at Midlife*, 60 STAN. L. REV. 2027, 2056–57 (2008).

research[39]) and whose debt loads have increased.[40] In the face of economic constraints, public interest lawyers have relied heavily on pro bono support for their work. Rhode's study showed that about four-fifths of leading public interest groups reported extensive or moderate collaboration with the private bar.[41]

Constraints on federally funded legal aid have also contributed to greater demand for pro bono services. The erosion in legal aid for the poor has resulted from reductions in federal funding and restrictions on advocacy. By 1996, congressional authorization for legal services had fallen to a level 50 percent below its peak in 1980.[42] That same year, Congress banned federally funded programs from engaging in a range of activities including litigation involving class actions, the representation of aliens, and recovery of court-awarded attorney's fees.[43] Legal services programs receiving federal subsidies were also prohibited from using nonfederal funds to engage in any of the banned activities.[44] Such limitations forced poverty lawyers to seek other revenue sources.[45] Despite successful efforts to diversify funding, the current civil legal aid system has remained chronically underfunded and, as a result, unable to adequately serve its client constituency.[46]

39 Ronit Dinovitzer et al., Am. Bar Found. & NALP Found. for Law Career Research & Educ., After the JD: First Results of a National Study of Legal Careers 43 (2004). Public interest salaries have declined in relation to law firm salaries. In the early 1970s, the ratio of private firm to public interest salaries was 1.5:1. In 2004, the ratio of private firm (more than 20 lawyers) to public interest salaries was roughly 3:1; the ratio of big firm (more than 250) to public interest salaries was 3.6:1. *Compare* Neil K. Komesar & Burton A. Weisbrod, *The Public Interest Law Firm: A Behavioral Analysis*, *in* Public Interest Law: An Economic and Institutional Analysis 80, 83 (Burton A. Weisbrod et al. eds., 1978), and Dinovitzer et al., *supra*, at 43.

40 Equal Justice Works, *supra* note 19, at 1.

41 Rhode, *supra* note 38, at 2070.

42 *See* Alan W. Houseman, *Civil Legal Assistance for Low-Income Persons: Looking Back and Looking Forward*, 29 Fordham Urb. L.J. 1213, 1222 (2002). As of 2008, federal funding was nearly fifty-three percent below what it was in 1980 when adjusted for inflation. Alan W. Houseman, Ctr. for Law & Soc. Policy, Civil Legal Aid in the United States: An Update for 2009, at 13 (2009), *available at* http://www.clasp.org/admin/site/publications/files/CIVIL-LEGAL-AID-IN-THE-UNITED-STATES-2.pdf.

43 Omnibus Consolidated Rescissions and Appropriations Act of 1996, Pub. L. No. 104–134, § 504(a)(7), (11), (13), 110 Stat. 1321, 1321–53 to –55.

44 *See* Brennan Ctr. for Justice, Restricting Legal Services: How Congress Left the Poor with Only Half a Lawyer 7 (2000), *available at* http://brennan.3cdn.net/3cbbeedd52806583b1_osm6blo8g.pdf.

45 Primary sources include grants from state and local governments, interest on lawyers' trust fund accounts, and private donors. *See* Alan W. Houseman, Ctr. for Law & Soc. Policy, Civil Legal Aid in the United States: An Overview of the Program in 2003, at 4 (2003), *available at* www.clasp.org/admin/site/publications/files/0153.pdf; Deborah L. Rhode, *Whatever Happened to Access to Justice?*, 42 Loy. L.A. L. Rev. 869, 908 (2009).

46 Legal Servs. Corp., Documenting the Justice Gap in America 1–4 (2d ed. 2007), *available at* http://www.lsc.gov/justicegap.pdf.

America's pro bono system has evolved against this backdrop. In 1981, the Legal Services Corporation required that its grantees make a "substantial amount" of funds available for private attorney involvement.[47] This requirement encouraged the expansion of programs designed to recruit, train, and connect pro bono volunteers with low-income clients. In 1980, about ninety such programs existed.[48] Today there are approximately 900.[49] Pro bono contributions to these programs constitute a significant part of the nation's civil legal aid structure, accounting for between one-quarter and one-third of overall legal aid services.[50] Large-firm lawyers play an increasingly prominent role in this pro bono system overall and provide crucial representation in matters that federally supported programs are barred from accepting.

The organized bar has actively promoted pro bono as a way to shore up gaps in legal aid and public interest representation, focusing special attention on large law firms. The ABA's Model Rule of Professional Conduct 6.1 provides that every lawyer "should aspire to render at least (50) hours of pro bono publico legal services per year," and that a "substantial majority" should assist "persons of limited means" or organizations that help them.[51] Additional assistance should go to activities that improve the law, legal profession or legal system, or that support "civil rights, civil liberties or public rights, or charitable, religious, civic, community, governmental and educational organizations" if payment of fees would "significantly deplete the organization's economic resources or would be otherwise inappropriate."[52] By giving preference to low-income and other underserved clients, the Rule seeks to channel pro bono work toward those who need help most. To encourage compliance with this aspirational standard, the organized bar has relied most heavily on recruitment and recognition initiatives. Professional initiatives have interacted with powerful market-based incentives for public service, particularly law firm rankings by major legal publications. In particular, *The American Lawyer*'s 1994 decision to begin publicly ranking firms based on the depth and breadth of their pro bono performance

47 Legal Servs. Corp., Adoption of Principles on Private Bar Involvement (1981). Under the program, Legal Services Corporation grantees are required to use 12.5% of their federal funds to support private attorney involvement. 45 C.F.R. § 1614.2 (2009).

48 *See* Meredith McBurney, The Impact of Legal Services Program Reconfiguration on Pro Bono 1 (2003); *see also* Esther F. Lardent, *Structuring Law Firm Pro Bono Programs: A Community Service Typology*, *in* The Law Firm and the Public Good, *supra* note 31, at 59, 75 (putting the number of pro bono programs at about fifty).

49 The American Bar Association's current directory of pro bono programs lists approximately 900 groups; there are 96 in California and 66 in New York. American Bar Association, Standing Committee on Pro Bono & Public Service and the Center for Pro Bono, Directory of Pro Bono Programs, http://www.abanet.org/legalservices/probono/directory.html (last visited Oct. 12, 2010).

50 Sandefur, *supra* note 31, at 102.

51 Model Rules of Prof'l Conduct R. 6.1 (2009).

52 *Id.*

dramatically altered firm behavior and contributed to a rise in organized pro bono programs at law firms and an increase in pro bono hours.

The rise of pro bono programs at large firms has not just contributed to a more "market-reliant" system of legal services delivery in the United States;[53] it has also reframed the professional project by underscoring new linkages between private lawyers' commercial and professional aims. A recent study I conducted with Deborah Rhode on the challenges faced by large-firm pro bono programs in the economic recession illuminated these connections.[54] In the face of the worst economic downturn since the Great Depression, law firms initiated a wave of deferrals, furloughs, and layoffs. As part of this restructuring, in 2009 more than fifty Am Law 200 firms offered incoming associates subsidies of up to $80,000 to spend a year working for nonprofits or government agencies.[55] The primary impetus for the placements was economic: Each deferred associate was estimated to save the firm up to $100,000 because the firms' costs in terms of salary and support would exceed revenue at junior billing rates. The deferrals would allow firms to quickly restock their associate ranks once the recession passed, with placed associates returning to the firms with relevant skills acquired while working in the public interest. These placement programs therefore underscored the increasing overlap between commercial and professional projects.

In general, the pro bono counsel we surveyed saw temporary placements as opportunities to reinforce commitment to pro bono work and to build a constituency for its support within the firm.[56] They believed that a stint in public service could make associates "more likely to think of it as a natural part of their practice." These lawyers could "at the very least be mentors to other lawyers here and … continue to do, as part of our pro bono program, the types of work they did during [their placement] year." Counsel were eager to take advantage of the knowledge accumulated during the year away from the firm: "My hope is that I have all these [associates] with areas of expertise [who] will come back knowing what it is to be a [public interest] advocate, [and who will] … continue to have deeper connections with groups that they went to work with." Other counsel hoped that the placements would influence associate attitudes concerning not only pro bono practice, but also professional life more broadly. At a minimum, the experience might "put to rest" the notion that "public interest lawyers are lazy and not effective." It might also reduce "feelings of entitlement" and provide skills that would give associates a competitive career advantage.

53 *See* Rebecca L. Sandefur, *Lawyers' Pro Bono Service and Market-Reliant Legal Aid, in* Private Lawyers and the Public Interest, *supra* note 29, at 95.

54 Scott L. Cummings & Deborah L. Rhode, *Managing Pro Bono: Doing Well by Doing Better*, 78 Fordham L. Rev. 2357 (2010).

55 Rachel Breitman, *Time Well Spent*, Am. Law., July 2009, at 15, 15.

56 Cummings & Rhode, *supra* note 54, at 2418.

Indeed, training was a key reason for the placements.[57] As surveyed counsel noted, providing placement opportunities for deferred associates enabled them to "continue to build their skills sets" while also meeting the urgent legal needs of vulnerable groups. One counsel summed it up this way: "The firm is pleased to be able to contribute to the public good through its attorneys involved in the placement program. The program also provides a way to develop attorney skill and manage firm resources." Toward this end, placements were designed to cultivate targeted skill sets. For litigators, pro bono counsel would look for opportunities with "courtroom time. For transactional lawyers, we look for large nonprofits with sophisticated legal departments. Our firm is looking at the back end of this. Otherwise what is the benefit?"

Partly because of the firms' economic motives, the placement programs generated some tensions, particularly when public interest organizations felt pressure to accept associates whose training, supervision, and administrative expenses would exceed what the groups could effectively supply.[58] The firms in our survey took different approaches to covering placement-related costs, with only one reporting that it was assuming "all costs associated with placed attorneys." An additional tension related to the awkwardness of placing junior associates in nonprofit groups to be supervised by senior public interest lawyers whose salaries were less than the associates' deferral stipend.

While the placement programs revealed some short-term economic benefits from pro bono volunteerism, they also underscored a deeper relationship between private interests and the public good. The institutionalization of pro bono programs has blurred the line between paid and unpaid work as the training, recruitment, and reputational functions of pro bono service are increasingly integrated into the economic framework of large law firms.[59]

Nowhere is this more evident than in the growing linkages between large-firm pro bono and career development programs.[60] The formality of this linkage between pro bono and training varied, but its importance was clearly apparent in law firms. At the most formal end of the spectrum was a firm that had revamped its first- and second-year associate program to require a substantial pro bono commitment linked to skills development.[61] To enhance its training function, the associate program was

[57] *Id.* at 2410.

[58] *Id.* at 2412–13.

[59] *See* Ronit Dinovitzer & Bryant G. Garth, *Pro Bono as an Elite Strategy in Early Lawyer Careers, in* Private Lawyers and the Public Interest, *supra* note 29, at 115 (referring to pro bono as a possible strategy of "demand creation" for law firms).

[60] *See* Stephen Daniels & Joanne Martin, *Legal Services for the Poor: Access, Self-Interest, and Pro Bono*, 12 Sociology of Crime, Law and Deviance 145, 154–55 (2009).

[61] Cummings & Rhode, *supra* note 54, at 2426–2427.

being restructured to run like a law school clinic, taught by pro bono counsel in conjunction with another firm lawyer whose background was in clinical teaching. Firm lawyers were selecting pro bono cases not only for their social impact but also for their pedagogical value in enhancing the "skills we want [associates] to get." Less formally, other firms were using pro bono cases as training vehicles.[62] One counsel in our study offered a typical description of this objective: "we match [pro bono cases] for three purposes: first, to provide as much free legal services as possible; second, so that lawyers' interests match; and third, to match lawyers' professional development goals.... I want to maximize interest in developing skills and align it with pro bono work." The economic crisis had prompted a number of firms to forge closer links between pro bono and training, which some counsel saw as a "long-term positive impact. The synergies between pro bono and professional development have been strengthened. The pressures from business clients not to pay for first- and second-year associates may help in making pro bono more attractive as a training vehicle." The incentive to mesh pro bono work with training goals was particularly noticeable in firms that had taken associates off lock-step compensation tracks. In the new model, pay reflects the acquisition of core competencies that can be achieved through pro bono cases.[63]

But training concerns were more pervasive, as was clear in the importance pro bono counsel ascribed to various factors in defining the objectives of pro bono programs and making case selection decisions.[64] For counsel who run pro bono programs, the primary stated objective is what the term implies: serving the public by assisting underrepresented groups. Making a social impact is also highly valued. Yet the programs also had major pragmatic goals. The most important was training associates, but aiding recruitment and retention, and enhancing reputation and rankings, were also significant. Similarly, for most firms, key factors guiding case selection are opportunities for training and appeal to associates.[65]

A less prominent, although still significant, objective of some firms was to link pro bono activity to fee generation. Our study found that some firms do collect fees when they are awarded by courts in pro bono cases.[66] And although most donate fees to nonprofit partner organizations, it is not uncommon for firms to keep a portion of fees to cover costs, fund ongoing pro bono program activities, or to pay for part of the attorneys' time. Although most firms did not think of pro bono in terms of profit potential, there were some that did.[67] One reported that it was launching

62 *Id.* at 2427.
63 *Id.* at 2428.
64 *Id.* at 2386.
65 *Id.* at 2392.
66 *Id.* at 2389.
67 *Id.* at 2428–29.

a new transactional initiative designed to address "development issues primarily in the third world," which also had fee-generating potential. As counsel noted, "There is a synergy between pro bono and paying work that can be better combined. So we can expand the reach of pro bono and capitalize ... by reaching out to groups that could pay fees.... There was a recognition by partners, that you could potentially make money while doing good."

This urge to unite profit and principle presents trade-offs that go to the heart of evaluating a system that relies heavily on market-based delivery. On the positive side of the ledger, private lawyers do a tremendous service representing poor clients in routine matters and lending their institutional resources to support the reform agendas of public interest groups. Their volunteer work ranges from the mundane to the transformative. But the central dilemma of pro bono remains. A system that depends on private lawyers is ultimately beholden to their economic interests. This means that private lawyers will avoid categories of cases that threaten relationships with paying clients. For example, half of the firms in our study indicated that they would not accept pro bono employment and labor cases because of the potential for real or positional conflicts. The importance of economic considerations also means that firms will take on pro bono cases for reasons that are disconnected from the interests of the poor and underserved – and often contrary to them. This is most apparent in the use of pro bono for law firm associate training. Associates who gain skills in the volunteer context may spend time using them to advocate *against* the interests served through pro bono representation.

There are other drawbacks. Pro bono lawyers do not typically invest heavily in gaining substantive expertise, getting to know the broader public interest field, or understanding the long-range goals of client groups. The partiality and narrowness of pro bono representation is striking, particularly in contrast to the way big-firm lawyers seek to understand and advance the goals of their client community. And the disparity in resources devoted to billable versus pro bono work – which, even at the most generous firm, rarely constitutes more than 5 percent of total hours – underscores the vast, persisting inequality in legal services. Indeed, there are no parallel resources available to press the interests of marginalized social groups, who are left to depend heavily on volunteer efforts to respond to their needs – a fact that distinguishes them from their adversaries, who spend lavishly to purchase the best legal counsel money can buy.

As the U.S. example suggests, the clash – and combination – of professional ideals and commercial aims produces a framework for legal services delivery, dependent on large-firm pro bono services, that represents a particular version of justice – one that expands resources for services while constraining their nature. Hence, a central paradox of professionalism: To the extent that lawyers assimilate their political project (doing good) to their commercial one (doing well), commercial ends define the limits of what legal means can achieve. The relationship between lawyers' political and commercial projects – and which ultimately gains ascendance – therefore has profound consequences for the quantity and quality of justice served.

THEORETICAL FRAMEWORK: WHICH PROFESSIONAL PROJECTS?

In analyzing the clash of professional projects, this volume intervenes in the rich professional and scholarly literature on lawyers. There are two main discussions. One is normative: It asserts that lawyers should be guided by a set of high ethical standards, laments the decline of these standards in the face of increasing commercialism, and offers proposals to "rekindle" the spirit of professionalism.[68] In this story, there are iconic lawyers – Brandeis, Story, Acheson – whose practice embodied a "lawyer-statesman" ideal of professionalism that rejected "hired-gun" neutrality in favor of independent judgment and public service.[69] The increasingly cut-throat nature of commercial practice promoted individualism and competitiveness – "eat what you kill"[70] – that eroded the institutional foundations of this ideal and pushed lawyers toward partisanship rather than public spiritedness, which must be reclaimed.

The other discussion about lawyers is essentially empirical: Rather than approaching professionalism as a theory to be defended, this literature takes professionalism as a set of ideas and practices to be studied. It therefore asks: How do lawyers understand and enact their professional duties in the context of their daily work lives? How should we judge their individual contributions to clients and their collective contributions to society? This empirical perspective still speaks to the desire to hold lawyers to higher standards – measuring the gap between professionalism in theory and professionalism in action may inform proposals for reform – yet the primary focus is on explaining why lawyers' behave as they do in the real world of practice and evaluating their social impact.

A core debate within this empirical domain centers on whether lawyers are, as a functional matter, a force for "justice" – or its foil. Of course, "justice" is, despite its frequent invocation by the bar, a fraught concept. I use it here to refer to two ideas identified in the literature. The first is a macrolevel conception of institutional justice associated with basic rule of law values: individual rights

[68] *See, e.g.*, AM. BAR ASS'N, ". . . . IN THE SPIRIT OF PUBLIC SERVICE:" A BLUEPRINT FOR THE REKINDLING OF LAWYER PROFESSIONALISM (1986), *available at* http://www.abanet.org/cpr/professionalism/Stanley_Commission_Report.pdf.

[69] *See* ANTHONY KRONMAN, THE LOST LAWYER: FAILING IDEALS OF THE LEGAL PROFESSION (1993).

[70] MILTON C. REGAN, JR., EAT WHAT YOU KILL: THE FALL OF A WALL STREET LAWYER (2005).

enforcement – encompassing both private (contract and property) and public (civil and political) rights, and requiring judicial independence and access to the legal process – as well as political accountability – associated with multiparty democracy, checks and balances, and robust civil society. Within this conception, it is essential that lawyers take a stand for public rights, provide equal access to justice, and serve as checks on political and economic power. The second conception of justice is a microlevel one associated with traditional notions of professionalism within the lawyer-client relationship. Justice in the context of particular matters requires representation by a lawyer who is zealous, competent, and ethical, but also willing to exercise independent judgment to ensure substantively fair and accurate decisions. As "public citizens," lawyers are asked to stand for these values. Do they?

Early sociologists of the profession presumed the answer to be yes. Lawyers, in a view generally traced back to de Tocqueville and expressed in Parson's structural functionalism, occupied an elevated social status as guardians of democratic values – a stabilizing force that modulates the passions of the masses while checking abuses of power.[71] Lawyers were accorded autonomy from the state precisely in order to prevent them from being captured by it. It was presumed that their commitment to craft would provide sufficient incentives to police and maintain internal standards of ethicality and expertise.

Yet, in the United States, this benevolent conception of lawyers has long stumbled upon uncomfortable facts: Too often, lawyers have been exposed as agents of abuse rather than champions of justice; manipulators of technicalities rather than promoters of values. Inspiring examples of lawyering for the good are matched by dispiriting stories of lawyering for the bad. The lawyers for Enron, hired to provide a thorough legal evaluation of the company in the face of concerns about "accounting scandals," famously limited the scope of their investigation to avoid "second-guessing the accounting advice" – placing its legal stamp of approval on the company just before its implosion.[72] Lawyers in the Bush Administration's Office of Legal Counsel, charged with giving independent legal advice to the White House, opined – in a striking display of interpretive license – that torture was not technically torture if an interrogator did not specifically intend to cause "severe pain or suffering," although he knew that it "was reasonably likely to result from his actions."[73]

[71] *See* Robert W. Gordon, *Are Lawyers Friends of Democracy?* (in this volume).

[72] Dan Ackman, *Enron's Lawyers: Eyes Wide Shut?*, Forbes.com (Jan. 28, 2002), http://www.forbes.com/2002/01/28/0128veenron.html.

[73] Jay S. Bybee, Assistant Attorney General, U.S. Dep't of Justice, Office of Legal Counsel, Memorandum for Alberto R. Gonzales, Counsel to the President 3–4 (Aug. 1, 2002).

Even outside individual occasions of misbehavior, broad structural problems persist: Those most in need of help often experience the market for professional services as itself abusive – or at least profoundly unfair. The "justice gap" in the United States is well documented: With one lawyer for every 6,415 poor people, "over four-fifths of the individual legal needs of low-income individuals remain unmet."[74] The scarcity of legal services on behalf of the poor contrasts with the deep investments in legal expertise by the powerful and contributes to unequal outcomes.[75] To make matters worse, even when lawyers are available, they do not always act with appropriate care,[76] leaving many vulnerable clients worse off: their legal problem unresolved, yet stuck with the lawyer's bill. What explains this divergence between the ideals of professionalism and the reality?

In the 1980s, Richard Abel set out to answer this question, launching a scholarly project stunning in its ambition, scope, and empirical rigor – one which would fundamentally transform our understanding of lawyers and their social role.[77] Abel's theoretical starting point was Weber, who posited that service providers become a "profession" through a project of "social closure" that involves both limiting competition ("market control") and enhancing status ("collective social mobility").[78] Beginning with a review of sociologist Magali Sarfatti Larson's classic, *The Rise of Professionalism*,[79] Abel embarked upon a decade-long effort to determine whether social closure could explain the development of legal professions in the United States, England and Wales, and a range of other common and civil law countries. His method was empirically grounded social science, which Abel used to marshal and analyze an enormous amount of data to shed light on the theory's validity, focusing specifically on how successful the bar had been in controlling entry to the profession ("the production *of* producers") and controlling competition within the profession ("production *by* producers").[80] The result was at once brilliant and

[74] Rhode, *supra* note 45, at 879.

[75] *See* Marc Galanter, *Why the "Haves" Come Out Ahead: Speculations on the Limits of Legal Change*, 9 LAW & SOC'Y REV. 95 (1974).

[76] *See* RICHARD L. ABEL, LAWYERS IN THE DOCK: LEARNING FROM ATTORNEY DISCIPLINARY PROCEEDINGS (2008); Lynn Mather, *How and Why Do Lawyers Misbehave? Lawyers, Discipline, and Collegial Control* (in this volume); Deborah L. Rhode, *Professional Regulation and Public Service: An Unfinished Agenda* (in this volume).

[77] Abel's seminal works during this period, include ABEL, AMERICAN LAWYERS, *supra* note 7; RICHARD L. ABEL, THE LEGAL PROFESSION IN ENGLAND AND WALES (1988); LAWYERS IN SOCIETY: THE CIVIL LAW WORLD (Richard L. Abel & Philip S.C. Lewis eds., 1988); LAWYERS IN SOCIETY: THE COMMON LAW WORLD (Richard L. Abel & Philip S.C. Lewis eds., 1988); LAWYERS IN SOCIETY: COMPARATIVE THEORIES (Richard L. Abel & Philip S.C. Lewis eds., 1989).

[78] ABEL, *supra* note 7, at 20.

[79] MAGALI SARFATI LARSON, THE RISE OF PROFESSIONALISM: A SOCIOLOGICAL ANALYSIS (1977).

[80] ABEL, *supra* note 7, at 27.

subversive: an astoundingly comprehensive portrait of how lawyers' private quest for economic and social status undermined their public commitment to service in the public good.

Abel's body of work from this period constituted an emphatic repudiation of the prevailing prosocial functionalist account of legal professionalism. Rather than viewing lawyers as motivated by public-regarding values adopted through training and professional assimilation, Abel argued that lawyers were engaged in a collective project to assert control over the market for their services and thereby enhance their wealth and status. In this account, the quest for economic gain was not opposed to, but rather formed the essence of, the professional project. This project – advanced by the organized bar –focused on efforts to extract monopoly rents by reducing the supply of lawyers and limiting competition, while simultaneously promoting a benevolent public image that abjured profit and embraced public service.[81] Abel's account of the professional project in the United States concluded that the organized bar achieved partial success at a substantial cost: The achievement of imperfect market control carried with it profound inequalities in the distribution of legal services and deep stratification within the bar.[82] He reached similar conclusions about the professional project across the span of other countries he and his collaborators studied.[83]

There have been a number of important responses to Abel's theory, all of which question the weight he gives to the economic movitations of lawyers in explaining the trajectory of professional developments.[84] Here, I focus on three responses that dispute the priority Abel gives to market control in order to recapture some theoretical space for professionalism as a public good.

The first directly challenges the theoretical power of social closure by positing that the professional project be understood in political rather than market terms: Instead of viewing lawyers as collectively oriented toward market control, we should instead

[81] Richard L. Abel, *Lawyers in the Civil Law World, in* Lawyers in Society: The Civil Law World, *supra* note 77, at 1, 9.

[82] Abel, *supra* note 7.

[83] *See, e.g.*, Lawyers in Society: The Common Law World, *supra* note 77.

[84] One type of response, exemplified by Kritzer's review of Abel's work, questions the "fit" between Abel's theoretical framework and his empirical evidence. *See* Herbert M. Kritzer, Abel and the Professional Project: The Institutional Analysis of the Legal Profession, 16 Law & Social Inquiry 529 (1991). Specifically, Kritizer suggested that the evidence – particularly that which showed the breakdown of market control in the United States and England after the 1960s – better supported an alternative theory of professionalism: what he termed "institutionalization," characterized by the development of "standard, universalistic procedures to govern recruitment and entry." *Id.* at 547. Kritzer notes the overlap between market control and institutionalization in the definition of boundaries between practitioners and nonpractitioners (the production of producers); yet he disagrees with Abel's assessment of why market control broke down (Kritzer sees an institutional logic where Abel sees external factors at play in trends like increased law school enrollment).

understand them as political actors engaged in the pursuit of fundamental values associated with the liberal state.[85] This perspective rehabilitates the public-regarding conception of professionalism, though on different grounds from the structural-functionalists: Lawyers do not embody democratic values, but they frequently fight for them. And, indeed, there is strong evidence, assembled by Halliday, Karpik, and Feeley, that lawyers have in fact often been in the vanguard of movements to both establish and expand basic legal freedoms and other features of political liberalism.[86] Abel does not disagree with this proposition and, indeed, has offered a powerful portrait of lawyers' quest for political liberalism in his comprehensive account of the role of South African human rights lawyers in the struggle against apartheid.[87]

The second main challenge to Abel's theory does not propose a unified alterative to market control, but rather suggests that the very notion of a coherent professional project is a chimera. Instead of professional unity, Nelson and Trubek argue that the profession itself is differentiated, "professionalism" is fractured and contested, and therefore to understand its meaning and practice, it is necessary to attend to lawyers' ideology in addition to the exogenous political and economic structures within which they work.[88] This emphasis on the relationship between external structure and lawyer agency, understood through the lens of ideology, represents another effort to redeem professionalism as a meaningful instrument of social justice. Whereas this perspective acknowledges that the rhetoric of professionalism – expertise, autonomy, and service – can be used to legitimate the inequities produced by market control, it argues that professionalism is not *just* legitimation. Rather, it is a set of competing ideas and norms, which may justify commercialism but may also point out ways to transcend it. This interpretive framework has led to a proliferation of "bottom-up" studies that focus on the construction of professional ideology across various professional arenas and practice sites, the factors that shape it, and the ways in which it may be mobilized to promote ethical and public-spirited lawyering.[89]

[85] Terence C. Halliday, Beyond Monopoly: Lawyers, State Crises, and Professional Empowerment (1987).

[86] *See* Fighting for Political Freedom: Comparative Studies of the Legal Complex and Political Liberalism (Terence C. Halliday, Lucien Karpik & Malcolm M. Feeley eds., 2007); *see also* Lawyers and the Rise of Western Political Liberalism: Europe and North America from the Eighteenth to Twentieth Centuries (Terence C. Halliday & Lucien Karpick eds., 1997).

[87] Richard L. Abel, Politics by Other Means: Law and the Struggle Against Apartheid, 1980–1994 (1995).

[88] Robert L. Nelson & David M. Trubek, *Introduction: New Problems and New Paradigms in Studies of the Legal Profession, in* Lawyers' Ideals/Lawyers' Practices: Transformations in the American Legal Profession 1, 18 (Robert L. Nelson, David M. Trubek & Raymond Solomon eds., 1992). For the classic account of the differentiated nature of the profession, see John P. Heinz & Edward O. Laumann, Chicago Lawyers: The Social Structure of the Bar (1994).

[89] Abel examines the contest over the meaning of professionalism by various sectors of the English bar in Richard L. Abel, English Lawyers Between Market and State: The Politics of Professionalism (2003).

A third response to Abel's professional project builds on the interpretive approach, but focuses on one slice of legal practice: cause lawyering. In his analysis of market control, Abel had asked whether U.S. legal aid and public interest law programs could be understood as strategies of "demand creation" – generating new business, promoting the profession's pledge of altruism, and reaffirming "a fundamental premise of liberal legalism – 'equal justice under law'"?[90] Although he concluded that such strategies were ultimately insufficient generators of new demand,[91] by locating legal aid and public interest law within the professional project, Abel suggested that they might serve a market control function. Sarat and Scheingold's cause lawyering framework, in contrast, reasserts the connection between lawyers in those fields to the profession's public role.[92] In doing so, they define cause lawyering not against profit-seeking practice, but rather against conventional professionalism – the so-called "ideology of advocacy" in which lawyers serve as amoral "hired guns" for their clients.[93] "At its core, cause lawyering is about using legal skills to pursue ends and ideals that transcend client service – be those ideals social, cultural, political, economic or, indeed, legal."[94] However, in challenging conventional ideology, Sarat and Scheingold argue that cause lawyers simultaneously help promote its public service aspirations by "asserting the political claims of professional authority."[95]

Each of these responses to Abel's emphasis on social closure has its own limits and lacunae, and none ultimately supplants it as an explanatory framework, but rather only reveals it as a partial lens. For instance, the pursuit of political liberalism is not incompatible with the quest for market control, and indeed, there are features of both projects that may be complementary. Specifically, to the extent that political liberalism embraces an individual-rights enforcement regime coextensive with free-market capitalism,[96] we might expect the legal complex to mobilize to expand basic legal freedoms in the political arena (including freedom of contract and property rights) while simultaneously seeking to limit competition by asserting restrictions on their services in the marketplace. It is therefore possible (and in some countries even likely) that the legal profession would be at once profoundly supportive of political liberalism while fiercely protective of their own economic prerogatives.

90 Abel, *supra* note 7, at 127.

91 *Id.* at 132–35.

92 Stuart Scheingold & Austin Sarat, Something to Believe In: Politics, Professionalism, and Cause Lawyering 28 (2004); *see also* Austin Sarat & Stuart Scheingold, *Cause Lawyering and the Reproduction of Professional Authority: An Introduction*, *in* Cause Lawyering: Political Commitments and Professional Responsibility 3 (Austin Sarat & Stuart Scheingold eds., 1998).

93 Scheingold & Sarat, *supra* note 92, at 3–7.

94 *Id.* at 3.

95 *Id.* at 47.

96 *See* David M. Trubek, *The 'Rule of Law' in Development Assistance: Past, Present, and Future*, *in* The New Law and Development: A Critical Appraisal 74 (David M. Trubek & Alvaro Santos eds., 2006).

The question then becomes how one assesses the consequences of each project in terms of different metrics of justice, such as rights enforcement and access to the legal process.

The limit of the interpretive approach to professionalism is that it exposes the multiple practices of professionalism from the bottom up but does not reach back to the general level to offer an overarching appraisal of their aggregate consequences. Indeed, the fragmentary and contested meanings of professionalism across smaller arenas of practice may nonetheless still sum to a larger picture of market control. To the degree that lawyers operate in a private market, in which outcomes are determined through competition, we can expect that wealth and status will be important factors within most arenas. Competition will invariably pit some groups of lawyers against others and it will generate conflict between lawyers and non-lawyers over the boundaries of legal services. Within market-based systems, there will be winners and losers; not all lawyers will benefit from any collective mobility project. Indeed, some will suffer – at times deliberately so (as we have seen in the United States with the restrictions on barratry and champerty designed to disadvantage nonelite, often immigrant, practitioners).[97] And there will be lawyers who actively resist a market-oriented vision. In the end, however, we may still find that these various projects settle into an overall pattern of professional organization and distribution of services that are at odds with the very public values that lawyers purport to embrace.

Focusing on cause lawyers' challenge to conventional professional ideology – whether they have "something to believe in" – is also a limited way of reframing the professional project. Defining a cause lawyer by her "political or moral commitment" raises questions about who *is not* a cause lawyer. What about the corporate lawyer who believes that her work defending against employee lawsuits reduces corporate costs and benefits consumers? Or the takeover specialist who believes his work promotes economic efficiency? Can one be a cause lawyer irrespective of whether the cause is in service of the economically powerful or the politically fringe? If so, cause lawyering would seem to be the exception that threatens to swallow the rule. Far from reconnecting legal practice to public values, cause lawyering in the service of corporate capitalism might actually subvert them.

Our approach in this volume seeks to bridge the competing conceptions of the professional project – commercial versus political; top-down versus bottom-up – by recognizing the multiplicity of projects while nonetheless trying to sort out which matter the most in appraising whether justice has been served at different times and

[97] Jerold S. Auerbach, Unequal Justice: Lawyers and Social Change in Modern America (1976). Also, the exclusion of women and racial and enthnoreligious minorities was a deliberate part of the status enhancement component of the professional project. *See* Abel, *supra* note 7, at 85–108.

in different locations. Toward this end, it rejects the standard binary formulation of the professional project – are lawyers a force for good or ill writ large? – and instead asks: Under *what conditions* do *which lawyers* advance *which projects*? And what are the consequences for social justice?

OVERVIEW OF THE BOOK

To understand the construction and contest of professional projects, this book is organized around the relationship of lawyers to three different types of justice claims, which correspond to the theoretical responses to Abel's theory of social closure presented above. The first is a claim to the *public good* understood in terms of the basic system of rules (on the books and in action) governing political and economic life. Within this domain, the key questions are, in the political arena, the degree to which lawyers act collectively and individually as guardians of the rule of law and, in the market, the extent to which they stand for and make possible equal access to justice. The second justice claim relates to the notion of *ethical practice*. Here, we ask how the quality of legal representation provided affects the quality of justice served. The questions revolve around the appropriate nature and extent of professional regulation in the production of zealous, competent, and ethical lawyers who are guided by fealty to client welfare but also a commitment to a broader set of professional values. The final claim is one of *transformative justice*. Which lawyers challenge the status quo in the service of a transformative vision of political change? What causes them to embrace radical possibilities and move beyond procedural fairness to envision the fair distribution of other types of social goods, often expressed in the concept of economic and social rights?[98]

Lawyers and the Public Good

The chapters in Part I, *Lawyers and the Public Good: The Fundamental Dilemma*, examine the basic contest between the public and market-oriented versions of the professional project. Robert Gordon begins with a sweeping historical assessment of the role of American lawyers in the development of democratic institutions. He concludes that the performance of American lawyers has varied across different epochs. "In their roles as Revolutionary spokesmen and Constitution-makers they have been among the world's most eloquent and effective architects of the institutions of rights-based democratic government.... As zealous servants of wealthy and

[98] *See* Lucie E. White, *African Youth Mobilize against Garbage: Economic and Social Rights Advocacy and the Practice of Democracy* (in this volume).

powerful clienteles, however, they have also effectively staffed the causes of conservative resistance to, or rollback of, access to equal justice and political power for workers, minorities, and other marginalized groups."

Terence Halliday turns us away from the American case to provide a comparative perspective on the professional project. Building upon his work on the legal complex, Halliday echoes the positive part of Gordon's story, arguing that around the world, lawyers can "often be found leading the charge toward a new kind of politics – the pursuit of political liberalism." Yet lawyers do not work alone. Indeed, as Halliday demonstrates, they often draw support and work in collaboration with religious groups. His chapter maps the nature of this conjuncture. Drawing on evidence of legal mobilization by lawyers in Asia, Latin America, and Africa, Halliday identifies the conditions under which religious groups stand for political liberalism and, alternatively, when the legal complex stands for religion. He concludes by suggesting the ways in which "religious groups mobilize in tandem with the legal complex on behalf of political liberalism" by lending their facilities as "reserve infrastructures" and "protected spaces for victims" and lawyers, monitoring abuse, restraining police, shaping rights' consciousness, leading civil society, and mobilizing the public.

Marc Galanter turns our attention to the increasing number of lawyers and its implications for justice by studying the "worldwide multiplication of legal professionals." He is concerned with "legalization" – reflected in the rapid growth of lawyers in countries around the world at rates much faster than the growth of courts and litigation. He concludes that this trend is related to the rise of "big time lawyering" – nonlitigation work for nonindividual clients, particularly "Artificial Persons – corporations, associations, and governments – rather than Natural Persons." One consequence of this (echoing the negative part of Gordon's story) is that "[l]awyers, especially in the growing corporate sector, are more loyal and committed to their clients and less to their firms or the guild: more 'hired guns' and less 'officers of the court.'" The impact of the growth of lawyers on justice is thus uncertain: More lawyers are available, but they may be appropriated by the powerful rather than the dispossessed.

John Nockleby's contribution to the debate about the relationship of lawyers to the public good is to focus our attention on lawyers for individuals – the antithesis of Galanter's big-time lawyering – and ask whether the conditions of their practice promote greater access to justice. His subject is tort lawyers who play a crucial role in defining and defending the compensatory and regulatory functions of our tort system--acting as gatekeepers of justice. In theory, tort lawyers allow an injured party to seek redress. In practice, this is often true, but Nockleby's analysis of the structure of litigation arrives at a troubling conclusion. Specifically, he notes that "the lawyer-as-gatekeeper affects the types of cases that are brought into the tort system, and the choices about cases to accept determine what cases are heard. Cases that cannot attract the contingency lawyer will not be brought, and this central fact means that many people's access to justice is limited by factors other than justice." Thus, even lawyers committed to challenging the power of Artificial Persons face economic tradeoffs that affect the scope of justice they can provide.

These contributions help map out some of the background factors influencing the contest of professional projects. First, they suggest that the relationship between lawyers and the form of government – its structure and its stage of development – is a crucial factor influencing the extent to which lawyers orient their projects toward the political rather than the commercial. Lawyers may have more at stake in building emerging democratic states than in maintaining basic liberties in highly developed ones. In addition, the type of political economy might influence how successful lawyers are in their different pursuits. Thus, lawyers in authoritarian states may be less likely to serve as checks on political power; in liberal capitalist ones, they may be less likely to check economic power.

Second, how lawyers orient their projects will depend on the organization and structure of the market for their services. To the extent that more lawyers serve more powerful interests, the less likely it is that they would be, as a collective, willing to stand against those interests in the name of some broader conception of the public good. In particular, where lawyers serve powerful corporate clients that are repeat players on which lawyers depend for wealth and status, those lawyers are unlikely to take political positions that fundamentally threaten corporate interests.

Lawyers and Their Clients

Part II, *Lawyers and Their Clients: Determinants of Ethical Practice*, explores the context-specific and structural factors influencing ethical lawyering. Lynn Mather starts by asking "how and why do lawyers misbehave?" She argues that we should focus not just on individual flaws but also on structural concerns. Mather looks at evidence of how lawyers view the extent of ethical practice across different substantive areas and finds that there is significant variation, with "[s]ubstantially more lawyers practicing in the areas of energy, banking, securities, real property, employee benefits, and estates agree[ing]...that their peers in the field were highly ethical than did lawyers practicing in the areas of labor relations, criminal law, insurance, immigration, and civil rights/discrimination...." To understand why this hierarchy exists, she proposes a perspective that focuses on "the structure, organization, and content of legal work itself." In particular, she considers how informal sanctions exerted through "collegial control" that emerge from different communities of legal practice interact with formal structures of lawyer discipline (such as professional liability and legal malpractice) to police lawyer misconduct.

Philip Lewis directs our attention to the microworld of the lawyer-client relationship, probing the external and endogenous factors that shape how lawyers implement professional values in practice. Drawing on studies conducted in a variety of practice settings, he argues that key features of the lawyer's role – the nature of expertise, the degree of control, and the relevance of other disciplines – are profoundly shaped by client influence and context. In so doing, he highlights the significant variation in professional values and identities across practice sites, and – like Mather – underscores the importance of informal controls and communities of practice in regulating lawyer conduct.

Deborah Rhode's chapter shifts the lens back to the macrolevel of formal professional regulation and asks what can be done – both within and outside the bar – to move it "toward more socially conscious policies." She focuses on two projects: pro bono and professional discipline. With respect to pro bono, she urges firms to adopt a more strategic approach to guide their pro bono contributions, rather than the "spray and pray" approach that has historically characterized their efforts. She chides firms for putting their own professional interests over the public interest and shrinking from "oversight and accountability." To move forward, she suggests the need for "more systematic processes for selecting and overseeing matters that take into account both participants' and public interests" and argues that "[c]ourts, bar associations, clients, academics, and the media can…do more to encourage and evaluate public service." With respect to professional discipline, she urges more transparency in bar proceedings, which rarely result in public sanctions and thus provide little guidance for consumers of legal services who want to evaluate possible lawyers.

Carrie Hempel and Carroll Seron conclude the section by considering the potential of legal education to reshape professional values toward public ends. They focus on the experiment by the newly formed University of California at Irvine School of Law to create a law school that operationalizes a commitment to experiential learning and interdisciplinarity toward the end of promoting public service. They describe the law school's goal of moving clinical education and professional responsibility from the margins to the mainstream of the curriculum, detail how it has been implemented, and evaluate the challenges that remain. "By making the concept of practice central to UCI's mission, there is the expectation that students' preparation for careers in the law will be more integrated and comprehensive." To do this, UCI has incorporated a Legal Profession course into its first-year curriculum; created an innovative first-year Lawyering Skills course that emphasizes broad skills such as interviewing, counseling, and negotiation; and required each student to take a clinical course. The challenge, as Hempel and Seron see it, lies in pursuing this mission within a highly developed professional field in which prestige and reputation are the name of the game, and in this game, "those who teach professional responsibility and clinical courses can rarely win."

Lawyers and Social Change

Part III, *Lawyers and Social Change: Mobilizing Law for Justice*, concludes the volume by analyzing how lawyers deploy law to produce social change. Penelope Andrews focuses on the iconic case of South Africa and asks whether the political and legal struggle to overturn apartheid has translated into real equality. She focuses specifically on the constitutional imperatives of promoting judicial independence and transforming the race and gender composition of the bench. She concludes that judicial independence has been advanced, seen in the role of courts in restraining state power, although courts have not yet lived up to their promise to reduce poverty and inequality. She is less sanguine about the effort to increase the representation of blacks and women on the bench, which "remains a central challenge."

Ann Southworth, Anthony Paik, and John Heinz look at how lawyers try to impact politics from a different perspective – namely, how they construct advocacy networks that attempt to influence national-level policymaking. Through a study of organizations and advocates that took positions on a set of controversial policy issues in the United States, the authors explore the characteristics of the lawyers, the strategies they deployed, and the lines of conflict and collaboration. They find relationships between professional status and causes served: "lawyers for liberal activist groups had the most prestigious academic credentials, while those serving conservative religious organizations were much less likely to have such credentials." They also found different patterns of collaboration. Their research "suggests that socially conservative advocates and organizations stand apart, not only from other conservatives but from the interconnected communities of lawyers and organizations that speak for most major players in national policymaking."

The section concludes with two stories of cause lawyering. Frank Munger turns to social movements in Thailand and elegantly maps the careers and work of lawyers who confront the state. He contrasts the experiences of lawyers working in the women's rights, environmental, and antipoverty movements, and asks how cause lawyering may promote "progress" outside the common law world – measured by increased "government accountability, respect for rights, and freedom to advocate change, consistent with a liberal interpretation of the 'rule of law.'" Muger's conclusions are clear-eyed yet optimistic. Although he acknowledges that "Thai cause lawyers continue to struggle to sustain their work," he finds "signs of progress" in the "administrative courts … and the still-strong network of NGOs and lawyers created by the October generation."

Lucie White offers an analysis of innovative lawyering for economic and social rights in Ghana. She focuses on a collaboration between community residents and lawyers (with the crucial help of law students) to reform health and sanitation systems in a very-low-income community called Nima. White describes in compelling terms the ravages of inadequate sewage treatment and the grassroots effort to challenge the "root causes" of community deprivation. She carefully reflects on the origins and execution of Nima's "Right to Health Campaign," which moved beyond traditional top-down strategies toward a "pragmatic multitactic program of human rights activism" that sought to transform sanitation practices while providing "a foundation for citizen participation in state-of-the-art welfare delivery institutions and systems over the long term." White concludes with observations about the degree to which the campaign was successful in achieving its aims, while also reflecting on the challenges of promoting equitable participation opportunities across differently situated members of Nima's community.

These contributions underscore important cause lawyering themes. In particular, they suggest that the most significant challenges to the status quo may come from those segments of the legal profession that are most marginalized from centers of power – and hence have the least to lose. This is of course not bound to always be the case because there will inevitably be lawyers who sacrifice their own standing in the name of advancing a cause. However, we would assume that a common pattern of challenge would be attacks on the center by those at the periphery. And we would also assume that those challenges are (precisely for this reason) frequently thwarted – or at least muted – and that the most successful challenges would be those that involve alliances between lawyers and other groups that, in the aggregate, are able to mount serious threats to the status quo.

This leads us to Richard Abel's powerful and synthetic epilogue, in which he asks whether and under what conditions law can, in fact, promote justice. In answering this question, Abel seamlessly weaves together the volume's three fundamental concerns: "the adequacy of the 'professional project' as a theory of the legal profession, the commitment of lawyers to the core notion of legality, and the possibility of equal justice in unequal societies." With respect to the professional project, Abel remains a committed Weberian and offers support for why he continues "to find Larson's theory of market control and status competition the most insightful and economical explanation for the continuing saga of common law legal professions." Although Abel is critical of the organized bar's pursuit of private self-interest and the barriers to justice that it creates, he is not ultimately dismissive of the possibility that justice may be achieved – at least sometimes. He therefore chooses to illuminate moments of possibility and honor the lawyers who seize them. While some lawyers thwart the rule of law, others rally to its defense. While some serve power, others dedicate themselves to challenging it. In the end, Abel eschews cynicism for inspiration, proclaiming that while law may offer only partial justice, it is a justice worth fighting for: "Any defense of the rule of law is better than capitulation to executive autarchy. Lawyers deserve praise for devoting effort to promoting justice – not criticism for failing to do more.... Victories, even small ones, inspire further resistance, not resignation to the status quo. The struggle for justice never ends; but each chapter inspires future generations to persevere."

Conclusion: An Unfinished Project

This volume is inspired by Abel's insistence that lawyers can – and should – do better. It therefore asks not just what the professional project has wrought, but what new visions it might create. Can lawyers lead us to a more just and equal world? What are the pathways and mechanisms by which lawyers may promote justice in the contemporary political and economic context? In the end, this volume does not answer these questions, but rather probes the openings for a revitalized approach to fusing law and justice while attending to the ongoing economic constraints embedded in the structure of the profession. In so doing, the contributors chart the new terrain of the professional project, asking whether the current moment is part of the inexorable march of commercialization – or may illuminate a meaningful way out.

PART I

LAWYERS AND THE PUBLIC GOOD: THE FUNDAMENTAL DILEMMA

2

Are Lawyers Friends of Democracy?

Robert W. Gordon

INTRODUCTION

Anyone who watched the pictures of Pakistani lawyers, in their dark business suits and ties, out on the street in the thousands to protest General Pervez Musharraf's 2007 removal of the country's chief justice, knew he was seeing something way out of the ordinary. We do not usually associate lawyers with street protests, or with popular politics of any kind. Do we even associate them with democracy?

In answering this question, I define "democracy" very loosely, to include much more than government by leaders or legislators elected (directly or mediately) by popular votes – though of course these are classical preconditions for democratic government. Societies are more or less democratic to the extent they exhibit institutional arrangements that enable ordinary people to get access to decision-making power – political, economic, or social – in matters that affect their lives; that enable people to lobby or petition power holders and to influence public opinion through the media; to organize in associations so that power holders will have to take account of them and bargain with them; to have access to effective procedures and representation to challenge decisions adverse to their interests in administrative proceedings and courts and private governments; to have resort to regular channels to resist enforcement of unpalatable laws; and to express dissent without fear of retribution.

Lawyers or lawyer equivalents are obviously important to democratic movements – both as enablers and as obstacles. In many societies (as in the United States for most of its history), they dominate the legislatures and bureaucracies that make the laws; and whether they do or not, lawyers in their private practices are one of the chief means for the ground-level interpretations of and responses – be it compliance, evasion, or resistance – to state law. Their aid and influence can amplify voice, organizational power, and capacity to manipulate the levers and negotiate the mazes of the institutional instruments of governance. In this respect, lawyers are much

Thanks for exceptionally helpful comments to Rick Abel and Scott Cummings.

like the other great mixed public-private associations that are the building blocks of democratic civil society – political parties, the media, churches, universities, trade associations, and labor unions. Whether a society is authoritarian, democratic, or torn apart by factional contest may essentially depend on the alignments of such associations: whether they are oriented toward and subservient to autocrats or oligarchs, or are independent power centers; whether they are agents of warring ethnic, tribal or ideological factions whose major aims are the eradication of their enemies. In most societies, most of the time, most lawyers are agents of the relatively powerful and wealthy – the state and powerful private associations like large landowners and corporations. You can usually – though not infallibly – predict what side lawyers will take in political contests by identifying the strategies and alliances of their principal patrons and clienteles.

A series of recent case studies of the role of lawyers in building liberal societies in modern times has generally concluded that lawyers are often a political force for legalism, following the rules laid down and the regular established procedures of the Rule of Law.[1] Historically in societies that have succeeded in building liberal institutions like parliaments, competitive elections, and relatively independent courts, lawyers are also a spearhead of bourgeois liberalism – promoters of the rights of property, assembly, and speech and free markets, and the right to freedom from arbitrary arrest and imprisonment. Especially where lawyers have achieved organization as independent self-regulating professions, they are more likely to resist new impositions of autocratic rule and persecution of political opponents.[2] (See, for example, the French bar's role in resisting Bonapartist governments through political defenses and restoring institutions of parliamentary government in the nineteenth century, or the Brazilian bar association's protests of abuses of military government in the 1980s.) This program is obviously friendly to democracy, because democratic movements and institutions require a basic infrastructure of enforceable rights that permit them to operate. The same studies however find that even liberal-minded lawyers are easily intimidated by authoritarian governments' claims to expanded powers in emergencies. And lawyers are not usually inclined to support expansions of popular participation in government, such as through a broader suffrage. They are even less likely to support movements from below that press the interests of labor or other subordinated groups. Representation of insurgent or outsider groups is generally the task, where it is taken up at all, of a few marginal or dissident members of the profession, like the South African lawyers who fought against apartheid.[3]

1 *See* FIGHTING FOR POLITICAL FREEDOM: COMPARATIVE STUDIES OF THE LEGAL COMPLEX AND POLITICAL LIBERALISM (Terence C. Halliday, Lucien Karpik & Malcolm M. Feeley eds., 2007).

2 Terence C. Halliday, Lucien Karpik & Malcolm M. Feeley, *The Legal Complex and Struggles for Political Liberalism*, *in* FIGHTING FOR POLITICAL FREEDOM, *supra* note 1, at 1.

3 RICHARD L. ABEL, POLITICS BY OTHER MEANS: LAW IN THE STRUGGLE AGAINST APARTHEID, 1980–1994 (1995).

This essay will be mostly about lawyers in the United States, whose story lines up with these general conclusions in some ways but departs from it in others. Most writers have followed Tocqueville in seeing American legal professions, and in particular the American institution of judicial review, as checks on, or counterweights to, popular democratic movements. This does not of course make American lawyers hostile to democracy as such. They may and often do support liberal or constitutional democracy, democracy within a framework of rights and restraints on powers. But they are associated with restraints on popular rule. If they support democracy it is by stabilizing it. In particular, as I detail in this essay, American lawyers are associated with:

- Constitutional checks on legislation, via gentry-staffed upper houses consisting largely of lawyers (the U.S. Senate was 80 percent lawyers throughout the nineteenth century) and judicial review; and the constitutional protection of rights of minorities, especially propertied but also sometimes marginal minorities, against encroachments by majorities.
- Alliances with monied and landed interests – in the United States specifically large-scale commercial interests (and, in the south, the planter slavocracy) – against populist-debtor, laborer, farmer, abolitionist, and other interests bent on taxing, regulating or redistributing business property; and with employers against employees.
- The guild interests of professionals in preserving or enhancing their privileges and status and limiting competition for their services, against those who would level distinctions based on education and special privileges.[4]

In what follows, I try to provide a rough and tentative sketch of successive phases in the complex relation between lawyers and democracy in the United States. In an initial phase of Revolution and Constitution-making, lawyers were the principal political movers in arguing the cause for the break with British rule, establishing institutions of rule by "the People," and at the same time building institutions to restrain what they considered popular excesses. In the nineteenth century, the legal profession's leaders embraced more expansive and inclusive forms of democratic participation as they themselves courted voters for election to legislative or judicial office. By the late nineteenth century, however, leading lawyers retreated from democratic ideals as they increasingly tied their careers and fortunes to the interests of corporate clients. This development prompted a split in the elite bar: Alarmed by the prospects both of special-interest corruption of republican government and populist revolt, "Progressive" lawyers led political movements, culminating in the New Deal, to enhance governmental capacity to make policy in the general interest. From

[4] Richard L. Abel, American Lawyers (1989).

1954–1975, an alliance of elite (judges on and advocates before the highest federal courts; Congressional leaders and executive appointees in liberal administrations) and marginal (black, female, Jewish, and labor) lawyers cooperated to produce the Rights Revolution, which helped bring excluded minorities into full citizenship; and to expand access to the legal system through legal services and public interest lawyering. Since the 1980s, however, the causes of equal justice and equal access to justice have gone into retreat as a result of conservative backlash; and leading attorneys once again devote themselves almost exclusively to the interests and agendas of business clients.

THE ROLE OF LAWYERS IN TOCQUEVILLE'S DEMOCRACY

The classic source and starting point for analysis of the relation between lawyers and democracy is Tocqueville, who gave a lot of thought to it in *Democracy in America*.[5] His answer was complicated. He discusses the legal profession in a chapter on counterweights to the "tyranny of the majority." In the United States, he says, lawyers are like the European aristocracy, an elevated class with conservative habits and instincts, who serve as a check on populist impulses. They love order and stability. Anglo-American lawyers in particular are professionally conservative because they are attached to the past through the common law method, with its respect for precedent.

If lawyers are not always friendly to democracy, democracies are friendly to them. Although lawyers may seem to be set above the ordinary mass of people because of superior education and knowledge, they spring from the people and have risen in a meritocratic career open to talent. Hence they are trusted as leaders of democratic movements and as leaders in democratic politics.

Lawyers, Tocqueville adds, do not play this role everywhere: It is a function of political situation and opportunities. In Europe, he says, "Sometimes they have been the tools of political authorities and sometimes they have made those authorities their tools."[6] If not included in governments, they may even lead revolutions! (Tocqueville is evidently thinking here of Robespierre and his associates.) In fact, a clever despot does well to include lawyers in his regime, because "having entrusted to them a despotism taking its shape from violence, perhaps he might receive it back from their hands with features of justice and law."[7] This is an important insight: Lawyers and the rule of law can be the instruments of enhancing autocratic rule and extending the state's authority, by lending it legitimacy and helping

5 Alexis de Tocqueville, Democracy in America (J.P. Mayer ed., George Lawrence trans., 1966).
6 *Id.* at 264.
7 *Id.* at 266.

it secure the cooperation it needs – for example, from important domestic factions to raise tax revenues to finance wars and other grand projects, or from foreign donors or governments who look for signs of compliance with the "Rule of Law." Indeed, in much of the world, this is exactly what lawyers do: They further their own interests by serving the interests of the ruling regime.[8] They uphold the legalist values of procedural regularity, adherence to precedent, strict formal readings of positive law. If the regime changes the law, lawyers go along with the change.

The same virtues that make lawyers useful to authority may, of course, also serve as brakes on utterly arbitrary applications of law, the targeting as enemies and arrest and detention of persons and groups for improvised or extralegal reasons. Especially in societies where lawyers have established independent judiciaries and bar associations, they may serve as centers of resistance to novel impositions of authority.[9]

In the United States, as elsewhere, lawyers have gained much of their authority through their association with a specific body of officials – the judiciary. The courts are staffed – as in Tocqueville's America the upper courts had come to be by the 1830s – with professional lawyers. Through judicial review, judges play a major political role, though their power is contained by having to be exercised case by case rather than wholesale. Tocqueville even credits lawyers with creating the public language of American democracy: Legal discourse spreads through the masses, in part through juries, until "the whole people have contacted some of the ways and tastes of a magistrate."[10] Not only is every lawyer a democrat, but every democrat is a lawyer.

Tocqueville's is a very good introduction to the complicated, antagonistic-but-also-sympathetic, and complementary relation of lawyers to democracy, not only in America but elsewhere in the world. Closer examination of the history of this relation shows it to be more complicated still.

REVOLUTIONARY LAWYERS

Something like Tocqueville's picture in short has come to be a standard picture of the relation of American lawyers to democracy. This picture, however, reliably captures the self-conception of a segment of the bar – Tocqueville's mostly Whig lawyer informants – and only at a particular point in time. This is, of course, a result of the occupational hazard of writing about "lawyers" generally or "the legal profession."

[8] *See* Dietrich Rueschemeyer, *Comparing Legal Professions: A State Centered Approach*, *in* LAWYERS IN SOCIETY: COMPARATIVE THEORIES 289 (Richard L. Abel & Philip S.C. Lewis eds., 1989); RULE BY LAW: THE POLITICS OF COURTS IN AUTHORITARIAN REGIMES (Tom Ginsburg & Tamir Moustafa eds., 2008).

[9] *See* Halliday, Karpik & Feeley, *supra* note 2.

[10] TOCQUEVILLE, *supra* note 5, at 270.

Law is many professions, fragmented by class origins and education, clienteles, and differential benefits from professional privileges.

In the Revolutionary phase of the republic, lawyers were friendlier to the popular element in democratic thought. They were, of course, articulate spokesmen for the basic principle of republican government, self-rule by the People. In part, this was a negative conception, antimonarchical, antiautocratic, and anti-feudal-distinctions based on caste or class. (This is actually the meaning Tocqueville himself gives to "democracy.") In the Revolutionary period, lawyers saw themselves playing the classical Ciceronian role of fearlessly independent spokesmen for republican liberty against tyranny, usually played out in defending individuals against encroachments on liberty. In this role, lawyers used (as Cicero had, as Thomas Erskine had in England in his defense of Thomas Paine, and as French lawyers repeatedly did in the 1760s) the opportunities presented by particular cases to make sweeping public arguments for the cause of liberty generally. The premier example was James Otis's great argument in the Writs of Assistance Case (1761) that Parliamentary acts authorizing general warrants were void because they were contrary to fundamental law.

But the revolutionary lawyers also became spokesmen for the far more radical proposition that the People oppressed by a government that repeatedly refused to reform itself and protect their liberties could dissolve that government and form another. This was a defense of the revolutionary and original role in creating governments of The People Themselves, or the People Out of Doors, assembling in crowd protests (much like the Pakistani lawyers' associations), juries, militias, and conventions of the people. As governments were the enforcers of ordinary law, the "people themselves" were enforcers, even against governments, of fundamental law.[11]

Indeed one of the most important contributions of lawyers for the radical Whig (in England) and revolutionary (in France and America) causes was their conversion of the specialized, technical, languages of law into a vernacular discourse of liberty and rights.[12] The common law, for example, was turned from a collection of writs and specialized sciences of pleading and property interests into a repository of public law maxims, the constitutional rights of freeborn Englishmen, and eventually of all men everywhere. Tocqueville himself noted both the attachment of lawyers

[11] *See* Christian G. Fritz, American Sovereigns: The People and America's Constitutional Tradition before the Civil War 11–46 (2008); Larry Kramer, The People Themselves 24–34 (2004); Pauline Maier, From Resistance to Revolution: Colonial Radicals and the Development of Opposition to Britain, 1765–1776 (1972).

[12] *See* David Bell, Lawyers and Citizens: The Making of a Political Elite in Old Regime France 105–128 (1994) (France); Daniel Hulsebosch, Constituting Empire: New York and the Transformation of Constitutionalism in the Atlantic World, 1664–1830, at 203–06 (2005) (United States); Steven Wilf, Law's Imagined Republic: Popular Politics and Criminal Justice in Revolutionary America (2010) (United States); Richard Ross, *The Commoning of the Common Law*, 146 U. Pa. L. Rev. 323, 446–61 (1998) (England).

to old common law forms and the diffusion of the language of law as a general public language, but missed the connection between them. Ironically, soon after lawyers helped convert law into a popular language of rights and self-government, the professional elite undertook to change it back again into a specialized science accessible only to the deeply and broadly educated.[13]

PROFESSIONAL INDEPENDENCE

American lawyers began to develop their more conservative Tocquevillian conception of the lawyer's function after the People, whether embodied as crowds or popularly elected legislatures, demonstrated in the elite's eyes that they too could act against their own long-term interests, for example, by storming courthouses to prevent them from collecting debts in recessions, enacting laws allowing payment in paper money, confiscating Loyalist property, or putting political opponents in jail. In particular, the concrete People demonstrated their unreliability by ceasing to defer to, and vote for, their betters in election contests. These developments opened a new role for elites – no longer defined in class terms but in institutional (federal representatives, senators, judges) and occupational (professionals) terms – as checks on popular excesses.[14] For example, Madison proposed first to give the Federal Congress a veto on state legislation; when that failed, he suggested federal judges as a substitute.

Lawyers of the Federalist persuasion also took the lead in state constitutional conventions in the attempt to resist expansion of the suffrage to men without property. James Kent, for example, warned against "a tendency in the poor to covet and to share the plunder of the rich; in the debtor to relax or avoid the obligations of contract; in the majority to tyrannize over the minority.... in the indolent and profligate, to cast the whole burthens of society upon the industrious and virtuous."[15]

But the Federalists were defeated nationally in 1800. The suffrage was expanded – despite their efforts – to include virtually all unpropertied white men (except paupers). And even elite lawyers found new uses for popular institutions. Tocqueville was alarmed by new movements to elect judges, which, he thought, could only sap the influence of his ersatz-aristos. The legal elites, however, rapidly came to appreciate elections as a means to strengthen the power and legitimacy of courts by giving judges a backing independent both of legislatures and of governors. In fact, it

[13] *See e.g.*, KRAMER, *supra* note 11, at 161–64.

[14] *See* FRITZ, *supra* note 11, at 119–52; *see also* GORDON WOOD, THE CREATION OF THE AMERICAN REPUBLIC, 1776–1787 (1969).

[15] James Kent, *Debates, New York Constitutional Convention of 182, in* DEMOCRACY, LIBERTY AND PROPERTY – THE STATE CONSTITUTIONAL CONVENTIONS OF THE 1820s, at 115–16 (M. Peterson ed., 1966).

was elected judiciaries, led by that of New York, that most aggressively exercised judicial review in the 1840s. In the wake of the public works scandals of the 1830s and 1840s, state constitutional conventions – dominated by lawyers – enacted new restraints on legislatures thought to be in league with corrupt corporations. Elected judges could thus plausibly claim to be the agents of the will of the People at large assembled in convention against the legislature.[16]

Elite lawyers in any case could hardly afford to disparage democratic politics because nearly all of them in this period ran for political office at both the state and federal level, as well as for judgeships. Four members of the U.S. Supreme Court of the 1860s aspired to run for President. Moreover, the elite's pretensions to being a special caste of aristos was – fortunately for the profession's future influence and standing – impaired by the Jacksonian destruction of closed bar associations, barriers to entry and competition. Although the highest precincts of practice – representing big commercial interests before upper courts, and posts in the federal and upper state judiciary – were de facto mostly occupied by college- and law-school-trained men of upper-middle-class background,[17] the legal profession was a career open to talent. And some men conspicuous for humble origins – for instance, Alexander Hamilton, Daniel Webster, and Martin van Buren – rose to fame and fortune within it. This contrasted strongly with the profession of English barristers, an insular club virtually closed off to any but men of independent means, dependent for advancement to judicial office on Crown patronage, committed to no cause larger than preserving its privileges and status, and not much of a force for the defense of rights or the promotion of democracy.[18]

The leading lawyers of the nineteenth century were indeed allied by business and political ties – and regular retainers – to dominant commercial interests: merchants, manufacturers, bankers, and insurance companies in the North, and slaveholding planters in the South. But they were still advocates who represented a diversity of clienteles and who tended to identify with the courts and their roles in public life, rather than with their clients, as the primary source of their prestige and power. Some leading lawyers in the North associated themselves with the antislavery cause, urged antislavery positions in the courts, and challenged laws and policies discriminating against blacks, often at the cost of losing some paying clients.[19] Until the

[16] Jed Handelsman Shugerman, The People's Courts (2008) (unpublished Ph.D. dissertation, Yale University) (on file with author).

[17] *See* Kermit Hall, *Social Backgrounds and Judicial Recruitment: A Nineteenth Century Perspective on the Lower Federal Judiciary*, 29 W. POLIT. Q. 243 (1976); Gary B. Nash, *The Philadelphia Bench and Bar, 1800–1861*, 7 COMP. STUD. IN SOC'Y & HIST. 203 (1965).

[18] *See* DAVID LEMMINGS, PROFESSORS OF THE LAW: BARRISTERS AND ENGLISH LEGAL CULTURE IN THE EIGHTEENTH CENTURY (2000).

[19] *See* J. Morgan Kousser, *The Supremacy of Equal Rights: The Struggle Against Racial Discrimination in Ante-Bellum Massachusetts and the Foundations of the Fourteenth Amendment*, 82 NW. U. L. REV. 941 (1988).

1880s, lawyers who regularly represented industrial interests such as the railroads also represented plaintiffs suing those interests.[20] Lawyers also identified with the political parties of which they were leaders and mainstays.

As political scientists have pointed out, the courts tend to be strongest and most independent in robust democracies in which parties alternate in power. Parties while in power want to use the courts to consolidate political gains, perpetuate their policies beyond their term in office, and cement in place allies against political persecution.[21] Parties at loggerheads over critical issues punt awkward and difficult issues to the courts for resolution so they do not have to take the heat for them – as, for example, the major parties hoped to do with the slavery issue in the nineteenth century, did with the dismantling of segregated schools after the 1950s, and to some extent continue to do with the abortion issue in the present.[22] Judges were pretty firmly under democratic controls. In most states, judges by the 1850s were elected. Federal judges, though appointed for life, were strictly limited in their jurisdiction – and hence their capacity to overturn state laws – by Congress, and were also recruited from and appointed to districts coterminous with states.[23] Moreover American lawyers of the early republic were trial lawyers, which meant that outside equity and admiralty practice, they had to have the knack of courting juries, and were thus invested in the system of jury trial. Adversary jury trial, as its historians have pointed out, puts lawyers in charge of adjudicative procedure.[24]

So after the first period of Federalist reaction, American lawyers were committed democrats – though, to be sure, relatively conservative democrats. In the many arguments over whether popular or professional elements should prevail in legal institutions, they usually took the professional side. Judges should be trained lawyers, not laymen; judges should be able to control and direct jury verdicts; commercial cases should generally be removed from juries; if the common law was to be codified, it should be through learned code commissioners rather than lay legislators. The sovereign People's will was best expressed not through their direct participation in civic life – as, for example, with the uprising resulting in the Dorr Rebellion in Rhode Island – but mediated through representatives, the separation of powers, and professional advocacy.[25] Lawyers were the primary movers of the

[20] *See* Robert W. Gordon, *The Lawyer-Citizen: A Myth with Some Basis in Reality*, 50 Wm. & Mary L. Rev. 1169, 1189–90 (2009).

[21] *See, e.g.*, Stephen Holmes, *Lineages of the Rule of Law*, *in* Democracy and the Rule of Law 19 (José María Maravall & Adam Przeworski eds., 2003).

[22] *See* Keith Whittington, Political Foundations of Judicial Supremacy: The Presidency, the Supreme Court, and Constitutional Leadership in U.S. History 82–160 (2007).

[23] *See* Howard Gillman, *How Political Parties Can Use the Courts to Advance their Agendas: Federal Courts in the United States, 1875–1891*, *in* Institutions and Public Law: Comparative Approaches 45–68 (Tom Ginsburg & Robert A. Kagan eds., 2005).

[24] *See* John H. Langbein, The Origins of Adversary Criminal Trial (2005).

[25] *See* Fritz, *supra* note 11, at 261–76.

transformations by which the informal, communal processes of local courts run by lay gentry justices (in which even weak stakeholders like slaves, apprentices, and women were allowed some participation) were gradually supplanted by the "rule of law" – professional-legal procedures of trials appealable up through a hierarchical, centralized court system that enforced a formal equality of rights but only among the classes of citizens who were accorded rights.[26]

A BAR DIVIDED

Lawyers of the Jacksonian era were divided among themselves about their appropriate relation to democracy. Generally the elites adopted a Tocquevillian conception of their role: The ideal lawyers were preferably college and law school graduates, steeped in classical and historical learning, and deep students of legal science. These characteristics equipped them to be democracy's necessary guardians: curators of legal and constitutional principle in restraint of popular excess, and disinterested stewards of the long-term interests of the People against their momentary "inclination[s]" or "ill humors."[27] The journeymen of the bar scoffed at the elite's pretensions and efforts to restrict entry. Lawyers were simply practical businessmen, who sold services to clients, and got ahead through enterprise and "hard work." "We are clever men of business, as a mass, and no more. It is our BUSINESS TALENTS, our PROMPTNESS, ACCURACY AND DILIGENCE, that commands success, respect, and influence."[28] Lawyers were not the guardians of democracy, but enactors of it, players in the primal democratic game, small entrepreneurs competing alongside others for success in the market.

Ironically it was in the period of the ascension of the elected judge that lawyers started talking about the countermajoritarian virtues of courts. Unfortunately, where forces were most needed to counteract the most vicious of popular impulses targeting unpopular minorities, the lawless dark underside of Jacksonian democracy – antiabolitionist mobs, white settlers expelling Indians from their lands, frontier vigilantes, disenfranchisers of free blacks – lawyers, with a few notable exceptions, were missing in action.[29]

In the later nineteenth century, the legal elite took a decidedly antipopulist turn and adopted strategies aimed at de-democratizing American politics and turning the direction of public policy over to a national business class. The elite bar at this

[26] *See* Laura F. Edwards, The People and their Peace: Legal Culture and the Transformation of Inequality in the Post-Revolutionary South 220–98 (2009); Richard E. Ellis, The Jeffersonian Crisis: Courts and Politics in the Young Republic (1971).

[27] The Federalist No. 78, Alexander Hamilton (1788).

[28] Maxwell Bloomfield, American Lawyers in a Changing Society, 1776–1876 151 (1976).

[29] *See* Daniel Walker Howe, What Hath God Wrought: The Transformation of America, 1815–1848 410–45 (2007).

point was becoming the captive of its business clienteles, chiefly the railroads, which demanded an exclusive loyalty to their interests.[30] On the whole, both Republicans and conservative Democrats were happy with a system that elevated corporate lawyers to the federal courts, there to serve as a bulwark against labor organizations, personal injury tort suits, a progressive income tax, Granger regulation of railroads and public utilities, and social legislation.[31] Lawyers in the South took the lead both as attorneys and legislators in promoting industrialization and in devising the legal architecture to give the appearance of compliance with the Reconstruction Amendments while disenfranchising and resubordinating their black populations.[32] Very few lawyers were connected with the Populist movements or labor organizations. In fact, Bryanite populists identified both judges and the elite legal profession as their natural enemies. Obviously the most important antipopular move was the disenfranchisement of blacks in the former slave states. This was matched by similar attempts to restrict the franchise to exclude poor, working-class, and immigrant citizens in the Northern states.[33]

LAWYERS IN THE PROGRESSIVE ERA

Legal professions have a direct relation to democratic movements and institutions as keepers of the gates of access and influence to legislatures and courts. The legal establishments generally did very little to promote access to the legal system for people of small means until the 1970s. Their funding of legal aid was stingy and conditional on polite nonadversarial behavior from those representing the poor.[34]

[30] For an exemplary study of a leading railroad's relations with its lawyers, see WILLIAM THOMAS, LAWYERING FOR THE RAILROAD: BUSINESS, POWER AND LAW IN THE NEW SOUTH (1999).

[31] This story is complicated. The upper judiciaries of the Gilded Age were never simply hirelings of plutocracy. Many were alarmed by the rise of giant consolidated enterprises and their corruption of republican politics and the rule of law. Their decisions did not always favor corporate business interests. But there is no question that such interests, especially in the federal courts, were likely to prevail over populists, labor organizations, and tort plaintiffs; and that the new national business class looked to those courts as its natural protector and preferred litigating forum. *See* EDWARD A. PURCELL, JR., LITIGATION AND INEQUALITY: FEDERAL DIVERSITY JURISDICTION IN INDUSTRIAL AMERICA, 1870–1958 13–27 (1992).

[32] *See* J. MORGAN KOUSSER, THE SHAPING OF SOUTHERN POLITICS: SUFFRAGE RESTRICTION AND THE ESTABLISHMENT OF THE ONE-PARTY SOUTH, 1880–1910 (1974).

[33] *See* ALEXANDER KEYSSAR, THE RIGHT TO VOTE: THE CONTESTED HISTORY OF DEMOCRACY IN THE UNITED STATES 117–171 (2000); Kermit Hall, *Progressive Reform and the Decline of Democratic Accountability: The Popular Election of State Supreme Court Judges, 1850–1920*, 9 AM. B. FOUND. RES. J. 345 (1984). These attempts at disenfranchisement were often defended in the language of democracy. The point was to recreate an electorate purified both of the influence of special interests and machine politics, and of ignorance and clan-based (as opposed to rational-individual) voting.

[34] Michael Grossberg, *The Politics of Professionalism: The Creation of Legal Aid and the Strains of Political Liberalism in America, 1900–1930*, *in* LAWYERS AND THE RISE OF WESTERN POLITICAL LIBERALISM 305–47 (Terence Halliday & Lucian Karpik eds., 1997).

Elite lawyers who dominated the early bar associations acted aggressively to purge from the profession lawyers who represented interests adverse to their clients, especially the new cadres of immigrant lawyers, mostly night-school graduates, who were the vanguard of the new personal injury bar. The organized bar from 1880 onward built organizations designed to restrict entry to the bar to all but the college trained (no more than 2 percent of the population in 1900) and to close down the night schools. (Fortunately it failed to achieve this, and the profession remained for some time a means of ascent for new groups, although the eventual triumph of the ABA's four-years-of-college-plus-three-of-law-school campaign ultimately narrowed the class basis of the profession.[35]) The bar's new "ethics" rules, such as its prohibitions of "ambulance chasing" and advertising, were also targeted at plaintiffs' lawyers.

The Progressive reformers – also mostly led by elite lawyers, often in league with vanguard business interests as well as social reformers – challenged the newly aggressive conservative courts and business dominance of the profession. But their remedy was the building of professions, technocracy, and the administrative state. They sought to put professional trusteeship, civil service appointments, and administrative commissions in place of patronage politics and advancement through party machines – and ultimately to shrink the effective domains of popular politics. Generally only marginal (Jews, blacks, women; the ACLU, the NAACP, the National Lawyers Guild), patrician renegade (Roger Baldwin, Moorfield Storey), and pariah (Communist Party) lawyers were willing to represent quasi-feudal undergroups like industrial labor, black laborers and tenant farmers, the farmworkers of the Imperial Valley, or left-wing political agitators. Bar associations strewed the path of cause lawyers, as they had of personal injury lawyers, with obstacles such as rules restricting solicitation and group legal practice, and refused to admit (or disbarred) lawyers with radical views and associations.

The New Deal produced new types of legal professionals and alliances among lawyers. A kind of Progressive paternalist democracy (Morton Keller's apt name for it is the "populist bureaucratic regime"[36]) flourished in the New Deal, which split the legal profession's elites. New Deal lawyers like Jerome Frank, William O. Douglas, and David Lillienthal saw the role of the new federal agencies as that of promoting the welfare of the common man over the obstruction of "economic royalists" and the business lawyers (such as the Lawyer's Committee of the Liberty League) and bar associations who represented them. The organized bar associations largely supported the business lawyers. The New Deal administrator saw himself a sort of trustee for consumers, farmers, and workers – countering the power of

[35] This story is authoritatively told in ABEL, *supra* note 4.

[36] MORTON KELLER, AMERICA'S THREE REGIMES: A POLITICAL HISTORY 201–280 (2007).

special interests.[37] Generally, FDR and his advisers preferred to promote the rights and security of working people, through new statutory regimes like Social Security and the Fair Labor Standards Act, rather than to encourage mobilized popular movements like industrial labor unions and southern tenant farmers. The New Deal did, however (thanks to a flood of unionized jobs in public works), integrate these movements into Democratic party politics and organizations – at least in the North.[38] The South was a different story, especially after FDR's failed "purge" of Southern conservatives in1938. The New Deal, as Jerold Auerbach put it, was a "lawyers' deal": It operated through heavily legalized processes and in consequence created whole new careers for government lawyers, public-policy-minded lawyers who moved in and out of government, a new cadre of labor lawyers, and business lawyers dealing with legislation and administrative agencies.[39]

THE RIGHTS REVOLUTION

The Rights Revolution of the postwar era was – as it appears in retrospect – an aberrant and anomalous era of judicial populism. Judges are not usually promoters or even supporters of insurgent social movements or the interests of the poor, marginalized, or subordinated in any society. (There are some notable exceptions, like the Indian, Israeli, and South African supreme courts, or the Latin American supreme courts that use a broad "amparo" jurisdiction to act on lay petitions from obscure plaintiffs at the bottom of the social ladder to do justice.[40]) In the 1960s and 1970s, as is well known, the federal judiciary – led from the top down by the U.S. Supreme Court under Justices Earl Warren and William Brennan – created new alliances between social movements, public interest lawyers, and the courts. Some analysts have come to see these alliances as fatally antidemocratic, or at best ineffectual because of their top-down character: The argument is that by foregoing political organization, and focusing their energies on getting courts to declare rights, lawyers failed to solidify their gains and ignited a backlash against measures perceived as top-down social engineering by liberal elites.[41] Yet the rights-promoting

[37] *See, e.g.*, William O. Douglas, Democracy and Finance (1940); Jerome Frank, If Men Were Angels: Some Aspects of Government in a Democracy (1942); David Lillienthal, TVA: Democracy on the March (1944).

[38] Lizabeth Cohen, Making a New Deal: Industrial Workers in Chicago, 1919–1939 (1991).

[39] Jerold Auerbach, Unequal Justice: Lawyers and Social Change in Modern America 191–230 (1976).

[40] For case studies of courts willing to act as aggressive enforcers of social rights, see Courts and Social Tranformation in New Democracies: An institutional voice for the poor? (Roberto Gargarella, Pilar Domingo & Theunis Roux, eds. 2006).

[41] *See, e.g.*, Joel Handler, Social Movements and the Legal System: A Theory of Law Reform and Social Change (1978); Stuart Scheingold, The Politics of Rights: Lawyers, Public

initiatives, as John Ely famously argued, served the "representation-reinforcing" cause of opening up democratic politics and increasing political participation of the previously excluded – for example, through the white-primary and reapportionment cases.[42] After a nasty interim of sustaining repressive measures against "subversives" in the Red Scares of the 1950s,[43] the federal courts extended broad umbrellas of legal protection for dissident speech and protest, which worked to the benefit of the street-level organizers and demonstrators of the civil rights movements.

Scholars of popular constitutionalism[44] and of cause lawyering[45] have largely refuted the picture of out-of-touch rights-activist lawyers by showing the links between social movement activism and changes in judicial doctrine in the area of civil rights. These lawyers were also engaged in mobilizing associations and popular constituencies, lobbying legislatures, and using litigation as one among many strategies to do so. Strategies of rights promotion through courts increased the leverage of out-groups, forcing interests who control the state to bargain with constituencies they could previously ignore altogether, or profit from demonizing. Decisions by judges did not invariably close down democratic dialogue or movement activism, but often provoked and nurtured them.[46]

Critics were certainly justified in saying that court decisions declaring rights often generated expectations far beyond the capacities of judicial institutions to satisfy – as the decade of massive resistance to racial integration between 1954 and 1964 conspicuously illustrates. But the same example also suggests that court decisions could help mobilize the groups they favored to engage in political organization and

Policy and Political Change (1974). For a comprehensive review and analysis of these critiques, see Scott L. Cummings & Ingrid V. Eagly, A *Critical Reflection On Law And Organizing*, 48 UCLA L. Rev. 443 (2001).

42 John Hart Ely, Democracy and Distrust: A Theory of Judicial Review (1980).

43 The legal profession, with isolated exceptions, failed utterly at performance of its Tocquevillian – or even simple advocacy ("everyone is entitled to legal representation") – roles during the Red Scares. Very few lawyers other than Communist lawyers and radical members of the National Lawyers Guild were willing to represent Communists. A handful of left-liberal lawyers undertook to represent those accused of Communism if satisfied the charges were false. Many state bar associations passed resolutions to expel or refuse to admit lawyers with ties to Communism. The ABA affirmed the advocate's creed that everyone is entitled to a lawyer, but took no practical steps to ensure representation. *See* Auerbach, *supra* note 39, at 231–62.

44 *See, e.g.*, Kramer, *supra* note 11; Jack Balkin & Reva Siegel, *Principles, Practices, and Social Movements*, 154 U. Pa. L. Rev. 927 (2006); Robert Post & Reva Siegel, Roe *Rage: Democratic Constitutionalism and Backlash*, 42 Harv. C.R.-C.L. L. Rev. 373 (2007).

45 *See, e.g.*, Cause Lawyers and Social Movements (Austin Sarat & Stuart Scheingold eds., 2006); Michael McCann, Rights at Work: Pay Equity Reform and the Politics of Legal Mobilization (1994).

46 *See, e.g.*, Thomas H. Sugrue, Sweet Land of Liberty: The Forgotten Struggle for Civil Rights in the North (2008) (documenting the encouragement given to civil rights activists in the Northern states by the Supreme Court's decision in *Brown v. Board of Education*).

lobbying to turn notional rights into real benefits. The Civil Rights Acts of 1964 and 1965 were most efficacious when they created enforcement authority in bureaucracies to withhold federal funds from institutions that discriminated and private rights of action that awarded attorney's fees to successful lawyers in employment discrimination lawsuits. The civil rights fee statutes in particular – like the labor law reforms of the New Deal – had the effect of creating a whole new class of practitioners, thus broadening participation in social change movements well beyond the tiny groups of left-wing idealists and reformers who had originally staffed them, to include ordinary lawyers making ordinary livings.

In the 1960s, President Lyndon Johnson created another new corps of lawyers with the federally funded Legal Services Program in the Office of Economic Opportunity as part of his War on Poverty. In 1965, there were 400 full-time lawyers in all U.S. legal aid programs, which had a combined budget of $5,375,890. By 1980, the federal legal services budget was $321 million (right before President Reagan cut it by a third), supporting 6,000 lawyers. In the early 1970s, foundations (led by the Ford Foundation) began making grants to "public interest firms," about half of whom identified the poor as their principal clientele. The lawyers often disagreed about what their objectives should be. Traditional legal aid lawyers and their supporters in the organized bar thought the main mission was a service function, taking care of clients' individual needs and not antagonizing local political or commercial power structures. Others favored a model closer to the Progressive settlement house, with "storefront" services located in poor neighborhoods, combining legal with other social work services, and focused on enabling families to move up and out of poverty.

Most of the new lawyers had a more ambitious vision of law as a means of broader social reform, which would work major structural changes in the situation of the poor. An important group favored test-case litigation directed at reforming the indifferent and repressive bureaucracies that served the poor. Others saw litigation as one component of a strategy directed at helping communities of poor people mobilize politically to articulate their own needs and demands, and to participate in making and applying policies of the new antipoverty agencies in the cities. The new poverty lawyers stirred up a hornets' nest. Established legal aid programs, local bar associations, charitable organizations, and local political machines saw them as threats to their own turf and patronage relations, and tried to close them down and restrict their operations to routine individual services. Several governors tried to abolish the programs in their states after legal services sued the states for violating their own laws and policies. President Reagan tried to abolish the federal program and succeeded in crippling it; it limps onward under many political restrictions on its systemic reform activities. The bar associations, however, switched sides and since 1975 have become staunch supporters of legal services, in part because the programs create jobs for lawyers, and in part because the bar wants the profession to look good.[47]

Like the activist lawyers of the Rights Revolution, public interest lawyers have attracted critics who doubt their democratic credentials. A common critique is that lawyers can only act as lawyers in a representative capacity and have no legitimacy as representatives of the public interest. There is no unitary public interest, and the lawyers' claim to be able to define one is sheer presumption. They are not elected, and the causes they claim to represent are not those chosen by any democratic decision-making processes. Other critics suggest more broadly that lawyering and democratic empowerment are inherently in tension when lawyers represent poor, powerless, and uneducated clients, because lawyers are bound to dominate such clients and control their choices and their definitions of their interests.

That is all true, but assumption of the self-appointed vanguard role is pretty much inevitable when one's constituency lacks political and organizational capacity. The vanguard does not necessarily think it knows better than its clients what their interests are (though admittedly, sometimes, vanguard lawyers do think so). Rather, it is trying to build a clientele it can represent, just as a vanguard of environmental lawyers and activists eventually built a broad-based constituency of supporters.

THE DECLINE OF THE DEMOCRATIC IDEAL

Successful legal and political strategies aggressively promoting the rights of marginal, outcast, or subordinated groups are bound to inspire popular backlash. Lawyers of the conservative countermovements set themselves against the Warren Court's rights revolution in the name of democracy, or at least of legislative and occasionally popular majorities. Judicial orders to bus school children were massively unpopular across the entire nation. Judicial decisions forbidding prayer in public schools and aid to religious private schools helped mobilize flocks of evangelical voters, especially in the South, to organize in support of resurgent conservative parties. New judicial protections for criminal suspects unluckily preceded a major crime wave and were held responsible for it. Richard Nixon used this upsurge of popular discontent to split the old Democratic coalition and rebuild the Republican Party, which has since used its control of the executive to restock the courts in most of the federal circuits with conservative judges.[48] But since gaining dominance of

47 On the new poverty lawyers, see Martha F. Davis, Brutal Need: Lawyers and the Welfare Rights Movement, 1960–1973 (1993); Earl Johnson, Jr., Justice and Reform: The Formative Years of the OEO Legal Services Program (1978); and Jack Katz, Poor People's Lawyers in Transition (1982).

48 *See* Barry Friedman, The Will of the People: How Public Opinion Has Influenced the Supreme Court and Shaped the Meaning of the Constitution 258–322 (2009).

the courts in most of the federal circuits, conservatives themselves have predictably adopted more countermajoritarian positions, invoking "original public meaning" jurisprudence to strike down unprecedented quantities of Congressional and state legislation, and using novel doctrines of federal preemption to strike down state regulatory legislation. They have also limited access to courts by restricting standing to sue and attorney-fee awards. In 2000, in a breathtaking assertion of judicial power trumping democratic political processes, the Supreme Court interrupted the counting of votes in Florida to decide the winner of the presidential election.

Elite lawyers in the corporate bar and bar associations, as previously mentioned, adopted as their own the causes that earlier in the century had been confined to marginal and pariah lawyers: civil rights, civil liberties, and representation of the poor. Bar organizations and elites have also been performing the Ciceronian role of asserting rule-of-law values and judicial restraints on executive power in representing casualties of the detention, abuse, and surveillance policies of the expanding national-security state.[49] Large law firms devote some resources to pro bono representation of clients and causes who would probably not otherwise have access to legal representation, though they steer clear of any causes that might annoy their own clients.[50]

In fact, where their own clients' interests are at stake, many precincts of the elite bar are reverting to the role they played in the Gilded Age: aggressive opponents of effective legal representation of adverse interests. Perhaps the most successful initiative has been the concentrated political and propaganda campaign against product liability tort suits, which has lobbied legislatures to cap tort attorney's fees, limit damage awards, make proof of liability more difficult and lawsuits easier to dismiss; has funneled political contributions to elect judges friendly to business tort defendants; and has promoted the use of mandatory arbitration in employment and consumer contracts to close off access to the courts and choke off class actions.[51] One of the most remarkable aspects of this campaign has been the explosion of expressions of contempt for the legal system, not only for regulatory legislation and administration (the standard rhetoric of the business bar in all ages), but for litigation, the jury trial, and the courts. The civil justice system is said to be awash in meritless claims brought by whining plaintiffs egged on by greedy lawyers, resulting in out-of-control damage awards that are destroying the competitiveness of American business.[52]

[49] *See* Richard L. Abel, *Contesting Legality in the United States after September 11* in, FIGHTING FOR POLITICAL FREEDOM, *supra* note 1, at 361–99.

[50] *See* Scott L. Cummings, *The Politics of Pro Bono*, 52 UCLA L. REV. 1 (2004).

[51] *See* WILLIAM HALTOM & MICHAEL W. MCCANN, DISTORTING THE LAW: POLITICS, MEDIA, AND THE LITIGATION CRISIS (2004).

[52] *See* Marc Galanter, *An Oil Strike in Hell: Contemporary Legends about the Civil Justice System*, 40 ARIZ. L. REV. 717 (1998).

The reason this is remarkable is because in most societies – including our own until relatively recent times – the influence of lawyers is closely tied to the prestige and standing of courts and the rhetoric of respect for the "rule of law." Courts especially are the distinctive institutional locus of lawyers' activity, their decisions the distinctive core of lawyers' knowledge, and their perceived independence is the main source of whatever perceptions there may be of the law's authority and autonomy. American lawyers are busily promoting the "rule of law" in foreign countries, by which they mean building independent courts, autonomous from political factions and interests, capable of neutral apolitical enforcement of property rights and contracts.[53] But at home, many of the lawyers occupying the highest positions in their profession are trashing the courts and financing campaigns to undermine not only the reality but even the perception of a judiciary free from corruption and independent of factional interests. Business lawyers have once again become, as in the Gilded Age, the captives of their clienteles, increasingly share their values, and identify their own interests with theirs.[54] Even after revelations of the recklessness and fraud contributing to major economic failures of recent years – the collapse of the savings-and-loan industry, the Enron bankruptcy, and the collapse of the banking and mortgage-lending industry that has led to a worldwide economic crisis – business lawyers continue to defend the work they did to enable corporate executives' actions and to help them influence governments to weaken regulations to prevent further failures. The leaders of the bar have once again become the uncritical servants of oligarchy. Maybe leading lawyers will once again form the vanguard of Progressive movements determined to open up the society to democratic participation or at least to rescue its public institutions from corruption by wealth. At present, however, there seems little prospect of this happening.

CONCLUSION

Observers of the U.S. legal profession have long engaged in debate about how to interpret the historical record of lawyers' relation to the democratic project. Is it a story best explained by the pursuit of the People's interest or simply crass self-interest? Among these observers, Richard Abel stands out for his dour view of what American lawyers have accomplished – and what we should expect from them. He is understandably skeptical of their claims to serve the public interest and the cause of justice, as he exhaustively documents the record of their organizations'

[53] For a concise review of the Rule of Law initiatives, their aims and limitations, see John Ohnesorge, *The Rule of Law*, 3 Ann. Rev. of L. & Soc. Sci. 99 (2007).

[54] *See* John Heinz, Robert L. Nelson, Rebecca L. Sandefur & Edward O. Laumann, Urban Lawyers: The New Social Structure of the Bar 179–202 (2005); Robert L. Nelson, Partners with Power: The Social Transformation of the Large Law Firm 231–69 (1988).

attempts to protect their markets, profits, and privileges.[55] But he has also taught us to be on the lookout for the inspiring exceptions, occasions in which lawyers have actively mobilized to make realities of the ideals they profess. Observed from the viewpoint Abel has recommended to us, American lawyers have turned in a mixed performance as friends of democracy. In their roles as Revolutionary spokesmen and Constitution-makers, they have been among the world's most eloquent and effective architects of the institutions of rights-based democratic government; and as advocates and political tacticians, of the expansion of rights to participate in democratic procedures and institutions by successive classes of the excluded. As zealous servants of wealthy and powerful clienteles, however, they have also staffed the causes of conservative resistance to, or rollback of, access to equal justice and political power for workers, minorities, and other marginalized groups. Still, in comparison to most of the world's legal professions, which tend on the whole to be very conservative defenders of state authority and powerful private interests, the many achievements of American lawyers in building the institutions of democracy and the rule of law and in promoting the rights of the dispossessed may seem more remarkable than their failures. In a period such as the one in which we live now, those achievements may help inspire a new vanguard of justice-seeking lawyers.

[55] *See* Abel, *supra* note 4.

3

"The Conscience of Society?"

The Legal Complex, Religion, and the Fates of Political Liberalism

Terence C. Halliday

"An independent little Republic at the heart of the state."
–Counselor to French Prime Minister (1731)

"The Church is the conscience of society.
If we do wrong and you keep quiet,
you shall answer for our mistakes."
–Jomo Kenyatta (1976)

INTRODUCTION

In the autumn of 1731, the Parisian Order of Barristers went on strike. Provocations for such a dramatic protest against royal justice had been building for several years as the bar progressively articulated ideas that intimated limits on royal power. The Crown initially counseled restraint despite its considerable exasperation with the Order as "an independent little republic at the heart of the state." But restraint disappeared when confronted with a legal brief that proclaimed the subversive doctrine that "all laws are contracts between those who govern and those who are governed."[1] The king's council threatened disbarment of the brief's author and thirty-nine fellow barristers unless they retracted the document. After negotiations failed to defuse the confrontation, lawyers walked out of the courts, thereby denying the Crown of a central

An earlier version of this chapter was presented as a lecture to the MacMillan Center Initiative on Religion, Politics and Society, Yale University, February 11, 2008. I am particularly indebted to my long-time collaborators, Lucien Karpik and Malcolm Feeley, together with the many contributors to our ongoing international and interdisciplinary collaboration on the legal complex and political liberalism.

[1] David A. Bell, *Barristers, Politics, and the Failure of Civil Society in Old Regime France, in* LAWYERS AND THE RISE OF WESTERN POLITICAL LIBERALISM: EUROPE AND NORTH AMERICA FROM THE EIGHTEENTH TO TWENTIETH CENTURIES (Terence C. Halliday & Lucien Karpik eds., 1997).

function – the dispensing of justice. Confronted with an obdurate profession, the Crown held out for three months and then effectively conceded the battle to the lawyers.[2]

The work stoppage symbolized a moment when the very foundations of royal absolutism began to be eroded, spurring the beginnings of a movement, said Voltaire, where "simple citizens triumphed, having no arms but reason."[3] Barristers brought royal justice to a standstill not because they had economic grievances, nor because they suffered slights to their status, nor because the royal courts themselves gave them cause for revolt. This insertion of the Paris bar into a politics of limited government, the opening of a public sphere, and the championing of basic rights had its origins not only in a certain concept of law, courts, and justice, but in a religious impulse. For students of western political liberalism, this "little republic" found its direction in, built its impetus on, and joined its arms with, religious insurgents. As historian David Bell and sociologist Lucien Karpik propose, the confluence of religious belief and lawyers' mobilization defined a critical moment in the evolution of western liberal politics.[4]

This episode, seemingly remote in time and doctrine, nevertheless points to a phenomenon repeated in subsequent centuries and across diverse forms of illiberal politics. It is the conjunction of religious belief and action with mobilization for a specific ideal – political liberalism. I say "conjunction" advisedly because it is not at all clear when and why religion and law are mutually supportive of political liberalism. Frequently they are not. Often they are. The theoretical problem is to account for the difference. Part of the puzzle that this chapter addresses turns precisely on the question of the conditions under which religious groups will join forces with lawyers to press toward political liberalism.

Let me set a context with the natural history of a long-term international collaboration. In the late 1980s, the sociology of professions on either side of the Atlantic had reached something of a realist consensus. Critics of an earlier functionalism asserted that professions must be seen through the lens of class conflict, economic self-interest, and control over work. The work of Richard Abel and Philip Lewis on market control featured heavily in the expression of this consensus for lawyers.[5] Beginning in the late 1980s and early 1990s, a revisionist turn brought together historians, sociologists, and legal scholars to demonstrate that lawyers must also be considered as *homo politicus*. In North America and Western

[2] Lucien Karpik, *Builders of Liberal Society: French Lawyers and Politics in*, LAWYERS AND THE RISE OF WESTERN POLITICAL LIBERALISM, *supra* note 1, at 101; *see also* LUCIEN KARPIK, FRENCH LAWYERS: A STUDY IN COLLECTIVE ACTION, 1274 TO 1994 (1998).

[3] VOLTAIRE, HISTOIRE DU PARLEMENT DE PARIS 284 (1775).

[4] DAVID A. BELL, LAWYERS AND CITIZENS: THE MAKING OF A POLITICAL ELITE IN OLD REGIME FRANCE (1994); Karpik, *supra* note 2; *see also* Bell, *supra* note 1.

[5] RICHARD L. ABEL, AMERICAN LAWYERS (1989); RICHARD L. ABEL, THE LEGAL PROFESSION IN ENGLAND AND WALES (1988); LAWYERS IN SOCIETY: THE CIVIL LAW WORLD (Richard L. Abel & Philip S.C. Lewis eds., 1988); LAWYERS IN SOCIETY: THE COMMON LAW WORLD (Richard L. Abel & Philip S.C. Lewis eds., 1988).

Europe, evidence accumulated that lawyers could often be found leading the charge toward a new kind of politics – the pursuit of political liberalism.[6] Abel himself began a "political turn" in the mid-1990s, initially with his research on lawyers in apartheid South Africa, and continuing with work on the legal complex in post-9/11 America.[7]

In these studies, an unexpected finding recurred. When we went looking for lawyers and liberalism, we often found religion. When we observed barristers, we saw priests and lay leaders, ministers and imams. When we studied bar associations, we encountered churches and mosques. When we analyzed jurisprudence, we were also confronted with theology. At least we found it often enough to warrant a closer investigation of these conjunctions between law and religious belief, or more precisely, the organized bar and religious groups.

This chapter sorts through fragments of evidence to set a research agenda for the conjunction of the legal complex, religion, and political liberalism. I proceed through four steps. First, I define briefly the core concepts political liberalism and the legal complex. Second, I review three principal conjunctions of religion and political liberalism that occur in our recent rounds of studies on Asia, Latin America, and Africa. Third, I summarize modes of mobilization for political liberalism that have involved both religious and legal groups. And fourth, I conclude by raising questions that must be at the heart of future research on lawyers, their collection action, and its political engagement with religion.

POLITICAL LIBERALISM AND THE LEGAL COMPLEX

Our project originates in empirical findings that lawyers orient themselves not only to markets but also to politics. Since "politics" itself is an enormously expansive concept, we limit ourselves to one configuration of politics, namely political liberalism.

6 Terence C. Halliday, Beyond Monopoly: Lawyers, State Crises, and Professional Empowerment (1987); Karpik, *supra* note 2; Lawyers and the Rise of Western Political Liberalism, *supra* note 1; Terence C. Halliday, *The Politics of Lawyers: An Emerging Agenda*, 24 L. & Soc. Inquiry 1007 (1999); Lucien Karpik, *French Lawyers and Political Liberalism, in* Lawyers and Political Liberalism (International Institute in the Sociology of Law ed., 1993).

7 It should be emphasized that a dichotomous contrast of *homo economus* with *homo politicus* is a conceptual convenience that vastly oversimplifies the complexity of bar politics. While it is true that a line of scholarship principally or entirely encapsulated lawyers' collective action as an economic project, it is more accurate to say that in some countries at some historical moments, different segments or strata of the bar pressed for different goals, some defending their market perquisites, others defending the fundamentals of political liberalism. Nonetheless, it still makes theoretical sense, based on empirical evidence of lawyers' collective action, to stylize the predominant tendency of a bar in one way or another. *See* Richard L. Abel, Politics by Other Means: Law in the Struggle Against Apartheid, 1980–1994 (1995); Richard L. Abel, *Contesting Legality in the United States after September 11, in* Fighting for Political Freedom: Comparative Studies of the Legal Complex and Political Liberalism 361 (Lucien Karpik, Terence C. Halliday & Malcolm M. Feeley eds., 2007).

We stipulate that political liberalism has three elements.[8] First, liberal political society turns on a *moderate state*, where power inside the state itself is fractured and substantial social power resides outside the state. Second, political liberalism is constituted by *civil society* that manifests itself both as webs of voluntary associations and a public sphere. Third, liberal political society creates and protects *basic legal freedoms*. These include: (a) so-called negative rights that restrain the state from arbitrary detention, torture, and killings through legal protections such as habeas corpus, legal representation of detainees, and due process of law more generally; (b) positive rights that include the foundational political rights of freedoms of speech, association, and movement; and (c) property rights. Political liberalism is to be distinguished from democracy, from expansive bundles of substantive rights, and also from narrow formal versions of the rule of law.[9]

Although our collaborative project began with the politics of lawyers, it became clear that lawyers alone do not adequately account for the mobilization of law to advance or defend political liberalism. The concept of "legal complex" helps capture a set of structures and dynamics that must be integral to a theory of legal mobilization. By "legal complex" we refer to relations among legally trained and legally practicing occupations that mobilize on a particular issue at a particular historical moment.[10] Although lawyers and judges are at the core of this complex, it can also include legal academics, prosecutors, and civil servants who are acting in their capacities as lawyers rather than as civil servants, administrators, or politicians. The legal complex configures itself in many different ways. Sometimes, the entire complex takes a concerted stand. At other times, the complex is fragmented.

It is especially important to note that we make no *a priori* assumptions about when and how the legal complex will mobilize on any issue at any time. We do *not* assume

8 Terence C. Halliday, *The Fight For Basic Legal Freedoms: Mobilization by the Legal Complex*, *in* Global Perspectives on the Rule of Law (James J. Heckman, Robert L. Nelson & Lee Cabatingan eds., 2009) [hereinafter Halliday, *The Fight for Basic Legal Freedoms*]; Terence Halliday, *Knowledge Mandates: Collective Influence by Scientific, Normative and Syncretic Professions*, 36 British J. of Sociology 421 (1985); Terence C. Halliday & Lucien Karpik, *Political Lawyering*, *in* International Encyclopedia of Social and Behavioral Sciences 11673–11678 (Neil J. Smelser & Paul B. Baltes eds., 2001); Terence C. Halliday & Lucien Karpik, *Politics Matter: A New Framework for the Comparative and Historical Study of Legal Professions*, *in* Lawyers and the Rise of Western Political Liberalism, *supra* note 1, at 15; Terence C. Halliday, Lucien Karpik & Malcolm M. Feeley, *The Legal Complex and Struggles for Political Liberalism*, *in* Fighting for Political Freedom, *supra* note 7, at 1.

9 Democracy places greater emphasis on political rights of suffrage, the contestation of political parties, and representation. We do not include mobilization by the legal complex on behalf of economic, social, and political (suffrage) rights, not because they are not important, but because the politics of the legal complex is qualitatively different in its legitimacy, organization, and impact on basic legal freedoms than wider substantive rights. In the former it can claim a singular epistemological and technical authority that it cannot in the latter, where it descends to the same level of playing field as any interest group in a pluralistic political regime. *See* Halliday, Karpik & Feeley, *supra* note 8, at 11; Lucien Karpik, *Postscript: Political Lawyering*, *in* Fighting for Political Freedom, *supra* note 7, at 468–9.

10 Halliday, *The Fight for Basic Legal Freedoms*, *supra* note 8.

that legal complexes everywhere are inherently disposed toward political liberalism. The conditions under which they mobilize *for* political liberalism is a subject for research and challenge for theory.[11]

CONJUNCTIONS OF THE LEGAL COMPLEX, POLITICAL LIBERALISM, AND RELIGION

Religious and legal groups relate to each other in varieties of ways, some more proximate to our theoretical agenda than others. Religious groups and the legal complex might mobilize to the same end but entirely independently, using similar or different methods. Religious groups might mobilize to accomplish a distinctively religious goal but whose byproducts prove constructive for lawyers. A case in point would be a defense of freedom of speech in which religion can thrive while also serving as a nursery for the political speech essential for liberal politics. Members of religious groups who are part of the legal complex, such as the Jansenists in the Paris Bar, might infuse the legal complex with political values consistent with those of the religious faith. And, most obviously, legal and religious organizations can join an alliance to pursue the same goals, using similar or different methods.

In the immediate instance, a politics of liberalism must identify at the outset direct relationships where religious and legal groups explicitly ally, or oppose each other, with respect to a common goal. This in itself would be a significant advance in the politics of lawyers and the legal complex. In other instances, however, research must identify those circumstances where there are indirect conjunctions of belief and action, which are complementary, but uncoordinated and unexpected. The variations on these direct and indirect conjunctions can be observed below.

Three orientations of the legal complex and religion toward political liberalism can be identified as: religion for political liberalism; the legal complex for religion; and religion against political liberalism.[12] I present illustrative fragments from Franco's Spain, Chile under Pinochet, Kenya during Moi's presidency, Brazil in the 1990s, and Egypt in last fifteen years.

RELIGION *FOR* POLITICAL LIBERALISM

There are two distinctive moments at which the advocacy of basic legal freedoms may vary systematically.

[11] Halliday, Karpik & Feeley, *supra* note 8, at 6–8, 12–36.

[12] I only treat episodes of religious mobilization that also involve the legal complex, that is, where there is a conjunction of both.

Resisting Oppression and (Re)Establishing Political Liberalism

In Spain's transition from Franco's authoritarianism, Lisa Hilbink has shown how a progressive group of judges, *Justicia Democrática* (JD), helped catalyze a shift toward political liberalism that mobilized diverse elements of the legal complex.[13] In 1971, they founded a clandestine bar association, *Círculo de Estudios Jurídicos*, which by 1974 became a national organization. JD mounted a critique of the judiciary's complicity with the regime and called for judicial independence and the restriction or abolition of military and special courts. JD sharply criticized infringements on rights and articulated the premises of a just rights regime.[14] Liberal judges declaimed the lack of procedural protections in the penal and military justice codes, assaults on free speech and repressive activities in universities, and the criminalization of political associations. In their place, JD advocated a state whose guiding principle would be "respect for the dignity, integrity and liberty of the human person," and that would guarantee citizens "rights to liberty of expression, correspondence, abode, assembly and association, security, habeas corpus, due process, and petition."[15]

The judges found allies in the Roman Catholic Church conventionally associated with Franco. In the 1950s and 1960s, two types of religious activists mobilized, seemingly at opposite ends of the political spectrum. From one wing came liberally minded Catholic academics who advocated social justice and the autonomy of intellectual ideas. They drew on both indigenous movements, such as the ACNP (*Asociación Católica Nacional de Progandistas*), which championed Catholics in positions of power, and on European movements led by prominent intellectuals such as Jacques Maritain and Pierre de Chardin. When repressed in the mid-1950s, their reputation soared all the higher in civil society. For instance, the progressive encyclicals of Pope John XXIII inspired Franco's former minister of education to form a critical journal of opinion, a platform from which he criticized the regime, arguing for democratic ideas, not least that legal professionals had an obligation to champion a justice that delivered authentic rule of law where the rights of the weak were protected against "the absolute power of the state."[16]

From another wing of the Church came technocrats influenced by the *Opus Dei* movement. As they came to dominate economic policy making and administration, they insisted that more liberal markets could function effectively, and could persuade Europe of Spain's fitness for membership in the European Economic Community, only if Spain were to develop an *Estado de Derecho*, a state of law. They embarked on

[13] Lisa Hilbink, *Politicising Law to Liberalise Politics: Anti-Francoist Judges and Prosecutors in Spain's Democratic Transition*, *in* Fighting for Political Freedom, *supra* note 7, at 403.

[14] *Id.*

[15] *Id.* at 414.

[16] *Id.* at 421.

a course of institution building that started with reform of administrative courts and spread into ordinary courts, including the Supreme Court, all premised on a subversive doctrine that law might prevail over political decisions in administrative cases.[17]

The Spanish case should not be overstated. Hilbink finds it is not at the center of the legal complex but at the margins where judges, lawyers, and their religious allies found common ground. Nevertheless, an alliance of marginal groups progressively moved toward a political center and moved Spain with it.

The church's engagement under Pinochet's state of siege takes a different form – although here again I work with limited materials that were not intended to explicate a holistic account of religious responses to the military coup. Chilean democracy was abruptly foreclosed by General Pinochet's military overthrow of the elected Allende government on September 11, 1973. In Pinochet's State of Siege, individual liberties were suspended, the Constitutional Court was dissolved, political opponents were deprived of citizenship, and thousands were seized, tortured, and summarily executed without due process – all this in a long-time democracy. Did the legal complex resist?

Javier Couso demonstrates just the contrary.[18] From the outset of the military government, the judiciary not only capitulated but aided and abetted the regime. Its "complacent attitude towards the abuses of power" was reflected in its resistance to *habeas corpus* writs filed by families of political prisoners and its blind eye to the government's parallel tribunals. Of the nearly 9,000 writs (*recursos de amparo*) that were filed by human rights lawyers between 1973 and 1990, only 30 were accepted.[19]

The celebratory mass for the military leadership in the first flush of the coup suggests that the Roman Catholic Church hierarchy threw its weight behind Pinochet from the outset. In fact, the Church itself was divided. Although conservative elements supported the military's overthrow of Allende's government, segments of the Church remained persistent irritants to the regime. Cardinal Silva Henriquez, Archbishop of Santiago, for instance, on numerous occasions allowed the cathedral in Santiago to be used as a safe haven by those fleeing arrest. From a legal standpoint, one of Cardinal Henriquez's most notable acts was to found the *Vicaría de la Solidaridad*, a church-based human rights organization that emerged as a critical NGO essentially immune from military intervention. Throughout the dictatorship, it advanced the struggle for human rights not by directly confronting the government, nor by bringing cases itself, but by systematically bearing witness to abuses of rights. Sometimes this took the form of critical commentaries on Pinochet's Decree Laws. On occasions, the *Vicaría* directly urged the courts to act on the *habeas corpus*

[17] Hilbink notes that this went only so far. It did not reach to the military and ad hoc courts to which the regime directed the most sensitive cases. *Id.*

[18] Javier A. Couso, *The Role of Chile's Legal Complex in the Configuration of a Moderate State, in* FIGHTING FOR POLITICAL FREEDOM, *supra* note 7, at 315.

[19] LISA HILBINK, JUDGES BEYOND POLITICS IN DEMOCRACY AND DICTATORSHIP: LESSONS FROM CHILE (2007).

briefs it customarily dismissed out of hand. In some high-profile cases, the *Vicaría* leadership met directly with the Supreme Court President to urge responsible reactions to apparently egregious abuses of rights.

But here, it seems, any alliance between the legal complex and the Church began and ended. A few dissident lawyers carried the torch for rights against the acquiescence of the bar and the accommodation of the judiciary to the excesses of the dictatorship. Law and religion met at the margins of each.

The struggles for political liberalism in Kenya unfolded in a regime type not atypical of postcolonial Africa – the emergence and consolidation of a "Big Man" regime. The British ruled Kenya from the late nineteenth century to the early 1960s. Following independence in 1963, founding President Jomo Kenyatta dismantled the independent constitutional regime and erected in its place a de facto one-party state and a loose authoritarianism that sought to domesticate lawyers without ostensibly offending core constitutional liberties.[20] Upon his death in 1978, his successor, former Vice-President Moi, progressively tightened the authoritarian noose. When Moi changed the constitution to institutionalize KANU (Kenya African National Union) as the only legitimate party, the Law Society of Kenya (LSK) roused itself to public dissent. But it was the bloody aftermath of an unsuccessful coup attempt in 1982 that brought lawyers and the church onto the public stage, where they would remain on and off for the next twenty years.

At the time of independence, the churches could arguably boast to be the most pervasive, most respected institution in Kenya. The majority of the population belonged to Protestant and Roman Catholic churches,[21] which were responsible for around 90 percent of education and a vast array of social services, ranging from health facilities and vocational training to welfare services and legal advice for the poor.[22] The leading denominations – the Anglican Church in Kenya (the Church of the Province of Kenya), the Presbyterians, and Roman Catholics – enjoyed great moral authority and counted leaders in the government and bar among their prominent members. The churches had extensive communication channels, including national radio and a variety of print publications, through which they could inform their own members from the pulpit. By the mid-1980s, it was said that the church was the best organized and most unified organization in the country.[23]

[20] Joel D. Barkan, *Kenya after Moi*, Foreign Affairs 83 (January/February 2004); Yash P. Ghai, *Law and Lawyers in Kenya and Tanzania: Some Political Economy Considerations, in* Lawyers in the Third World: Comparative and Developmental Perspectives (Clarence J. Dias, Robin Luckham, Dennis O. Lynch eds., 1981).

[21] In 1997, there were approximately 25 million Christians out of a population of 34 million.

[22] Galia Sabar-Friedman, *"Politics" and "Power" in the Kenyan Public Discourse and Recent Events: The Church of the Province of Kenya (CPK)*, 29 Can. J. of Afr. Stud. 429 (1995).

[23] Galia Sabar-Friedman, *Church and State in Kenya, 1986–1992: The Churches' Involvement in the "Game of Change,"* 96 Afr. Aff. 25 (1997).

When Moi unleashed his forces of repression after the 1982 attempted coup, he was taken aback by the dogged resistance of a few prominent lawyers who launched active and aggressive defenses of the mutineering soldiers, challenging post-coup detentions and lodging a series of appeals to the High Court.[24] In 1986, the church joined civil society's interlocutors with the government by opposing, through the National Council of Churches in Kenya, a proposal by Moi to change procedures in voting from secret ballots to a public method whereby, it was alleged, voters would be more susceptible to partisan pressure. That same year, the government sought to push through a constitutional amendment to reduce the independence of the Attorney-General, Controller, and Auditor-General, a move that brought together the Law Society and churches with human rights advocates. This initial cooperation put in place an alliance for mobilization that recurred repeatedly over the next fifteen years as Kenya struggled toward multiparty politics and a revised constitution.

Consolidating and Defending Political Liberalism

The incompleteness of political liberalism in countries where competitive electoral systems are in place and the retreat from foundational rights in long-established liberal polities underscore the continuing salience of the most basic freedoms in countries whose polities may otherwise contrast quite markedly.[25]

In his impressive recent book, Daniel Brinks uses the prevalence of police violence in Latin America to demonstrate the limits to a liberalism that had been supposed to accompany the restoration of democracy after military dictatorships.[26] Brinks shows that in several large cities in Brazil and Argentina, police kill large numbers of victims who are disproportionately poor and weak. In 1992, police killed nearly 1,500 people in Sao Paolo – about 30 per week – or around a quarter of all homicides in the city. Similar patterns could be found in Salvador and Buenos Aires, and in smaller cities elsewhere in Brazil. Yet police seldom were held accountable for their actions. Prosecutors would not prosecute. Judges would not convict.

Many Latin American countries permit private citizens to bring prosecutions on behalf of victims, either when public prosecutors refuse to act or to support a public prosecution. Brinks found that the involvement of a private prosecutor in Sao Paolo lifted the conviction rate of police from almost zero to 32 percent. A message was sent to police that they were not immune from prosecution and to the community that justice might protect those least able to defend themselves.

[24] Robert Maxwell Press, Establishing a Culture of Resistance: The Struggle for Human Rights and Democracy in Authoritarian Kenya, 1987–2002 (2004) (Ph.D. Dissertation, University of Florida) (on file with author).

[25] Guillermo A. O'Donnell, *Democracy, Law and Comparative Politics*, 36 Stud. Comp. Int'l Dev. 7 (2001).

[26] Daniel M. Brinks, The Judicial Response to Police Killings in Latin America (2008).

The organizational leader for holding police accountable is the *Centro Santa Dias*, established in 1980 by the Archdiocese of Sao Paulo, under the leadership of its public rights advocate, Cardinal Paulo Everisto Arns. The center employs lawyers who work on behalf of victims of police violence. It has been remarkably successful. The Center's effects on prosecution for police violence are salutary not only because they put pressure on state prosecutors to perform their jobs zealously, but because the Center's private prosecutors will share the burden of bringing cases. The Center has credibility as an organ of the Church and offers protection and cover for parties to cases associated with it. Yet the Center is reluctant to engage in collective action: It does not participate in demonstrations to pressure judges to make the "right" decision or engage in direct political activity. Rather it insists that legal precepts be upheld, legal procedures followed, and corruption of the criminal process resisted.

And where was the U.S. legal complex and religion in the aftermath of 9/11? Suffice it to note here the tantalizing comment by Richard Abel on religious groups that filed amicus briefs in key federal courts: "Unitarians and Quakers predictably defended detainees; more surprising was support for Muslims from the Churches of Christ and Reform Judaism (though a Jewish group also filed for the government)."[27] Abel's passing allusion to these religious groups puts on the agenda the far bigger question: How did religious groups align themselves with opposing fragments of the legal complex as they wrestled with torture and abrogation of basic legal freedoms in the wake of the events of September 11, 2001?

THE LEGAL COMPLEX *FOR* RELIGION

Religion, not infrequently, is rather more the beneficiary of mobilization by the legal complex than its agent. Take the case of Mubarak's Egypt since 1990. Tamir Moustafa (2007) shows that the Supreme Constitutional Court become the institutional springboard for lawyers, civil society groups, and rights organizations to combat repression and compel reforms that edged Egypt, inconsistently, in a liberal direction.[28] Islamists played a quite equivocal role in this movement. Fear of Islamic extremism fueled the worst excesses of Mubarak's security apparatus. Any manifestation of political Islam, whether in the Muslim Brotherhood, in Islamic-leaning or Islamic-dominated political parties, or through Islamic leadership of key professions, drew scrutiny at best and repression at worst.

Since political Islamic lawyers, activists, and politicians were among those targeted by the security apparatus, any mobilization by the legal complex on behalf of victims of arbitrary arrest, torture, or killing disproportionately benefited political

[27] Abel, *supra* note 7, at 395.

[28] Tamir Moustafa, *Mobilising the Law in an Authoritarian State: The Legal Complex in Contemporary Egypt, in* FIGHTING FOR POLITICAL FREEDOM, *supra* note 7, at 193.

Islamist victims. When Islamist lawyer and member of the Egyptian Organization for Human Rights, 'Abd al-Harith Madani, was abducted, tortured, and killed by the security forces in April 1994, hundreds of lawyers gathered at their Syndicate to protest. So many were arrested and so vocal were their criticisms that international human rights groups – Human Rights Watch, the Center for the Independence of Judges and Lawyers, and the Lawyers' Committee on Human Rights – strongly criticized the government. Islamist groups similarly were prime beneficiaries of the battle over press freedoms that was waged by the Supreme Constitutional Court, rights groups, and opposition parties.[29] However, Moustafa offers no evidence that Islamic groups either formed religiously based human rights organizations themselves or that leading Muslim religious authorities provided moral or other support for civil society groups that indirectly defended their cause.

Explicit relationships of support or mutual benefit can be found in the electoral politics in Egypt from the 1990s through 2005. Although suffrage and elections are outside our theoretical frame, calls by the bar for participation in clean elections were embedded in broader claims for rights and more open civil society. In the months leading up to the 1996 parliamentary elections, for instance, eighty-five Islamist figures were brought before a military court to intimidate and remove them from contesting the election. In the first round, more than half of the complaints came from the Muslim Brotherhood and the Labor Party that was sympathetic to Islamist interests. In the second round, flagrant violations of election standards disproportionately victimized Islamist candidates. Many people were killed and hundreds seriously injured.[30] The courts became the only formal venue where abuses could be aired and some hope of legal redress offered.

By the time of the 1999 presidential elections and 2000 People's Assembly elections, reformers prepared by joining opposition parties with NGOs to call for not only free and fair elections, but the freedom of political speech through the media and the independence of civil society.[31] The Supreme Constitutional Court, says Moustafa, waded into battle with a "bombshell ruling" that demanded the regime permit full judicial supervision of elections for the first time in Egyptian history.[32] Although its promise was not fully realized, again it was Islamist targets of government persecution that stood substantially to gain from any added protections.

This potentially protective role of the legal complex for religious believers and groups has a parallel in contemporary China. Although our research is still at an early stage, Liu and I are finding cases where Christian lawyers are developing specialized practices, as a form of Christian vocation, to defend Christians arrested or harassed

[29] *Id.* at 140–45.

[30] *Id.* at 156–61.

[31] *Id.* at 188.

[32] *Id.* at 193–281.

for exercise of religious practice, including meetings in unauthorized churches.[33] We do not know how widespread is this conjunction, but a disproportionately high number of notable human rights lawyers who are being actively persecuted by the regime are Christians. However, these actions appear less to be collective mobilization by religious groups than the actions of a network of religious lawyers who find common cause in defense of basic legal freedoms.[34]

RELIGION *AGAINST* POLITICAL LIBERALISM

While religion not infrequently aligns with movements of political liberalism, it often can be found either to be silent about, or complicit in, political illiberalism. Several modalities appear in our cases.

Complicity

On a number of occasions, the Roman Catholic Church hierarchy aligned itself with absolute monarchs, authoritarians, and military dictators. We observe a complicity of the church with illiberalism in the Roman Catholic Church hierarchy of seventeenth-century France, in the Roman Catholic Church hierarchy of fascist Spain, in the early days of Pinochet's military dictatorship, and in Argentina's Dirty War. Such alignment endows legitimacy on fragile regimes and offers symbolic cover for actions that in normal times would be offensive to publics with a democratic heritage, as in Chile. In Spain and Chile, it allowed leaders to claim their regimes had Christian foundations or accorded with Christian ethics or in effect defended the Christian faith. Moreover, it placed religious weapons in the hands of political leaders or their compliant religious allies.

Indifference

Indifference reveals itself less as explicit actions designed to buttress illiberal regimes and more as a failure to take action or give voice in ways that question the legitimacy of illiberal rulers and their abrogation of rights. The contrasting orientations of the Roman Catholic Church in Brazil and Argentina during their respective military dictatorships offer cases in point. The absence of religiously based human rights centers or monitoring commissions represents an organizational expression of indifference.

[33] Terence Halliday & Sida Liu, *Birth of a Liberal Moment? Looking through a One-Way Mirror at Lawyers' Defense of Criminal Defendants in China*, *in* FIGHTING FOR POLITICAL FREEDOM, *supra* note 7, at 65.

[34] These preliminary findings are from a five-year study of lawyers and political liberalism, principally as it is expressed through criminal procedure law and practice across China, funded by the National Science Foundation and American Bar Foundation.

Silence

Another modality, perhaps a variant of indifference, is captured in Gad Barzilai's provocative argument that silence from a profession that makes a living by talking can connote more than indifference.[35] In his discussion of political liberalism in contemporary Israel, Barzilai argues that a very large, politically salient, commercially vigorous legal profession becomes strangely mute when certain basic civil rights are abused. He finds silence by the legal complex in three areas: "the legitimacy and legality of Israel as a Jewish republic, the place of the Arab-Palestinian minority in this context, and national security issues."[36] In some cases, says Barzilai, silence by lawyers can mean dissent. More often, silence means an acceptance of the status quo, a quiet form of legitimation of dominant beliefs and hegemonic understandings, not least, he says, the nonliberal preference given constitutionally and practically to Judaism as the state religion.[37] When Jewish Israeli lawyers are confronted by these three challenges to their liberalism, it is their "Jewishness" that prevails, not a commitment to the fundamental rights of political liberalism. Concomitantly their silence also robs civil society of debate and denies publics of leadership. To that extent, religious infusions of the conception of the state hinder "lawyers from having an active role in publicly debating and forming issues linked with human rights."[38]

Division

National religious groups not infrequently divide internally on issues of basic legal freedoms. That division can lead to simultaneous vocal expressions of support and opposition to the state's orientation toward core rights, or it can lead to vocal expression on the part of one faction and silence on the part of others. The direct and indirect effects of internal dissent play out in complex ways. The internal doctrinal divisions within the seventeenth-century French Church opened up a dissident minority to formulate and promulgate ideas that fostered liberalism. Yet the struggle of the Jansenist with the Roman Catholic Church hierarchy also shows that the religious capture of one part of the legal complex can lead to the deformation of its capacity to mobilize on behalf of political liberalism.[39] Whereas the early years of Jansenist leadership of the Paris Bar redounded to the expansion of liberal

[35] Gad Barzilai, *The Ambivalent Language of Lawyers: Between Liberal Politics, Economic Liberalism, Silence, and Dissent*, *in* FIGHTING FOR POLITICAL FREEDOM, *supra* note 7, at 247.

[36] *Id.* at 267.

[37] *Id.* at 252.

[38] *Id.* at 261.

[39] For more on the Jansenist struggles, see BELL, *supra* note 4; KARPIK, *supra* note 2.

ideas and civil society, the dominance of the Bar by a vocal minority eventually led to a backlash and the Bar found itself increasingly threatened by anti-Jansenist forces. Non-Jansenists lost their sympathy for Jansenist leaders thought too radical for the main body of the profession. A religion-induced division within the bar or the legal complex on issues of political liberalism, therefore, can subvert the distinctive epistemological claims that lawyers and judges can make to a special authority on matters of basic legal freedoms.[40]

MODES OF MOBILIZATION

What do these cases reveal about ways that religious groups mobilize in tandem with the legal complex on behalf of political liberalism?

Reserve Infrastructures

The Monserrat Abbey served a critical role for the political opposition in Catalonia and Spain. Said one influential judge:

> One thing is clear: during our clandestine period, if it hadn't been for the help of the Catholic Church, our capacity to respond would have been far weaker. We didn't have the capacity to disseminate our clandestine programs, because the risk was enormous. Keep in mind that we printed our publications in the abbey at Montserrat. One of the meetings of the Democratic Assembly of Catalonia, which united the entire clandestine political opposition, took place in the abbey at Montserrat! We had a very fluid dialogue with sectors of the Church. They supported us in a variety of concrete ways.[41]

In this sense, church facilities can function as "reserve infrastructures" for a movement.[42] They lower the organizational barriers of cost and commitment, effectively allowing groups that are poor or must remain underground nevertheless to benefit from facilities that are critical for mobilization.

Protected Spaces for Victims

Centers for religious worship themselves can serve as a sacred space, a sanctuary into which governments are loath to intrude. From the Cathedral in Santiago, Chile, to the grounds of an Anglican church in Kenya, religious leaders can offer

[40] HALLIDAY, BEYOND MONOPOLY, *supra* note 6.

[41] Hilbink, *supra* note 13, at 425.

[42] Terence C. Halliday, Michael Powell & Mark Granfors, *Minimalist Organizations: Vital Events in State Bar Associations, 1870–1930*, 52 AM. SOC. REV. 456 (1987).

what is often the only physical space in repressive regimes that security forces will be reluctant to invade arbitrarily.

Monitors of Abuses

Church agencies, such as the Chilean *Vicaría*, may be granted symbolic protection to exercise moral authority. In its systematic and thorough recording of human rights abuses, which were published in monthly reports, the Roman Catholic Church functioned as a warning and witness. By plainly notifying political leaders that flagrant abuses of rights were being assiduously recorded, the *Vicaría* signaled that security apparatuses and their political masters were being held accountable and, indeed, might one day be brought to justice when its evidentiary archive would provide the basis for prosecution.

Protective Shelters for Lawyers

During the worst of the repression, Chile's *Vicaría* provided protective cover for those few lawyers, some of them future leaders of Chile, who dared use the law against a regime that steadfastly pronounced its commitment to the rule of law.

Restraining Police

Sao Paulo's *Centro Santo Dias* employed a legal staff to mobilize law on behalf of victims' families, in this case to defend basic legal freedom through private prosecutions of police officers who had killed citizens without cause and, hitherto, with complete impunity.

Shaping Rights' Consciousness

The *Centro Santo Dias* symbolized a more diffuse commonality of purpose shared by religious and legal groups. By bringing private prosecutions and putting police officers in jail, it shaped public consciousness of legal rights. The persistent pursuit of difficult cases by Church agencies on behalf of weak and marginal citizens shapes rights' consciousness in social spheres where rights customarily have been enforced only in the breach.

Leading Civil Society

It has been said that in Brazil during the military dictatorship of the 1960s, the Brazilian Bar Association and the Roman Catholic Church were the only two institutions left relatively untouched within civil society.[43] On another continent, one scholar concluded that at the height of Moi's abuses of rights in the late 1980s Kenya, "only the Church … had the courage to speak on behalf of the people" in the face of a "culture of fear."[44] Arguably the most significant contribution of religious groups to civil society comes when they transcend their own denominational divisions and join together with each other and sympathetic non-religious groups, as they did in Kenya.

Organizational Mobilization

One of the principal threats to authoritarians is the capacity of groups outside state control to mobilize publics in key locations or across the country. As the Kenya churches also exemplified, religious groups frequently have extensive capacities to coordinate action, to disseminate information through their own religious channels, and to underwrite alternative media outlets. It was the shock of Falun Gong's capacity to do this outside China's Party leadership compound, and unbeknownst to the security apparatus, that so galvanized the savage official backlash against its adherents.

SETTING A RESEARCH AGENDA

The legal and religious complexes, theology and jurisprudence, and the metaphysical claims of religion and law exist in uneasy tension. Our studies in Europe, the Americas, and North East Asia do not seek to revisit the vast scholarship on religion and politics in general, but rather on that aspect of their intersection that engages the legal complex in action on behalf of political liberalism. The fragments of evidence from our many case studies put on the agenda the following questions.

1. *Which religious beliefs invigorate the legal complex for action toward political liberalism?*

To explain when the legal complex or any of its fragments will mobilize or not in conjunction with religious groups demands a deeper inquiry into the theological and ethical bases of that action. Which theological ethics sustain an orientation toward political liberalism by religious leaders that is congruent with the jurisprudence and ideological motivations of the legal complex? And where are there theological intersections across world religions that might enable them to coexist in any

[43] Joaquim Falcao, *Lawyers in Brazil*, *in* LAWYERS IN SOCIETY: THE CIVIL LAW WORLD, *supra* note 5, at 400.

[44] Sabar-Friedman, *supra* note 23.

society, protected by core civil rights, in ways that infuse or buttress action by the legal complex?

2. *Do religious ethics place more emphasis on some aspects of the legal complex's political agenda than others?*

There is some evidence that religious groups are less interested in the moderate state, including the independence of the judiciary, than the defense of civil society and basic legal freedoms. Like the bar, religious groups frequently can survive illiberal regimes, often better than other civil society groups. Like the bar, religious groups provide a potential basis for mobilization on behalf of the rest of society. To do this, however, requires the defense of core political rights. Freedom of speech and association permit religious observance, and whereas the basic legal rights are at the heart of legal liberalism, those same rights also protect religious believers when they are in the minority or persecuted. Hence it appears that a conjunction of action around basic legal freedoms is more likely than over a moderate state.

3. *When does religion subvert the drive of the legal complex for political liberalism?*

In one reading, liberal politics can exist only when there has occurred a historical differentiation of politics from religion.[45] This delinking of institutional politics from institutional religion creates an autonomous political sphere that does not rely on the theological foundations of a given religion. Yet the engagement of religion with politics recurs in struggles by the legal complex over political liberalism. How is this disengagement and reengagement to be managed? Does the legal complex become a collective agent to define the terms of that delicate balance? While a legal complex may accept the religious neutrality of the state, might it still ally with religious groups in a coalition of civil society actors?

4. *How does the state affect the capacity of religious groups to become allies of the legal complex on behalf of political liberalism?*

In general, poorly institutionalized states offer social space for religions to substitute their own organizations for delivering education, health, social support, and identity formation. The substitution of religious for state infrastructure has potentially adverse consequences for liberalizing tendencies of the legal complex. First, by reinforcing religious loyalties and identities, an administrative infrastructure may work against the universalities of identity inherent in legal liberalism. Second, if the state is underdeveloped, it is likely that the justice system will also be truncated in its substantive reach, restricted in its geographical scope, and contested by other legal

[45] Karpik, *supra* note 9.

orders. Third, poorly institutionalized states will be less likely to stimulate a supply of highly trained and prestigious lawyers, judges, and prosecutors. Finally, powerful religious institutions that substitute for an absence of a state infrastructure may resist the emergence of a robust state machinery.

CONCLUSION

These questions, and the case studies I have ransacked for material, do little more than hint at an intellectual terrain that begs for exploration. Nonetheless, this exploration has consequences that reach far beyond theory and the academy. They touch on the fundamentals of social life free from arbitrary arrest, disappearances, torture, state-perpetrated sexual violence, perpetual detention, religious persecution, political oppression, Dirty Wars, States of Siege, and Emergency Powers. In these struggles for political freedom, evidence accumulates that a religious and legal alliance on behalf of, or against, liberal politics can be decisive.

4

More Lawyers than People

The Global Multiplication of Legal Professionals

Marc Galanter

"If the current rate of increase continues, by 2000 this country will have more lawyers than people."[1]

INTRODUCTION

Looking back, I am impressed by how many institutions that once seemed bedrock foundational parts of the world – railroads, corner stores, newspapers – have disappeared or morphed into things quite different. But it is not always easy to tell which things are in decline and which are in the ascendant. At mid-century, it appeared to many observers in the United States that law had reached its maturity. Litigation was in a deep trough.[2] Knowledgeable judges and practitioners lamented its decline.[3] As late as 1963, the Dean of the Wisconsin Law School observed that "law is a dwindling profession. In numbers it has remained fairly constant while everything else grows."[4] But through the corrective lens of hindsight we can see that at that very

This is a revised and expanded version of my keynote address to the International Conference of the Israeli Law and Society Association, Jerusalem, December 24–26, 2008. I am grateful to Swethaa Ballakrishnen for assistance with the initial collection of data, to Anders Carlson for expanding and maintaining the archive, and to Frances Raday and Rick Abel for helpful comments on the Jerusalem version.

1 American Lawyer Joke *circa* 1990s.

2 Molly Selvin and Patricia A. Ebener, Managing the Unmanageable: A History of Civil Delay in the Los Angeles Superior Court (1984); Marc Galanter, *Contract in Court: Or, Almost Everything you May or May Not Want to Know About Contract Litigation*, 2001 Wisc. L. Rev. 577 (2001). Comparable declines occurred in England, see Christopher W. Brooks, *The Longitudinal Study of Civil Litigation in England 1200–1996 in* Litigation Past and Present 38 (Wilfred Prest & Sharyn Roach Anleu, eds., 2004), and in India, see Marc Galanter, *'To the Listed Field …' The Myth of Litigious India*, 1 Jindal Global L. Rev. 65 (2009).

3 Charles D. Breitel, *The Quandary in Litigation*, 25 Mo. L. Rev 225, 225 (1960); David W. Peck, *The Future of the Trial Lawyer*, 40 J. Am Judicature Soc'y 38 (1956).

4 Dean George H. Young, quoted in Owen Coyle,*'Benchers' Group Aiding Needy Law School Scholars at UW*, Capital Times, Oct. 28, 1963, at 1 (Green Section).

time, law in the United States – and elsewhere – entered a period of unprecedented growth on a number of dimensions – the amount of litigation, the number of lawyers, the density of legislation and regulation, expenditures on law, and its presence in public consciousness.[5] I think it is fair to refer to this growth as legalization.

At least one part of this legalization complex – an increase in the presence of lawyers – is not confined to the United States, or to advanced industrial countries, or to common law jurisdictions, but is visible across a great part of the world. Lawyers everywhere are multiplying. After documenting this, I compare this growth to the trajectories of other dimensions of legalization. Then I shall suggest how other features of societies and legal institutions are related to this growth. I then make a number of surmises about the implications of these trends for the development of the legal profession and the law. I emphasize that these remarks are speculative: My generalizations are based on fragmentary data and subject to modification as I learn more about the variety of local conditions. There is, as you may suspect, a North Atlantic and common law bias since the United States and the United Kingdom are, along with India, the legal professions with which I am most familiar. I hope to present a wide panorama – a bit blurry and containing many blank spaces – rather than a precise portrait.[6] If this galactic view suppresses differences and overstates similarities, I hope it has the compensating virtues of generating plausible hypothesis and inspiring collaboration in filling in those blank spaces.

It should not be surprising to approach changes in law and its place in society by examining changes in the number, organization, and work of lawyers. Lawyers are, after all, an incarnation of the law, its products and its agents. Oliver Wendell Holmes famously observed, "When we study law we are not studying a mystery but a well-known profession."[7] Does this work the other way around? Can the study of lawyers tell us about law as an institution? Does the increasing density of lawyers portend that the world is getting more "legalized" as well as more lawyerized? And what does this mean? Does it refer to a normative condition in which the exercise of power is channeled and restrained by legal standards? Or are we just talking about the presence and prominence of distinctively legal institutions – laws and courts and lawyers and lawsuits? Certainly the recent past has brought us more legality in the second, behavioral sense – a more prominent *role* of law in society – but what does it say, if anything, about the *rule* of law?[8] Does it mean that events are increasingly

5 Marc Galanter, *Law Abounding: Legalisation Around the North Atlantic*, 55 MODERN L. REV 1 (1992).

6 "Is an indistinct photograph a picture of a person at all? Is it even always an advantage to replace an indistinct picture by a sharp one? Isn't the indistinct one often exactly what we need?" LUDWIG WITTGENSTEIN, PHILOSOPHICAL INVESTIGATIONS §71 (1958).

7 Oliver Wendell Holmes, *The Path of the Law*, 10 HARV. L. REV. 457, 457 (1897).

8 For an illuminating discussion, see Robert M. Gordon, *The Role of Lawyers in Producing the Rule of Law: Some Critical Reflections*, 11 THEORETICAL INQUIRIES IN LAW 441 (2010).

controlled by legal principles or legal procedures? Or does it simply mean that law "reigns" in the sense of supplying the language or idiom through which rule is exercised or appears to be exercised.

MORE LAWYERS

> "I suppose that in all Christendom are not so many pleaders, attorneys and men of the law as be in England only, for if they were numbered all that belong to the courts of the Chancery, King's Bench, Common Pleas, Exchequer, Receipt and Hell [record repository in Westminster Hall], and the bag-bearers of the same, it should amount to a great multitude. And how all these live, and of whom, if it should be uttered and told it should not be believed.[9]"

I have managed to compile figures from twenty-two countries, most for years that include the period 1970 to 2000, some for only part of that period, some for even longer. For purposes of comparison, I looked at this thirty-year period or the best approximation of it, to see what has happened to the number of lawyers. As Table 4.1 shows, that number increased in every country, just about doubling in Austria and Japan but growing ten times over in several Latin American countries and three or four times over in a number of countries including Canada, Germany, the Netherlands, Spain, Portugal, Israel, South Korea, the United States, and the United Kingdom. The professions in Australia, France, and Italy more than doubled in size over this period.

These figures have to be discounted in several ways: Some may be artifacts of changes in educational systems, producing many nominal lawyers in addition to those actually engaged in the practice of law. Then there is the question of how to define "the practice of law"? Would we include the Japanese scriveners? American paralegals? English managing clerks? The legal professions of the world are cousins, not identical twins. Whether we adopt the most exacting local definition or impose a standard definition of our own, we are not counting exactly the same thing in each place. In some places, the count includes all those with legal training, in others persons on a roll of those admitted to practice, whereas in still others those that are currently licensed. In some places, the count includes only those in private practice, whereas in others it includes government and corporate lawyers, judges, retired lawyers, and unadmitted trainees. For purposes of the present study, I have not concerned myself with counting exactly equivalent things in each country, but instead have been concerned that within each country we are counting the same thing at each point of time. That is, each country is being compared primarily with itself

[9] W. Caxton, *Game and Playe of the Chesse* (1474), *quoted in* J. H. Baker, The Legal Profession and the Common Law 75 (1986).

TABLE 4.1. *Total number of lawyers in selected countries*

Year	Austria [a]	Australia [b]	Brazil [c]	Canada [d]	Chile [c]	China [e]	Costa Rica [c]	France [f]	Germany [g]	Israel [h]	Italy [f]	Japan [i]	Mexico [c]	Netherlands [j]	Pern [k]	Poland [l]	Portugal [m]	South Korea [n]	Spain [o]	U.K. [p]	U.S.A. [q]	Venezuela [r]
1950			15666	9038	1475				12844		29400	5883			1970					17035	221605	
1960	2301 [1961]	6636 [1961]	30066	12068	2602				18347	2303	36916	6327	8426	1946	2960			450		19069	285933	4256 [1961]
1970	**2017**	**12580** [1975]	**37710**	**16315** [1971]	**4306**		**968**	**14890** [1973]	**22882**	**4853**	**41639**	**8520**	**14669**	**2063**	**4080**	**5722** [1968]	**2573**	**719**		**24407**	**326842**	**8102** [1971]
1980	2170	26007 [1986]	85710	34120 [1981]	6546 [1982]	**31629** [1985]	1700		36077	7245		11494	141539	3726		5640	5134	940	**27983**	37832	574810	16045 [1981]
1990	2887		148671 [1991]		9308 [1992]	41383	4400	**42092** [1998]	56638	10697	**98258** [1996]	14173		6368		7085 [1992]	11319	1803	55076	54734	755694	31350
2000	**3969**	**36124** [2002]		**81237**	**11400**	**90011**	**10800**		**104067**	**23127**		**16340** [1997]	**200000** [1998]	**11033**	**67205*** [2002]	**7216** [1998]	**13809** [1996]	**4228**	**96000** [1998]	**79503** [1999]	**1022462**	**82939** [2001]
More Recent	5129 [2008]		**547037** [2007]	99617 [2007]		136014 [2007]			142830 [2007]	38017 [2007]	119267* [2006]							5533 [2003]		96757 [2004]	1180386 [2009]	
% Change*	97%	187%	1351%	398%	165%	185%	1016%	183%	355%	377%	136%	92%	1263%	435%	1547%	26%	437%	488%	243%	226%	213%	924%

* Change from 1970 to 2000 or closest approximation, indicated in bold

Source Note: All data sources are in the Appendix to this chapter. The source is referenced by the bracketed lower-case letter following each listed country. For example, the reference to the data source for Austria is indicated by [a]. Dates that appear in brackets below numbers in the table refer to the exact year of data collection (when different from the year indicated in the left column).

over time. Rough comparisons across countries may be suggestive, but clarification of who is being counted is necessary in order to rely on such comparisons.

Table 4.2 shows that in every instance, the population of lawyers is growing faster than the underlying population, so the number of lawyers per 100,000 of the population continuously increases. From 1970 to 2000, the number of lawyers per capita doubled in the United States, Australia, France, Israel, and Italy; tripled in Canada, Spain, and the United Kingdom; and quadrupled in Germany, the Netherlands, and Portugal. Countries in many parts of the world – civil law and common law jurisdictions, countries that started with few lawyers and those that started with large lawyer populations – all share this feature. Of the countries for which data was found, the only one with virtually no growth was Poland, which spent two-thirds of the period under communist rule and a command economy.

In some places lawyer numbers begin to take off as early as 1970; in others, the take-off is within the most recent decades. Everywhere this growth is fed by, and in turn drives, a great increase in the number and enrollment of legal educational institutions, ranging from university law faculties to freestanding proprietary law schools. The number of law students started rising in the 1970s in many places, later in others (see Table 4.3).

With training at the university level in increasing favor, systems of apprenticeship/clerkship and practitioner training (which were prevalent in much of the common law world until the post–World War II era) have been abandoned or reduced in scope. Although some clerkship requirements remain, law is now a university subject. (This is one of the ways in which the common law world has converged with the civil law world.) This in turn has meant the burgeoning of a class of academic lawyers where they did not exist before – and in at least some places, the growth of a body of legal intellectuals detached from legal practice and increasingly part of academic rather than practitioner communities. The growing legal academy produces not only practical instruction but reams of theory as well, some of it critical of existing practice.

When the expansion begins, the profession becomes younger, because larger cohorts enter and smaller numbers retire or die. But within the course of a generation, as the larger cohorts pass through the pipeline, the profession starts to become older once more. For example, in the United States, a sharp increase in the number of lawyers in the 1970s soon led to a situation in which there were almost three times as many lawyers in their thirties as in their fifties; but as the larger cohorts aged, that ratio dropped to about 1.3 to 1 now and will approach equality in 2020.[10] This will happen later elsewhere and it has tremendous import

[10] Marc Galanter, *Old and In the Way: the Coming Demographic Transformation of the Legal Profession and Its Implications for the Provision of Legal Services*, 1999 Wisc. L. Rev. 1081 (1999).

TABLE 4.2. *Lawyers per 100,00 residents in selected countries*

Year	Austria [a]	Australia [b]	Brazil [c]	Canada [d]	Chile [c]	China [e]	Costa Rica [c]	France [f]	Germany [g]	Israel [h]	Italy [f]	Japan [i]	Mexico [c]	Netherlands [j]	Peru [k]	Poland [l]	Portugal [m]	South Korea [n]	Spain [o]	U.K. [p]	U.S.A. [q]	Venezuela [r]
1950			30	65	24				19		57	7			25					34	146	
1960	32 [1961]	63 [1961]	42	66	34				25	108	73	7	24	17	31			2		36	158	54 [1961]
1970	27	91 [1975]	41	74 [1971]	44		57	29 [1973]	29	167	76	8	30	16	32	18	28.45	2		44	159	73 [1971]
1980	29	164 [1961]	72	137 [1981]	58 [1982]	3 [1985]	75		46	194		10	174	26		16	52.51	2	75	67	252	106 [1981]
1990	37		101 [1991]		70 [1992]		157		71	239	171 [1996]	11		42		18 [1992]	114.07	4	140	95	302	162
2000	49	185 [2002]		261	75	7	309	70 [1998]	127	378		13 [1997]	208 [1998]	70	250 [2002]	19 [1998]	136.72 [1996]	9	241 [1998]	134 [1999]	362	348 [2001]
More Recent	63 [2008]		282 [2007]	302 [2007]		10 [2007]			173 [2007]	544 [2007]	295* [2006]							12 [2003]		161 [2004]	384 [2009]	
% Change*	81%	102%	588%	253%	70%	138%	442%	141%	330%	126%	125%	59%	593%	337%	681%	6%	381%	305%	222%	206%	127%	379%

* Change from 1970 to 2000 or closest approximation, indicated in bold

Source Note: All data sources are in the Appendix to this chapter. The source is referenced by the bracketed lower-case letter following each listed country. For example, the reference to the data source for Austria is indicated by [a]. Dates that appear in brackets below numbers in the table refer to the exact year of data collection (when different from the year indicated in the left column). For standardization purposes, figures for lawyers per 100,000 residents were created by relating the total number of lawyers from Table 4.1 to the country population from the International Database of the U.S. Census Bureau.

TABLE 4.3. *Law students in selected countries*

Year	Argentina [f]	Brazil [f]	Chile [f]	Costa Rica [f]	France [f]	Italy [f]	Mexico [s]	Peru [f]	Spain [f]	U.K. [t]	U.S.A. [u]	Venezuela [f]
1950			2284	205		27035		1392	16853		43057	1000
1960		23519 [1961]	3431 [1961]	328 [1961]	45511 [1961]			4624 [1961]			35769	6766 [1961]
1970	29045				131460 [1978]	67387	57973 [1979]		21009		64416	
1980										1608 [1982]	117297	
1990		190712 [1994]		4262 [1994]			111025 [1991]		180516 [1988]	5969 [1993]	124471	
2000	163881 [1998]		24478		180490 [1998]	324889 [1996]	155332 [1997]			9324	125184	40000
More Recent							190338 [2001]	41192 [2002]		13803 [2008]	141719 [2008]	

Source Note: All data sources are in the Appendix to this chapter. The source is referenced by the bracketed lower-case letter following each listed country. For example, the reference to the data source for Argentina is indicated by [f]. Dates that appear in brackets below numbers in the table refer to the exact year of data collection (when different from the year indicated in the left column).

for the shape of lawyers' careers. For with the units of practice becoming larger and more hierarchic (see further in this chapter), we can imagine that these structures require relatively fewer generals and colonels and more captains, sergeants, and privates, leading to a surplus of high-caliber older lawyers under mounting pressure to retire earlier.

An even more dramatic demographic change is the arrival of women in the world of lawyering after a long slow start during the previous century. Around 1970, women began to enter legal education in ever-escalating numbers. By the end of the century, they were about half the lawyers in Mexico, Argentina, France, Greece, Hungary, and Portugal – and just a bit less in the United Kingdom (see Table 4.4). And women were a solid majority of law students in many countries, so a continuing gender shift was in the pipeline. The distribution of women in various legal roles is uneven. For example, in the United States and a number of other countries, the proportion of women is higher in government work and in corporate legal offices and lower in private practice firms, especially in their partnership ranks. Overall women lawyers earn less than their male counterparts. Assessing the difference that the presence of women makes in the output of the legal system is one of the great unanswered questions for law and society research.

Beyond gender, the changing demographics of the profession are more difficult to discern. The kinship element that played an important role in the original growth of large law firms gradually declined in the United States,[11] first in New York and later in regional centers. A comparable shift in England occurred later, and the growing large-firm sector is going through that transition now in India, Latin America, and probably elsewhere as well. In the United States, the earlier exclusion and marginalization of disfavored racial, ethnic, and religious groups has declined, dramatically in some cases and slowly in others.[12]

COURTS AND LITIGATION

Judicial establishments have also grown as shown in Table 4.5. Their growth, however, has been much slower than the growth of lawyers (as shown in Table 4.6). In civil law countries that traditionally had a much higher ratio of

[11] Marc Galanter & Thomas Palay, Tournament of Lawyers: The Growth and Transformation of the Big Law Firm 14 (1991); William Delany & Alan H. Finegold, *Wall Street Lawyer in the Provinces*, 15 Admin. Sci. Q. 191 (1970);); Marc Galanter & Simon Roberts, *From Kinship to Magic Circle: The London Commercial Firm in the Twentieth Century*, 15 Int'l J. Legal Prof. 143 (2008); Eli Wald, *The Other Legal Profession and the Orthodox View of the Bar: The Rise of Colorado's Elite Law Firms*, 80 U. Colo. L. Rev. 605 (2009).

[12] Erwin O. Smigel, The Wall Street Lawyer: Professional Organization Man? 370–73 (1969); Eli Wald, *The Rise and Fall of the WASP and Jewish Law Firms*, 60 Stan. L. Rev. 1803 (2008).

TABLE 4.4. *Women as a proportion of lawyers in selected countries*

Year	Australia [b]	Brazil [z]	Canada [d]	China [e]	Germany [bb]	Israel [x]	Japan [aa]	Netherlands [y]	Poland [l]	South Korea [n]	U.K. [v]	U.S.A. [w]
1960	3.9% [1961]		2.6% [1961]		>2%	7.0%	0.7%	8.0%				3.0%
1970	7.5% [1976]	18.3% [1975]	4.8% [1971]		4.5%	18.0%	2.2%	11.0%	12.8% [1968]	0.4% [1975]		3.0% [1971]
1980	11.4% [1981]	25.2%	15.1% [1981]		8.0%	28.0%	3.8%	18.0%	19.0%	0.3%	14.4% [1985]	8.0%
1990	25.1% [1991]	33.7%	22.0% [1986]		14.7% [1989]	36.0%	5.9% [1991]	26.0%	27.4% [1992]	1.0%	23.2%	20.0% [1991]
2000		37.8% [1995]		16.2%	24.6%	36.0%		30.0% [1993]	29.5% [1998]	3.1%	35.1% [1999]	27.0%
More Recent				19.2% [2005]	27.9% [2003]					5.5% [2003]	45.2% [2009]	

Source Note: All data sources are in the Appendix to this chapter. The source is referenced by the bracketed lower-case letter following each listed country. For example, the reference to the data source for Australia is indicated by [b]. Dates that appear in brackets below numbers in the table refer to the exact year of data collection (when different from the year indicated in the left column).

TABLE 4.5. *Number of judges in selected countries*

Year	Austria [cc]	Belgium [cc]	Canada [cc]	Chile [cc]	China [cc]	Costa Rica [cc]	Denmark [cc]	Germany [g]	Israel [h]	Italy [cc]	Japan [cc]	New Zealand [cc]	Panama [cc]	Poland [cc]	Portugal [m]	South Korea [n]	U.S.A. [cc]
1970									176						422	406 [1971]	
1980	**1501** [1986]			427 [1986]		249 [1986]		16657 [1981]	237	6735 [1986]	2800 [1986]	113 [1986]	137 [1986]		612	546 [1979]	
1990	**1544**	**1152**	**1994** [1998]	461	**194836**	295	**653** [1997]		276	7140	2823	137	208	**4794**	1018	1048 [1991]	**11009**
2000		2293 [2001]	2011 [2001]	544	219952 [2001]	581	648	20880	457	6221 [2001]	3019	160 [2001]	239	7614 [2001]	1231 [1996]	1393	29023 [1999]
More Recent	**1674** [2006]	2381 [2002]	2068 [2003]	804 [2004]	204096 [2002]	720 [2004]	697 [2004]	20395 [2005]	577 [2007]	7107 [2004]	3094 [2002]	159 [2002]		9756 [2004]		1708 [2003]	31320 [2001]
% Change*	12%	99%	1%	27%	13%	133%	–1%	25%	93%	–8%	8%	42%	74%	59%	101%	155%	164%

* Change from 1980 to 2000 or closest approximation, indicated in bold

Source Note: All data sources are in the Appendix to this chapter. The source is referenced by the bracketed lower-case letter following each listed country. For example, the reference to the data source for Austria is indicated by [cc]. Dates that appear in brackets below numbers in the table refer to the exact year of data collection (when different from the year indicated in the left column).

TABLE 4.6. *Growth in number of lawyers compared to growth in number of judges, 1980 to 2000*

Country	% Growth Lawyers	% Growth Judges
Austria	83%	12% [1986–2006]
Chile	74% [1982–2000]	27% [1986–2000]
Germany	188% [1981–2000]	25% [1981–2000]
Israel	219%	93%
Japan	42% [1980–1997]	8% [1986–2000]
Portugal	169% [1980–1996]	101% [1980–1996]
South Korea	350%	155% [1979–2000]

Source Note: These numbers were calculated using the data from Tables 4.1 and 4.5. Dates that appear in brackets below numbers in the table refer to the exact range of years during which growth was measured (when different from the base range of 1980 to 2000).

judges to lawyers, that ratio has fallen, approaching the kind of ratios found in common law countries. For example, in Germany in 1970, there was one judge for every 2.2 lawyers, but by 2005, there were 6 lawyers for every judge. In Israel, judges increased 2.8 times from 1970 to 2007, but lawyers increased 8 times over the same period. Judges kept up with the growth of population, but lawyers outstripped it. It is possible that the gap represents and encourages a diffusion of judicial authority, with dispute resolution functions moving from the "regular courts" to special-purpose tribunals,[13] alternative dispute resolution, and to forums within or adjacent to organizations that display legal forms but are organized to achieve management goals.[14]

[13] *See* Judith Resnik, *Migrating, Morphing, and Vanishing: The Empirical and Normative Puzzles of Declining Trial Rates in Courts*, 1 J. EMPIRICAL LEGAL STUDIES 783 (2004) (noting that, in the United States, dispute functions are moving into administrative forums which handle far larger caseloads than the "courts" proper).

[14] Lauren Edelman & Mark Suchman, *When the "Haves" Hold Court: Speculations on the Organizational Internalization of Law*, 33 LAW & SOC'Y REV. 941 (1999).

It also seems to be correlated with an enhancement of judicial powers of case management.[15]

Observers have marked the advance of a "juristocracy" in which courts play a larger role in governance. We might think this would be reflected in changes in the rate and role of litigation. In many places, litigation increased significantly in the later part of the twentieth century. But the increase trails far behind the increase in lawyers.[16] And in the recent past, civil litigation seems to be declining – in some cases absolutely and in many places when adjusted for population. In the United Kingdom, civil litigation is falling absolutely, while the lawyer population continues to grow.[17] In Israel, cases in the district courts increased only half as much as the lawyer population from 1970 to 2005.

Litigation rates register growth that is much smaller than the increase in lawyer populations. Most of the growth comes in the early part of the period under consideration. In the most recent decades, litigation growth has been tapering off or even shrinking. These are rates for the core governmental institutions that are denominated courts, so they do not take into account the relocation of litigation in other agencies denominated agencies or tribunals. These rates also do not take account of the stakes in litigation, which may have become larger or smaller; nor do they account for the changing role of judicial pronouncements in governance.

In the common law world at least, the litigation that remains at the central core of government courts is increasingly truncated. Cases terminate at some point short of their formally prescribed culmination. The portion of cases eventuating in a trial has declined precipitously in the United States, in the United Kingdom, and in Ontario, Canada.[18] In the U.S. federal courts, there are about five times as many civil cases as there were fifty years ago but about one-third fewer trials. In the United Kingdom, both filings and trials are declining.[19]

[15] Adrian A.S. Zuckerman, *Justice in Crisis: Comparative Dimensions of Civil Procedure*, *in* Civil Justice in Crisis 47 (Adrian A. S. Zuckerman, ed., 1999) ("The clearest trend emerging from the different national accounts is a general tendency toward judicial control of the civil process.").

[16] *See, e.g.*, David Bamford, *Litigation Reform 1980–2000: A Radical Challenge? in* Litigation Past and Present, *supra* note 2, at 146 (showing declining filings in South Australia); Robert Dingwall & Emilie Cloatre, *Vanishing Trials? An English Perspective*, 2006 J. Disp. Resol. 51 (showing declining filings in England and Wales); Ted Wright & Angela Melville, *Hey, But Who's Counting? in* Litigation Past and Present, *supra* note 2, at 96 (showing declining filings in New South Wales).

[17] Hazel Genn, Judging Civil Justice 33–35 (2010).

[18] Dingwall & Cloatre, *supra* note 16; Marc Galanter, *The Hundred-Year Decline of Trials and the Thirty Years War*, 57 Stan. L. Rev 1255 (2005); Marc Galanter, *The Vanishing Trial: An Examination of Trials and Related Matters in Federal and State Courts*, 1 J. Empirical Legal Studies 459 (2004); Marc Galanter, A *World Without Trials*, 2006 J. Disp. Resol., 7 (2006); Herbert M. Kritzer, *Disappearing Trials? A Comparative Perspective*, 1 J. Empirical Legal Studies 735 (2004).

[19] Dingwall & Cloatre, *supra* note 16.

BIG-TIME LAWYERING

If we have significantly more lawyers but fewer lawsuits, what are all these lawyers doing? Presumably something other than litigating – transaction planning, compliance, bargaining, mediating, and lobbying rather than adjudication. And who are they doing it for? Increasingly their effort is expended to provide services to Artificial Persons – corporations, associations, and governments – rather than Natural Persons. The increasing predominance of organizations as users of law is dramatically displayed by Heinz and Laumann's studies of the Chicago bar. They estimated that in 1975, "53 percent of lawyers' time was allocated to the corporate fields …, while 40 percent was devoted to the personal client fields…."[20] When the researchers returned to the field twenty years later, they found that there were roughly twice as many lawyers working in Chicago. But in 1995, about 64 percent of the total effort of all Chicago lawyers was devoted to the corporate client sector and only 29 percent to the personal/small business sector.[21] Since the number of lawyers in Chicago had doubled, this meant that the total effort devoted to the personal sector had increased by 45 percent. But the corporate sector grew by 126 percent. To the extent that lawyers serving the corporate sector were able to command more staff and support services with their effort, these figures understate the gap in services delivered.

This pattern is not confined to Chicago. The generality of both the contours of distribution and the patterns of change are suggested by U.S. Census data. As the size of the legal services "pie" was increasing, businesses were buying a greater share of that pie. In 1967, individuals bought 55 percent of the product of the legal services industry and businesses bought 39 percent. In 2002, individual purchases had fallen to 41.4 percent and business purchases had risen to 47.4 percent of a much-enlarged total.[22]

Legal forums are populated increasingly by Artificial Persons (corporations, associations, and governments). They enjoy formidable advantages in the use of legal processes. Not only do these entities tend to prevail in most legal encounters, but

[20] John P. Heinz, Robert L. Nelson, Rebecca L. Sandefur & Edward O. Laumann, Urban Lawyers: The New Social Structure of the Bar 43 (2005).

[21] John P. Heinz et al., *The Changing Character of Lawyers' Work: Chicago in 1975 and 1995*, 32 Law & Soc'y Rev. 751, 765 tbl.3 (1998).

[22] From 1967 to 1992, with each subsequent five-year period, the business portion has increased and the share consumed by individuals declined. Marc Galanter, *Planet of the APs: Reflections on the Scale of Law and Its Users*, 53 Buff. L. Rev. 1369, 1383–1384 tbl. 1 & fig. 3 (2006). A change in the method of compiling these totals led to an apparent sharp reversal in 1997, but in 2002, the shift away from expenditures by individuals to expenditures by businesses and government resumed.

they are better prepared for legal contingencies before the transaction or contest.[23] The superior legal agency of these Artificial Persons derives in good measure from the scale and continuity of their resort to legal services: They can plan transactions in advance by employing specialized legal services, utilizing advanced intelligence, developing expertise, and cultivating facilitative informal relations with institutional incumbents. Artificial Persons consume an increasing portion of legal services, disproportionately provided by elite practitioners, on a continuous basis.[24] Indeed, representation of these entities is closely associated with both income and professional prestige. It is routine for these services to empower corporate entities to navigate the law-thick world as capable legal agents. Gillian Hadfield spells out the contrast with the situation of ordinary individuals, which is especially acute in the case of the poor and friendless:

> Most corporate work is before-the-fact, everyday advice on what contracts to sign, which regulations apply, how conduct is likely to be interpreted by enforcement authorities or in the event of litigation, what the options are for modifying the extent of legal liability, how to manage a dispute before it becomes a lawsuit, and so on. But for ordinary citizens in the U.S. there is almost no functioning legal system in this ex ante sphere.[25]

An increasing portion of legal services are supplied to corporations, governments, and other institutional actors. The lawyers who supply these services are more likely to practice in larger units, and the size of these units has been increasing steadily. In 1970, the largest firms contained about 200 lawyers; today, the largest firms have more than 3,000 lawyers. In many places, firms in the corporate sector have adopted (or are moving toward – by de-emphasizing kinship) the tournament model of promotion that contains a built-in growth imperative. At the same time, in the United States and United Kingdom, firm growth and an information system that promotes lateral mobility are transforming the tournament model into a more hierarchic and corporate model.[26] Lawyers, especially in the growing corporate sector, are more loyal and committed to their clients and less to their firms or the guild – more "hired guns" and less "officers of the court."

Specialization and coordination among lawyers have also increased outside the format of the large firm. There are more specialized advocacy groups – such as

[23] *Id.* at 1385–98.

[24] *Id.* at 1381–85.

[25] Gillian K. Hadfield, *Higher Demand, Lower Supply: A Comparative Assessment of the Legal Resource Landscape for Ordinary Americans*, 37, FORDHAM URB. L.J. 129, 132 (2010). *Cf.* JOHN P. HEINZ & EDWARD O. LAUMANN, CHICAGO LAWYERS: THE SOCIAL STRUCTURE OF THE BAR 322–323 (1982).

[26] Marc S. Galanter & William D. Henderson, *The Elastic Tournament: A Second Transformation of the Big Law Firm*, 60 STAN. L. REV. 1867 (2008).

public interest law firms, human rights groups, and other nongovernmental organizations (NGOs). Improved communications technology, more information resources, and more capital increase the amount of legal product per lawyer, so legal product increases even faster than the number of lawyers. (But since lawyers make work for each other, the net product delivered to clients does not increase correspondingly.)

There is more hierarchy – both in the profession as whole and within firms. Within firms, there are increasing disparities in power and earnings as the relatively stable lifetime partnership among a small number of lawyers in face-to-face relationships is supplanted by much larger units dispersed over a wider area, in which the power of mobile partners to exit displaces voice and loyalty as the master control.[27] The hierarchy in the profession – formerly emphasizing prominence as advocates and counselors – is now displaced by distinctions based on earnings and the prestige of clients.

Legal work is more "global" and mobile. There is accelerated cross-border adoption of practices, norms, and doctrine.[28] Firms have become transnational. Whereas firms from the metropole follow capital to multiple far-flung locations, most of the lawyers in these branches are locals. The metropole also exports legal education to students from the periphery,[29] which in turn exports legal services to the metropole by migration of talent and by outsourcing.[30] With a few exceptions, the globalization of law practice involves firms that represent corporate entities; lawyers that represent individuals remain largely locked in their national compartments.

THE WIDER LEGAL AND SOCIAL SETTING

Lawyers, courts, and litigation are shaped by the wider legal and social setting in which they reside. This preliminary essay cannot undertake to trace the multiple and intricate connections, but I want to note just a few that seem widespread, plausible, and relevant to the present inquiry.

27 Albert O. Hirschman, Exit, Voice, and Loyalty: Responses to Decline in Firms, Organizations, and States (1970).

28 Wolfgang Weigand, *Americanization of Law: Reception or Convergence? in* Legal Culture and the Legal Profession (L.M. Friedman & H.N. Scheiber eds., 1996); J. Gillis Wetter, *The Case for International Law Schools and an International Legal Profession*, 29 Intl. & Compar. L. Q. 206 (1980).

29 Like outsourcing, legal education in the recipient countries may move up the food chain, providing education that equips graduates to function in the world of transnational lawyering. Examples include the U.S.-style Peking University School of Transnational Law in Shenzhen, China, About STL, http://blogs.wsj.com/chinajournal/2008/06/06/an-american-law-school-inchina/, and India's Jindal Global Law School, About Jindal Global Law School, http://www.jgls.org/lawschool/aboutjgls.asp.

30 Jayanth Krishnan, *Outsourcing and the Globalizing Legal Profession*, 48 Wm. & Mary L. Rev. 2189 (2007).

Perhaps the most important development in the law is the increasing prominence of Artificial Persons (APs) – corporations, organizations, and governmental bodies – as actors in society and in its legal arenas.[31] These APs have an affinity for the legal order – not surprisingly considering that they are, in some sense, its creatures. They have become "legalized" by internalizing (some) legal norms[32] at the same time that they generate and administer systems of faux/private law, from health care regulations to frequent-flyer program rules. Public forums in turn incorporate standards from these APs. For structural reasons, APs are more proficient players of the legal game[33] and command resources to play the game on a scale that enables them to realize these advantages.[34]

As public/state law – in the form of legislation, regulations, and decisions of courts and tribunals – becomes more abundant,[35] it is increasingly surrounded by "soft law" and, paradoxically, more indeterminate. Indeterminacy is fostered by the ever-expanding accumulation of conflicting norms, interests, and commitments embedded in the ever-growing corpus of authoritative materials.[36] Parties have increasing incentives and means to make greater investments in the decision-making process and legislators, judges, and lawyers have more incentive to innovate to enrich or distinguish themselves.[37]

In addition to the indeterminacy about what the authoritative decision makers will decide and propound, a second layer of indeterminacy suffuses legal prescriptions. Legal decisions are typically made – or at least justified – instrumentally, on the premise they will produce certain favored results or will prevent certain disfavored ones.[38] However, instrumentalism provides no guarantee that the desired

[31] Galanter, *supra* note 22.

[32] Lauren Edelman, *Legal Environments and Organizational Governance: The Expansion of Due Process in the Workplace*, 95 AM. J. SOCIOLOGY 1401 (1990).

[33] Marc Galanter, *Why the 'Haves' Come Out Ahead: Speculations on the Limits of Legal Change*, 9 LAW & SOC'Y REV. 95 (1974).

[34] Gillian Hadfield, *The Price of Law: How the Market for Lawyers Distorts the Justice System*, 98 MICH. L. REV. 953 (2000).

[35] Galanter, *supra* note 5.

[36] Mirjan Damaska, *Structures of Authority and Comparative Criminal Procedure*, 84 YALE L.J. 480 (1975) (observing that "there is a point beyond which increased complexity of law, especially in loosely order normative systems, objectively increases rather than decreases the decision-maker's freedom. Contradictory views can plausibly be held and support found for almost any position."). *Cf.* RICHARD POSNER, THE FEDERAL COURTS: CRISIS AND REFORM 110 (1985) (noting the declining ability of judicial decisions to command assent).

[37] HEINZ & LAUMANN, *supra* note 25; *see also* Anthony d'Amato, *Legal Uncertainty*, 71 CALIF. L. REV. 1 (1983) (suggesting that the incentives of legal actors support an inherent entropic tendency of legal rules to become "increasingly vague, inapplicable, remote, ambiguous, or exception-ridden").

[38] On instrumentalism as the increasingly favored mode of legal reasoning, see BRIAN TAMANAHA, LAW AS A MEANS TO AN END: THREAT TO THE RULE OF LAW (2006). A collateral development of the embrace of instrumental reasoning is that the discourse of law becomes less differentiated from that of business and of politics.

results will actually be attained. Much instrumental reasoning is flawed, embraced without reliable evidence about context or effects, but rather based on supposition or ignorance of other forces at play, so that the actual results of instrumentally designed legal decisions and enactments frequently diverge widely from anticipated results. A very prominent example of inadvertent and perverse consequences is the United States's "war on drugs."[39] A judicial counterpart might be the decision of the U.S. Supreme Court in *Bates v. State of Arizona*,[40] striking down bar rules that forbid advertising by a low-cost legal clinic and setting in motion flows of information that helped bring about a transformation of law practice far beyond the results imagined by the members of the court.[41]

PEERING INTO THE FUTURE

> "It takes considerable effort to see facts (and remember them) while withholding and resisting explanations."[42]

The last half-century has seen a great increase in the world's population, economic growth, an accelerating proliferation of new technologies, environmental degradation, globalization of trade and communications, and the spread of democratic government. These developments, as we have seen, have been accompanied by a marked increase in the presence of lawyers.

It is frequently suggested that lawyers inhibit rather than promote growth: "Lawyers are indeed bad, and engineers good, for growth."[43] The detrimental effect of lawyers may be attributed to misallocation of talent[44] or to their facilitation of rent seeking.[45] However, credible research suggests that the presence of lawyers is associated with economic growth.[46] Whether or not lawyers promote growth, it appears that growth promotes the presence of lawyers.

We should not assume that the growth of legal professionals over the past half-century is destined to continue along the same trajectory. The longer history of the

[39] Robert J. MacCoun & Peter Reuter, Drug War Heresies: Learning from Other Vices, Times, and Places (2001).

[40] 433 U.S. 350 (1977).

[41] Galanter & Palay, *supra* note 11, at 71–73.

[42] Nassim Nicholas Taleb, The Black Swan: the Impact of the Highly Improbable 64 (2007).

[43] Kevin M. Murphy, Andrei Shliefer, & Robert W. Vishny, *The Allocation of Talent: Implications for Growth*, 106 Q.J. Econ. 503 (1991).

[44] *Id.*; *see also* Derek C. Bok, *A Flawed System of Law Practice and Training*, 33 J. Legal Educ. 570 (1983).

[45] Stephen P. Magee, William A. Brock & Leslie Young, Black Hole Tariffs and Endogenous Policy Theory (1989).

[46] Frank B. Cross, *Law versus Economics?* 17 Law & Soc. Inquiry 653 (1993); Charles R. Epp, *Do Lawyers Impair Economic Growth?*, 17 Law & Soc. Inquiry 585 (1992).

profession – for example, the collapse of lawyer activity and prosperity during the Great Depression – gives no such assurance. Indeed, the history of professions portends a drastic restructuring of the world of lawyering. There is a strong possibility of yet to be identified further developments in knowledge and communication technologies that will have profound effects on the cost, scale, location, and organization of legal work.[47] Australia and Britain have already broken with the old requirement that law firms must be financed by themselves (with bank credit), and have allowed for raising capital from outside investors. If provisions for the enhanced inflow of capital become more general, we can expect a surge of innovation in law firm practices and a further shift from artisanal to corporate models.

Finally, might we imagine any change in the relation of lawyers to justice/injustice? The official view is that lawyers are a means to justice, so the more lawyers you have, the more justice. There is a long countertradition that asserts that the more lawyers, the more injustice. My own view is that both are right. Injustice increases with the capacity of human society to remedy conditions that are seen as unjust. As inventiveness, technology, and social organization cumulatively enlarge the capacity of human society to remedy conditions that are seen as unfair and onerous, what was once regrettable but unavoidable becomes a matter of unfairness or neglect. If justice is the remedy for, or removal of, injustice, we can expect to experience an increase of both injustice and justice as more situations move from the realm of inalterable fate into the realm of human control and social choice. There is an inevitable struggle over whose claims for justice are going to be attended to. Lawyers may be major or minor players in this struggle, depending on how much of this distributive politics is located in or adjacent to the courts. As societies become more legalized/juridified, the relation of lawyers to justice (and injustice) may become closer.

Will these or other changes appear in the coming decades? We do not know – and no amount of careful dissection of the data about lawyers can yield answers because the moving forces are, in large measure, outside the legal sphere – in the unpredictable collisions of politics, technology, economics, and culture. People may like law to look and talk as if it is autonomous, but that does not make it so. Of course, the forms of autonomy – imposing courthouses, oracular robed judges, impenetrable jargon – will survive and flourish. Perhaps more will be invested in these forms to maintain the illusion of autonomy.

In looking ahead, we should recall how the coming enlargement of the legal realm was hidden from all those well-placed mid-century observers. We are reminded that figures at central locations in the legal world are not vouchsafed advance tidings of impending changes. So, we must wait and see – and resist being seduced by the idols

[47] Richard Susskind, The End of Lawyers? Rethinking the nature of Legal Services (2008); Richard Susskind, The Future of Law (1996).

of overconfident knowledge and their priests. Here I turn to the words of Romain Rolland, a great literary figure of the early twentieth century, who reports: "Never do I hesitate to look squarely at the face that every passing hour unveils to us, and to sacrifice the false images of it formed in advance, however dear they may be."[48]

APPENDIX: DATA SOURCES FOR TABLES 4.1–4.6

[a] E-mail from Alexander Christian, Bar Association of Austria, to Anders Carlson, Law Student, University of Wisconsin (June 29, 2010) (on file with author).

[b] Sharyn Roach Anleu, *Women in the Legal Profession: Theory and Research*, *in* Women and the Law: Proceedings of a Conference Held 24–26 September 1991 193, 195 (Patricia Weiser Easteal & Sandra McKillop ed., 1991), *available at* http://www.aic.gov.au/publications/previous%20series/proceedings/1–27/~/media/publications/proceedings/16/anleu.ashx. In Tables 4.1 and 4.2, for the 2002 number, see Law Council of Australia, September 2004 Snapshot of the Legal Profession (on file with author). In Table 4.4, for 1986 and 1991, full-time-only figures were used.

[c] Rogelio Pérez Perdomo, Los Abogados de América Latina: Una Introducción Histórica 194 (2004). In Tables 4.1 and 4.2, Brazil's 2007 figure is taken from Organization for Economic Cooperation and Development, Competition Restrictions in Legal Professions: Brazil 2 (OECD 2007), *available at* http://www.seae.fazenda.gov.br/destaque_ingles/daf-comp-wp2-wd-2007–42-legal-professions-brazil-cade.pdf (last visited June 8, 2010).

[d] David A.A. Stager with Harry W. Arthurs, Lawyers in Canada 149 (1990). For 2000 and 2007, see 2000 and 2007 Law Societies' Statistics, *available at* http://www.flsc.ca/en/lawSocieties/statisticsLinks.asp (last visited Nov. 24, 2010).

[e] Ethan Michelson, Gender Inequality in the Chinese Legal Profession, Paper Presented at the Law & Society Ass'n Annual Meeting, Denver, Colorado (May 28–31, 2009) (on file with author). For some dates, there are numerous reports given from different sources. For the purposes of this paper, these were averaged to provide one estimate.

[f] Rogelio Pérez-Perdomo & Lawrence Friedman, *Latin Legal Cultures in the Age of Globalization*, *in* Legal Culture in the Age of Globalization: Latin America and Latin Europe 1 (Lawrence M. Friedman & Rogelio Pérez-Perdomo eds., 2003). In Tables 4.1 and 4.2, the data are taken from Pérez-

[48] Romain Rolland, Journey Within (1947).

Perdomo & Friedman, *supra*, at 10. Note that for Italy, the reported number from 2006 is the average of two numbers. The first number was computed from a per capita number provided in EUROPEAN COMMISSION FOR THE EFFICIENCY OF JUSTICE, EUROPEAN JUDICIAL SYSTEMS 214 (Council of Europe Publishing, 2008). The second number was provided in Council of Bars and Law Societies of Europe, Number of Lawyers in CCBE Member Bars (2006), http://www.ccbe.org/fileadmin/user_upload/NTCdocument/table_number_lawyers1_1179905628.pdf (last visited Nov. 24, 2010). In Table 4.3, the data are taken from Pérez-Perdomo & Friedman, *supra*, at 8.

[g] Ulrike Schultz, *Legal Education in Germany—A Never-Ending Story of Resistance to Change*, *in* HIGHER LEGAL CULTURE AND POSTGRADUATE EDUCATION IN EUROPE 125 (Vittorio Olgiati ed., 2007). In Tables 4.1 and 4.2, the data are from Schultz, *supra*, at 136. In Table 4.5, the data are from Schultz, *supra*, at 133.

[h] Statistical Abstract of Israel 2008, Tbl. 11.2: Judges, Judges in Rabbinical Courts, Lawyers, Israel Police and Prison Service, http://www.cbs.gov.il/reader/shnaton/templ_shnaton_e.html?num_tab=st11_02&CYear=2008 (last visited Nov. 24, 2010). In Table 4.5, we do not include rabbinical judges in our tallies.

[i] Yukiko Hasebe, *Civil Justice Reform: Access, Cost and Expedition. The Japanese Perspective*, *in* CIVIL JUSTICE IN CRISIS: COMPARATIVE PERSPECTIVES OF CIVIL PROCEDURE 235, 256 (Adrian A.S. Zuckerman ed., 1999).

[j] Fred J. Bruinsma, *Judges and Lawyers in the Netherlands: An Overview from 1970 till 2000*, *in* REORGANISATION AND RESISTANCE: LEGAL PROFESSIONS CONFRONT A CHANGING WORLD 67, 71 (William L. F. Felstiner ed., 2005).

[k] Maria Ines Bergoglio, Transformations in the Legal Profession in Latin America: Law Firms and New Types of Professional Discourse, Paper Presented at the Law & Society Ass'n Annual Meeting, Baltimore, Maryland (July 6-9, 2006) (on file with author).

[l] Malgorzata Fuszara, *Women Lawyers in Poland under the Impact of Post-1989 Transformation*, *in* WOMEN IN THE WORLD'S LEGAL PROFESSIONS 371, 382 (Ulrike Schultz & Gisela Shaw eds., 2003).

[m] Maria Manuel Leitao Marques, Conceicao Gomes & Joao Pedroso, *The Portuguese System of Civil Procedure*, *in* CIVIL JUSTICE IN CRISIS, *supra* note [i], at 413, 438.

[n] Dai-kwon Choi, *A Legal Profession in Transformation: The Korean Experience*, *in* REORGANISATION AND RESISTANCE, *supra* note [j], at 171. In Tables 4.1, 4.2, and 4.3, the data are taken from Choi, *supra*, at 175. In Table 4.5, the data are taken from Choi, *supra*, at 184.

[o] Jose Juan Toharia, *The Organization, Functioning, and Evaluation of the Spanish Judicial System, 1975–2000: A Case Study in Legal Culture*, *in* LEGAL CULTURE IN THE AGE OF GLOBALIZATION, *supra* note [f], at 377, 390.

[p] RICHARD L. ABEL, THE LEGAL PROFESSION IN ENGLAND AND WALES 406, 407 (1988). For numbers after 1980, see The Law Society, Annual Statistical Report, http://www.lawsociety.org.uk:80/aboutlawsociety/whatwedo/researchandtrends/statisticalreport.law (follow link for desired year) (last visited Nov. 24, 2010).

[q] E-mail from Kathy Genens, Manager of Legal Information & Department Administration, Am. Bar Ass'n, Market Research Department, to Anders Carlson, Law Student, University of Wisconsin (Mar. 19, 2010) (on file with author) (indicating that the data were retrieved from the ABA Archives (prior to 1998) and the ABA Market Research Department's National Lawyer Population Survey (1998 and forward)).

[r] Rogelio Pérez-Perdomo, *Venezuela, 1958–1999: The Legal System in an Impaired Democracy*, *in* LEGAL CULTURE IN THE AGE OF GLOBALIZATION, *supra* note [f], at 414, 464.

[s] Hector Fix-Fierro & Sergio Lopez Ayllon, *Legal Professionals Aplenty, but No Legal Profession? Law and Lawyers in Contemporary Mexico*, *in* REORGANIZATION AND RESISTANCE, *supra* note [j], at 237, 240.

[t] The Law Society, Annual Statistical Report, http://www.lawsociety.org.uk:80/aboutlawsociety/whatwedo/researchandtrends/statisticalreport.law (follow link for desired year) (last visited May 31, 2010). The numbers provided in the table are the number of law graduates from England and Wales for each year, and do not represent the total enrollment for each year. The data do not include modular or joint honour degrees.

[u] Am. Bar Ass'n, First Year and Total J.D. Enrollment by Gender 1947–2008, *available at* http://www.abanet.org/legaled/statistics/charts/stats%20-%206.pdf (last visited Nov. 24, 2010).

[v] For the 1985 and 1990 numbers, see VERITY LEWIS, TRENDS IN THE SOLICITORS' PROFESSION: ANNUAL STATISTICAL REPORT 1996 10 (1996), *available at* http://www.lawsociety.org.uk/secure/file/180109/e:/teamsite-deployed/documents/templatedata/Publications/Research%20Publications/Documents/trendsasr1996report.pdf (last visited Nov. 24, 2010). For the 1999 number, see BILL COLE, TRENDS IN THE SOLICITORS' PROFESSION: ANNUAL STATISTICAL REPORT 1999 9 (2000), *available at* http://www.lawsociety.org.uk/documents/downloads/ASRreport99_v1.pdf (last visited Nov. 24, 2010). For the 2009 number, see BILL COLE, NINA FLETCHER, TARA CHITTENDEN & JOANNE COX, TRENDS IN THE SOLICITORS' PROFESSION: ANNUAL STATISTICAL REPORT

2009 9 (2009), *available at* http://www.lawsociety.org.uk/secure/file/183555/e:/teamsite-deployed/documents/templatedata/Publications/Research%20Publications/Documents/asr2009report.pdf (last visited Nov. 24, 2010).

[w] Clara N. Carson, American Bar Foundation, The Lawyer Statistical Report: The U.S. Legal Profession in 2000 3 (2004).

[x] Bryna Bogoch, *Lawyers in the Courtroom: Gender, Trials and Professional Performance in Israel, in* Women in the World's Legal Professions, *supra* note [l], at 247, 250. Bogoch's numbers were averaged by decade.

[y] Leny E. de Groot-van Leeuwen, *Women in the Dutch Legal Profession (1950–2000), in* Women in the World's Legal Professions, *supra* note [l], at 341, 342.

[z] Eliane Bothelho Junqueira, *Women in the Judiciary: A Perspective from Brazil, in* Women in the World's Legal Professions, *supra* note [l], at 437, 439.

[aa] Yuriko Kaminaga & Jörn Westhoff, *Women Lawyers in Japan: Contradictory Factors in Status, in* Women in the World's Legal Professions, *supra* note [l], at 467, 471. Except for the percentage of women lawyers in 1991, Kaminaga and Westhoff provide only the total number of women lawyers in the given years. Percentages listed for all other years were configured using Kaminaga and Westhoff's total number of women lawyers and the total number of lawyers (both men and women) provided in Hasebe, *supra* note [i], at 256.

[bb] Ulrike Schultz, *The Status of Women Lawyers in Germany, in* The World's Legal Professions, supra note [l], at 271, 275. Note that the 2003 number comes from Ulrike Schultz, *Growth as an Agent of Change, in* Reorganization and Resistance, *supra* note [j], at 93, 94.

[cc] United Nations Surveys on Crime Trends and the Operations of Criminal Justice Systems, http://www.unodc.org/unodc/en/data-and-analysis/United-Nations-Surveys-on-Crime-Trends-and-the-Operations-of-Criminal-Justice-Systems.html (last visited Nov. 23, 2010).

5

Faces of the Tort Pyramid

Compensation, Regulation, and the Profession

John T. Nockleby

INTRODUCTION

To what extent does the efficacy of the tort system depend on the plaintiff's tort bar? In this chapter, I address how the regulatory function of the tort system is skewed by structural features of the legal profession.

The tort system serves at least two separate functions. First, it provides for compensation for a limited class of injured persons. Second, it serves to regulate safety. In addition to these two functions, the tort system reflects a particular moral view of responsibility for injury. For any of these roles to be served, the tort system requires significant lawyer energy. Although it is possible for nonrepresented plaintiffs to file suit, in fact most people do not sue without the aid of a lawyer. More to the point, few unrepresented plaintiffs are ever successful.

In this chapter, I ask how well the twin functions, as well as the moral sensibility, are served by looking at the role of lawyers in the tort system. My conclusion is that, on account of the peculiar way in which the legal profession intersects with the tort system, this system cannot adequately serve the functions presently assigned it. Before assessing the role of lawyers, it will be helpful to describe in general terms the compensatory function and the regulatory function of the present tort system.

THE COMPENSATORY FUNCTION

Much scholarship addresses the compensation function of the tort system, which annually generates billions of dollars in compensation, or transfer payments.[1]

[1] For critiques of tort law, see Richard L. Abel, A *Critique of American Tort Law*, 8 BRITISH J. L. & SOC'Y 199 (1981); Richard L. Abel, A *Socialist Approach to Risk*, 41 MD. L. REV. 695 (1982); Richard L. Abel, *Pound's of Cure, Ounces of Prevention*, 73 CALIF. L. REV.1003, 1023 (1985); Richard L. Abel, *Should Tort Law Protect Property Against Accidental Loss?*, 23 SAN DIEGO L. REV. 79 (1986); Marc Galanter, *Real World Torts: An Antidote to Anecdote*, 55 MD. L. REV. 1093, 1116–20 (1996); George

Undoubtedly this accounts for just a fraction of actual injuries that are potentially compensable, and a small portion of the actual cost of accidents.

Although the evidence about the actual operation of the tort system is sparse,[2] we know that several million *civil* cases are filed annually in state courts – not all of these are tort cases – and that a majority of torts are automobile accident cases.[3] In simplest terms, a tort suit seeks to hold another party responsible for the claimant's injury. Finding liability goes to the heart of the tort compensation system. In the absence of a determination of fault or other responsibility, no compensation is awarded. Therefore, we need to probe deeper into the tort litigation process.

Marc Galanter visualizes successful tort litigation as the pinnacle of a pyramid that contains many layers.[4] At the bottom, we find all the injuries that might potentially be claimed. However, some injured persons do not recognize they have a potential claim; others are fearful or ambivalent about pursuing a claim, or blame themselves or fate. The next level of the pyramid – grievances – thus contains just a fraction of those injured. Some grievances are resolved; others are disputed. The next level of the pyramid represents a portion of the disputed claims that are pursued further, perhaps by consulting a lawyer. Some of those claims are dropped or resolved at this stage, and a few are pursued to the next level, filing suit. At this stage, the plaintiff's tort bar plays a critical gatekeeper role.

I will have much more to say later about the lawyer's role, but for now, it is important to note that, effectively at this stage, the decision to pursue a claim is no longer in the hands of the injured person. Tort litigation typically requires a lawyer's involvement; people are free to file claims on their own, but such claims rarely succeed.

As we proceed up the levels of the "pyramid," the number of claims drops significantly. We can see this empirically. For example, studies have shown that of all

L. Priest, *The Current Insurance System and Modern Tort Law*, 96 Yale L.J. 1521, 1552–53 (1987); *see also* Deborah R. Hensler, Mary F. Vaiana, James S. Kakalik & Mark A. Peterson, Trends in Tort Litigation: The Story Behind the Statistics 26–29 (1987); Deborah R. Hensler, *Reading the Tort Litigation Tea Leaves: What's Going on in the Civil Liability Justice System?*, 16 Just. Sys. J. 139, 140–41 (1993); Stephen D. Sugarman, *Doing Away With Tort Law*, 73 Cal. L. Rev. 555, 604 (1985).

[2] *See, e.g.*, Hensler et al., *supra* note 1; Theodore Eisenberg, *The Need for a National Civil Justice Survey of Incidence and Claiming Behavior*, 37 Fordham Urb. L.J. 17, 21 (2010); Michael J. Saks, *Do We Really Know Anything About the Behavior of the Tort Litigation System – and Why Not?*, 140 U. Pa. L. Rev. 1147 (1992).

[3] *See* Hensler et al., *supra* note 1; Lynn Langton & Thomas H. Cohen, *Civil Bench and Jury Trials in State Courts, 2005*, Bureau of Justice Statistics, 1–2 (Oct. 2008), http://bjs.ojp.usdoj.gov/content/pub/pdf/cbjtsc05.pdf; Eisenberg, *supra* note 2; John T. Nockleby, *How to Manufacture a Crisis: Evaluating Empirical Claims Behind Tort Reform*, 86 Or. L. Rev. 533 (2007).

[4] Galanter, *supra* note 1; *see also* Tom Baker, The Medical Malpractice myth (1995); William L.F. Felstiner et al., *The Emergence and Transformation of Disputes: Naming, Blaming, Claiming…*, 15 Law & Soc'y Rev. 631 (1980–81); Herbert M. Kritzer et al., *The Aftermath of Injury: Cultural Factors in Compensation Seeking in Canada and the United States*, 25 Law & Soc'y Rev. 499, 501–02 (1991).

those injured by likely medical malpractice over several years in a particular hospital, about 3–4 percent ended up filing claims.[5] We do not have good evidence about what percentage of "deserving" victims who surmount all the hurdles recover compensation, but it is clear that except in certain well-known areas, such as automobile accidents, it is typically 50 percent or less.[6]

Scholars have identified many hurdles individuals face in pursuing claims. Some of those injured do not understand law sufficiently to recognize that their injuries may be compensable. Cultural factors may inhibit others. Some may distrust the legal system or associate all law with the police or criminal prosecution. Others may be vulnerable to political or legal pressures (such as undocumented immigrants or workers who fear their employer might find out) and thus unwilling to seek relief. Most of those injured will lack funds to hire a lawyer and thus must have a sufficiently viable and valuable claim to attract a contingency lawyer to represent them. Most of those who seek assistance – especially if they have small claims – will have difficulty finding a lawyer. All these impediments (cultural, logistical, and transactional) to making claims necessarily undermine the utility of the tort system in fulfilling its compensatory function: If you do not recognize you have suffered a legally compensable tort injury, you will not receive compensation. If a defendant refuses to pay and you cannot find a lawyer to represent you, you will likely go uncompensated.

Therefore, if our goal is primarily to obtain compensation for injured parties, it is clear that the tort system does not function well as a system of social insurance. Too many persons are left outside the compensatory scheme, and of those who do make claims, many do not receive compensation because they either cannot establish causation or cannot identify a responsible entity that is at fault. Also, at a critical juncture in the process, the decision whether to pursue a claim lies in the hands of a lawyer, whose calculations understandably do not focus on the desperate straits of the claimant. Thus, even though "providing compensation" is a frequently stated objective of the tort system, it does not in fact do this. Instead, tort creates a mechanism for finding responsible parties. Tort operates more as a system of attributing responsibility for injury than as a system designed to compensate injury.

The tort system assigns blame and awards compensation only to those who "deserve" payment within the tort framework of causation and whose claim is considered sufficiently attractive to a plaintiff's lawyer to be worth investing time and money to pursue. From the injured person's perspective, perhaps it makes the person feel better to be able to identify a wrongdoer who must pay. However, one might suspect that in the vast majority of cases, an injured person would prefer to

5 BAKER, *supra* note 4, at 69.

6 Langton & Cohen, *supra* note 3, at 4.

have adequate medical care and a pension if she were unable to support herself as a result of the injury.

The tort system also locates a potential pocket from which funds for medical care can be drawn. One advantage of assigning blame through tort law is that (at least until the time of tort reform) the state's role in creating these transfer payments is obscured. When payments are made, they are defined as "private" transfers, not "public." The transfer is legitimated by the requirement of proof of fault (or excessive risk taking in the case of strict-liability transfers). Tort thus helps maintain the illusion that the costs of accidents involve private disputes, with no public monies involved. In an era when the cost of government and the cost of social insurance are under attack, tort can accordingly be legitimated as a "private" system of compensation.

One suspects, therefore, that a workers' compensation model of tort – a no-fault system – has not received widespread support because no-fault systems shift transfer payments onto public budgets, making the state ultimately responsible for the liquidity of the system.[7] With many government social programs already underfunded, it is unlikely that developing further insurance schemes to cover accidental loss will occur in the present political climate. Thus, the second-best solution to the lack of compensation for most injuries may be to press forward with improvements to the tort structure.

TORT LAW'S REGULATORY FUNCTION

Tort law also serves a regulatory role, and the lawyers within the system are crucial enforcers of tort norms.[8] The tort system sets important default regulatory standards when not preempted by government statutes or regulations. In the tort system, judges and juries set standards of behavior and enforce them across a wide spectrum of behavior. This regulatory function engenders significant hostility from those subject to the regulatory spur. The most recent organized movement against this regulatory function is the so-called tort reform movement.[9]

[7] For example, the California No-Fault auto insurance ballot initiative of the 1990s went down to defeat.

[8] I thus take issue with some of the dispute-resolution literature which overemphasizes the function of tort law as primarily a forum for resolving micro-conflicts between Person A and Person B, sometimes to the exclusion of the regulatory apparatus. In addition, I think it is important to underscore how tort law regulates behavior rather than merely providing incentives to act in an "optimally safe way," as some of the law and economics tort literature puts it.

[9] At one time, these costs were hidden in the balance sheets of insurers and companies. However, tort reform proponents have emphasized that the tort system creates costs that may be passed on to consumers. American Tort Reform Association, http://www.atra.org (last visited June 8, 2010); U.S. Chamber of Commerce Institute for Legal Reform, http://www.instituteforlegalreform.com/ (last visited Nov. 26, 2010).

A few examples may help illustrate the comprehensiveness of the tort regulatory framework. Because tort law is taught within a doctrinal framework (intentional torts, negligence, strict liability), it is easy to forget the sheer number of contexts in which the tort system has created detailed rules and standards of behavior. Tort rules and standards serve an important role by operating as the default regulatory framework against which significant human activity takes place.

Consider how tort law affects the major life activities of every person. Tort law establishes the standards of care businesses must exercise for their visitors' safety, whether from the physical surroundings or from potential threats posed by others. Tort sets the default standards of care for travel and vehicular operation – whether by auto, train, bus, truck, moped, airplane, or foot. We know what minimal care the medical profession must provide to patients and their families by examining medical malpractice standards.

All tangible "things" sold as products to consumers or businesses must meet the default standards of safety set through tort law. The safety level of products governed by tort ranges across the entirety of every object one encounters in daily life: coffeemakers, beds, cars, irons, clothing, pharmaceuticals, electrical outlets, machinery, computers, chairs, tools, and devices of every type. Ergonomics studies the interface between humans and objects; part of the design of every product incorporates the analysis of the safety features of that product in order to comply with tort standards. Tort law also sets standards regulating other human relationships. The communication torts (defamation, privacy, assault) mark boundaries of what one can say about or to another. The physical torts (battery, false imprisonment, infliction of emotional distress, negligence) govern spatial relationships among people, setting standards that, at least in theory, protect against injury.

The limit of property rights is defined by tort law in conjunction with other rules. We test ownership rights through the property torts such as trespass, trespass to chattels, and conversion. Family relationships, once immune from much tort law, today provide background operating rules governing "discipline" of children (though the "discipline" of wives is no longer the province of tort) and, along with the criminal law, regulate what constitutes consensual behavior between adults regarding sexual practices.

It would be fair to say that, in the absence of other preempting regulation, tort law defines a limited set of default standards of behavior for significant human interaction. However, although every lawyer knows about the reach of tort law, the fact that tort law establishes the background operating rules against which human activity takes place is obscured by several important characteristics of the system.

First, to say that tort sets systemic default background operating rules is not the same as saying that these rules can be consulted like volumes of the tax code. Tort rules operate much like cultural norms: People do not generally spit on crowded public sidewalks, nor do they routinely bump each other on the street. It is only when someone is bumped or hurt by another's conduct that tort rules come to mind. It is only when someone departs from the standard set by the tort law that the occasion arises to consider the rules.[10]

Second, tort law places the power of enforcement in the hands of individual claimants. Tort rules are not enforced in the same way that speed limits are. No agent checks for violations; whether a claim is brought rests in the hands of an injured person. For this reason, even though the aggregate of tort law sets standards of behavior, tort claims have historically been viewed as "private" disputes, not public controversies. (Tort reform proponents are challenging this view of tort law, and on this issue they are right.) Individualized enforcement of tort norms obscures this public regulatory function by making it appear in every instance that a tort suit is a dispute between an individual claimant and an individual defendant. The norm-setting function of tort law is hidden in the myriad sets of individual disputes.

Third, tort rules are typically set at a high level of generality.[11] Defining what sorts of behavior are "negligent" or "unreasonable" requires contextual information about the particular practices. The requirement of detailed information about a specific incident suggests that the problem is localized, not common to everyone. Indeed, with many torts, and particularly with respect to the negligence tort, it is very difficult to set out detailed behavioral rules in advance.[12] In the realm of unintentional harms, tort law employs standards of behavior, not rules.[13] This requires case-by-case analysis, further obscuring how safety standards are being set.

In sum, many features of the tort law obscure its public role as regulator of harms created in the marketplace and enforcer of public safety.

THE SYMBIOTIC RELATIONSHIP BETWEEN COMPENSATION AND REGULATION

Thus far, I have described the compensatory and regulatory functions of tort law as dichotomous features of the tort system. In fact, however, the two functions are intertwined in ways that make it impossible to disaggregate one from the other. Compensation and regulation are integrally related to each other in ways that obscure the normative issues. We can approach the matter from both directions.

[10] *See, e.g.*, Felstiner, et al., *supra* note 4.

[11] Tort judges did not set out to define the background operating rules. These rules developed over time through accretion and periodic synthesis. *See* OLIVER WENDELL HOLMES, JR., THE COMMON LAW 128–129 (Mark DeWolfe Howe ed., 1963) (1881) (stating that law judges did not set out a general theory of tort).

[12] For analysis of the "featureless generality" of the negligence action, see *id.* at 89.

[13] *See, e.g.*, Duncan Kennedy, *Form and Substance in Private Law Adjudication*, 89 HARV. L. REV. 1685 (1976) (discussing the form of legal commands as rules or standards).

The regulatory function of tort is to set standards of safety. A key question, however, is how much safety is enough? This is a knotty problem that law and economics purports to answer by claiming there is an "efficient" or optimal outcome to the inquiry.[14] Other literature emphasizes a restorative goal: The objective is to correct a moral imbalance between two parties.[15] Regardless of whether one's perspective is economic or moral, the classic Learned Hand formula from negligence law shows how the two functions are related.

Under the Learned Hand formula, a defendant is said to be negligent when the burden of precaution is less than the probability that the loss from the injury will occur.[16] To an economist, the formula asks one to compare the costs and benefits of imposing liability versus the costs of compensation.[17] Presumably if the costs of compensation were reduced, the regulatory burden would also be reduced. That is, we "know" whether an enterprise should have invested in safety by asking "how much" compensation would be required to reinstate victims to their prior position. Thus the amount of anticipated loss (or, if suit becomes necessary, compensation) is necessarily part of the analysis of whether given conduct is or is not negligent.

Coming at the relationship from the compensation side, the anticipated damage award provides the incentive to sue – and thus to establish and enforce the regulatory standards. A contingency lawyer will typically file suit on behalf of a claimant only if she thinks the investment of time and energy will result in an award. Accordingly, without compensation, there would be no meaningful regulation of behavior through tort. The monies a defendant might pay in compensation create the incentive to comply with the community standards set through tort.

Thus, given the mutual incentives and measuring sticks on both sides of the compensation/regulation dichotomy, it is impossible in fact to separate the two functions. They are mutually constitutive of each other: "How much" safety is sufficient to satisfy the legal standard is answered by "however much compensation" is required to make victims whole.

14 Much law and economics literature focuses on this question, but the claim of optimality obscures the normative nature of the question. *See* Duncan Kennedy & Frank I. Michelman, *Are Property and Contract Efficient?*, 8 Hofstra L. Rev. 711 (1980).

15 *See, e.g.*, Jules Coleman, Risks and Wrongs (1992).

16 In *United States v. Carroll Towing*, 159 F.2d 169 (2d Cir. 1947), Judge Learned Hand posited a formula to show the relationship between compensation and safety. Under that formula, a defendant is said to be negligent if the burden of precaution is less than the probability times the amount of anticipated loss, or $B<PL$. *Id.*

17 For present purposes, it does not matter whether the Learned Hand formula is employed to decide a specific case (such as whether a store is responsible for a plaintiff's fall by cleaning up a spill) or employed to decide standards for an entire class of cases (such as whether stores should be expected to clean up spills within a few minutes of their occurrence regardless of whether they are on notice of them).

By channeling the regulatory apparatus through litigation, over time and case by case, the tort system thus tends to obscure the normative questions raised in every case. For example, what types of injuries do people suffer that constitute compensable "injury" within the meaning of tort? Being fired from a job? Suffering emotional distress but not physical injury because you fear contracting cancer from the chemical to which the defendant exposed you? Defining cognizable injury is a normative question that, because litigation proceeds individualistically, tends to be obscured by the litigation process.

THE LAWYER'S ROLE IN CONSTRUCTING THE TORT REGULATORY SYSTEM

From this brief overview, we can begin to assess the effectiveness of tort law as a system of rule making and enforcement. We can also begin to tease out how the plaintiff's tort bar plays a central role in enabling the system to function *at all* while simultaneously limiting those same functions.

If we review how the tort bar finds clients, we note that plaintiff's lawyers employ various filters. Some accept only certain types of cases. Others look for high-volume cases or screen for high-value cases. For our purposes, we need merely to understand in a general way how these screens operate. The screens determine who among the injured have effective access to the tort system. But they also determine what types of cases are brought – and what types of cases are brought constitutes the tort regulatory system.

Suppose an injured person finds his way to a lawyer and seeks representation. In virtually all instances, the lawyer is asked to take the case on a contingency basis, so the lawyer receives a fee only if someone pays a claim. Meanwhile, the lawyer understands that by taking the case, she can ordinarily expect to front money to investigate the underlying events leading to the injury, and perhaps to hire experts who can assess the claim more effectively. These costs – which can be substantial – will not be paid unless the lawyer is able to secure a settlement or a judgment.

Contingency lawyers typically employ a merits screen at the outset, and about half the cases tend to be rejected at this stage.[18] Once past the initial screen (that is, once a case has been determined to have merit), many cases are still rejected. Studies of the plaintiff's bar show that, past the initial screen, the principal determinants of whether a tort case is worth the lawyer's time and expense are: (1) the amount of damage the plaintiff suffered; (2) whether there is a "responsible party" who has sufficient funds to pay those damages; (3) the amount of expense likely to

[18] *See generally* HERBERT M. KRITZER, RISK, REPUTATIONS, AND REWARDS: CONTINGENCY FEE LEGAL PRACTICE IN THE UNITED STATES (2004).

be required to secure a settlement or a judgment; and (4) the amount of time and effort the lawyer is likely to be required to invest, and over what period of time. The fifth factor – how meritorious a judge and jury are likely to see the claim to be – may appear to the outsider to be the most important in the lawyer's decision to accept or reject a case, but, surprisingly to many, it tends to be less important to the ultimate decision once the case has passed the initial screen. The economic calculation a contingency lawyer undertakes focuses largely on whether the case is economically viable. Even meritorious claims require investment of time and money because the lawyer must assume the defendant will contest the claim.

Determining how these factors intersect with each other is a critical part of the lawyer's decision-making process in choosing whether to accept or reject a case. These are the factors over which the injured person has no control and may not even understand. Even more importantly, these factors have little to do with the underlying tort regulatory functions. The screening criteria – How much will the case cost? How many hours will it require? – are essential inquiries for the lawyer deciding whether to accept a case, but the filtering process greatly skews the nature of the claims that eventually are brought. How much – and when – a lawyer is likely to be paid turns out to be the critical determinant of whether a tort rule is enforced. Indeed, in more complex tort cases, plaintiff's lawyers accept somewhere between 5 and 20 percent of the claims for which people seek representation.[19] Many cases are rejected because they lack merit, but the plaintiff lawyer's economic calculation means that many potentially meritorious cases will not be filed.

We can evaluate the effects of the filtering system by examining several different characteristics of the lawyer's decision-making process, and their impact on the efficacy of tort as a regulatory regime.

The "Ideal" Plaintiff

In a familiar populist trope, it is said that a remarkable feature of our civil law system is that it permits an individual person to haul the most powerful institutions in the country into court – and sometimes win. Injured persons can obtain compensation and simultaneously enforce public norms against powerful interests.

A quick survey of twentieth-century tort law developments demonstrates that tort litigation does have bite. Tort lawyers overturned many rules protecting the medical establishment from malpractice (such as locality rules and expert-witness limitations) and created an informed-consent tort. Claims of emotional distress were recognized for the first time. Toxic exposures and suits for products liability, including

[19] *See, e.g.*, Herbert M. Kritzer, *Contingency Fee Lawyers as Gatekeepers in the Civil Justice System*, *in* Judicial Politics: Readings from Judicature 132 (Elliot E. Slotnick ed., 2d ed. 2005).

product design, became subjects of litigation. Doctrinal changes expanded the field of tort law, such as the abandonment of immunities and rules constricting suits on account of lack of privity, the expansion of duty and joint and several liability rules, and the development of comparative fault. Class-action suits allowed many types of tort claims to be addressed that previously were left aside.[20]

On the other hand, tort cannot serve its regulatory function without litigation.[21] Even if we agree that the current tort rules are the best available (a contestable claim), the only enforcement mechanism available requires that an injured person file a lawsuit. The dual requirements that someone both suffer injury and then file suit about it limits the effectiveness of tort law as a mechanism for setting safety standards.

Consider again Galanter's "pyramid" of tort: Some who have been injured do not recognize they have suffered cognizable injury; of those who do, some do not pursue the claim; of those who do consult a lawyer, some drop it before filing suit; of those who are able to persuade a lawyer to accept the case, many settle; of those who sue and do not settle, half lose; of those who prevail at trial, some lose on appeal. In short, the narrowing categories from the class of injured persons to those who ultimately prevail means that much injury will not go redressed, and thus tort norms may go underenforced.

Of course, the threat of tort litigation (as opposed to actually being sued) can itself operate as an inducement to invest in safety precautions. Further, even if a suit is compromised or ultimately unsuccessful, litigation itself can spur greater safety or serve as an example to others to rectify unsafe practices. The point is not that litigation does not work to incentivize safety (indeed it can and does work), but rather that unlike other regulatory regimes, litigation is essential to enforcement of tort norms. Put another way, in the absence of litigation, the norms are neither established nor enforced. Seen in another context, gender and race discrimination were rampant until civil rights litigation forced businesses and schools to change their practices.

Moreover, an individual must have standing to sue in tort. Standing is provided by injury. Yet the requirement of proving an injury disqualifies all but those suffering injury from serving as a private attorney general and actually assessing whether institutions are being careless and risking injury. In contrast, the Occupational Safety and Health Administration does not need an injury to find a violation. The tort system, however, requires it. Thus, tort has limited utility as regulatory regime designed to forestall injury.

[20] *See generally* John T. Nockleby & Shannon Curreri, *100 Years of Conflict: The Past and Future of Tort Retrenchment*, 38 Loy. L.A. L. Rev. 1021 (2005).

[21] Litigation is central to enforcement. Thus, the "tort reform" community, comprised largely of business interests seeking to be free of regulation by tort, attacks litigation generally.

Further, we have created an enforcement mechanism that most people cannot afford to utilize. Few people can afford to hire a lawyer outright,[22] and the evidence shows that most unrepresented plaintiffs cannot win against a represented defendant.[23] So most tort plaintiffs turn to the contingent fee lawyer.

The contingent fee lawyer is an entrepreneurial lawyer.[24] She accepts cases with an eye toward the merits of the case, but a large part of the assessment process focuses on her own economic calculations such as how much time and money she must invest in the case, gauged against the likely settlement value or verdict value of the case. Many cases with significant harms also require huge (often multimillion-dollar) investments by the plaintiff's lawyer, so many contingent fee lawyers are priced out of high-value cases because they lack capital. Many other lawyers cannot afford to invest thousands of hours developing complex cases. As a result, many lawyers who work the plaintiff's side actually operate as referral lawyers – and accept a small percentage of the eventual contingency fee in return for "finding" and referring the case.

The "ideal" plaintiff is also well known in the legal community. Obviously, the plaintiff whose case evidences strong liability is desired, but compelling liability is not critical, nor is it even the most important consideration. Indeed, plaintiffs whose case evidences compelling liability but who suffered modest damages will struggle to find a lawyer to take their case.

For example, in the Los Angeles region, many lawyers will turn down even routine tort cases (for example, slip and fall), whose value is below a range of $20,000 to $50,000. The exact cut-off depends on complexity, who the defendant is, and how clear liability is. Many medical malpractice lawyers will not accept a case valued at less than $300,000 to $500,000.[25] The expenses of litigation, plus the hours required

[22] Finding ways to provide equal access to justice in civil litigation has proven extremely challenging. *See, e.g.*, DEBORAH L. RHODE, ACCESS TO JUSTICE (2004); Scott L. Cummings, *The Politics of Pro Bono*, 52 UCLA L. REV. 1 (2004).

[23] Russell Engler, *Shaping a Context-Based Civil Gideon from the Dynamics of Social Change*, 15 TEMP. POL. & CIV. RTS. L. REV. 697 (2006).

[24] *E.g.*, KRITZER, *supra* note 18; Mary Nell Trautner, *Personal Responsibility v. Corporate Liability: Evaluating and Accepting Personal Injury Cases*, 12 SOCIOLOGY OF CRIME, LAW & DEVIANCE 203 (2009).

[25] These generalizations are based on many conversations with plaintiff's lawyers in the Los Angeles area. Obviously the market for contingency lawyers differs from one geographic region to another. The market also varies from one specialty to another. For example, some firms have routinized classes of tort cases, such as auto accident cases, and these may be processed by armies of paralegals working under a single lawyer, so the actual settlement value of any individual fender-bender need not be great in order to provide adequate inducement for lawyers to accept the case. Moreover, there are always exceptions to these generalizations. Some lawyers will take a case with low damages for settlement value, but if the case does not settle, they will not invest the time and money to develop the case. And some elite-firm lawyers will accept low-value contingency cases as their "pro bono" contribution to the profession. In any event, the significant point is not the exact amount of damages required to attract

to develop a case, make such low-value cases unattractive because they are not economically viable.

The most important consideration from the plaintiff's lawyer's perspective is the amount of potential damages. The plaintiff with a reasonable chance of establishing liability is always preferred, but the "ideal plaintiff" has serious injuries requiring substantial, long-term medical care, and which prevent her from performing a high-paying job she would have held for many years.[26]

The "Responsible" Defendant

In theory, anyone can commit a tort and be held liable to another. In practice, only those who have resources to pay judgments are likely to be sued. In general, this means deep-pocketed institutions or individuals carrying insurance tend to become defendants. The search for a responsible defendant has undoubtedly contributed to the expansion of many tort duties. For example, in the last few decades, courts have expanded duties to protect customers and employees from third-party criminal behavior; extended *respondeat superior* to include "foreseeable" behavior by employees; and (at least before tort reform targeted the practice) flexibly imposed joint and several liability rules.[27]

In turn, this also means that tort suits tend to not be filed against those without resources (except as a deterrent, such as in stalking cases; or to establish a principle, such as the civil suit against O.J. Simpson). There is not much point in seeking compensation from someone who is judgment-proof or whose assets are out of reach.

As an enforcement mechanism, tort law works only if a defendant has the resources to compensate an injured person. Thus, the tort system tends to be dysfunctional as a regulatory mechanism whenever a defendant is indifferent to suit.

Skewing Tort Regulation toward "Ideal" Plaintiffs and "Responsible" Defendants

Together, the legal requirements of proving individual injury (and thus placing the power of enforcement of tort norms in the hands of injured persons) and finding a

a contingency lawyer, but that there is a dollar-value limit necessary to attract contingency lawyers in many types of tort cases.

26 Most injured plaintiffs are entitled to the amount of money required to restore them to their prior position. Such sums typically include the present value of lost income to date and into the future; medical expenses to date and anticipated; and some amount for pain and suffering. In many jurisdictions, damage caps have severely restricted the amounts available as pain and suffering.

27 Nockleby & Curreri, *supra* note 20, at 1028, 1066–67; Marc Galanter, *The Turn Against Law: The Recoil Against Expanding Accountability*, 81 Tex. L. Rev. 285, 287 (2002);. Priest, *supra* note 1, at 1536.

responsible defendant deeply affect what types of tort suits are filed. When we also consider the pragmatic requirements of the lawyer hoping to be paid out of the recovery, the types of cases that end up in court are skewed in significant ways: Some behaviors that cause significant injury are far more likely than others to be litigated and thus will tend to be more highly regulated.

Many types of cases are not typically litigated within the tort system. Cases of serious injury in which causation cannot easily be proved (such as toxic contamination), or in which injuries have low economic value (primarily affecting poor people or the elderly), tend not to be brought. In such instances, the necessity of establishing a responsible defendant who can pay substantial compensation eviscerates the effectiveness of tort law as a regulatory regime.

Examples of such skewed regulation abound. Some torts go unlitigated because there are no economic incentives to attract contingency lawyers. Decrepit rental housing, or rats in the stairwell, or mold under the rug may violate the law, but people will not be able to attract a private lawyer to enforce the tort unless someone can prove significant economic damage.

Lucinda Finley's work shows that harms to women, children, and the elderly often are underenforced.[28] The unemployed, noncitizens, and workers in marginal employment also tend not to sue or to be unable to obtain lawyers. In part, this is because the tort law privileges economic losses, such as lost wages, over pain and emotional distress damages.[29]

Finley's focus, however, is on the inequity of the compensatory structure. Other scholars have also shown how, on the compensation side, tort law advantages well-off people who can establish fault over the impoverished or the elderly.[30] What has not been fully appreciated, however, is how the skewed nature of compensation greatly affects the regulatory side as well.

That the power of enforcement is individualized also means that individuals face substantial hurdles in enforcing tort norms, and this of course raises significant access-to-justice questions. Not all individuals are equally situated; not everyone understands their rights; many do not have access to lawyers or information about how to enforce their rights.[31] Endemic depression that accompanies poverty undermines one's energies and capacities to assert rights. Medical malpractice

[28] Lucinda Finley, *Female Trouble: The Implications of Tort Reform for Women*, 64 TENN. L. REV. 847 (1997); Lucinda Finley, *The Hidden Victims of Tort Reform: Women, Children, and the Elderly*, 53 EMORY L.J. 1263 (2004).

[29] Martha Chamallas, *Removing Emotional Harm from the Core of Tort Law*, 54 VAND. L. REV. 751 (2001).

[30] *Id.*

[31] *See generally* IN LITIGATION DO THE "HAVES" STILL COME OUT AHEAD? (Herbert M. Kritzer & Susan Silbey eds., 2003).

claims illustrate the low enforcement rate in certain areas: Studies have shown that of those likely injured through malpractice, only between 4 percent and 7 percent file suit.[32]

The critique of formal rights applies to the enforcement of tort norms: The capacity to name a wrong and to make a claim is not equally distributed among the population. This unequal access to knowledge also leads to the skewed development of tort law. For example, tort law involving products (automobiles) or services (medical malpractice) that threaten the safety of the middle class is more likely to be developed than tort law involving slum housing (lead paint), police misconduct, or child abuse.

Evaluating the Mechanisms of Setting Tort Standards

In theory, tort law provides an ongoing review of a wide range of behavior. This means that we do not need the panopticon of the government to sniff out violations. We do not need traffic cops patrolling grocery stores on the lookout for slip-and-falls about to happen. By dispersing the authority of the regulatory state among the population, we deputize individual citizens to confront hazardous conditions and to work to repair them. Needless to say, these citizens and their lawyers are motivated by a desire for individual compensation, but this is not reason to object to their enforcing common safety standards.

Moreover, the system has evolved so that today we have a cadre of experienced professionals – lawyers who operate independently of the state and who look for hazards that injure people. For all its limitations, the plaintiff's tort bar typically represents people without requiring payment for services (beyond the contingency fee). The expertise represented in the plaintiff's tort bar ranges across the tort regulatory landscape: from medical malpractice, highway design, toxic torts, and consumer fraud to elevators, drugs, auto safety, and nursing homes.

Nonetheless, the individualized nature of the tort litigation process also raises significant questions about whether the very public function of enforcing safety standards should be left to private tort plaintiffs. Should we be relying on individual claimants pursuing individual interests to enforce safety standards that affect all of us? Are the incentive structures sufficiently in place so that the public's safety is not compromised by individual self-interest in the pursuit of millions of individual lawsuits?

Consider, as an example, the confidentiality of documents produced during individual tort litigation. A defendant desires to settle but seeks as a condition that the parties return all documents produced during the litigation and promise

[32] Baker, *supra* note 4.

confidentiality. From the standpoint of the plaintiff and her lawyers, this is an easy question. Talk about a "Getting to Yes" moment: We have a classic case in which what the defendant wants is worth a lot to the defendant, yet it appears costless to the individual plaintiff to agree to confidentiality and to the destruction of the records.

From the public's perspective, however, destroying the smoking-gun memo or hiding the practices that may have affected many others is a social cost. The plaintiff's tort bar is politically opposed to such confidentiality agreements but believes that as a matter of zealous representation (and getting a settlement worth a lot to their clients), they have to concede the issue when it comes up in individual cases.

How torts are actually litigated parallels the document destruction example. Strategically, a plaintiff and her lawyer are best advised to seek maximum relief on the narrowest possible grounds rather than to fight for the broader principle. In part, this is due to the inherent conservatism of case-by-case adjudication. But it is also due to the inherent incentive structures built into individualistic lawsuits. Each individual litigant is expected to maximize her individual utility, not to seek broad rules that might improve the conditions for many others (and the ethics rules require that lawyers defer to the client's choice of ends).

In this respect, in its operation, tort law resembles a market mechanism and is therefore subject to similar criticisms that can be directed at other market-based allocation and distribution mechanisms. For example, markets work only if you have money, and the currency in tort is cognizable injury. The more cognizable the injury, the more resources you can command in the litigation marketplace. Thus, the market for medical malpractice suits with significant damages is vibrant, whereas the market for slumlord housing and toxic torts is not so lively.

Finally, one can also question the effectiveness of random enforcement of tort norms for certain types of injuries. If some types of harms are heavily litigated and others not at all, does the tort system work well enough to incentivize appropriate levels of care? The answer is that in some arenas, the tort system probably creates excessive safety incentives (for example, promoting the practice of defensive medicine), whereas other arenas go unregulated for all of the reasons previously identified.

Inefficient enforcement of tort standards does not necessarily mean that the regulatory function has been undermined. The periodic or even random nature of large, well-publicized tort damage awards may create sufficient incentive for enterprises at least to consider the safety features of their activities or products, even though not every tort will be compensated.

Still, the tort system decentralizes enforcement of regulatory norms, and this may be its most important feature, if not its saving grace. Much has been written about regulatory capture of federal agencies. The electoral process is corrupted by the necessity of raising huge sums from those who will be benefitted or harmed by a candidate's decisions. The legislative process is heavily influenced by those with money to hire lobbyists. Judicial elections, too, are becoming far more politicized and corrupted by the same practices that afflict other electoral processes. But it is much harder to stack the deck against the plaintiff's bar and the jury system. Juries are democratic, nonrepeat players.[33] Not that individual juries always get it right, but it is much harder to influence the one-off jury.[34]

CONCLUSION: UNDERSTANDING AND REMEDYING THE SKEW

The same flaws that afflict tort as a compensatory system also undermine the efficacy of tort law as a regulatory regime. Pursuing social regulation through tort has many advantageous features – particularly its open-ended nature that allows new types of claims to be brought – but it is apparent that we need to rethink how to enable the system to function better.

My goal in this chapter has been to pose a number of questions about the architecture of the tort system. I have suggested that the compensatory and regulatory functions of the tort system are intertwined with lawyers' case-selection filters, so that the regulatory function is skewed in important ways. We can see how the lawyer-as-gatekeeper affects the types of cases that are brought into the tort system, and the choices about cases to accept determine what cases are heard. Cases that cannot attract the contingency lawyer will not be brought, and this central fact means that many people's access to justice is limited by factors other than justice.

Paying attention to the architecture of the tort system may lead us to imagine ways of creating alternative pathways to justice. If the tort system does not work well for small cases, or for the elderly and the disempowered, then we should consider alternative structures that would provide greater access to justice.

[33] Heather Gerken, *Second-Order Diversity and Disaggregated Democracy*, 118 Harv. L. Rev. 1099 (2005).

[34] John Nockleby, *What's a Jury Good For?*, 11 Voir Dire 6 (Summer 2005).

PART II

LAWYERS AND THEIR CLIENTS: DETERMINANTS OF ETHICAL PRACTICE

6

How and Why Do Lawyers Misbehave?

Lawyers, Discipline, and Collegial Control

Lynn Mather

A fundamental principle of professional labor is that the members of a specialized occupation, as professionals, enjoy autonomy. In sociologist Elliot Freidson's words, professionals "control their own work."[1] The practitioners themselves decide what constitutes acceptable or appropriate behavior. Professions establish rules and systems of self-regulation to teach and enforce the expected standards of conduct on their members. One way, then, to assess legal professionalism is to ask how well lawyers regulate themselves. The extensive literature on lawyer regulation paints a negative picture.

The Watergate scandal of the early 1970s brought renewed scrutiny to the legal profession. Although a variety of changes have occurred since then to improve lawyer regulation, numerous problems remain. Law schools now require students to take legal ethics, but such courses generally lack stature and respect. Bar discipline was reorganized in the 1970s to transfer some control from bar associations to agencies of state supreme courts.[2] State discipline agencies in turn have increased their investigation of grievances filed against lawyers. But the vast majority of grievances continue to be dismissed. Much professional discipline is private (such as a warning letter, reprimand, or confidential diversion program), which undermines public trust and confidence in the system.[3] Further, even the most common forms of public sanctions on lawyers (public censure, suspension, or disbarment) are specific to

I appreciate the feedback on an earlier draft from faculty and students in Justice Studies, University of New Hampshire; Justice, Law, and Society, George Mason University; and Legal Studies, Brown University. Special thanks to Rick Abel, Scott Barclay, Ellen Butterfield, Ross Cheit, Ellen Cohn, Scott Cummings, Leslie Levin, Mark Suchman, Eli Wald, and Jim Wooten for their helpful comments. I am grateful to David Chambers for data and analysis of ethical conduct from surveys of Michigan law graduates.

1 Eliot Freidson, Professionalism Reborn: Theory, Prophecy and Policy 173 (1994).

2 Michael J. Powell, *Professional Divestiture: The Cession of Responsibility for Lawyer Discipline*, 1986 ABF Res. J. 31 (1986).

3 Leslie C. Levin, *The Case for Less Secrecy in Lawyer Discipline*, 20 Geo. J. Legal Ethics 1 (2007).

that state, and nothing prevents a sanctioned attorney from seeking bar admission in another state (although they would be required to disclose any prior sanctions).

Suits for legal malpractice have multiplied and now provide a significant parallel source of regulation over lawyers.[4] Indeed, some attorneys specialize in professional liability law, unlike decades ago when very few lawyers were willing to represent a client in a suit against a professional colleague. Yet it is still difficult to win a legal malpractice suit, and some lawyers who lack insurance say they avoid it out of a belief that it will reduce their chances of being sued.[5] A growing number of jurisdictions are requiring lawyers to disclose whether they carry malpractice insurance, and the proportion of lawyers with such insurance varies considerably by practice area and by state.[6] Only Oregon mandates it for lawyers. Insurance companies have increasingly become important regulatory actors for the legal profession.

Other sources of lawyer regulation have also emerged in recent years, such as criminal prosecution for egregious lawyer misconduct, more aggressive judicial oversight over lawyers for rude, careless, or otherwise unprofessional conduct, and requirements imposed on lawyers who interact with certain administrative agencies (such as securities lawyers and the SEC). In short, multiple overlapping regulatory systems operate to monitor attorney conduct. Some of these alternatives (or additions) to bar discipline have emerged because of public hostility toward lawyers and a lack of evidence that the legal profession is able to regulate itself.

Despite the expansion of these regulatory structures, we still lack answers to basic empirical questions about lawyer behavior. How much lawyer misconduct is there? And are there any general patterns to it? Analysis of the data from state disciplinary board actions and legal malpractice claims provides one way to evaluate legal professionalism, by focusing on lawyer deviance. In this chapter, I explore the ethical violations lawyers commit, with the aim of increasing our understanding of the legal profession and its capacity to regulate itself. Besides considering formal sanctions resulting from bar grievances and legal malpractice claims, I examine informal sources of regulation and discipline for lawyers, including socialization, networks, and social norms that exist in different areas of legal practice. I conclude with two examples of how formal and informal discipline work together to produce and enforce norms of professionalism in practice.

4 *See, e.g.*, Manual Ramos, *Legal Malpractice: The Profession's Dirty Little Secret*, 47 Vand. L. Rev. 1657, 1661 (1994) (noting that, from 1970 to 1989, the number of lawyers sued for legal malpractice increased more than five times).

5 Lisa G. Lerman & Philip G. Schrag, Ethical Problems in the Practice of Law 134 (2nd ed. 2008).

6 Estimates of lawyers who carry malpractice insurance range from 65 to 90%, according to recent state bar surveys. *Id.*

PROFESSIONAL CONDUCT AND DEVIANCE

Assessing the extent of attorney misconduct is challenging both as a matter of definition and data. The lack of a universal definition for *professional* lawyer conduct that applies across the entire legal profession creates a conceptual problem for any analysis of attorney *mis*conduct. The ethical rules adopted by each state, typically based on the ABA's Model Rules of Professional Conduct, ostensibly define behavioral standards for all lawyers. But the rules only set bare minimums.[7] And, as numerous critics have argued, the rules are also indeterminate, vague, contradictory, and ignore the factual differences lawyers face across diverse legal work settings.[8]

At the same time, the secrecy of state bar disciplinary processes and the fact that malpractice cases are usually resolved through insurance settlements, not public trials, limit the availability of empirical data on this question. Even evidence of increased complaints to the bar or lawsuits filed against lawyers does not necessarily mean greater deviance because the increase could simply reflect more publicized regulation and/or general antilawyer sentiment in popular culture. Moreover, discipline numbers paint an incomplete picture of deviance because individuals are more likely to go to the bar with their grievances, whereas corporate clients might use market mechanisms to complain about attorney service – for example, seeking a fee reduction or simply taking their law work to another firm. And within a large law firm, unprofessional conduct is likely to be handled internally to avoid embarrassment to the firm. Thus, although bar discipline falls most heavily on solo practitioners and small firm lawyers, and proportionately less on large firm lawyers, "one cannot judge the prevalence of misconduct from the imposition of lawyer discipline."[9]

7 *See, e.g.*, Deborah L. Rhode, *Institutionalizing Ethics*, 44 Case W. Res. L. Rev. 665, 731 (1994) (criticizing the bar's insistence on uniform ethical rules that produce "higher levels of abstraction and lower common denominators in regulatory standards than is desirable for ethical guidance"); *see also* Richard L. Abel, *Why Does the American Bar Association Promulgate Ethical Rules?*, 59 Texas L. Rev. 639 (1981).

8 *See, e.g.*, David Wilkins, *Legal Realism for Lawyers*, 104 Harv. L. Rev. 468 (1990); *see also* Paul G. Haskell, Why Lawyers Behave As They Do (1998). As an example of ambiguity in the Model Rules. compare two rules on the lawyer/client relationship. Rule 1.2 (a) requires a lawyer to "abide by a client's decisions," but Rule 2.1 says to "exercise independent judgment and render candid advice." Taken together, the Rules thus allow lawyers to act as a "hired gun" *or* to follow a more independent model of representation, according to their own ideology of legal practice and client expectations. The meaning of "professional" representation in the attorney-client relationship has become a matter for academic debate in theory and attorneys' discretion in practice. *See* Lynn Mather, *Fundamentals: What Do Clients Want? What Do Lawyers Do?* 52 Emory L. J. 1065 (2003); *see also* Abel, *supra* note 7.

9 Lisa Lerman, *The Slippery Slope from Ambition to Greed to Dishonesty: Lawyers, Money, and Professional Integrity*, 30 Hofstra L. Rev. 879, 913 (2002); *see also* Leslie C. Levin, *The Ethical World of Solo and Small Law Firm Practitioners*, 41 Hous. L. Rev. 309 (2004); State Bar of California, Investigation and Prosecution of Disciplinary Complaints Against Attorneys in Solo Practice, Small Size Law Firms and Large Size Law Firms (2001).

Lawyer Deviance: Case Studies from New York

Richard Abel's recent book, *Lawyers in the Dock*, provides an important new analysis of lawyers' professional conduct by asking, "how and why lawyers misbehave."[10] Through detailed investigation of the disciplinary proceedings against seven New York lawyers, Abel examines the personality, background, family, and work pressures that led these men (all his cases were male) to betray their clients or engage in other professional misconduct and, ultimately, to be sanctioned by the New York bar. Abel acknowledges that his cases were not randomly selected; indeed, after reading more than 200 discipline files, he selected "extreme" cases that were "arguably more revealing."[11] The vivid portraits of these seven attorneys do show clearly how easily they made mistakes, large and small – often for what they believed to be good reasons. Nevertheless, even such rich, detailed cases cannot show the full extent and general characteristics of lawyer misconduct.

Abel describes the lawyers' deviance as their "betrayal of trust," yet the book never explicitly defines this fundamental notion, creating what Eli Wald describes in his book review as "a conceptual confusion" throughout the study.[12] This confusion is not surprising considering that it parallels the difficulty of defining professionalism in such a way as to clearly delineate the conduct expected from *all* lawyers, regardless of the type of legal work that they do, the cases they handle, or the clients they represent. Most of Abel's narrative and the lengthy cases themselves suggest that the "trust" these attorneys betrayed was their loyalty to clients. Abel has since explained that he meant "trust" to incorporate a broader meaning, including "attorney loyalty to other constituencies such as courts, opposing counsel, the legal system, and the public."[13] Finding the appropriate balance of loyalty to these different (and potentially conflicting) constituencies creates an uncertain range of ethical conduct.

Following the individualistic focus of the book's research, Abel concludes that "character is destiny,"[14] and one must only "look for greed or need (which often are indistinguishable)"[15] to explain what led the disciplined lawyers into such deep trouble. Deviance among attorneys is no different from deviance in other occupations, he suggests. It reflects some combination of a person's psychological makeup and

[10] Richard L. Abel, Lawyers in the Dock: Learning From Attorney Disciplinary Proceedings 53 (2008).

[11] *Id.* at 57.

[12] Eli Wald, *Book Review*, 59 J. Legal Educ. 311, 331 (2009) (reviewing Abel, *supra* note 10).

[13] *Id.* at 334–335. Abel gave his more expansive definition in a recorded interview at the Baldy Center for Law & Social Policy, see *id.* at 334, and in a published response to other reviews, Richard L. Abel, *Author Response*, 11 Legal Ethics 126 (2008),

[14] Abel, *supra* note 10, at 496.

[15] *Id.* at 492.

upbringing, severe stress or crisis, or other economic, family, and social pressures, often combined with substance abuse and depression.

Abel also looks beyond the individual stories to assess the social controls that exist to discipline lawyers in various work settings, and he is especially harsh on attorneys in solo practice. The book cites critics of the bar's disproportionate investigation of solo and small firm practitioners and notes that the harms of misconduct by large firm attorneys may in fact be more serious and "cost many more people much more money."[16] Yet, Wald argues that "by only selecting solo and small firm practitioners" for their deviance "the whole book sends an implicit message that this is where ethical lapses occur."[17] Even more than that, the book sends that message explicitly in its conclusion. Abel writes, "it is not clear that any lawyer should" practice *alone* today, given the difficulty of making appearances in court while also being in the office, the ease of missing deadlines without a calendar system in place, and the lack of financial incentive that a partner might provide to maintain a reputation.[18] Yet each of these arguments could apply to attorneys working in firms, both small and large: Multiple demands on lawyers prevent them from meeting court obligations; calendar systems are only as good as the people who create and employ them; partners who take advantage of their clients might also be willing to cheat on a partner.[19]

Instead of focusing solely on the personal history and details of individual lawyers, or on the difference in lawyers' professionalism according to firm size, I suggest we look more closely at the structure and culture of legal practice to see if there are patterns in lawyers' misconduct. In particular, I focus on the context in which lawyers work – that is, the work conditions, clients, law and legal institutions, and social networks commonly found in specific areas of law practice.

Lawyer Deviance and Collegial Control

Consider the wide variation in the perceived "ethical conduct" of lawyers across forty-two areas of practice in Cook County, Illinois, as reported in a well-known 1995 survey by John Heinz, Robert Nelson, Rebecca Sandefur, and Edward Laumann.[20]

16 *Id.* at 54–55.

17 Wald, *supra* note 12, at 322.

18 Abel, *supra* note 10, at 525.

19 *See* Leslie C. Levin, *Bad Apples, Bad Lawyers or Bad Decisionmaking: Lessons from Psychology and from* Lawyers in the Dock, 22 Geo. J. Legal Ethics 1549, 1589 (2009); *see also* Lerman, *supra* note 9, at 910 (commenting that although law partners might be deterred from taking firm funds through loyalty, "the glue of partner loyalty may be weaker than it used to be").

20 John P. Heinz, Robert L. Nelson, Rebecca L. Sandefur & Edward O. Laumann, Urban Lawyers: The New Social Structure of the Bar (2005). The survey asked professors and legal researchers in Chicago to evaluate each field of legal work on several different dimensions, including

The *most* ethical attorneys in this reputation-based survey practiced in the areas of civil rights/civil liberties, international law, intellectual property, general family practice/poverty law, general corporate law, estates, and securities. By contrast, the attorneys who ranked the *lowest* on ethical conduct practiced in the areas of divorce, plaintiff personal injury, personal bankruptcy, and criminal defense. Moreover, this ranking of legal specialties based on ethical conduct changed very little between 1975 and 1995, according to Heinz and Laumann's identical survey, conducted twenty years earlier.[21]

This ranking, however, is based solely on *reputation* as judged by outside academics, so it does not provide direct evidence of ethical behavior. Nevertheless, its results can be compared with a ranking derived from a survey of law graduates from the University of Michigan law school based on their observation and knowledge of fellow practitioners in each legal area.[22] The Michigan survey also shows a hierarchical ranking of lawyers' ethical conduct according to different substantive legal fields.

In annual surveys conducted between 1980 and 2006 of Michigan law graduates 15, 25, and 35 years out of law school, 6,108 graduates answered a question asking the extent to which they agreed with the statement, "the lawyers with whom I deal (other than those in my own office) are highly ethical in their conduct."[23] Substantially more lawyers practicing in the areas of energy, banking, securities, real property, employee benefits, and estates agreed (mildly to strongly) that their peers in the field were highly ethical than did lawyers practicing in the areas of labor relations, criminal law, insurance, immigration, and civil rights/discrimination (which ranked lowest).[24] Other areas of practice such as corporate, intellectual property, environmental law, and domestic relations fell in between.

The Michigan survey data, although not without problems, provide stronger evidence of variation in ethical conduct by area of law since they are based observations

intellectual challenge, public service, freedom of action, and ethical conduct (described as "the reputation for ethical behavior of the lawyers doing the work"). *Id.* at 86.

21 *Id.* at 86; *cf.* JOHN P. HEINZ & EDWARD O. LAUMANN, CHICAGO LAWYERS: THE SOCIAL STRUCTURE OF THE BAR (1982). The correlation between the 1975 and 1995 rankings was .90 based on twenty-seven specialties. HEINZ ET AL., *supra* note 20, at 328.

22 This previously unpublished analysis of the survey data from 6,108 Michigan law graduates was done by David Chambers. Survey questions and results reported here are on file with the author. It is difficult to directly compare the 1995 survey data reported by Heinz, Nelson, Sandefur, and Laumann with the Michigan survey since the latter examines twenty-three categories of substantive law practice while Heinz and his colleagues examine forty-two specialties, and some of the specialties themselves were defined differently.

23 *Id.*

24 Overall, 59% of the Michigan lawyers surveyed agreed that their peers in the field where they spent the most time working were highly ethical, whereas 66% or more of lawyers practicing in the areas of energy, banking, securities, real property, employee benefits, and estates agreed with this statement, compared to 52% or fewer of the lawyers in the areas of labor relations, criminal law, insurance, immigration, and civil rights/discrimination.

by lawyers practicing in each area.[25] What might explain this hierarchy? Why should the area of law practice make such a difference? If *individual* characteristics (character, substance abuse, or family stress) are key to professional misconduct, then shouldn't the bad apples be spread more randomly across the legal profession? The alternative perspective that I propose here shifts the focus from the individual lawyer who misbehaves to the structure, organization, and content of legal work itself. That is, instead of taking a microview that looks at bad apples, we should take a macroview and look at "bad barrels" – conditions that foster attorney misconduct.[26]

I suggest in this chapter that we explore the work conditions, interactions, and values of lawyers in different communities of practice and situate lawyer deviance in each particular work context. Legal specialization, along with the stratification of the profession, impacts lawyers' understandings of what constitutes professional conduct and misconduct. That is to say, defining *un*professional conduct first requires a definition of *professional* conduct, and that depends on the context of lawyers' work. A conception of lawyer deviance that defines professionalism according to legal context, integrates two bodies of literature. On the one hand are the critics of the official ideology of the profession, an ideology that assumes universal ethics for all lawyers, influencing their conduct from the top down. In David Wilkins' classic critique, "we must abandon the traditional model's commitment to general, universally applicable ethical rules" in favor of midlevel principles for the regulation of lawyers.[27] Similarly, Judge Stanley Sporkin drew on his experience in securities law to call for separate codes of professional conduct for the various specialties, which would acknowledge the facts, problems, and responsibilities unique to each of them.[28] Robert Nelson and David Trubek argued, "there are multiple and competing visions of what it means to be a 'professional'"[29] and proposed instead that we examine different "arenas of professionalism," that is, "particular institutional

25 Lawyers may not share a common standard for "highly ethical conduct" that is independent of the area in which they practice. Also, the most ethical fields tend to involve counseling and transactional work, whereas the least ethical fields involve adversarial negotiations or litigation. The former is less likely to be observed by professional peers than the latter. And it may simply be less possible to perceive highly ethical conduct in adversarial legal settings. Finally, these data come from graduates of only one elite law school.

26 Blake E. Ashforth, Dennis A. Gioia, Sandra L. Robinson & Linda K. Trevino, *Introduction to Special Topic Forum: Re-Viewing Organizational Corruption*, 33 Academy of Mgmt. Rev. 670, 673 (2008); *see also* Levin *supra* note 20.

27 Wilkins, *supra* note 8, at 515.

28 Stanley Sporkin, *The Need for Separate Codes of Professional Conduct for the Various Specialties*, 7 Geo. J. Legal Ethics 149 (1993).

29 Robert L. Nelson & David M. Trubek, *Arenas of Professionalism: The Professional Ideologies of Lawyers in Context*, *in* Lawyers' Ideals/Lawyers' Practices: Transformations in the American Legal Profession 177, 182 (Robert L. Nelson, David M. Trubek & Rayman L. Solomon eds., 1992).

settings in which groups construct, explicitly or implicitly, models of the law and of lawyering."[30]

There is also a growing empirical literature describing the shared expectations and professional values of particular legal cultures and subcultures: divorce attorneys,[31] plaintiff personal injury networks,[32] criminal court workgroups,[33] solo and small firm attorneys,[34] legal services organizations,[35] prosecutors and government lawyers,[36] corporate litigators,[37] bankruptcy lawyers,[38] and even different law firms and the practice groups within them.[39] These distinct "communities of practice," as my colleagues and I have suggested, consist of "groups of lawyers with whom practitioners interact and to whom they compare themselves and look for common expectations and standards."[40] Such communities are multiple and overlapping. Experienced attorneys learn to navigate among them as they represent different types of clients or find themselves working in different practice areas or institutional contexts. It is within these diverse communities that we can identify "*varieties* of professionalism in practice."[41] This bottom-up perspective on legal professionalism reveals lawyers'

[30] *Id.* at 179.

[31] *See, e.g.*, Lynn Mather, Craig A. McEwen & Richard J. Maiman, Divorce Lawyers at Work: Varieties of Professionalism in Practice (2001); Austin Sarat & William L. F. Felstiner, Divorce Lawyers and Their Clients: Power and Meaning in the Legal Process (1995).

[32] *See, e.g.*, Herbert M. Kritzer, Risks, Reputations, and Rewards: Contingency Fee Legal Practice in the United States (2004); Stephen Daniels & Joanne Martin, *It Was the Best of Times, It Was the Worst of Times: The Precarious Nature of Plaintiff's Practice in Texas*, 80 Tex. L. Rev. 1781 (2004); Sara Parikh, *Professionalism and Its Discontents: A Study of Social Networks in the Plaintiff's Personal Injury Bar* (2001) (unpublished Ph.D. Dissertation, University of Illinois at Chicago).

[33] *See, e.g.*, James Eisenstein, Roy B. Flemming & Peter F. Nardulli, The Contours of Justice: Communities and their Courts (1988); James Eisenstein & Herbert Jacob, Felony Justice: An Organizational Analysis of Criminal Courts (1977); Lynn Mather, Plea Bargaining or Trial? The Process of Criminal Case Disposition (1979).

[34] *See, e.g.*, Carroll Seron, The Business of Practicing Law: The Work Lives of Solo and Small Firm Attorneys (1996); Levin, *supra* note 9.

[35] Ann Southworth, *Lawyer-Client Decisionmaking in Civil Rights and Poverty Practice: An Empirical Study of Lawyers' Norms*, 9 Geo. J. Legal Ethics 1101 (1996).

[36] Milton Heumann, Plea Bargaining: The Experiences of Prosecutors, Judges, and Defense Attorneys (1978); Patrick Schmidt, Lawyers and Regulation: The Politics of the Administrative Process (2005).

[37] Duffy Graham, The Consciousness of the Litigator (2005); Kimberly Kirkland, *Ethics in Large Law Firms: The Principle of Pragmatism*, 35 U. Mem. L. Rev. 631 (2005); Mark C. Suchman, *Working Without a Net: The Sociology of Legal Ethics in Corporate Litigation*, 67 Fordham L. Rev. 837 (1998).

[38] Milton C. Regan, Eat What You Kill: The Fall of a Wall Street Lawyer (2004).

[39] Michael J. Kelly, Lives of Lawyers (1994); Michael J. Kelly, Lives of Lawyers Revisited: Transformations and Resilience in the Organizations of Practice (2007); Emmanuel Lazega, The Collegial Phenomenon: The Social Mechanisms of Cooperation among Peers in a Corporate Law Partnership (2001).

[40] Mather et al., *supra* note 31, at 6.

[41] *Id.* at 176 (emphasis added).

shared expectations and norms in particularized practice settings, expectations that are socially constructed by attorneys working with specific clients, knowledge, legal rules, social networks, institutions, and workplace organizations.

Within these communities, lawyer behavior is constrained by the norms and practices of colleagues. This "collegial control" over work involves multiple dimensions:

> It includes *shared languages, knowledge, and identities* that together reinforce common understandings of the challenges of particular kinds of legal work. It involves *internalized norms of conduct* learned in life, in law school, and during *socialization into practice*. It includes *pressures from peers* to behave in particular ways in order to function effectively in a system of *reciprocal relationships*. It involves *formal norms of conduct* and the *threat of sanction* for violating these norms. *Collective organization* and identity strengthen collegial control over work.[42]

These mechanisms of collegial control emerged from research on communities of practice among divorce attorneys in New England. Other aspects of control within communities of practice include the need to maintain a good reputation to attract clients – for example, in personal injury practice[43] – and lawyers' advice networks – groups of lawyers who provide information and judgment to attorneys early in their careers and help shape expectations for solo and small-firm lawyers.[44]

Large law firms also have embedded controls built into the way they are organized and operate. Ethical consciousness among corporate litigators in large law firms, according to Kimberly Kirkland, is constructed through an organizational logic that depends on situational factors, following the "choice of norm" rule: In light of the varying informal expectations in a large firm, a lawyer learns to follow the guidelines of the partner or group for which she is working, and the best associates not only identify the appropriate norms but can navigate easily among them.[45] Mark Suchman found corporate litigators to have rather weak material controls within the firm, and somewhat stronger controls through culture – particularly, the selection, socialization, and interaction of associates and partners. But he notes that even these internal collegial controls, which used to sustain the firm as a community, have weakened as large firm practice has become more market driven.[46]

Although collegial control may be the most effective means of regulating lawyers, it is vulnerable on numerous counts. Lawyers not embedded in their firm or practice specialty may choose to defect from the norms of the community, or lawyers who

[42] *Id.* at 178 (emphasis added).

[43] *See* Kritzer, *supra* note 32. For discussion of reputation as a constraint on attorney escalation of conflict, see Ronald J. Gilson & Robert H. Mnookin, *Disputing Through Agents: Cooperation and Conflict Between Lawyers in Litigation*, 94 Colum. L. Rev. 509 (1994).

[44] Levin, *supra* note 9, at 328–32.

[45] Kirkland, *supra* note 37.

[46] Suchman, *supra* note 37.

are unfamiliar with an area may be ignorant of the particular practices that guide successful specialists there. The next section explores two types of formal regulation of attorney conduct with an eye to what they might show about variation in misconduct across different areas of practice.

FORMAL SANCTIONS AND AREAS OF PRACTICE

Bar Discipline

Most states do not publish summary data about the characteristics of attorneys facing grievances. But data that are available show the top three practice areas for complaints about attorney misconduct to be in family law, criminal law, and personal injury, followed by real estate and probate, with the precise ranking of areas varying by state and method of counting.[47] Investigations against attorneys in Illinois in 2004, for example, were most frequent in matters of criminal law, domestic relations, tort, and real estate, in that order; only 6 percent of investigations ended with formal charges filed for attorney misconduct.[48] Such extensive screening is typical for attorney grievances. According to an analysis of state data submitted to the ABA for 2006, the average state agency investigates only 58 percent of the grievances it receives, only a fraction of those result in charges, and only 7.8 percent of investigations yield public discipline.[49] Some grievances are referred to other agencies such as fee arbitration or consumer protection, whereas others are dismissed or resolved informally without investigation.

Although criminal law and domestic relations usually top the charts for grievances or investigations, those areas typically drop in the rankings when it comes to disciplinary charges filed against lawyers. In Illinois in 2004, for example, although the ranking of *investigations* (in declining order of frequency) were (1) domestic relations, (2) criminal, (3) tort, and (4) real estate, the last two areas (tort and real estate) emerged as numbers one and two for *charges* filed. Similarly, reports from Maine and New Hampshire showed attorneys in criminal law and family law to have the highest proportion of docketed complaints against them (close to half of

[47] *See* Craig McEwen & Lynn Mather, *Client Grievances and Client Relationships: Central Challenges of Divorce Practice*, Paper Presented at Conference on Lawyers in Practice: Ethical Decision Making in Context (April 23, 2010) (noting that a search of websites for twenty states' grievance offices showed that most did not publish summary statistics on the nature of complaints, charges, and final sanctions).

[48] *See* Attorney Registration & Disciplinary Commission of the Supreme Court of Illinois, ARDC Organizational Information, http://www.iardc.org/orginfo.html (last visited Feb. 18, 2010).

[49] Analysis of the ABA data was done by HALT, a legal reform group. *See* HALT, *Attorney Discipline Report Card 2006*, http://www.halt.org/reform_projects/lawyer_accountability/report_card_2006/index_2.php (last visited Feb. 20, 2010).

all complaints came from just these two areas), but proportionately fewer family law and criminal attorneys were found guilty of misconduct.[50]

Professional discipline involves "*both* deviant behavior and agency response," as Bruce Arnold and John Hagan conclude after comparing Canadian lawyers prosecuted for misconduct with an equal number of lawyers who received complaints but were not prosecuted.[51] Just as any understanding of crime rates rests on the nature of both defendant and police/prosecutorial behavior, the same holds true for explaining lawyer deviance. Arnold and Hagan found certain characteristics of attorneys (for instance, solo practice and inexperience) make them particularly vulnerable targets for complaints but that discipline agencies were also more likely to prosecute certain kinds of offenses – such as those involving financial harm to client or violation of trust accounts.[52] Similar to Canada, reports of discipline in the United States suggest a high likelihood of sanction for attorneys who have committed more serious professional violations, especially involving the abuse of financial trusts.[53] Other frequently sanctioned misconduct includes neglect, failure to communicate, and fraud.[54] Who gets disciplined depends in part, on "which misconduct the disciplinary agencies see fit to investigate" and on "whether the disciplinary agency has the resources to investigate misconduct where the perpetrator is a large firm lawyer."[55]

What characterizes family law, criminal law, and personal injury such that attorneys handling these cases are more vulnerable to bar grievances? Since it is clients who most frequently initiate complaints (as opposed to other lawyers or judges), and these are personal plight areas of law, it is easy to see why individuals with few other outlets for complaints might turn to discipline agencies. Divorce, criminal, and personal injury cases involve emotional turmoil, high stress, pain, and suffering. Consequently, some client complaints against attorneys might simply be venting, scapegoating their lawyers for the fact that life has not gone as planned. Also, attorneys engaged in these areas of practice enjoy great autonomy due to the imbalance of information between the one-shot client and the experienced lawyer. Moreover, these attorneys usually work in sole practice or small firms where there is little or no oversight and little support staff. And in some of these areas (such as

[50] Maine Board of Overseers of the Bar, 2007 Annual Report; New Hampshire Supreme Court, Attorney Discipline System, 2008 Annual Report. The 2008 New Hampshire report does not show the area of law for sanctioned attorneys but this pattern is shown in an earlier analysis by New Hampshire bar counsel. *See* Thomas V. Trevethick, *Is There a Pattern in the Madness? A Statistical Survey of Conduct Complaints*, 36 N.H. B.J. 13 (1995).

[51] Bruce L. Arnold & John Hagan, *Careers of Misconduct: The Structure of Prosecuted Professional Deviance Among Lawyers*, 57 Am. Soc. Rev. 771, 779 (1992).

[52] *Id.* at 777.

[53] *See, e.g.*, New Hampshire and Maine reports, *supra* note 50.

[54] *Id.*

[55] Lerman, *supra* note 9, at 913.

criminal defense or divorce practice with a working-class clientele), there are class differences between lawyer and client that accentuate the power of the attorney. Thus, there are few obvious controls over attorney conduct in these personal plight areas, at least by comparison with lawyers in large law firms who work in bureaucratic structures surrounded by peers and staff, with sophisticated clients (general counsel or the financial officer for a corporation).

Nevertheless, we know from research on the different communities of practice in the divorce, criminal defense, and personal injury areas that informal collegial controls do exist and influence attorney conduct. Shared identities and knowledge, repeated interactions in social networks, informal norms, and the need to maintain a quality reputation in order to attract clients all contribute to lawyer professionalism in these particular areas of practice. Moreover, specialists in these fields know the risks of client complaints and incorporate defensive strategies in their practices where they can. Attorney deviance, in the macroview that I suggest here, could be explained in two ways: by attorney participation in subcultures of specialists with deviant norms, or by the activities of general practitioners without experience or knowledge in the specific area of law.

On the one hand are the subcultures of law practice that maintain and transmit norms that "in some cases, directly contribute to deviant behavior."[56] Several of the cases of lawyer deviance described by Abel involved specialists who had learned sloppy or shady behavior from other lawyers. Leslie Levin, for example, discusses the impact on the lawyers in Abel's book of particular community norms in real estate (a "pressurized place" with little help for a new lawyer), immigration (high-volume practice with clients from "travel agents"), and personal injury (with kickbacks to expedite settlements).[57] In each case, lawyers had observed practice norms from other attorneys with similar clients and work situations in these subcultures. Among divorce lawyers, for example, are a few specialists who handle an extremely high volume of cases for low fees and who struggle to provide competent representation to all their clients.[58] Other specialists in divorce include the small subgroup of attorneys who acknowledged being "unreasonable," more litigious, and more likely to do whatever their client wanted.[59] Given that some divorce clients seek vengeance and may want to use the legal process to punish their spouse – by hiding assets or making false charges – divorce lawyers who follow a client's wishes without question may find end up facing grievances from opposing counsel or the court. Lawyers in all of these examples specialize in the particular area of law but share a professional

[56] Levin, *supra* note 3, at 29.

[57] Levin, *supra* note 19, at 1558–59.

[58] Mather et al., *supra* note 31, at 25–30.

[59] *Id.* at 51, 127–30.

ideology and type of practice, similar clients, and working conditions. That is, they develop their own community of practice, a subculture within the larger community of specialists, which embraces norms more likely to lead to professional deviance.

Nonspecialist practitioners constitute a second group of lawyers who, I suspect, are also especially vulnerable to grievances in fields such as divorce, criminal defense, personal injury, or real estate. The general practitioner who specializes in "doorway law" – taking whichever client walks through the doorway – is taking a professional risk. As one New York attorney explained, attorneys in general practice often engage in "naked malpractice" since "most people don't know what they don't know."[60] Recent studies of small firm and solo practitioners have all found increased specialization among them, as a strategy for getting clients, a way to achieve competence, and a means to maintain a professional reputation. "The days of the solo or small-firm 'general law practice' appear to be over (or at least numbered)."[61]

Like general practice lawyers, specialists might be at greater risk if they take on clients outside of their specialty, such as the real estate lawyer who accepts a divorce client or a personal injury specialist who accepts a criminal case. Why would they do this? For the money – to pay the bills and generate some income for a business that is struggling.[62] Or as a favor – to provide full service perhaps to a family friend, business acquaintance, or previous client. Data on lawyers working outside of their normal specialty is difficult to obtain, let alone data to confirm my hunch that these lawyers receive a higher proportion of grievances. In research my colleagues and I conducted on divorce, we found that a surprisingly large proportion of divorce clients are represented by nonspecialists. Analysis of the dockets of over 4,000 divorce cases revealed that most lawyer names (66 percent in New Hampshire and 55 percent in Maine) appeared in only one or two divorce cases over a four-year period.[63] Such lawyers who represent only an occasional divorce client might consult with peers in the community for advice and information. But they also might decide to simply handle the case on their own and assume they can learn all they need to know,

60 Levin, *supra* note 3, at 7.

61 Karen L. Pascale, *Small Wonders: Lessons from Delaware's Small Firms and Solo Practitioners*, 19 DEL. LAW. 17, 17 (2001); *see also* SERON, *supra* note 34; Levin, *supra* note 9.

62 I recognize that an individual focus on deviance here could help explain why certain practitioners would choose to practice outside of their area of competence, just as a microlevel perspective could help answer why certain subcultures develop their own deviant norms. My point, which I return to in the conclusion, is that *both* perspectives are needed to understand attorney deviance and that the current focus rests too much blame on the individual practitioner, ignoring the complicity of law firms and the legal system itself.

63 By contrast, a relatively small group of lawyers handled the majority of divorce representations. The 20% of the lawyers who were listed most frequently appeared in 56% of the New Hampshire cases and 65% of the Maine cases. MATHER ET AL., *supra* note 31, at 47–48. Note that, because we sampled counties in the two states, some of the lawyers with few cases may have been listed more often in a neighboring county or state.

taking a risk that they have the competence to identify and respond to the particular challenges of a divorce case.

Legal Malpractice

Professional liability provides another set of formal controls over lawyers, along with the discipline of state agencies. And here too, certain fields of law appear to top the list in generating complaints. In 1985, the ABA Standing Committee on Lawyers' Professional Liability began to collect and publish statistics on claims against attorneys for malpractice, using data supplied by national insurance companies. In its latest study (2007), the ABA has data from more than twenty-five insurance companies, but because some companies do not participate (e.g., Attorneys' Liability Assurance Society), mid- and large-size law firms are underrepresented in their analysis.[64] Nevertheless, as in lawyer discipline, claims against attorneys for legal malpractice show a "remarkable consistency" over time by the area of law.

Plaintiff personal injury and real estate ranked first and second in the distribution of claims (with family law often third) in every ABA survey between 1985 and 2007.[65] Indeed these three legal areas supplied over one-half of the 40,486 claims against attorneys in 2007.[66] Some cautions about these data are in order, beside the fact that they overrepresent solo and small-firm attorneys. Since the data are based on insurance *claims*, it is obvious that attorneys without insurance are not included, nor are many large-firm lawyers who are insured through ALAS. As noted earlier, the likelihood of attorneys having malpractice insurance varies significantly by state and firm size. Moreover, proof of legal malpractice requires a finding that "but for" the negligence of the lawyer, the client would have won his case. Such a standard is especially difficult in a criminal case, in which criminal defendants must essentially prove their innocence if they are to succeed in a malpractice claim against an attorney. Indeed, very few malpractice claims are filed in criminal matters (5% in 2007). Finally, the likelihood of a malpractice claim also depends on the extent of the damages and on the ease of translating damages into monetary terms.

In their analysis of the claim data by field of law, the ABA cautions that additional information is necessary before concluding that certain areas are riskier than others. We lack the data, the report explains, to conclude that the high percentage of claims in personal injury cases "is disproportionate to the overall time spent in this area of legal practice."[67] But a comparison of malpractice claims in Florida with data on the Florida bar (using Martindale-Hubbell and membership in specialty bar sections)

[64] Am. Bar Ass'n, Standing Comm. on Lawyers' Prof. Liability, Profile of Legal Malpractice Claims: 2004–2007 2, 17 (2008).

[65] *Id.* at 4.

[66] *Id.*

[67] *Id.* at 3.

done by Manuel Ramos in 1995 suggests that claims do *not* occur disproportionately in particular areas of law, such as personal injury and real estate.[68] On the other hand, a study of liability claims at firms of thirty-five or more attorneys found that "a firm's type of practice, geographic region, and size *were* significantly related to both the total number and aggregate dollar amount of claims resolved from 1992–1996," with corporate practice having the greatest exposure.[69]

Whether or not claims data demonstrate *disproportionate* risk for certain practice areas, it is clearly the case that insurance companies believe in variation by legal fields and they set their premiums accordingly. For example, one application form for lawyers' professional liability insurance, which runs more than ten pages plus supplements, asks first about total billings and size of firm.[70] The very next set of questions probes a lawyer's area of practice in great detail. There is a matrix listing eighteen areas of law in one column – banking, general corporate, tax, employment, copyright/patent, domestic relations, oil and gas, among others – and next to each area is space to indicate the percentage of total gross billings derived from that area of practice for two separate years. Further information on the nature of clients (plaintiff versus defense, creditor or debtor, management versus union) is requested for *each* area of law that represents more than 10 percent of the applicant's practice. According to the executive vice-president of a large Connecticut insurance company, "area of practice plays a large role in the underwriting and pricing of legal malpractice risks, as do other factors such as geography and firm size."[71] And an attorney with over twenty years experience in insurance law said, "I learned quickly that there are five areas of law you don't touch unless you do it all the time. You need to specialize or else you can get yourself in Big Trouble." When asked to name those five areas, he responded, "tax, patents, domestic relations, ERISA, and corporate real estate."[72]

DEFENSIVE STRATEGIES IN DIVORCE AND CORPORATE PRACTICE

How does the interaction of collegial control with the formal structures of lawyer discipline and professional liability work? This section presents two examples of

[68] Manuel R. Ramos, *Legal Malpractice: No Lawyer or Client Is Safe*, 47 Fla. L. Rev. 1, 52 (1995).

[69] *Harris Study Confirms Value of Risk Management for Law Firms*, http://www2.prnewswire.com/cgi-bin/stories.pl?ACCT=104&STORY=/www/story/9–11–97/315250&EDATE (last visted Sept. 8, 2009) (emphasis added).

[70] *See* Application for Lawyers Professional Liability Insurance for Lloyd's Insurance (December 2, 2001) (on file with author).

[71] E-mail from Executive Vice-President of large Connecticut insurance firm that handles professional liability policies (Sept. 9, 2009) (on file with author).

[72] Confidential Interview with Maryland lawyer (Jan. 7, 2009) (on file with author).

informal practices described by divorce attorneys and by lawyers in corporate law work: Choose Your Client Carefully and Cover Your Ass (CYA). Both of these strategies address ethical challenges, as attorneys see them, and help constitute professionalism in practice. That is to say, these are everyday practices used by experienced, specialized lawyers in response to what they perceive can get them into trouble.

Choose Your Client Carefully

The importance of client selection typically ranks high on any listing of advice for lawyers, whether in solo or small-firm practice or in large firms. "Pick the right clients,"[73] cautions Pascale, and avoid "the 'bad' client,"[74] writes Levin, since it is clients who often push attorneys to engage in unethical conduct or have unreasonable expectations. Divorce clients "often sought to underreport their income on financial disclosure statements," according to lawyers interviewed in New York.[75] In interviews with divorce lawyers in New England, my colleagues and I asked whether they screened clients, and more than 90 percent said they did.[76] Some attorneys said that they used their initial interview as an opportunity both to hear the client's expectations and to explain their style of divorce representation. "They decide if they can work with me and I decide if I can work with them," as one lawyer said.[77] Other lawyers mentioned using their secretaries to report rude or obnoxious behavior from clients as they sat in the waiting room or complained about having to wait for an appointment. The most common adjective attorneys used to describe a client who might be rejected was "difficult." One type of "difficult" client was the vengeful, unrealistic, or stubborn spouse who was "totally out for blood." Because most divorce lawyers prided themselves on being "reasonable," they were wary of potential clients who were not. "Difficult" clients also included those who would be especially demanding of the attorney's time:

> [p]eople ... who look like they are going to think they are my only clients.... [s]omeone who is going to want to be able to pick up the phone and call you four, five, six times a week and want you there to hold their hand and to talk with them about everything.[78]

A "red flag" signaling a difficult divorce client was the person who had a prior divorce attorney. The fact that the client was unhappy with one lawyer suggested that she

[73] Pascale, *supra* note 61, at 18.

[74] Levin, *supra* note 9, at 338.

[75] *Id.* at 338.

[76] Mather et al., *supra* note 31, at 213 n.12.

[77] This quote and the material following comes from Mather et al., *supra* note 31, at 93–95. I also draw directly from our lawyer interviews. For details on data and methods of this study, see *id.* at 195–201.

[78] *Id.* at 94.

might also be dissatisfied with the next one. As one lawyer explained her screening process:

> I do not represent people who have previously had another attorney and want to get rid of that attorney. Under no circumstances. Because the reason they are leaving is probably because they don't like what they are being told. And if I have general respect for that attorney, I will not get myself involved in someone else's garbage.[79]

Another attorney said, "If you've got somebody coming in from another office, then you instinctively smell trouble.... If they have been a pain in the rump to another lawyer, then they are going to be a pain in the rump to you."[80]

What is interesting about these comments is not whether divorce lawyers *actually* turn away "difficult" or "recycled" clients – obviously many do not – but instead, what they reveal about how lawyers *think about* choosing clients. Experienced divorce attorneys have learned that overly demanding clients – especially those who lack the funds to properly compensate the attorney – can be a risk to represent. Who wants to return phone calls from someone who is unrelenting in their demands, their anger, or their grief? Such difficult clients are precisely the ones who might file a grievance with the bar for an attorney's lack of communication. Moreover, the social network of other divorce lawyers provides a warning sign to alert lawyers to clients who might pose problems for them. Interestingly, this informal knowledge among divorce lawyers echoes advice on how to prevent malpractice claims:

> Many malpractice claims can be avoided by identifying and refusing to work with problem clients. Experienced practitioners recognize the following characteristics as *"red flags"*:
>
> - The client is changing attorneys in the middle of a case;
> - The case already has been rejected by one or more firms;
> - The client wants to proceed with the case out of principle, regardless of cost....[81]

Although most divorce lawyers self-identified (and were named by their peers) as "reasonable" lawyers who shared the same generally cooperative approach in divorce negotiation and tried to avoid scorched-earth tactics, some attorneys specialized in a more adversarial or litigious style. Clients who left their first divorce lawyer were more likely to seek out and ultimately retain an attorney with a more litigious approach.[82]

[79] Confidential Interview (on file with author).
[80] *Id.* at 94–95.
[81] Stephen M. Blumberg, *Risk Management: Preventing Malpractice Claims*, 13 Legal Econ. 52, 52 (1987) (emphasis added).
[82] In divorce cases where both parties are represented (which was less than half the cases), about 10% of the parties had more than one attorney listed as attorney of record in the case docket. Analysis of the docketed cases for the lawyers we interviewed showed that lawyers who were most likely to be the

The economics of divorce practice led some lawyers to take whatever clients they could get, regardless of how difficult these clients might be. Attorneys with high-volume, low-fee divorce practices could not afford to be selective. These lawyers were especially at risk for misconduct, especially neglect, because of taking on more cases than they could handle. One lawyer admitted sheepishly that his caseload was too high:

> Well, I think it would be healthier for me and for the clients if I decreased it some, maybe charged a little more, or something. And wasn't quite so on the edge here as far as getting things done. Risking doing sloppy work.... I mean, I've got some cases that are seriously neglected here. And I keep promising people I'll get to it.[83]

Other attorneys, perhaps just starting out in practice or coming from a different legal specialty (for example, to handle a divorce for a friend or colleague), lacked the knowledge to read the cues about problem clients in divorce and might not have realized the difficulties that some clients could bring. In sum, experienced divorce attorneys learned that one way to avoid complaints about misconduct was to be selective in accepting clients, but not all practices allowed lawyers that strategy.

Corporate attorneys also learn the importance of choosing clients carefully. In large law firms, avoidance of conflict of interest is key in taking on a new client. Office organizational policies institutionalize such screening, for instance, by saying "you cannot get a billing number until you get a conflicts clearance."[84] Screening clients helps lawyers avoid bar grievances and protects against complaints of malpractice. According to the ABA's *Risk Management: Survival Tools for Law Firms*,

> The best time for lawyers and firms to protect themselves is when a client first seeks to engage them.... Many sources of potential risk posed by clients ... can be readily identified at or before the time of engagement.[85]

The authors of this ABA guide draw on the Kaye Scholer malpractice case to emphasize such issues as the competence of the firm to handle the case and the scope of services to be provided. Kaye Scholer was sued by (and ultimately settled with) the federal Office of Thrift Supervision for the law firm's role in keeping Lincoln Savings & Loan afloat even when the bank was no longer solvent. Had the law firm focused on banking regulation and defined the scope of their representation accordingly, they might have acted differently and thus avoided liability.[86] Similarly,

second lawyers scored significantly higher on seeing litigation as an important skill in divorce practice than did lawyers who were first lawyers. MATHER ET AL., *supra* note 31, at 85.

83 *Id.* at 26

84 Elizabeth Chambliss & David B. Wilkins, *Promoting Effective Ethical Infrastructure in Large Law Firms: A Call for Research and Reporting*, 30 HOFSTRA L. REV. 691, 692 (2002).

85 ANTHONY E. DAVIS & PETER R. JARVIS, RISK MANAGEMENT: SURVIVAL TOOLS FOR LAW FIRMS 5 (2d ed. 2007).

86 *Id.* at 4–6

a popular legal ethics text cites client selection as one of two practices that carry a high risk of triggering professional liability: "accept any client and any matter that comes along."[87] The Harris survey of large law firms (discussed earlier) provides empirical support for such advice. The survey found that one of the two most effective risk management practices to reduce claims costs in large firms involved client screening. Specifically, "firms that have a separate partner or committee to oversee the acceptance of new clients and engagements, on average, paid out approximately $800,000 less for their largest claim."[88]

Attention to client selection helps lawyers maintain professional standards and avoid complaints against them by rejecting problem clients and seeking to establish an appropriate match between lawyer and client *before* representation begins. Once engaged by a client, how do lawyers address potentially problematic situations or gray areas of conduct? Many examples abound. Defensive strategies described by attorneys as CYA in divorce law practice and in corporate litigation show that the same label refers to very different conduct in these two communities of practice. Examination of these strategies sheds light on the values and institutional constraints lawyers face in these two areas.

Cover Your Ass

In any area of legal practice, there are bound to be ethical challenges that require discretionary judgment and where poor decisions can get an attorney in trouble. From experience and through their peers, lawyers learn to identify these situations and to protect themselves, taking precautions to "cover your ass" should a complaint be brought. The risk of complaint depends on the area of practice. Here, I explore two different domains, divorce and corporate litigation, where lawyers report systematic use of CYA.

Divorce attorneys frequently face disagreement with their clients over settlement.[89] The most common conflict arises between vengeful, unrealistic clients who insist on more than they are entitled to and ask their lawyer to use the legal process to strike back at their spouse. But the reverse occurs as well. A client, whether out of guilt, sorrow, or fatigue, sometimes wants to sign an agreement for much less than he or she is entitled to. When presented with these two hypotheticals, divorce lawyers report that they would try to educate and persuade clients in both situations to be reasonable – to soften expectations in the first situation and to have more backbone in the second. If persuasion was not successful, lawyers faced the difficult choice of whether

87 Lerman & Schrag, *supra* note 5, at 130. The second high-risk practice that they mention, discussed earlier, is to "practice outside your area of expertise."

88 *Harris Study Confirms Value of Risk Management for Law Firms*, *supra* note 69.

89 This section draws on Mather et al., *supra* note 31, at 87–109.

to continue to represent the client. Some would continue representation in both situations. But lawyers were more than twice as likely to say they would withdraw from the case when the client was making unreasonably high demands than when the client was selling herself short. Collegial controls in the form of peer pressure from other lawyers, lawyers' interest in maintaining a reputation for reasonableness, and judicial disapproval steered many lawyers away from making excessive demands for clients in court. The reverse situation, however, led to a different response.

If, after an attorney's best efforts at persuasion, clients were adamant about selling themselves short to obtain the divorce, lawyers typically said they would continue to represent the client, with some explicitly invoking the ethical rule in favor of client self-determination. Most lawyers added that they would also write a CYA letter explaining that the client was accepting the divorce agreement against the lawyer's advice. As one divorce attorney put it:

> If the client insists on going through with it, then what I would generally do is write a long letter that I will require them to sign before I'll continue representation. That serves a couple of purposes. When they see it in writing and show it to some friends, by and large, they will change their mind and decide not to go through with it. But in the event that they do go through with it, I won't be sued for malpractice.[90]

Although 60 percent of lawyers interviewed said they would write CYA letters when faced with these situations, analysis of lawyers' responses showed that those most specialized in family law were most likely to write them. Family law specialists (devoting 75% or more of their practice to family law) were twice as likely as nonspecialists (devoting less than 25% of their practice to family law) to refer to CYA letters when the client wanted less than the lawyer recommended. Lawyers embedded in the network of family law specialists undoubtedly shared horror stories of grievances and malpractice complaints from clients who later complained about getting an unfair divorce settlement. These lawyers knew the value of CYA, in contrast to attorneys lacking experience in divorce who thought they could protect themselves simply by saying it was the client's choice to settle.

Corporate litigators also report disagreement with their clients, portraying them as "amoral, short-sighted and excessively aggressive."[91] In private conversations with one another, litigators share what Duffy Graham calls the "two rules of practice. The first rule is The Client is the Enemy. The second rule is Don't Forget the First Rule."[92] Overt tensions between lawyer and client do not arise because of fear of malpractice, according to Graham. Instead, Kirkland explains, litigators shape their conduct according to the expectations of different audiences (clients, partners,

[90] *Id.* at 105.
[91] Suchman, *supra* note 37, at 848.
[92] Graham, *supra* note 37, at 55.

judges, the media) constituted by what the situation demands.[93] How do litigators respond to clients who expect overly aggressive discovery and no-holds-barred litigation? Suchman found one group of litigators among his informants deferred to their clients, adopting an agency or hired-gun approach, and another group saw themselves as fiduciaries who "would make at least a cursory effort at moral suasion if they felt their client was in the wrong." Some litigators in the second group added, "that a 'CYA [cover-your-ass] letter' might suffice to discharge the attorney's advisory obligations."[94] Given the relative power of clients over litigators and the relative weakness of judges in sanctioning attorneys, litigators see their biggest risk as not sufficiently deferring to their clients.

In-house counsel, speaking on behalf of the corporate clients they work for, not surprisingly see any efforts of outside litigators to exercise independent decision making in counseling to be "at best redundant with the in-house counsel's own moral stewardship – and, at worst, subversive of the very principle of client control ... either an unethical waste of resources or an unethical attempt at manipulation."[95] Litigators must walk a fine line between excessive aggressiveness and excessive caution. But the informal norms of their practice see zealous advocacy as a litigator's central responsibility and allow it to trump other ethical rules. The organizational logic of large law firms reinforces unquestioning client loyalty, as Kirkland writes,

> Junior lawyers are agents for the lawyers who supervise them ... not autonomous counselors who consult internal or fixed standards ... and advise their superiors about the appropriate course of action. Large-firm litigators approach their relationships with, and obligations to, their clients the same way. They must understand their client's will and they have an affirmative moral obligation to zealously advance that will.[96]

Litigators can express any moral qualms in a CYA letter but they know that they must act in accordance with their client's wishes and aggressively play the game of litigation as defined by their peers and opposing counsel.

What do these two examples from two very different areas of practice suggest? First, experienced divorce lawyers and corporate litigators both recognize the risks posed by unquestioning acceptance of any client, and some institutionalize ways of screening clients to avoid problems. Second, when conflict arises between attorney and client over uncertain choices of judgment, many informal constraints – from peers, the firm, opposing counsel, the court, and the market for clients – influence a lawyer's decision making. Third, the matrix of collegial control operates differently

[93] Kirkland, *supra* note 37, at 713–15.

[94] Suchman, *supra* note 37, at 849.

[95] *Id.* at 850.

[96] Kirkland, *supra* note 37, at 719.

in the two areas of practice. In divorce, it reinforces the lawyer's independent judgment over client demands for overly aggressive representation. But in corporate litigation, collegial control reinforces the lawyer as agent of the client and encourages aggressive representation. Finally, a lawyer's attempt at self-protection through a CYA letter is aimed at avoidance of a grievance or malpractice claim in divorce, where such oversight is common. The CYA letter in corporate litigation is aimed at self-protection for an attorney in the unlikely event of investigation from a senior partner, outside agency, or court. In short, there is a dramatic divide between professionalism in these two communities of practice. What is considered unprofessional conduct in one is praised in the other.

CONCLUSION

Assessing how well the American legal profession regulates itself is a more complicated task than first appears. Although individual stories of lawyer deviance point to glaring weaknesses, systematic data is difficult to obtain. Individual states control their own disciplinary processes and few publish aggregate data that includes details on characteristics of attorney, firm size, nature of grievance, area of law, and the type of discipline imposed, including private sanctions. Data on legal malpractice claims are similarly limited. Many insurance companies, especially those covering large law firms, will not share information with the ABA for its report, leading to a skewed picture of legal malpractice. Even with more complete and better data on discipline and claims, we still would lack a clear picture of attorney misconduct without knowing something about the complaint process. How often do clients or others come to perceive attorney misconduct and then decide to do something about it, and in which cases and practice areas does this occur? Ideally we would have a survey like the Civil Litigation Research Project, which traced the trajectory of citizen grievances in different areas of law to discover which became lawsuits.[97]

Using the limited data available, I have outlined a picture of lawyer deviance that situates *un*professional conduct within the informal professional norms found in various communities of practice. Instead of individual explanations for deviance, I have suggested a focus on the social networks and collegial controls in particular areas. I do not believe that most lawyers who misbehave can be identified simply by their poor character or greed. Indeed, studies of white-collar crime dismiss those as "folk theories" and instead emphasize the social context in which criminal activity

[97] The Civil Litigation Research Project conducted a survey of households about grievances to understand how disputes became civil lawsuits. See results and discussion in the *Special Issue on Dispute Processing and Civil Litigation*, 15 LAW & SOC'Y REV. 485. In 1976, a study was published about client perceptions and complaints about attorney conduct. *See* Eric H. Steele and Raymond H. Nimmer, *Lawyers, Clients and Professional Regulation*, 1976 AM. B. FOUND. RES. J. 917 (1976).

occurs and the available rationales or techniques of "neutralization" that individuals use to justify their actions to themselves and others:

> What the criminology literature tells us ... is that it is not about character and it is not about values. On the contrary, it is various aspects of the *situation* that individuals find themselves in, what they *think* about this situation, and what they *expect others* to think about the situation, that plays the major role in determining how they conduct themselves.[98]

By looking at particular situations of client representation in context, looking at what lawyers think about those situations and, most importantly, what they expect others to think and to do, we can better understand attorney misconduct.

Collegial control provides cues to reinforce professionalism even if some of those communities of practice push the boundaries of what others would consider professional conduct. The very breadth of "legal professionalism" and its claim to universality provides lawyers working in different areas with the tools to neutralize their conduct. Thus, corporate litigators who push boundaries for their clients with their zealousness can overlook their moral qualms and point to client self-determination as they engage in what might be questionable conduct. Communities are fluid and overlapping, however, and attorneys may go back and forth among them, just as the dynamics of a large law firm continuously force attorneys to attend to shifting expectations of those around them.

Finally, an emphasis on professionalism *in practice* might help in "the rekindling of lawyer professionalism"[99] by redirecting attention to the multiple ways that lawyers learn and are taught to behave in their everyday practices. Informal collegial control selectively incorporates and reflects what lawyers think about formal discipline and about what they think other lawyers think about it.

[98] Joseph Heath, *Business Ethics and Moral Motivation: A Criminological Perspective*, 83 J. of Bus. Ethics 595, 610 (2008). Heath draws on criminological works such as J.W. Coleman, The Criminal Elite: The Sociology of White Collar Crime (1989) and Gresham Sykes & David Matza, *Techniques of Neutralization: A Theory of Delinquency*, 22 Am. Soc. Rev. 664. Abel cites this criminological literature in his opening chapter as well. Abel, *supra* note 11, at 28–38.

[99] Am. Bar Ass'n, In the Spirit of Public Service: A Blueprint for the Rekindling of Lawyer Professionalism (1986).

7

Aspects of Professionalism

Constructing the Lawyer-Client Relationship

Philip Lewis

INTRODUCTION

In policy discussions, professionalism has usually been considered in general terms as a quality, value, ideology, or state of affairs applying to or based in the whole of a particular profession.[1] Sociolegal and empirical work on the topic, however, has tended to focus more narrowly and to explore the ways in which particular working contexts are associated with different professional ideologies and approaches to practice.[2] Nevertheless, work on "arenas of professionalism,"[3] which categorizes areas in which ideologies are developed and compete, has picked out as significant "arenas" the institutions of the profession as a whole as well as the locally situated "workplace." Similarly, work on the origins of professional behavior has found them within the institutions of the legal profession as a whole, including "general professional identities, formal training and rules of conduct,"[4] and also elsewhere in lawyers' economic incentives, their personal identities and values, and the organizational and practice contexts within which they work.

I am grateful to Scott Cummings for inviting me to contribute, and to him, Robert Gordon, and Richard Abel for penetrating and helpful comments on an earlier draft. In further comments, Scott Cummings wisely forced me to reconsider many points in the argument. I owe an intellectual debt to Carroll Seron, Lynn Mather and her colleagues, Austin Sarat and Bill Felstiner, and Robert Nelson and Laura Beth Nielsen, without whose work this chapter would not have been possible. My great gratitude is also due to Lauren Edelman and the Center for the Study of Law and Society at Berkeley for their hospitality and the opportunity to reflect on the issues in this chapter.

1 *See generally* LAWYERS' IDEALS/LAWYERS' PRACTICES: TRANSFORMATIONS IN THE AMERICAN LEGAL PROFESSION (Robert L. Nelson, David M. Trubek & Rayman L. Solomon eds., 1992).

2 LYNN M. MATHER, CRAIG A. MCEWEN & RICHARD J. MAIMAN, DIVORCE LAWYERS AT WORK: VARIETIES OF PROFESSIONALISM IN PRACTICE (2001); Robert L. Nelson & David M. Trubek, *Arenas of Professionalism: The Professional Ideologies of Lawyers in Context, in* LAWYERS' IDEALS/LAWYERS' PRACTICES, *supra* note 1, at 177.

3 Nelson & Trubek, *supra* note 2.

4 MATHER ET AL., *supra* note 2, at 4.

This chapter focuses on the workplace, though it follows the view that the factors shaping workplace behavior and ideology may lie outside it. Although the significance of the context in which lawyers work for their sense of ethical obligations and what is permissible was demonstrated in the 1960s[5] and made very clear in the work of Landon on small-town practice in the 1980s,[6] the concept of a "workplace" was not clearly articulated until the work of Abbott,[7] who recognized it as one of the three sites in which professions competed for "jurisdiction." His examples tend to focus on professionals' positions in organizations,[8] in line with his recognition of the significance of bureaucracies, though his approach is not limited to organizations. Shortly afterwards, Nelson and Trubek's treatment of the "workplace" as one of the "arenas of professionalism," taking off from Carlin's work on legal practice in Chicago in the 1960s,[9] focused on lawyers' practice and employment situations, in particular the large law firm, corporate legal departments, and legal services for the poor.[10]

For all its success as an analytical tool, if the "workplace" in which ideologies of professionalism are developed or jurisdiction is gained is just a general expression for the context of practice we may lose some helpful detail. This chapter focuses on one aspect of the workplace: lawyers' relationships and interactions with clients (whether or not they may be thought to raise issues of professionalism), although it includes factors that explain their form, nature, and content, and which may be outside the workplace.[11] These factors should be relevant to inquiries focused on professionalism. It also contains an element of comparison or contrast in its reliance on material drawn from quite different working contexts and national backgrounds.[12]

The chapter examines relationships and interactions between lawyers and clients as shown in four pieces of research that I carried out or in which I was involved.[13]

[5] Jerome Carlin, Lawyers' Ethics: A Survey of the New York City Bar (1966); Jerome Carlin, Lawyers on Their Own: A Study of Individual Practitioners in Chicago (1962).

[6] Donald D. Landon, Country Lawyers: The Impact of Context on Professional Practice (1990).

[7] Andrew Abbott, The System of Professions: An Essay on the Division of Expert Labor (1988).

[8] *Id.* at 153.

[9] Carlin, *supra* note 5.

[10] Nelson & Trubek, *supra* note 2 (citing Eve Spangler, Lawyers for Hire: Salaried Professionals at Work (1986)); *see also* Jack Katz, Poor People's Lawyers in Transition (1982).

[11] It is theoretically possible to distinguish between lawyer-client relations, covering the relationship as a whole, and lawyer-client interactions – the actual exchanges between lawyer and client – and it is certainly possible to see how particular interactions are affected by the relationship between lawyer and client. For instance, the content of an exchange can be affected by the need or lack of need to establish trust, or previously acquired shared knowledge of the subject matter. Nevertheless the distinction is not generally made here.

[12] *Cf.* Nelson & Trubek, *supra* note 2.

[13] All these projects involved interviews with lawyers, and one, for which lawyer-client relationships were the focus (the project on U.K. government lawyers), with clients too.

The first was research between 1975 and 1982 on the U.S. legal services program and its history, the second was research on lawyers in Silicon Valley before the dotcom collapse,[14] the third was on the development of expertise in computer law in England and Wales, and the last was on government lawyers in the United Kingdom.[15] The main focus of the first was on the way in which the mission of helping to fight poverty was affected by entrusting it to the legal profession. At the local level, both lawyers and leading members of relevant local organizations were interviewed. The Silicon Valley research was aimed at elucidating the part played by lawyers in significant technological and economic change; interviews were exclusively with lawyers.[16] The research on computer law in England and Wales[17] was based on work by Dezalay[18] on the use by lawyers of new forms of expertise as a means of competition; interviews were also exclusively with lawyers. The field of U.K. government lawyers was originally chosen for research because their clients often have a great deal of legal knowledge and thus the imbalance of legal expertise between lawyer and client assumed by the classic sociology of the professions might be absent. To assess the effect of this on lawyer-client relations, interviews were carried out with both lawyers and clients. The clients in this research were the so-called "administrators," mainly in the higher reaches of the civil service, whose main function is to formulate workable and politically acceptable policy, usually on the basis of the requirements of the governing politicians, and then make recommendations for action to the politicians who make the decisions.[19]

In analyzing lawyer-client relations in these contexts, I adopt a cultural or interpretive approach,[20] in which the lawyer's relationships and interactions with her

[14] Lawrence M. Friedman, Robert W. Gordon, Sophie Pirie & Edwin Whatley, *Law, Lawyers, and Legal Practice in Silicon Valley: A Preliminary Report*, 64 INDIANA L. J. 555 (1988). This research was carried out principally by Robert Gordon and Lawrence Friedman, and I am grateful to them for allowing me to use their data.

[15] Interviews are cited by project initials and year. The project initials are as follows for research on: the U.S. legal services program (LSP); lawyers in Silicon Valley (SVRP); computer law in England and Wales (ECL); and government lawyers in the United Kingdom (GL). I am grateful to the Economic and Social Research Council for supporting the latter two.

[16] There was significant review of secondary sources, particularly on the context of Silicon Valley legal practice.

[17] Philip S.C. Lewis, *Knowing the Buzzwords and Clapping for Tinker Bell: The Context, Content and Qualities of Lawyers' Knowledge in a Specialised Industrial Field, in* THE HUMAN FACE OF LAW: ESSAYS IN HONOUR OF DONALD HARRIS 151 (Keith Hawkins ed., 1997).

[18] *E.g.* Yves Dezalay, *Introduction: Professional Competition and the Social Construction of Transnational Markets, in* PROFESSIONAL COMPETITION AND PROFESSIONAL POWER: LAWYERS, ACCOUNTANTS AND THE SOCIAL CONSTRUCTION OF MARKETS 1 (Yves Dezalay & David Sugarman eds.,1995).

[19] The United Kingdom has a non-political Civil Service at all levels, even the most senior. The research focused on policy making, mainly, but not exclusively, leading up to legislation rather than on the making of particular decisions, though there is some similarity in principle.

[20] A description of these approaches, which has guided me, is in MATHER ET AL., *supra* note 2, at 200.

clients are seen as constructed and negotiated rather than the product of determined and fixed roles. Using this framework, Nelson and Nielsen show how the roles of in-house business lawyers are constructed, rather than given,[21] and point out the similarity to the "contingent, shifting, complex, and constantly negotiated" relationships of divorce lawyers and their clients described by Sarat and Felstiner.[22]

A number of themes emerged from a review of these four research projects that help explain how lawyer-client relationships are constructed and managed. These themes are: the construction of expertise, the exercise of control, the lawyer's role, the influence of practice communities, the impact of context, and finally the relation between law and other fields of knowledge and practice. In general, the review suggested that client influences were often (but not invariably) more significant than the literature has suggested, and that the influence of background and context is pervasive. Although the themes are used to organize the material presented here they are interrelated. For instance, assertions of and challenges to expertise are involved in the constitution and operations of the various "law and . . ." divisions and boundaries. For that reason, I present some situations showing how things work out in practice; all are drawn from the research on U.K. government lawyers.

In the first example, an employee of the U.K. customs office calls a departmental lawyer on a hotline to know whether he can seize a debtor's vehicle. The lawyer is recognized as an expert on such seizures within the department, and the hotline has been established as a resource for field operatives who may have no knowledge or previous experience of the lawyer. Nevertheless, even the field operatives have to have sufficient knowledge and understanding to recognize a situation not covered by their training or instructions and to describe it to the "expert." Since the facts are limited, the interaction is brief, and the lawyer's advice is accepted without question, in view of his status as a departmental lawyer and designated "expert," as well as a considerable difference in terms of civil service rank. The nature of the interaction is shaped by expertise, organization, and the nature of the situation in which advice is sought.

Compare another situation that, on the face of it, seems very different. Here the lawyer is dealing with an administrator (a specialist in his subject area, with some understanding of the legal position) who has to make a recommendation on the

[21] Robert L. Nelson & Laura Beth Nielsen, *Cops, Counsel, and Entrepreneurs: Constructing the Role of Inside Counsel in Large Corporations*, 34 Law & Soc'y Rev. 457, 460, 489 (2000); *see also* Kenichi Yoneda, *Developmental Processes of Corporate Legal Staffs in Japan: The Pluralizing Mechanism on Legal Practices Within an Organization*, 40 Hogaku Ronshu of Kagashima U. 75 (2006), *available at* http://ci.nii.ac.jp/naid/110004994292/en.

[22] Austin Sarat & William L.F. Felstiner, Divorce Lawyers and Their Clients: Power and Meaning in the Legal Process (1995).

much more complex matter of approving legislation passed by governments in the Channel Islands; though they are constitutionally independent, their legislation needs Royal Assent. Though the legislation raises constitutional questions, the request for legal advice might take no more than half a page. The lawyer and administrator have dealt with such questions together before, and the lawyer knows what issues to look at. There is a shared approach, based on previous experience, and an understanding of the policies of the U.K. government, the Islands' legislatures, and the European Union. The organization has created the specialty and the expertise, and though the situation is much more complex, it has been simplified by previous analyses. Here, as in the customs context, there is not any negotiation of roles as between lawyer and client.

Now take a lawyer working on a piece of legislation. Two junior administrators come to her to describe their policy aims, which the lawyer will then turn into instructions to Parliamentary Counsel, who will actually draft the bill. However, the administrators are inexperienced and unfamiliar with their field; in effect, they are coming to the lawyer for advice on how to proceed. In another department they might meet a lawyer who would be unhelpful to administrators who were not prepared, and only be helpful to those who seemed to have done their best. Here, however, it is different: Whether because of the lawyer's personality, the culture of her department, or the enormous time pressure this legislation is under, the lawyer is proactive in getting the administrators to formulate their aims and warning them of pitfalls in approaches they seem to be considering. In the lawyer's words:

> [some administrators] don't really have the expertise in their subject area that I would normally expect, and it's become obvious to me, just in the dealings I've had with them thus far, that they don't really understand how the particular tax that they're responsible for actually works. Knowing that has meant that, for my own – to save work later on – I'm trying to pick up some of the things they're saying to me, and trying to work out what they're thinking of at the moment, and where I think they're thinking of things that I know might not work.... [I'm] [t]rying to stop them from going off and developing a whole intricate policy that's based on a fundamental misconception.[23]

This is very different from the closely defined interaction in the previous two examples. Even with experienced and knowledgeable administrators, the lawyer might have to probe: Legislation is a social practice in the United Kingdom that requires an exactness in policy aims that the administrators may not have. As the same lawyer put it, "[Q]uite often you have to go back and really question [administrators] about exactly what is it that they want, and have they realized that if they do this, it might have the knock-on effect of that, somewhere else, or if they do it in this way, there

[23] GL 2001.

might be a loophole, or this might be ambiguous?"[24] One reason for this problem is that the policy making, especially the refinement of policies agreed in general terms, has been pushed down to lower-level administrators less familiar with the process and sometimes the subject matter.[25] A result is the need for the lawyers to be increasingly proactive in their relationships with such administrators, and to go further into the administrators' area of "policy." This illustrates how lawyers may expand their reach, but an explanation would have to include the managerial initiative on policy making. With the understanding that no firm lines can be drawn, I turn to the different themes.

EXPERTISE

In an essay relating to a general approach for lawyers engaged in problem solving, Gerald López poses the question: "Which institutions and which groups of people do we regard as 'expert' sources of valuable knowledge?"[26] His use of the word "valuable" hints at the idea that expert knowledge has to be useful in a particular social context. That there are different forms of legal expertise in different practice contexts is, of course, well known. But the framing of his question to include "regard" takes us further – toward recognizing that who is an "expert" in a particular context is itself a social construction, not just as to identity, but also as to the content, degree, and relevance of the expertise.

The sociology of the professions has focused on the imbalance of legal expertise between lawyer and client, as if the knowledge of one could be weighed against the other. Mather, McEwen, and Maiman draw attention to the doubts expressed in the literature about the reality of legal expertise,[27] but those doubts are not in issue here. Instead, I argue that in the competition for clients and in the course of lawyer-client interactions, it is the client perception of expertise that is significant.[28] There are realities in the outside world that have to be communicated to the client;[29]

[24] *Id.*; *see also* E.C. Page & W.I. Jenkins, Policy Bureaucracy: Government With a Cast of Thousands (2005).

[25] Chris Clifford, who took a substantial part in the government lawyers project, made and developed this point in an unpublished paper: Of Bees and Honey: Professionals, Policy-Making and the Role of the Government Lawyer (on file with author).

[26] Gerald P. López, *Shaping Community Problem Solving Around Community Knowledge*, 79 N.Y.U. L. Rev. 59, 73 (2004). I am grateful to Scott Cummings for this reference.

[27] Mather et al., *supra* note 2, at 64.

[28] This approach is nearer to Mather, McEwen, and Maiman's reference to "both legal expertise and the *idea* of legal expertise," though that is at a more general level. *Id.* at 65. Lawyers also need to be recognized as expert by third parties with whom they deal, for instance, other lawyers with whom they are negotiating.

[29] For an example of the difficulty of seeing what those realities are, see Ethan Michelson, *The Practice of Law as an Obstacle to Justice: Chinese Lawyers At Work*, 40 Law & Soc'y Rev. 1 (2006). *Cf.*

in so doing, the lawyer must persuade the client that he or she has the necessary expertise to opine on those realities – a process that is often more negotiation than imposition.[30]

The Clients' View

What do clients look for from lawyers? One administrator, who was very familiar with law, referred to the lawyers' knowledge of "nuances" that he acknowledged he did not have. Another regarded interpretation as a field for lawyers, and one lawyer said he was looked to for assessments of legal "risk." There were also cases where lawyers' analytical input was prized, for instance, where the lawyer showed that proposals had an unintended but significant effect in policy terms, or showed how a complicated situation could be understood in terms of the governing legislation.[31] More often, however, the administrators looked to lawyers for special knowledge on topics that were either general or outside their own often considerable knowledge. One significant example was on the applicability of human rights law. Though administrators had received significant training in the subject and policies favored their being able to deal with human rights issues themselves, even administrators familiar with the impact of human rights law on their own areas felt that lawyers' general knowledge of this legal field made it necessary to ask their advice on human rights issues.

None of the research projects provided useful information on why clients accept that lawyers are experts. For instance, in the U.K. government context, lawyers' advice – although treated skeptically by some high-level department ministers[32] – was on the whole accepted by administrators. There might be two reasons: First, that clients thought that there was an area of knowledge that lawyers possessed; second, that their advice had to be accepted because the organization had allocated the

Lauren B. Edelman, Steven E. Abraham & Howard S. Erlanger, *Professional Construction of the Legal Environment: The Inflated Threat of Wrongful Discharge*, 26 LAW & SOC'Y REV. 47 (1992).

30 SARAT & FELSTINER, *supra* note 22, at 53–84; *see also* MATHER ET AL., *supra* note 2, at 90, 96.

31 An administrator with great knowledge of the relevant law said: "We can get some really, really complex issues ... There was one ... and it was almost impossible to get round, and the sort of the cold towel round the head sort of thing, but ... she came back and she brought out this advice that was absolutely beautiful – the model of clarity." GL 2002.

32 Consider the evidence of a government lawyer speaking about the reluctance of the Foreign Secretary to take his advice: "I think the first thing was that we had a bilateral meeting, I think, at which he took the view that I was being very dogmatic and that international law was pretty vague and that he wasn't used to people taking such a firm position. When he had been at the Home Office, things had often – he had often been advised things were unlawful and he had gone ahead anyway and won in the courts, this kind of a line, which is what he recorded in the minute to me." Testimony of Sir Michael Wood, Legal Advisor, Foreign and Commonwealth Office, 2001–2006, Transcript at 31 (Jan. 2010) (speaking of former Foreign Secretary Jack Straw).

authority to determine legal questions to the lawyers. The first view seemed prevalent, but some experienced administrators who would not accept legal advice until it had been validated at the top of the government legal hierarchy seem to have come close to the second.

On the other hand, in the same organization, there existed at some levels considerable hostility toward lawyers for the unconstructive way in which advice had been given or seen to be given. But a change from handing down "tablets of stone" was well established by the time of the research: Lawyers should not just say "No," but offer alternative legally possible courses of action that would forward the client's aims. A Silicon Valley lawyer had anticipated them by years: "When we got [a big client company], I was with a firm that was only six people. But we had 80 percent of their business. Why? Because my managing partner said to me 'people don't want to hear what they can't do. You can tell them that, but you'd better follow it up, my son, with what they can do. And you'd better have three alternatives. Alternative A is easy; I want to hear Alternatives B and C."[33]

I suggest that a lawyer's apparent willingness to forward the client's aims in this way is a major element in enabling a client who is comparatively ignorant of the law to trust the lawyer's assertion of his knowledge of it. Another factor, mentioned below, is the lawyer's acceptance of management initiatives.[34]

"Nonlegal" Knowledge

Lawyers have, and often need, in order to work, knowledge of things about which they are not seen as experts – for example, an understanding of business or the ways of Whitehall (the home of the U.K. civil service). In some contexts, this knowledge may be very significant, as my research on the role of lawyers in the development of English computer law shows. A substantial part was played by certain lawyers who used their knowledge of the technology to develop legal concepts appropriate for its use. An academic described this "blue sky" thinking as analogous to academic work, and said that one lawyer's draft clauses had "normative force."[35] In Silicon Valley, one lawyer noted that "the underlying premise of the practice is that most of the stuff that I do requires and involves a high level of understanding of technology and the relationship between technology and what a company is doing."[36]

[33] SVRP 1996 (speaking of the early 1980s).

[34] Similarly, it has been argued that the pre-dotcom success of some Silicon Valley law firms resulted from their successful promotion of client trust by assertions of common membership in a "community." Lesley Barnhorn, Lawrence Friedman and Philip Lewis, Tales from the Valley: Law, Lawyers and Culture in an Innovation Center, Paper Presented at Canadian Law & Soc'y Ass'n Annual Meeting (June 2, 2000).

[35] CLE 1992.

[36] SVRP 1991.

Knowledge of the client and the client's concerns has long been recognized as affecting client relationships, which clients may experience as a "sunk cost"[37] affecting their incentive to change lawyers.[38] In the government lawyer context, one administrator noted that a lawyer's ability to suggest alternative ways of achieving client objectives when the administrator's original proposal was disapproved depended on the lawyer's deep understanding of what the administrator was trying to achieve. In addition, simple common sense and commercial savvy may be critical to a lawyer's ability to provide effective advice. For example, one administrator I interviewed emphasized the crucial importance of his lawyer's "common sense and commercial nous" in helping to unravel the consequences of a large government investment disaster.[39]

Sometimes, however, the clients look directly to the lawyer for nonlegal knowledge – for example, what is important for the company on the other side of a proposed transaction, what is normal in an industry, for instance, the going rate for licensing royalties, or the common ways of dealing with a particular business situation. This was a feature of practice in the research on Silicon Valley, where problems were recurrent, patterns of behavior became settled,[40] clients' experience was often in engineering rather than business, and for a long time it was unusual for early-stage companies to have an in-house lawyer. Because of their previous experience of local companies and transactions, local law firms often possessed this nonlegal knowledge and could use it for their clients.[41] One lawyer viewed his nonlegal knowledge of the business environment as "very important to our clients":

> In fact, the big companies that I represent tend not to be local companies and they come to me to represent them entirely because I know and understand small companies and the issues associated with small companies and what they need out of doing deals and what the pitfalls are and what they need to be worried about. And similarly my small company clients think it's very important that I know and understand big companies and what they want and how they do these deals and the sorts of things that are important to them. And it is because your clients are looking for more from you than telling them what the contract law is or what the antitrust law is. They really need to know five creative solutions to how you deal with this

[37] Gillian Hadfield, *The Price of Law: How the Market for Lawyers Distorts the Justice System*, 98 MICH. L. REV. 953 (2000).

[38] Toni Hilton & Stephen Migdal, *Why Clients Need, Rather Than Want, Lawyers*, 12 INT'L J. LEGAL PROF. 145 (2005).

[39] GL 2003.

[40] Mark C. Suchman & Mia L. Cahill, *The Hired-Gun as Facilitator: The Case of Lawyers in Silicon Valley*, 21 LAW & SOC. INQUIRY 679 (1996).

[41] Mark C. Suchman, *Dealmakers and Counselors: Law Firms as Intermediaries in the Development of Silicon Valley*, *in* UNDERSTANDING SILICON VALLEY: THE ANATOMY OF AN ENTREPRENEURIAL REGION 71–97 (Martin Kenney ed., 2000).

impasse on how to calculate royalties that they've come up with. Unless you've done lots of different kinds of transactions, it's harder for you to figure out what those five creative solutions might be.[42]

"Strategic" Knowledge

Beside knowledge that can easily be categorized as legal or nonlegal, there is also knowledge of the effects of particular forms of law or legal action. An example in the U.K. government context was a paper prepared by a lawyer on legal mechanisms available for achieving policy objectives, discussing, for instance, the relative merits of statutory and self-regulation, the need to take into account the existing regulatory environment, how to formulate substantive requirements, and the advantages and disadvantages of various types of sanctions and enforcement mechanisms that might be employed. In theory, this might be expected to be within the boundaries of a lawyer's expertise; however, in Whitehall practice, it falls directly within the realm of "policy" that is seen as being for administrators. This ambiguity is reflected in how the paper was distributed. An administrator who knew the lawyer well and valued his conclusions eagerly circulated copies to his colleagues. But the senior legal civil service, perhaps avoiding the appearance of a wish to challenge administrators' general policy-making authority, presented it generally as no more than a prompt to take advice from lawyers early in the law-making process. Administrators could, however, in the right circumstances be very receptive to strategic advice. A senior lawyer, who saw himself as generally trusted by his administrator colleagues, told me that in one area where government had long been bogged down in detail, he had been able to suggest how a far-reaching and novel legislative change could give it flexibility and that this was welcomed.[43]

This kind of knowledge can be complex and reflexive, as in the case of the cause lawyers described by Cummings.[44]

Conclusion

Some of the expertise discussed in this section may be taken for granted by clients, such as nonlegal knowledge of the working environment; it may be important for

[42] SVRP 1991.

[43] GL 2002.

[44] *Cf.* Scott L. Cummings, *Mobilization Lawyering: Community Economic Development in the Figueroa Corridor*, *in* Cause Lawyers and Social Movements 302 (Austin Sarat & Stuart Scheingold eds., 2006) (describing how cause lawyers in a specific campaign were aware of the opportunities that a credible threat of litigation could give to the client organizations, but also of the limitations of legal expertise as compared to the importance of creating coalitions and negotiating outcomes). I am grateful to Scott Cummings for this reference.

the success of the lawyer's work, but it is not something for which clients are looking. Knowledge of areas of the law will usually be looked for expressly. But other nonlegal and strategic knowledge may be important only to particular clients in particular contexts, but their expressed need for it may encourage lawyers to expand their roles.

CONTROL

The subject of control has until recently been at the center of the study of lawyer-client relationships, and focus on it has led to penetrating and sensitive studies, particularly of immediate lawyer-client interactions. The techniques of control in these interactions (and of the resistance to it) have been well studied, and there has also been some work on the circumstances affecting the locus of control.[45] Some more recent work seems less focused on control, whether because of actual changes in practice brought about by the cause lawyering movement,[46] or the methodological advances of Sarat and Felstiner.[47]

I am also treating the issue of control as less central. Although Sarat and Felstiner seem now most often cited for the way in which lawyers "trash" the legal system to create a need for clients to trust them, the main significance of their work is their emphasis on the interaction of lawyer and client, with each trying to gain recognition for the territory they can regard as their own.[48] Such an emphasis on negotiation rather than the balance of forces at the individual level gives us a helpful parallel to the work of Nelson and Nielsen on the constitution of the roles of in-house counsel in U.S. corporations.[49]

Research on three very different types of lawyers – lawyers both in large and small firms advising technology companies in Silicon Valley before the dotcom collapse, U.S. poverty lawyers in the 1970s and 1980s, and U.K. government lawyers – reinforces this view of lawyer-client negotiation. In Silicon Valley, for instance, one lawyer tried to persuade a client to adopt a contractual termination provision in an

[45] Richard L. Abel & Philip S.C. Lewis, *Putting Law Back into the Sociology of Lawyers*, *in* LAWYERS IN SOCIETY: COMPARATIVE THEORIES 478, 495 (Richard L. Abel & Philip S.C. Lewis eds., 1989); *see also* Lynn M. Mather, *What Do Clients Want? What Do Lawyers Do?*, 52 EMORY L. J. 1065 (2003) (summarizing the research on control).

[46] COREY S. SHDAIMAH, NEGOTIATING JUSTICE: PROGRESSIVE LAWYERING, LOW-INCOME CLIENTS, AND THE QUEST FOR SOCIAL CHANGE (2009) (presenting a picture rather more in the direction of cooperation between lawyer and client).

[47] SARAT & FELSTINER, *supra* note 22.

[48] *Id.* at 7–8, and *passim*.

[49] Nelson & Nielsen, *supra* note 21, at 490 ("A lawyer's behavior is shaped by past experiences in the corporation. When lawyers are criticized by businesspeople or when businesspeople resist legal advice in various ways (by not going to lawyers at all, or by choosing to go to a different lawyer within the corporation, or by complaining to higher ups that the lawyers are not 'team players') it affects how the lawyer will behave the next time.").

agreement despite the client's belief that he had a strong relationship with the other party at the time and thus such a provision was unnecessary. The lawyer prevailed by offering examples of "horribles" that had occurred in similar cases, specifically analogizing the situation to a married couple who later get divorced.[50]

In my research on the early period of the U.S. legal services program, I was not able to observe interactions at the lawyer-client level or to interview clients. However, my research did point to evidence that challenged the view of early legal services lawyers as overly dominant. First, it was not always the case that legal services clients were isolated and unprotected. The head of a local alcoholism organization, who described himself as "interested in the uniqueness of the individual and how it can be conveyed" also described himself as a "pressure-source on attorneys, with some success... I am on the arses of the lawyers. We tell the lawyer."[51] Though he was complimentary about all the lawyers, one he described as "really noble.... Really serves people. He doesn't ever give up on clients."[52]

Second, my work on a local legal services program included interviews with senior members of client organizations that put pressure on lawyers to take on proactive roles.[53] There were, in the program's most active phase, internal policies to ensure lawyer proactivity and community involvement. Such activities in other programs have been criticized by those hostile to the legal services program nationally, and also by academics, as attempts by lawyers to arrogate decision-making to themselves. Yet a leading local activist I interviewed thought that it would be wrong to see changes in program activity as lawyer-determined; rather, he thought that they corresponded to ebbs and flows in pressures coming from the community.[54] Therefore, we should not be too ready to assume that lawyers were always in effective control.

Evidence of lawyer-client negotiation also emerges from my study of U.K. government lawyers. In that context, the power of administrators was constrained by their dependence on government lawyers. Whereas in the United States, business people in a corporation could affect individual in-house lawyer behavior – by not going to lawyers, choosing different ones, or making complaints–in the United Kingdom, government administrators would usually have to go to lawyers eventually, had little or no choice of the lawyer with whom they were to deal, and ultimately had very few complaints about the lawyers with whom they dealt.[55]

[50] SVRP 1991. In another case, pressure on the clients to clarify what would happen in certain future circumstances got the parties themselves to come up with an innovative solution. "Getting clients to a level where they are willing to look at issues like that, sort of very pragmatically look, in terms of their own internal procedures and their reality of the sorts of disputes that may arise, is very difficult to do." SVRP 1991.

[51] LSP 1976.

[52] *Id.*

[53] Katz, *supra* note 10, at 84–85 (suggesting a similar picture).

[54] LSP 1976.

[55] This is very unlike the situation described in Nelson & Nielsen, *supra* note 21, at 481–83.

At the highest levels, there were practically no client-side initiatives touching on lawyer-client relations. Instead the head of the Government Legal Service took the initiatives in this area, and some administrator-led management buzz-words, such as "diversity"[56] and "joined-upness" (i.e., collaboration),[57] played to the legal department's strengths,[58] thus creating greater confidence among the administrators with whom it dealt. As this suggests, outside the individual lawyer-client relationship, there may be broad policy choices that shape the nature of lawyer-client interactions – effectively constituting a process of negotiation writ large.

ROLES

Roles are sometimes negotiated in lawyer-client interactions, but more settled roles, which may give rise to client expectations, are constituted more variously.[59] Organizations are obviously significant, whether they be law firms, or other organizations employing lawyers as such.[60] In the case of U.K. government lawyers, there is now a clear modeling of the lawyer's role, at a basic level, on private practice, with a lawyer-client relationship assumed between lawyer (responsible for law) and administrator (responsible for policy), and ultimately the relevant minister (the political official) for the department for which the lawyer works.[61] This would not be a familiar concept to lawyers in the French,[62] Italian,[63] or German civil service, for whom

[56] The administrator head of a department with a large legal staff, and many law-rich functions thought that the success with which the lawyers advanced the careers of ethnic minorities and women (rather than any legal achievements) contributed considerably to the regard in which the whole department was held in Whitehall. GL 2003.

[57] The latter was promoted by the White Paper, Cabinet Office, Modernising Government (1999).

[58] The existence of the Government Legal Service, extending across departmental boundaries, as well as a natural willingness of lawyers to cooperate, and some mechanisms for producing cross-departmental networks, was an example of "joined-upness" without trying.

[59] Plainly clients' expectations are significant for their relationships with lawyers. *See* Abel & Lewis, *supra* note 45. Narratives of lawyer control place emphasis on their creation by the lawyers themselves in the course of their interaction with the client, but it seems unlikely that clients come into the relationship without any preexisting expectations. Perhaps in some cases it is lawyer self-promotion, for in the competition for clients assertions are made about who the lawyers are and how they can help potential clients.

[60] Robert L. Nelson & Rebecca Sandefur, *From Professional Dominance to Organizational Dominance: Professionalism, Inequality, and Social Change Among Chicago Lawyers, 1975–1995, in* Reorganization and Resistance: Legal Professions Confront a Changing World (William F. Felstiner ed., 2005).

[61] How contingent this is can be seen from the fact that I was told that lawyers in Scotland owe loyalty not to a particular minister, but to the constitutional settlement embodied in the devolution of powers from Westminster, and to the Lord Advocate as guardian of that settlement.

[62] On a study visit in France, no French equivalent could be found to the position of a senior Departmental Solicitor.

[63] Terence Daintith & A.C. Page, The Executive in the Constitution: Structure, Autonomy, and Internal Control 324 (1999).

there is no such "law/policy" divide. This role has been reinforced by recent managerial initiatives emphasizing the need for "client" satisfaction.[64] Most government lawyers were happy to use this terminology, though one objected that it separated the lawyers off too much.[65]

The most substantive change of role was from lawyers' issuing opinions in the form of "tablets of stone" to participating actively in both policy making (in particular by saying: "Not A that you have suggested, but B or C would meet your intended ends") and delivery (ensuring that policy developments became effective). Both were the result of lawyer and client responses to managerial initiatives[66] that thus affect the way that roles are "constituted."[67]

COMMUNITIES OF PRACTICE

"Communities of practice" operate indirectly rather than directly on lawyer-client relationships, by shaping lawyers' ideas of how to behave.[68] In some contexts, as Mather, McEwen, and Maiman have shown, they have, to a substantial extent, replaced both professions, organizations, and even the workplace as sources of norms for lawyers' practices.[69] What are these communities? Mather, McEwen, and Maiman's study focused on divorce lawyers from comparatively small firms, engaged in litigation and negotiation with others like themselves. The contexts I have studied, though having very different characteristics, also showed indications of relevant communities.

Both in the U.S. legal services program[70] and the U.K. government,[71] some lawyers regarded themselves expressly as part of a separate legal profession or subprofession.

64 Treasury Solicitors Department, Quinquennial Review Report, Stage Two (2001).

65 GL 2002.

66 A senior government lawyer took part in the introductory course for government lawyers, emphasizing that their job was "problem-solving," and an earlier head of the Government Legal Service suggested that promotion choices were used to weed out the unwilling. GL 2002, 2003.

67 Nelson & Nielsen, *supra* note 21, at 490 ("Although we have emphasized the ways corporate counsel 'construct' their roles, it is important to recognize that this is a reciprocal process among the lawyers, their 'clients,' and other members of top management.").

68 Mather et al., *supra* note 2.

69 Nelson & Sandefur, *supra* note 60. The structural factors described in Robert W. Gordon, *The Ethical Worlds of Large-Firm Litigators: Some Preliminary Observations*, 67 Fordham L. Rev. 716 (1998), are also related to workplace organizations.

70 Alfred Feinberg, *The Birth of a New Profession*, 3 Clearinghouse Rev. 165 (1969); *see also* Craig W. Christensen, *Legal Services and the Organized Bar*, 3 Clearinghouse Rev. 35 (1969) (criticizing legal services lawyers for not being concerned with their bar associations). In the program I studied in detail, the lawyers played a fair part in the bar association, and their involvement was significant for their work and their local status.

71 *See, e.g.*, Interview with a former Departmental Solicitor (GL 2002) ("The Government Legal Service is a different species, if you like, of lawyer. It's almost a separate profession I think in itself. It's perhaps

In both cases, the lawyers were part of an organization with a wider purpose. Silicon Valley lawyers also saw themselves as separate from other lawyers (particularly those in the East[72]); Suchman and Cahill have illustrated not only their special knowledge but their special conceptions of professionalism.[73] All of my research showed institutions for developing and sharing knowledge special to the lawyers involved. The legal services program had well-defined intermediary groups to share knowledge and best practices. Similar institutions existed in Silicon Valley, among English computer lawyers, and in the Government Legal Service, which also ran systematic training on topics such as legislation.

However, one of the best illustrations of communities of practice can be found in the "public interest" and "cause lawyering" movement and literature. It has been said that "[p]ublic interest law ... is in itself a network of Deweyesque 'social interactive learners,' in which lawyers learn from each other, from communities, and from shared experiences...."[74] This is a fair description of a process in which questions about ends, means, the relevance of knowledge (legal and strategic), control, and other aspects of lawyer-client relationships are debated, and the results of the debate fed back into practice.

Identity and Meaning

Mather, McEwen, and Maiman speak of how lawyers find meaning in divorce work and the part that communities of practice play in validating lawyers' own assessments.[75] In the research on Silicon Valley and U.K. government lawyers, I found additional evidence related to how lawyers identify themselves and what gives them satisfaction. For example, a Silicon Valley lawyer emphasized that she enjoyed helping start-up companies, which she viewed as providing an important service: "[T]here's nothing more satisfying than sitting down with some small company clients about to do their first deal and explaining to them what it all means and what they ought to get out of it and why, and why it's important to the business that they're trying to develop. That sort of participation and entrepreneurship is extremely gratifying."[76]

a sub-profession of lawyers, who have to understand both the workings of government and the intricacies of the legal machinery of government.").

72 A sense of difference between Silicon Valley ways and those of the East was not confined or original to lawyers. Examples can be found in ANNALEE SAXENIAN, REGIONAL ADVANTAGE: CULTURE AND COMPETITION IN SILICON VALLEY AND ROUTE 128 (1994).

73 Suchman & Cahill, *supra* note 40.

74 Helen Hershkoff & Benedict Kingsbury, *Crisis, Community, and Courts in Network Governance: A Response to Liebman and Sabel's Approach to Reform of Public Education*, 28 N.Y.U. REV. L. & SOC. CHANGE 319, 326 (2003).

75 MATHER ET AL., *supra* note 2, at 157–74.

76 SVRP 1991.

A government lawyer derived satisfaction from his involvement in high-level politics and exposure to all kinds of out-of-the-ordinary activities. "I've had a fascinating time here. I've dealt with about 25 odd bills. I've been out to Strasbourg [European Court of Human Rights] lots of times, [as well as] Luxembourg [European Court of Justice]. I can't imagine anything more interesting really. You feel you're at the center of the law making process here, which, as a lawyer, what could be more interesting?"[77]

Professional identity is not monolithic; lawyers see themselves in various ways. Sometimes, the same lawyer may view himself in more than one way.[78] Lawyers within the same organization may also have different accounts of their professional role. For instance, some U.K. lawyers view themselves as "government lawyers," and others as lawyers for a particular department (where their obligations lie). The Government Legal Service emphasizes the first conception, especially in its training courses, because of the organization's efforts to make a career path not confined to one department and also to develop the idea of the Government Legal Service as a community of interest in Whitehall. Rarely someone thinks of himself simply as a lawyer who happens to be working in government.[79]

BACKGROUND AND CONTEXT

A model for considering the effect of background and context on the construction of the lawyer-client relationships is the work of Seron,[80] who explains how a particular kind of practice was made possible by technology and suburbia. Less directly, as Nelson and Trubek point out,[81] the work of Carlin showed the relationships between clientele and employment or group membership and attitudes toward ethical problems.[82] More recently Landon showed how pressures of practice might affect the relationships of small-town lawyers and their clients.[83]

Sometimes background and context are significant in themselves, but sometimes there is a choice by lawyers to see features of background and context as significant,

[77] GL 2002.

[78] Interview with the senior lawyer at an English computer company (ECL 1992). On the other hand, "the salience of business concerns did not detract from their self-identification as lawyers." Nelson & Neilsen, *supra* note 21, at 489.

[79] As one lawyer put it, "I think, having a background at the bar, my instincts are towards being independent. I think I was quite resistant initially to seeing myself as a civil servant, but I suppose it creeps up on one by degrees. I still see myself as a lawyer, first and foremost, who happens to be working in the civil service." GL 2002.

[80] Carroll Seron, The Business of Practicing Law: The Work Lives of Solo and Small-Firm Attorneys (1996).

[81] Nelson & Trubek, *supra* note 2.

[82] Carlin, *supra* note 5.

[83] Landon, *supra* note 6.

though others might have chosen to neglect them. One example is the recognition by public interest lawyers that new relationships and tactics could take advantage of changes in forms of regulatory governance.[84]

My research has reinforced the importance of contextual factors. Above all, Silicon Valley practice was shaped by the Valley's spatial limits and its associated ways of doing business. The growth and form of English computer law practice was shaped by the expansion of U.S. companies and law firms into England, and one major aspect of practice, the negotiation and drafting of computer contracts, was greatly affected by the breakdown in the dominance of the mainframe computer. The falling away of restrictions on competition allowed law firms to present themselves in different ways, from being technologically oriented specialists to being specialists in particular types of business, such as media companies. Some part of the success of the U.S. legal services program was due not so much to the initiatives of particular program directors as to local government, bar association, and community support. And the character of the relations between U.K. government lawyers and their administrator clients was affected not only by a range of legal factors (such as the growth of judicial review and the increasing importance of European Human Rights law), but also by managerial changes in the U.K. civil service, of which the lawyers took advantage.

An important example of relevant context is whether or not the client has an in-house lawyer. If so, there will be the complex relationships between the in-house lawyer and those with whom he or she deals within the organization.[85] In addition, when the in-house lawyer interacts with outside counsel, there is no such imbalance in legal knowledge between client and lawyer as is posited in the sociology of the professions, and the in-house lawyer has the ability to develop defined goals and use client resources to manage the relationship. Where there is no in-house lawyer, as was often the case in the earlier days of Silicon Valley, there may, at one extreme, be a one-off relationship with outside counsel, or at the other, a sustained relationship in which the outside lawyer becomes general counsel for the client business.[86] Conversely, the relationship of in-house lawyer and client can be affected by the lawyer's ability to recruit outside support. If challenged by an administrator or a Minister, U.K. government lawyers could call in a specialist outside barrister (Treasury Counsel) or the more politically powerful Attorney-General.

[84] Louise G. Trubek, *Crossing Boundaries: Legal Education and the Challenge of the "New Public Interest Law"*, 2005 Wis. L. Rev. 455 (2005). I am grateful to Scott Cummings for this reference.

[85] Nelson & Nielsen, *supra* note 21.

[86] One Silicon Valley lawyer noted that his role evolved into general counsel for a number of businesses: "The rest of my time [was spent] acting as general counsel to a large number of emerging company clients, both public and private and doing a full range of corporate and technology services for them." SVRP 1991.

LAW AND...

In a workplace situation involving lawyer and client, the distinction between law (the province of the lawyer) and other domains of knowledge (sometimes the province of the client) often arises. This boundary, always contested, has to be managed and perhaps negotiated. Sometimes, this negotiation relates to the issue of lawyer-client control discussed earlier. Other times, however, the divide between law and nonlaw shapes professional identity in other ways. For example, in the legal services context, questions of law and politics frequently arose, but not primarily in the context of the lawyer-client relationship. Instead, assertions of law, legality, and legal ethics were used as defenses against accusations of political activity.

For lawyers in commercial practice, the boundary between law and business is pervasive. It is unlikely that any business lawyer can be successful without understanding a great deal about business. The interest is in decisions that seem to involve both law and business. How are they taken, and how is responsibility for aspects of the decisions allocated?[87] In the early days of Silicon Valley, many of the start-ups were being run by engineers who had (and would accept that they had) less business knowledge than lawyers who had seen other start-ups fail or succeed. It was this comparatively greater experience that Suchman and Cahill argued allowed lawyers to play a significant normative and stabilizing role in Silicon Valley.[88] Sometimes, a distinction was made formally, as with one lawyer, who said that he would advise on business matters, but that he would say clearly, when doing so, that he had to take off his lawyer's hat.[89] It is not my impression, however, that this attitude was common. A lawyer responding to a question about a software entrepreneur who had praised the advice she got from him said that he had merely given her common sense business advice.[90]

Law and technology seem very far away from each other, but often converged in my research on legal practice. Silicon Valley lawyers emphasized their knowledge of technology as a way to build credibility. Similarly, the U.K. computer law experts discussed earlier in this chapter were very familiar with technology and would not have been able to engage in their creative, "blue sky" thinking without that knowledge. It was not that they were appropriating the knowledge of others to maintain control, but that new legal concepts fitting the technology had to be developed if legal transactions were to be effective. It did not appear in either context that lawyers

[87] This is discussed in Nelson & Nielsen, *supra* note 21.

[88] Suchman & Cahill, *supra* note 40.

[89] SVRP 1991.

[90] SVRP 1993. Elsewhere the lawyer described his organization as "a hybrid of a startup law firm, a venture capital firm, a consulting firm and an investment bank." Susan Orenstein, *Lawyers Need Equity, Too*, Industry Standard, Apr. 10, 2000, at 142.

had been directly involved in technological discoveries or decisions, or that there were any tensions around the interaction of law and technology. Rather, there was evidence that lawyers contributed indirectly to technological development by asking technologists to elucidate what they intended in order to put those intentions into legal shape, such as in the case of licensing agreements. However, on rare occasions, lawyers played a more central role. For instance, one Silicon Valley engineer was pushed by a patent attorney into thinking of possible further patent claims in connection with an invention that ultimately became a major technological advance.[91]

The distinction between law and policy was central to the lawyer-client relationships investigated in my research on U.K. government lawyers. The "ideology of separate spheres" is alive and well in Whitehall.[92] Policy making was central to the administrators' self-definition, and although it was their role to make policy recommendations to ministers, that activity often involved the participation of lawyers, who, as we have seen, needed an understanding of policy. What were the responsibilities of each if both "law" and "policy" were involved? The distinction had to be managed, and conceptions had to be developed. Was there a dividing line, and if so, was it purely theoretical (and unknowable) or fuzzy and debatable? Were there situations in which both law and policy were involved? One administrator said that there was a line, and although it was important that lawyers had an understanding of the policy issues, they should observe the line carefully to retain their objectivity:

> There is, clearly there is a line, and there has to be a line. I guess in a sense it's one that perhaps lawyers need to guard almost more jealously than administrators do on the other side, because … there are occasions obviously when there is a drive in terms of the policy to deliver something, sometimes by a particular route because ministers are particularly attracted to that route for whatever reason, but where there are clearly legal problems and so I think colleagues in legal advisors branch, quite rightly, do need to be conscious of their independence and the need for an objective view. There is potentially a danger that the more you blur the line between the two, the more difficult it can be to stand back and actually say no, that really isn't going to work.[93]

There was, however, no systematic way in which these questions were answered, only (more or less) contested approaches. For instance, although it was understood that lawyers did, in fact, get involved in policy making, it remained an area of sensitivity among the lawyers themselves – as revealed by one lawyer who conceded that lawyers did more policy making than they would like recognized. Gordon suggests

[91] Leslie Berlin, The Man Behind the Microchip: Robert Noyce and the Making of Silicon Valley 109 (2005).

[92] Sarat & Felstiner, *supra* note 22, at 6.

[93] GL 2002.

that the lawyers do not want to take responsibility for policy decisions or be criticized for making "political" rather than "autonomously legal" decisions.[94] On the other hand, though law was their province, government lawyers were reluctant in their interactions with clients to assert the primacy of law, preferring instead to frame their legal advice in terms of the likelihood of adverse responses in the legislative process or in public opinion. As one lawyer put it, "I think lots of being a lawyer is rather than coming at people and saying, 'This is the law,' I often try to come up to people and say, 'We are going to have to go to parliament, and your minister is going to have to justify this. [A minister, without legal expertise] is going to have to justify this on the floor of the House of Lords, with all manner of eminent Law Lords or other former lawyers kicking around who might take an interest in it.'"[95] Gordon has similarly observed that lawyers "exhibited a positive allergy to moral language," perhaps because their clients did not want to be "preached at."[96] For government lawyers, the corresponding feeling seems to be that their clients might see the lawyer's judgment as unreliable, or the law as uncertain, or, worse still, a mere "technicality."

CONCLUSION

This chapter has sought to describe the range of factors that shape lawyer-client relations. It has concentrated on expertise, particularly the part played by client perceptions, and on roles and how they are constituted, by interaction between lawyer and client, by the involvement of management and other third parties, and by the communities of practice in which lawyers participate and from which, in part, they derive their professional identities and the meaning they find in their work.[97] It has given somewhat less attention to control, on which the professionalism literature has focused until recently, but it has described research suggesting that lawyer and

[94] Private Communication between Robert Gordon, Chancellor Kent Professor of Law and Legal History, Yale Law School, and Philip Lewis, Associate Research Fellow, University of Oxford Centre for Socio-Legal Studies (Oct. 2, 2009). Generally lawyers shared the view that it was for administrators to take responsibility for policy recommendations (though very occasionally lawyers might explicitly be asked to take the lead on policy issues with a strong legal flavor or content). However, an official attempt to increase team-working to include lawyers rejected the idea that any blurring of responsibilities should be avoided. Sir Robert Andrew, Review of Government Legal Services 5 (1989).

[95] GL 2002.

[96] Gordon, *supra* note 69, at 732–33.

[97] This is a partial working out of Richard Abel's linkage of lawyer-client relationships, including issues of control and the inconsistent expectations of lawyer and client, with broader issues of what lawyers do. Abel & Lewis, *supra* note 45, at 494–95 (inquiring into "*when* lawyers do *which* things for *which* clients"). His approach forces us to take a more integrated view of the various aspects of lawyer-client relations and their connection with lawyer practice and functions, and in this chapter I have tried to follow his example.

client can be on more equal terms or can negotiate their positions, as Sarat and Felstiner showed, but in a wider context than that of matrimonial law. It has shown that contest and negotiation over the boundaries between law and other knowledge domains are also pervasive in legal practice. Finally, it has emphasized the important part that background and context can have in shaping lawyer-client relations, taking further work of Carlin and Landon which has been somewhat neglected recently.

What has been said here of the nature of and influences on lawyer-client relations in general is likely to apply to those subsets of them that scholars have singled out in their descriptions of professionalism, whether that be the development of ideologies or changes in behavior. To that extent, the themes discussed here may be a guide to future research. A particular lesson should be that even if there is a focus on professionalism in the workplace, the influences on it may lie outside, in the wider background and context.

8

Professional Regulation and Public Service

An Unfinished Agenda

Deborah L. Rhode

INTRODUCTION

When I began teaching and writing about legal ethics some three decades ago, the field was barely a field. "General piffle" was how an early scholar of the profession described the field.[1] Some leading exceptions are represented in this volume. Unlike much of the pompous moralizing that had previously characterized the field, this new work drew on research in law and society and critical legal theory. And unlike more conventional professional responsibility approaches, this scholarship tended to be skeptical of incremental reform, particularly the bar's efforts to reform its regulatory structures and promote public service. Shoring up a bankrupt structure was how many of us saw it.

So what were the alternatives? Here accounts differed. In a 1981 law review symposium, Richard Abel, one of the most influential voices, presented deficiencies in lawyers' ethics as inherent in a liberal capitalist system that privileged profits and value-free conceptions of professional roles.[2] On the prospects of reforming that system, he was diplomatically silent. By contrast, I suggested that "to affect significant improvements in the cost, quality, and delivery of legal services, the bar must accept fundamental changes in its regulatory structures," changes in which the public would have a much greater voice.[3] On how those changes could be achieved, I was similarly silent.

If I had any illusions about the adequacy of this reform agenda, I lost them quickly. For the final exam in my first legal ethics course, I circulated a draft of my symposium article, without identifying myself as the author, and asked for comments. A star student in the class offered an observation that remains with me after three

[1] George P. Costigan, Jr., *The Teaching of Legal Ethics*, 4 AM. SCHOLARLY REV. 290, 295 (1917).

[2] Richard L. Abel, *Why Does the ABA Promulgate Ethical Rules?*, 59 TEX. L. REV. 639 (1981).

[3] Deborah L. Rhode, *Why the ABA Bothers: A Functional Perspective on Professional Codes*, 59 TEX. L. REV. 689 (1981).

decades. If, as the article had suggested, the only way to obtain substantial improvements in professional regulation was to reduce the bar's control over the process, why was the author writing in a law review? Surely lawyers would not voluntarily relinquish control on matters where their status and economic interests were so directly implicated. Pressure for reform would need to come from the public, and their political representatives, who were unlikely readers of law reviews. The problem with the essay, he suggested, was that it was written for law professors; if the goal was reform, the author's energy would have been better spent writing op-eds and lobbying legislatures.

I gave him an A for the course, but prudently ignored his advice until after receiving tenure. I've since devoted a fair amount of effort to professional reform and found the results frustrating at best. I don't know whether this makes me more or less radical than my younger self, but I have grown increasingly impatient with calls for fundamental transformation unaccompanied by plausible strategies for getting from here to there. Although in some contexts, incremental reforms may divert attention from broader change, they can also lay foundations for achieving it. Pending a revolution, incrementalism is all we have.

Moreover, experience over the last quarter-century suggests that the project is not entirely hopeless. Forces external to the legal profession can play a powerful role in nudging the bar toward more socially conscious policies. Academics can support those efforts through both applied research and curricular initiatives that prepare the next generation to address challenges that remain unmet. This chapter explores two areas in which such opportunities arise: pro bono work and bar regulatory structures.

PRO BONO SERVICE

In the 1981 symposium, those of us representing the new, more critical approach to professional regulation expressed skepticism about the bar's pro bono initiatives. Abel described its efforts as follows:

> [E]very study that has investigated the matter has reconfirmed that these efforts are trivial – in comparison to the work a lawyer does for pay, in comparison to the need for pro bono services, and in terms of what a lawyer could do while still "earning a satisfactory living".... Elite lawyers with an inflated sense of their self-importance view such work as insignificant; most lawyers lack the training to qualify them to represent pro bono clients; and socioeconomic stratification and racial segregation prevent most pro bono clients from ever approaching most lawyers. Finally, the Rules ignore the most obvious reason why lawyers do not offer more pro bono services: simple greed.[4]

[4] Abel, *supra* note 2, at 685–86.

My own account was similarly scathing:

> Nowhere is the disparity between rhetoric and reality more apparent than in the assertion of both the Model Rules and Code that the "basic responsibility for providing legal services for those unable to pay rests upon the individual lawyer." If the nation had relied exclusively upon the private bar to assume that responsibility, the legal services movement undoubtedly would still be in an incipient stage. The most comprehensive survey of lawyers' pro bono activity revealed that about three-fifths of respondents devoted less than five percent of billable hours to such work and half of this group spent no time at all.... Moreover the vast bulk of these contributions did not redound to the advantage of chronically underrepresented interests. One-third of individual pro bono clients were relatives and friends. Of the organizations receiving assistance, eighty-two percent were churches, hospitals and middle class-oriented community groups.... Only five percent were legal aid and public defender organizations. Considering the extent to which most attorneys now manifest their "responsibility to those unable to pay," the Commission's rhetorical posturing is at best rank hypocrisy. At worst it is counterproductive, insofar as it deflects attention from more fundamental questions about the distribution of legal talent.... An entity concerned more with substance than self-image would have invested its energy in proposals with greater potential for enhancing access to justice, such as alternative forms of dispute resolution or regulation of the professional monopoly.[5]

Over the last quarter-century, much has changed and much has remained the same. On the positive side, the amount and quality of pro bono work for those who need it most has risen substantially.[6] Although precise estimates are impossible to come by, a 2008 ABA study found that almost three-quarters of lawyers provided some pro bono assistance to persons of limited means or organizations serving them, for an average amount of forty-one hours per year.[7] The average contributions of the nation's largest firms have more than doubled since the turn of the twenty-first century.[8] Moreover, as Scott Cummings has noted, pro bono work has become professionalized.[9] About half of large firms now have full-time coordinators for such work, and a growing number of bar and nonprofit organizations are devoting substantial resources to matching practitioners with causes and clients.[10] These efforts

[5] Rhode, *supra* note 3, at 699, 701.

[6] ABA surveys have found an increase in the number of lawyers who engage in pro bono work, as well as in their amount of service over the past five years. *See* Am. Bar Ass'n Standing Committee on Pro Bono & Public Service, Supporting Justice II, A Report on the Pro Bono Work of America's Lawyers 21 (2009).

[7] *Id.* at 3.

[8] Nate Raymond, *A Silver Lining*, Am. Law., July 2008, at 101.

[9] Scott L. Cummings, *The Politics of Pro Bono*, 52 UCLA L. Rev. 1 (2004).

[10] About half of the nation's 200 most profitable firms have at least one full time pro bono coordinator. Daphne Eviatar, *Pro Bono Pros*, Am. Law., July 2008, at 104.

can no longer be described as "trivial"; indeed by some estimates, the contributions to civil legal aid programs alone are equivalent to between a quarter and a third of the time provided by full-time lawyer staff. [11]

Yet neither is this increase in public service grounds for complacency. Measured by the need for services and by what lawyers could reasonably provide while "earning a satisfactory living," participation rates still reflect a dispiriting gap between bar rhetoric and reality. Only a quarter of lawyers in the ABA's study met its aspirational norm of fifty hours of assistance per year to persons of limited means or to organizations that serve them.[12] Only about two-fifths of lawyers in the nation's 200 most profitable firms have contributed at least twenty hours a year.[13] Moreover, the rise in pro bono work pales in comparison to the magnitude of unmet needs. Virtually all the bar studies that have surveyed the problem find that at least four-fifths of the individual legal needs of the poor are not addressed.[14] Those estimates do not include collective problems for which a lawyer's representation is critical. It is a shameful irony that the country with the world's highest concentration of lawyers has done so little to make legal assistance available to those whose needs are greatest.

Increases in pro bono work are, of course, only part of the solution. Having volunteers dabble in poverty and public interest law is not the most cost-effective way to deliver assistance. Even if all attorneys made substantial contributions, they would still come nowhere close to meeting current needs. As I have argued endlessly elsewhere, we need a fundamental restructuring of our system of delivering legal services, including procedural simplification and greater access to specialized non-lawyer providers.[15] But given all the obstacles to achieving those reforms, increasing the quality and quantity of pro bono work should remain a priority. Not only can

[11] Rebecca Sandefur, *Lawyers' Pro Bono Service and American Style Civil Legal Assistance*, 41 Law & Soc'y Rev. 79, 85 (2007).

[12] The ABA's current Model Rules of Professional Conduct, Rule 6.1, asks that lawyers "aspire" to provide at least fifty hours of pro bono work each year or the financial equivalent. A "substantial majority" of their contributions should go to "persons of limited means" or organizations assisting them. Additional assistance should go to activities that improve the law, legal profession or legal system, or that support "civil rights, civil liberties or public rights, or charitable, religious, civic, community, governmental and educational organizations" if payment of fees would "significantly deplete the organization's economic resources or be otherwise inappropriate." Model Rules of Prof'l Conduct R. 6.1. The Comment to the Rule also allows firms to satisfy their lawyers' obligations collectively.

[13] *The American Lawyer* uses a standard developed by the Pro Bono Institute, which tracks the Model Rule but excludes activities designed to improve the law or legal profession, such as bar committee work. Aric Press, *In House*, Am. Law., July 2008, at 13; Raymond, *A Silver Lining*, *supra* note 8, at 101.

[14] *See* Legal Services Corporation, Documenting the Justice Gap in America 4–11 (2005); Deborah L. Rhode, Access to Justice 3 (2004).

[15] Rhode, Access to Justice, *supra* note 14; Deborah L. Rhode, *Whatever Happened to Access to Justice?*, 42 Loy. L.A. L. Rev. 869 (2009).

such public service make a crucial difference in protecting fundamental rights, it can also give lawyers a better sense of how the legal system functions, or fails to function, for the have-nots. And that experience can help broaden support for more fundamental reforms.

What stands in the way of greater pro bono commitments? Greed is one explanation, but it is part of the solution as well as the problem. Much of the recent increase in pro bono work has been fueled by bottom-line concerns. For individual attorneys, such unpaid assistance can bring valuable contacts, trial experience, and expertise in a field in which they would like to obtain paid work.[16] For firms, pro bono programs can enhance recruitment, retention, recognition, and career development efforts.[17] Improvements in these programs are partly attributable to their increased visibility in the media. For example, *The American Lawyer* rates the pro bono contributions of the nation's 200 most profitable firms based on the number of hours per lawyer and the percentage of lawyers who contribute more than twenty hours annually. A firm's pro bono rating also accounts for a third of its score in the competition for membership on *The American Lawyer*'s coveted "A-List" of the nation's top twenty firms. Other national and local periodicals showcase outstanding public service. Nonprofit organizations and bar associations give awards. And a student-run organization, Building a Better Legal Profession, has begun to rank law firms on their pro bono performance.[18]

As a firm's reputation for public service becomes more visible, it also becomes more important to clients and potential recruits.[19] Moreover, in the current economic downturn, pro bono opportunities have also become increasingly valuable as way stations for underemployed or furloughed attorneys. This, of course, makes public service easier to sell as a purely financial proposition. As one lawyer in an American Bar Foundation study put it: "Law firms do not support pro bono unless there is a business reason to do so. The bottom line on this question is the

[16] Deborah L. Rhode, Pro Bono in Principle and Practice 131–32 (2005); Robert Granfield, *The Meaning of Pro Bono: Institutional Variations in Professional Obligations Among Lawyers*, 41 Law & Soc'y Rev. 139 (2007); Karen Lash, *Pitching Your Pro Bono Projects: Getting to "Yes" with the "Big Firm"*, DePaul J. for Social Justice 8 (forthcoming).

[17] *See* Am. Bar Found., New Approaches to Access to Legal Services: Research, Practice & Policy 10 (2006), *available at* http://www.americanbarfoundation.org/uploads/cms/documents/rlmoserfund.pdf; Brent Harris, Fulfilling the Promise of Law Firm Pro Bono (2008) (unpublished manuscript on file with the author).

[18] Building a Better Legal Profession, http://www.betterlegalprofession.org/ (last visited Apr. 27, 2009).

[19] *See* Eviatar, *supra* note 10 (quoting Ron Tabak, pro bono coordinator for Skadden, Arps, Slate, Meagher & Flom, about the increasing number of external constituencies, "including potential recruits, who now care about how big or successful a pro bono program you have"); *see also* Stephen Daniels & Joanne Martin, *Legal Services for the Poor: Access, Self-Interest and Pro Bono*, 12 Soc. of Crime, L. & Deviance 145, 154 (2009) (noting that there remains a "war for talent," and "many if not most of the lawyers these firms want to hire" expect public interest opportunities).

bottom line."[20] Another attorney was equally candid: "We're not running a charity. This is good business ... for large firms.[21]

In one sense, such views are neither surprising nor problematic. In principle, pro bono publico is about what is "good for the public." But in practice, it has also been about what is good for lawyers. From most bar leaders' perspective, that is not cause for concern. To borrow British philosopher Bernard Williams' example, when a man gives money to famine relief, why should we care whether his motive is to enhance his standing with the Rotary Club?[22] So too, what difference does it make if law firms volunteer time less out of concern for social justice than a desire to improve their recruitment, reputation, and rankings in *The American Lawyer*? The point is to get their contributions.

The risk, however, is that focusing on the profession's interest may too often shortchange the public's. A chronic difficulty stems from the inadequacy of oversight and accountability. Law firms and media ranking systems compile information on the quantity, not quality, of pro bono work, and clients often lack the knowledge or leverage to raise concerns. Particularly where pro bono cases are seen as training opportunities for junior lawyers, and supervisors have little incentive to monitor performance, the results may be ineffective or inefficient service. Problems arise when young associates don't know how to take a deposition or become overcommitted with paying matters.[23] In my own recent survey of leading public interest legal organizations, almost half reported extensive or moderate problems with quality in the pro bono work they obtained from outside firms.[24]

A further difficulty involves programs that pressure attorneys to participate in public service without providing sufficient choice or credit. In a large national study I conducted on pro bono involvement, almost half of the attorneys expressed dissatisfaction with the kind of work their firms permitted.[25] Favors for clients, other lawyers, firm employees, or partners' "pet organizations" struck many associates as "not truly" in the public interest.[26] Many surveys find that attorneys are foreclosed from accepting cases that would offend the political sensibilities of firm leadership or major clients, or are sometimes drafted for matters that hold no interest.[27]

[20] AM. BAR FOUND., *supra* note 17, at 6.

[21] Daniels & Martin, *supra* note 19, at 153.

[22] BERNARD WILLIAMS, MORALITY: AN INTRODUCTION TO ETHICS 66 (1972).

[23] Deborah L. Rhode, *Public Interest Law: The Movement at Midlife*, 60 STAN. L. REV. 2027, 2072 (2008).

[24] *Id.* at 2070.

[25] RHODE, *supra* note 16, at 148.

[26] *Id.*

[27] For the reluctance of firms to subsidize work that may conflict with client interests or values, see *id.* at 146; Cummings, *supra* note 9, at 122; Rhode, *supra* note 23, at 2073; Norman W. Spaulding, *The Prophet and the Bureaucrat: Positional Conflicts in Service Pro Bono Publico*, 50 STAN. L. REV. 1395

A related problem involves the lack of strategic focus in formulating selection standards. Despite all the discussion about the "business case" for pro bono, most firms are strikingly unbusinesslike in the way that they structure their programs. The result is missed opportunities for both the profession and the public. Research on strategic philanthropy in general and public interest legal efforts in particular suggests that the most effective approach is to be systematic in identifying goals, designing cost-effective strategies to address them, and developing criteria to measure their achievement.[28] By this standard, most lawyers' pro bono work falls short. Relatively few firms engage in any systematic assessment of community needs, the social impact of their work, or the most efficient use of resources. That is true even among the most well-supported pro bono programs. In Scott Cummings' and my recent survey of pro bono counsel, none reported formal systematic efforts to solicit feedback from nonprofit organizations or to gauge client satisfaction.[29] In one of my earlier surveys, when asked about how effectiveness is measured, one Wall Street partner expressed a common view with uncommon candor: "we are not able to answer this question as it is posed.... we cannot opine as to which of our pro bono programs effectively contribute to the community."[30] The result is often a "spray and pray" approach, which spreads assistance widely in the hope that somehow something good will come of it.[31] Something usually does, but the result is not necessarily the most cost-effective use of resources.

Significant improvement in pro bono programs will require greater strategic direction and public accountability. Firms need more systematic processes for selecting and overseeing matters that take into account both participants' and public interests. For example, are they meeting needs that experts or client groups consider most compelling, or bringing some special expertise to the table? How many individuals are they assisting and how satisfied are clients or nonprofit partners with the assistance provided? If the matter involves policy work or impact litigation, what are the chances of a long-term legal or political payoff? To promote quality as well as participation, pro bono programs need to ensure that unpaid work is effectively supervised, credited toward billable hour requirements, and valued in promotion and compensation decisions.[32]

(1998); David Wilkins, *Doing Well by Doing Good? The Role of Public Service in the Careers of Black Corporate Lawyers*, 41 Hous. L. Rev. 1, 77 (2004).

28 Peter Frumkin, Strategic Giving: The Art and Science of Philanthropy 5–7 (2006).

29 Scott L. Cummings & Deborah L. Rhode, *Managing Pro Bono: Doing Well By Doing Better*, 78 Fordham L. Rev. 2357, 2401–05 (2010).

30 Paul Saunders, member of the Pro Bono Committee at Cravath, Swaine and Moore, quoted in Brent Harris, Fulfilling the Promise of Law Firm Pro Bono 24–25 (Unpublished Manuscript, Stanford Law School, 2008).

31 Frumkin, *supra* note 28, at 371.

32 Rhode, *supra* note 16, at 150; *see also* Michael Aneiro, *Room to Improve*, Am. Law., July 2006, at 100.

Courts, bar associations, clients, academics, and the media can also do more to encourage and evaluate public service. Requiring lawyers to report their contributions can result in substantial improvements in hours and financial assistance.[33] So can enlisting clients to consider pro bono records in allocating legal work.[34] Legal publications can work with researchers and bar organizations to develop ways of evaluating firms on the effectiveness as well as quantity of pro bono work.[35] As research on strategic philanthropy demonstrates, those who want to make a difference cannot afford to conflate good intentions with good results.[36] Yet lawyers have a tendency to do just that. They often assume that anything given pro bono *is* pro bono; unpaid representation is taken as a good in and of itself, regardless of cost-effectiveness. The challenge now is to find more ways of holding participants accountable for the quality of their contributions.

Legal education can also do more to promote pro bono service. Here again, enormous progress has occurred over the last two decades. When I entered the field, virtually no law schools supported organized pro bono programs. Students who wanted to do volunteer work generally had to identify opportunities themselves.[37] Now the vast majority of schools have such programs. Yet only a minority of students participate.[38] Only about ten percent of schools require service, and the amounts demanded are sometimes quite minimal: Half of those responding to an ABA survey required only ten to twenty hours from students.[39] Moreover, the quality of some programs is open to question. Many students lack on-site supervision or a classroom opportunity to discuss their work or pro bono issues generally. In my own national pro bono survey, only 1 percent of attorneys reported that the issue received coverage in their law school orientation programs or professional responsibility

[33] Since Florida has required reporting of pro bono work, the number of lawyers providing assistance to the poor has increased by 35%; the number of hours has increased by 160% and financial contributions have increased by 243%. Standing Committee on Pro Bono Legal Service, Report to the Supreme Court of Florida, The Florida Bar, and The Florida Bar Foundation on the Voluntary Pro Bono Attorney Plan (2006).

[34] Rhode, *supra* note 16, at 167–69; Wilkins, *supra* note 27, at 83–84.

[35] For example, the ABA Standards for Programs Providing Civil Legal Services to Persons of Limited Means (Standard 2.12) identifies useful assessment strategies. They include collecting not just data on individuals served and results obtained, but also evaluations from participants, clients, and referring or collaborating organizations.

[36] Paul Brest & Hal Harvey, Money Well Spent: A Strategic Guide for Smart Philanthropy 247 (2008).

[37] Cynthia F. Adcock & Alison M. Keegan, A Handbook on Law School Pro Bono Programs: The AALS Pro Bono Project 7 (2001); *see also* Rhode, *supra* note 16, at 22.

[38] Law School Survey on Student Engagement, Student Engagement in Law Schools: A First Look 8 (2004). Only about 10% of schools require service by students, and fewer still impose specific requirements on faculty. Only two schools reported faculty requirements. Am. Bar Ass'n Standing Committee on Professionalism, Report on Survey of Law School Professionalism Programs 46–47 (2006).

[39] *Id.*

courses; only 3 percent observed visible faculty support for pro bono work.[40] An American Bar Foundation survey of recent law graduates ranked pro bono last on a list of educational experiences that practitioners felt had assisted them significantly in practice.[41] In the words of a Commission of the Association of American Law Schools on public service opportunities: "law schools should do more."[42]

SELF-REGULATION

Bar efforts at regulatory reforms reflect a similar trajectory. In the 1981 Model Rules symposium, Abel wrote:

> [S]tudy after study has shown that the current rules of professional conduct are not enforced. Misconduct is rarely perceived. If perceived, it is not reported. If reported, it is not investigated. If investigated, violations are not found. If found, they are excused. If they are not excused, penalties are light. And if significant penalties are imposed, the lawyer soon returns to practice, in that state or another.... Lawyers can hardly present their travesty of a penal system as an effective deterrent. [43]

My view was similar: "Every major study of bar disciplinary agencies has found them grossly unresponsive both to serious misfeasance and to garden-variety complaints about the cost and quality of services.... So long as disciplinary proceedings remain firmly under professional control, substantial improvement is unlikely."[44]

That prediction has proved all too accurate. There has, to be sure, been progress over the last quarter-century. Many jurisdictions have significantly increased the resources available to disciplinary authorities, provided greater insulation from bar influence, and instituted informal dispute resolution procedures for complaints involving fees and "minor" misconduct.[45] But the basic structural problem remains: Any regulatory process controlled by the group to be regulated is bound to fall short. Nothing in the history of the legal profession suggests it to be an exception.

[40] Rhode, *supra* note 16, at 161–62. Only 62% of those responding to the ABA survey reported the availability of on-site supervision. ABA Standing Committee, *supra* note 38, at 45.

[41] Ronit Dinovitzer et al., After the J.D.: First Results of a National Study of Legal Careers 81 (2004).

[42] Commission on Pro Bono and Public Service Opportunities in Law Schools, Ass'n of American Law Schools, Learning to Serve: A Summary of the Findings and Recommendations of the Commission on Pro Bono and Public Service Opportunities in Law Schools 2 (1999).

[43] Abel, *supra* note 2, at 648–49.

[44] Rhode, *supra* note 3, at 718–19.

[45] For example, many states have transferred regulatory authority from bar associations to commissions that report directly to the state supreme court. About half the states have such commissions. For these and other reforms, see Richard L. Abel, Lawyers in the Dock: Learning from Attorney Disciplinary Proceedings 505 (2008); Deborah L. Rhode & David Luban, Legal Ethics 982–86 (5th ed. 2009).

As John Coffee puts it, "private self regulation of attorneys through bar associations means the continued government of the guild, by the guild, and for the guild."[46] In his 2008 study of lawyer disciplinary proceedings, Abel came to much the same conclusion that he had reached decades earlier: "There is a systematic mismatch between the harms clients most commonly suffer (primarily neglect) and the willingness of disciplinary authorities to impose significant penalties."[47] The view of most experts is that "too little unethical behavior is named, blamed, claimed, and punished.... [H]owever, many lawyers believe just the opposite – that discipline is unfair, oppressive, and counterproductive."[48]

As was true a quarter-century ago, virtually all independent studies show a wide gap between the protection that consumers need and the oversight that the bar supplies. Bar ethical rules requiring lawyers to report evidence of serious misconduct are widely ignored and rarely enforced. Only about 10 percent of the complaints to disciplinary bodies come from the profession.[49] Yet one survey found only four disciplinary actions over two decades for failure to report ethical violations.[50] As a consequence, most agencies rely solely on clients as a source of information about misconduct – an approach that is clearly inadequate given these individuals' frequent lack of information or incentives to file a grievance. Even those clients who are aware that their attorneys have violated ethical standards often doubt that complaining to the bar will produce effective remedies.

Those clients are generally right. Fewer than 5 percent of the cases brought to disciplinary authorities result in public sanctions.[51] Fewer still end in permanent disbarment. Except in egregious circumstances, many disciplinary agencies decline jurisdiction over the kinds of conduct generating most consumer grievances: neglect, negligence, and fee disputes. Bar oversight is limited because of both resource constraints and an assumption that other remedial alternatives are available through malpractice actions. However, malpractice litigation is too expensive for most of these matters, and the lawyers most likely to be subject to complaints frequently lack civil liability insurance.[52] Although a growing number of states have alternative dispute resolution systems for minor client grievances and fee disputes, not all

[46] John C. Coffee, Jr., *The Attorney as Gatekeeper: An Agenda for the SEC*, 103 Colum. L. Rev. 1293, 1316 (2003). For similar views, see Anthony E. Davis, *Professional Liability Insurers as Regulators of Law Practice*, 65 Fordham L. Rev. 209, 2231 (1996).

[47] Abel, *supra* note 45, at 500.

[48] *Id.* at 505.

[49] *Id.* at 502.

[50] *See* Lance J. Rogers, *Conference Panelists Call for Clarification of Obligation to Report Peer Misconduct*, 23 ABA/BNA Lawyers' Manual of Professional Conduct 297 (2007).

[51] Rhode & Luban, *supra* note 45, at 982.

[52] An estimated 20% to 50% of lawyers lack liability insurance. *See* Rhode & Luban, *supra* note 45, at 1016.

of these programs are mandatory and not all are perceived as effective by many clients.[53] Many states also lack effective diversion systems or remedial approaches that respond to the causes of ethical violations. Attorneys receive reprimands or mediated solutions for individual grievances rather than the training and oversight that will assist them in averting future problems. The twenty states that have diversion programs generally fail to track or publish statistics on the effectiveness of these programs in preventing misconduct.[54]

The problem is compounded by the absence of transparency. Most ethical violations by lawyers or inadequacies in bar responses are not visible to the public. Except in four states, bar disciplinary agencies will not disclose the existence of a complaint unless they have found a disciplinary violation or probable cause to believe that a violation has occurred. Lawyers with as many as twenty complaints under investigation have received a clean bill of health when a consumer asked for information about their records, and it has sometimes taken as many as forty-four complaints over a decade to get a practitioner disbarred.[55] Even where sanctions are imposed, the public lacks a ready way of discovering them. Not all states publish information concerning disciplinary sanctions, and many do not do so online or in formats that are accessible to consumers.[56] Because the vast majority of complaints never result in public sanctions, and the vast majority of malpractice actions never result in published opinions, consumers lack crucial knowledge about lawyers' practice histories. The profession and the public also lack information that would enable them to assess the fairness of disciplinary processes. Many practitioners believe that the system is biased against small firms, solo practitioners, and racial and ethnic minorities; the studies to date have been inadequate to evaluate those concerns.[57]

[53] For disciplinary systems' lack of attention to performance issues and the rates of client dissatisfaction, see DEBORAH L. RHODE, IN THE INTERESTS OF JUSTICE 159, 181(2000); *see also* Deborah Rosenthal, *Every Lawyer's Nightmare*, CAL. LAW., Sept. 2002, at 23, 24. In Oregon's system, a majority of clients were not satisfied, although it is unclear how much of that dissatisfaction was related to unrealistic expectations. OREGON STATE BAR, ANNUAL REPORT OF THE OREGON STATE BAR CLIENT ASSISTANCE OFFICE (2006).

[54] For failure to address underlying causes, see Vivian Berger, *Mediation: An Alternative Means of Processing Attorney Disciplinary Complaints*, 16 PROF. LAW. 21, 24 (2005). For the absence of data on diversion programs, see Leslie C. Levin, *The Case for Less Secrecy in Lawyer Discipline*, 20 GEO. J. LEGAL ETHICS 1 (2007).

[55] RHODE, *supra* note 53, at 159–60; Levin, *supra* note 54, at 2 n.9, 19.

[56] Levin, *supra* note 54, at 20–21; Vesna Jaksic, *Attorney Discipline Web Data Uneven*, NAT'L L. J., Sept. 10, 2007, at 1, 7.

[57] For example, almost half of Oregon lawyers believe that the disciplinary system is biased, largely based on the size of the lawyers' firm. A majority of African-American lawyers in Illinois believed that race played a factor in disciplinary decisions, but only a small minority of white lawyers believed that race played a role in the disciplinary process. Levin, *supra* note 54, at 6–7. For the inadequacies of the studies, see *id*.

We do not lack for reform proposals. One cluster of strategies would attempt to make disciplinary processes more visible, proactive, and effective. The jurisdiction of disciplinary agencies should be broadened to include concerns of neglect, negligence, and fees, and resources should be increased to ensure adequate investigation and remedial responses, including client compensation. Rather than relying almost exclusively on client complaints (supplemented by felony convictions), regulatory officials should initiate investigations based on malpractice filings, judicial sanctions, and random audits of trust funds. More should be done to publicize the complaint process, to assist individuals in filing grievances, and to develop effective alternative dispute proceedings. Expert panels could be available to give clients a second opinion on the reasonableness of proposed fees or business dealings with attorneys.[58] Lawyers should be required to carry malpractice insurance. Support services and diversion programs for lawyers with mental health, substance abuse, office management and short-term financial difficulties should help these practitioners establish an appropriate remedial plan and supervise their compliance.[59] More efforts should also be made to track the effectiveness of these programs and to deal with recidivists.

A second set of reforms could focus on increasing public knowledge. Lawyers should be required to provide information to clients concerning their disciplinary and malpractice records, as well as information about clients' rights and remedies.[60] Centralized data banks and toll-free hotlines should provide information about judicial sanctions, disciplinary actions, and malpractice judgments. Useful models could be the online clearinghouses for physicians required in about half the states. These clearinghouses include information such as education, practice area, professional affiliations, criminal convictions, disciplinary sanctions, malpractice actions, and liability insurance. Four-fifths of surveyed Americans express a desire for such a resource concerning lawyers, and the nation's single commercial provider that has begun offering some of this information does not meet the need.[61]

Attorneys object to these data banks on the grounds that potential clients may attach undue importance to partial information or to minor transgressions, and that the reputations of practitioners would be unjustly impaired. However, no evidence for that claim has been forthcoming, and minor indiscretions rarely trigger public disciplinary action or malpractice judgments. In other comparable contexts, Americans' preferred response to incomplete information has been to encourage

[58] Abel, *supra* note 45, at 514–516.

[59] *Id.* at 514; Rhode, *supra* note 53, at 163–64; Diane M. Ellis, A *Decade of Diversion: Empirical Evidence that Alternative Discipline Is Working for Arizona Lawyers*, 52 Emory L. J. 1221 (2002).

[60] Abel, *supra* note 45, at 514; Rhode, *supra* note 53, at 163–64.

[61] Steven K. Berenson, *Is It Time for Lawyer Profiles?*, 70 Fordham L. Rev. 645, 651–57, 680 (2001). For these and other reforms, see Rhode, *supra* note 53, at 163–64.

more rather than less, and regulation of the legal profession should be no exception. Databases can include background materials that would help consumers put profiles of particular lawyers in appropriate context. Moreover, by identifying practitioners with good records and adequate malpractice insurance, such clearinghouses would create additional incentives for appropriate conduct.

Another strategy for increasing accountability is to make disciplinary complaints public if the agency finds probable cause for investigation. Although lawyers have generally opposed this proposal on the ground that disclosure of unfounded complaints would unjustly prejudice their reputations, no evidence has demonstrated those harms in the minority of states with open processes. If civil complaints and police arrests are matters of public record, it is not clear why grievances against lawyers should be subject to special protection.[62] Because consumer surveys find deep suspicion about closed-door proceedings, even the ABA's own disciplinary commission has recommended public disclosure of complaints.[63]

Yet that recommendation, like the other reform proposals, has met with strong opposition from the bar's rank and file, and with indifference from state supreme courts, which have asserted inherent power to control the regulation of the profession. The central challenge is how to overcome those obstacles to change. On that point, most academic critics remain silent. For instance, Abel's 2008 study offers a sensible agenda for modifying bar disciplinary processes, and then concludes with a question: "Can the profession muster the political will to reform?"[64]

If history is any guide, the answer is not promising. Much of the progress that has occurred in professional regulation over the last several decades, both in the United States and elsewhere, has been the product of external intervention, not internal initiatives. In the United States, many of those initiatives have supplemented or supplanted bar disciplinary oversight through legislative or agency rulemaking. For example, lawyers' complicity in some of the major financial scandals of the early twenty-first century led Congress to require – over the ABA's vehement objections – that counsel make internal reports of potential fraud to corporate leadership.[65] Other federal and state agencies have imposed ethical standards beyond what bar rules require, prosecutors have brought criminal proceedings where disciplinary authorities have failed to act, and insurance companies have insisted on additional ethics-related

[62] Levin, *supra* note 54, at 22–23

[63] Am. Bar Ass'n Commission on Evaluation of Disciplinary Enforcement, Lawyer Regulation for a New Century (1992); Levin, *supra* note 54.

[64] Abel, *supra* note 45, at 528.

[65] *See* Deborah L. Rhode & Paul Paton, *Lawyers, Enron and Ethics*, *in* Enron: Corporate Fiascos and their Implications 625, 628 (Nancy Rappaport & Bala G. Dharan eds., 2004); *see also* Susan P. Koniak, *When the Hurly Burly's Done: The Bar's Struggle with the SEC*, 103 Colum. L. Rev. 1236 (2003); Fred C. Zacharias, *The Myth of Self Regulation*, 93 Minn. L. Rev. 1147, 1170, n.109.

safeguards as a condition of malpractice coverage.[66] As John Leubsdorf summarizes the trend: "more and more regulators have sought to regulate the bar … and have become increasingly unwilling to defer to either bar associations or courts."[67]

Other countries with similar legal systems have moved in the same direction. Some have established co-regulatory structures in which the bar shares authority with more publicly accountable entities. England has an independent Legal Services Board, chaired by a lay person, which has oversight over an Office for Legal Complaints, also headed by a lay Chair. The Office has broad power to ensure effective responses to individual complaints, including compensation for injuries resulting from professional misconduct.[68] In Australia, widely publicized scandals also helped prompt some state governments to create more consumer-oriented regulatory processes. The New South Wales Independent Legal Services Commissioner receives all complaints about a lawyer and refers them either to consumer-oriented mediation or to the bar's own regulatory bodies. Complainants who are unsatisfied with the results may seek review by the Commissioner, who has the power to substitute a new decision. The Commissioner also oversees the process for handling complaints and may take over a particular investigation or recommend more general changes.[69] Queensland, Australia has an independent Legal Services Commission headed by a nonlawyer. Its disciplinary system includes a Client Relations Center, which resolves minor disputes, and a Legal Practice Tribunal, composed of a Supreme Court Justice, one nonlawyer, and one practitioner. Problems of competence and diligence can be subjects for discipline, and all disciplinary actions are published on the Legal Service Commission website.[70]

Similar reform proposals in this country have bumped up against several obstacles. The first is that state supreme courts have claimed inherent authority to regulate the

[66] Anthony Davis, *Professional Liability Insurers as Regulators of Law Practice*, 65 FORDHAM L. REV. 209 (1996) (noting role of insurance companies in mandating risk management practices as a condition of malpractice coverage); Bruce A. Green, *The Criminal Regulation of Lawyers*, 67 FORDHAM L. REV. 327 (1998) (noting role of criminal prosecutions in lawyer regulation); Paul F. Rothstein, *"Anything You Say May be Used Against You": A Proposed Seminar on the Lawyer's Duty to Warn of Confidentiality's Limits in Today's Post-Enron World*, 76 FORDHAM L. REV. 1745, 1749 n.16 (2007) (noting increased trend toward criminal prosecutions of lawyers in connection with clients' crimes); Zacharias, *supra* note 65, at 1169–70 (discussing agency rules and criminal prosecutions).

[67] John Leubsdorf, *Legal Ethics Falls Apart*, 57 BUFF. L. REV. 959, 961 (2008).

[68] *See* Judith L. Maute, *Revolutionary Changes to the English Legal Profession or Much Ado about Nothing?*, 17 PROF. LAW. 1, 8–9 (2006); Richard Parnham, *The Clementi Reforms in a European Context: Are the Proposals Really That Radical?*, 8 LEGAL ETHICS 194, 199 (2005).

[69] DAVID NICOLSON & JULIAN WEBB, PROFESSIONAL LEGAL ETHICS 86 (1999); CHRISTINE PARKER & ADRIAN EVANS, INSIDE LAWYER'S ETHICS 54–55 (2007); Deborah L. Rhode, *In the Interests of Justice: A Comparative Perspective on Access to Legal Services and Accountability of the Legal Profession*, 56 CURRENT LEGAL PROBS. 93 (2003).

[70] Legal Profession Act of 2007; *see also* PARKER & EVANS, *supra* note 69, at 56; Leslie C. Levin, *Building a Better Lawyer Discipline System: The Queensland Experience*, 9 LEGAL ETHICS 187, 193–94 (2006).

profession but have insufficient time, incentives, or capacity to exercise that authority effectively. Most justices face crushing caseloads and have neither the resources nor expertise to construct adequate oversight processes.[71] Nor do they have much reason to challenge the organized bar on matters that hold great importance for lawyers but are not priorities for the general public. Judges share the background and world view of those they claim to regulate. As social theorists note, a group's distinctive norms, thought patterns, and behaviors construct an institutional identity that shapes decision making.[72] Moreover, most state judges are elected and depend on lawyers for endorsements, rankings, and campaign contributions.[73] Even in states where judges are selected through merit processes, state and local bars exercise substantial influence.[74] The judiciary is also dependent on support from the organized bar concerning salaries and budgets, and is readily accessible to lawyer lobbying at conferences, annual meetings, and social gatherings.[75] By contrast, consumer activists rarely have such opportunities for influence.

A second obstacle to reform involves voters' lack of information concerning the judiciary's role in regulating the profession and the absence of organized interest groups that could make such issues relevant in judicial elections.[76] HALT, the only national consumer organization that focuses on reforming the legal profession, has only about 50,000 members; its resources and influence pale in comparison to state, local, and national bar associations.[77] Part of the problem is that clients and third parties who are most vulnerable to lawyers' misconduct also lack the resources and incentives to mobilize around the issue. Most are "one shot" players who use lawyers episodically, and seldom the same one twice. Although only about a third of Americans believe that the bar does a good job disciplining lawyers, few have sufficient reasons to do anything about it.[78]

[71] Benjamin H. Barton, *An Institutional Analysis of Lawyer Regulation: Who Should Control Lawyer Regulation – Courts, Legislatures, or the Market?*, 37 GEO. L. REV. 1167, 1204, 1207 (2003).

[72] WENDELL GORDON, INSTITUTIONAL ECONOMICS (1980). For the influence of legal training and experience on judicial goals and thought processes, see LAURENCE BAUM, THE PUZZLE OF JUDICIAL BEHAVIOR 33–34 (1997). For application of such theories to regulation of the legal profession, see Barton, *supra* note 71, at 1176; Benjamin H. Barton, *Do Judges Systematically Favor the Interests of the Legal Profession?*, 59 ALA. L. REV. 453, 456, 459 (2008).

[73] Barton, *supra* note 71, at 1186, 1195; Barton, *supra* note 72, at 458.

[74] Kelly Armitage, *Denial Ain't Just a River in Egypt: A Thorough Review of Judicial Elections, Merit Selection and the Role of State Judges in Society*, 29 CAP. U. L. REV. 625, 656 (2002); Barton, *supra* note 71, at 1199.

[75] Barton, *supra* note 72, at 458; Barton, *supra* note 71, at 1200.

[76] Barton, *supra* note 71, at 1203.

[77] *See* HALT, http//:www.halt.org. The American Bar Association alone has about 369,000 members. *See* AM. BAR ASS'N, MONTHLY REPORT, *available at* http://www.abanet.org/leadership/executivedirector/reports/monthly_progar_report_june_2009.pdf.

[78] AM. BAR ASS'N., PERCEPTIONS OF THE U.S. JUSTICE SYSTEM 77 (1999); RHODE, *supra* note 53, at 158.

In other reform contexts, the constituency that has been most effective in mobilizing consumers or representing their interests on regulatory issues has been public interest lawyers. But the success of such efforts often depends on financial support and pro bono contributions from the private bar.[79] Such assistance is hard to come by on issues that put the bar's own interests at risk.[80] In this political climate, there appears little chance of mustering the necessary support for state constitutional amendments that would replace the judiciary's inherent regulatory authority with a more publicly accountable structure.

Yet to acknowledge the obstacles to significant structural reform is not to abandon all hope for progress. Many leaders of the profession would like to see the oversight system function more effectively. They might readily respond to external pressures for change, or to opportunities for collaborative partnerships that might create such pressures. These partnerships could bring together a broad base of stakeholders including state supreme court justices, heads of consumer and bar organizations, government regulators, disciplinary officials, and legal scholars.[81] Academics who specialize in the field could do more to help launch such collaborations and to educate students and the public about the need for reforms. More scholarship could also focus on the performance of the disciplinary system and on the effectiveness of alternative models from other nations and other professions.

CONCLUSION

In his celebrated 1934 address on the "Public Influence of the Bar," U.S. Supreme Court Justice Harlan Stone noted that legal academics were the segment of the profession "most detached" from pressures that had compromised the social responsibilities of the profession.[82] With that position came unique opportunities for disinterested analysis of the "bar as an institution … [including] the performance of its public functions and … [the] ways of stimulating a more adequate performance. …"[83] The need for such analysis is no less urgent today. Collections like this one underscore the importance of scholarship in the spirit of Wallace Stevens' *The Man with the Blue Guitar*: "I cannot make the world quite round/I patch it as I can."

[79] *See* Rhode, *supra* note 23.

[80] The only public interest legal organization that has been significantly involved in reforming the legal profession is Public Citizen, and the resources it has been able to devote to the issue are extremely limited. Its total budget is only $13 million, its legal staff is only fifteen, and lawyer regulation is only one of its issues. *Id.* at 2094.

[81] For a similar proposal, see Susan Sturm, *Constructing the Practices of Accountability and Professionalism: A Comment on* The Interests of Justice, 70 Fordham L. Rev. 1903, 1910 (2002).

[82] Harlan F. Stone, *The Public Influence of the Bar*, 48 Harv. L. Rev. 1, 11 (1934).

[83] *Id.*

9

An Innovative Approach to Legal Education
The Founding of the University of California, Irvine, School of Law

Carrie Hempel and Carroll Seron

INTRODUCTION

Legal practice requires credentialed expertise, hands-on skill in working with clients, and appreciation of the special responsibilities society grants to professionals. For the better part of the twentieth century, there has been an informal division of labor between law schools, which are in the business of credentialing knowledge, and first employers responsible for passing on the skills of day-to-day practice. Along the way, through both formal and informal channels, professionals are socialized to take seriously their special responsibilities to society.

Beginning in the 1960s, this informal division of labor between the tasks of credentialing, apprenticing, and developing professional identity began to shift as law schools played a more prominent role in passing on the skills of practice and teaching legal ethics. The demands for reform often came from stakeholders outside the legal academy, including elite leaders of the bar and, during the 1960s, students themselves. But, we argue, the basic assumptions of this informal architecture have remained in place; we have seen tinkering around the edges of legal education but relatively little fundamental change.

With the recent publication by the Carnegie Foundation of *Educating Lawyers: Preparation for the Profession of Law*, there is yet again a call for reform.[1] In many respects, the Carnegie Report draws similar conclusions to earlier reports

We thank the faculty who shared their experiences of teaching at the UCI School of Law: Mario Barnes, Jennifer Chacon, Catherine Fisk, Trina Jones, Stephen Lee, Christopher Leslie, and Ann Southworth. We thank Dean Erwin Chemerinksy for agreeing to be interviewed for this work and for providing thoughtful feedback on earlier drafts. Rick Abel and Scott Cummings each raised important questions, for which we are most appreciative. Finally, we thank Kevin Chicas for his valuable research assistance, and Laura Fry who came to our rescue to clean up our citations and to edit the text.

1 William M. Sullivan, Anne Colby, Judith Welch Wegner, Lloyd Bond & Lee S. Shulman, Educating Lawyers: Preparation for the Profession of Law (The Carnegie Foundation for the Advancement of Teaching 2007) [hereinafter the Carnegie Report].

that resulted in very little meaningful change in legal education. What sets this call for reform apart from earlier efforts – or at least provides a wedge issue that has the potential to develop a "new" division of labor – is the call for what we term an *integrated* approach to legal education, or one that gives *equal* space *within* the legal academy to credentialing expertise, hands-on practice, and the development of professional identity. The Carnegie Report coincides with the opening of a new law school at the University of California, Irvine (hereinafter UCI or the Law School). In many respects, the design of the curriculum at this new law school echoes the framework proposed in the Carnegie Report – one where the faculty as a whole will take seriously the responsibility to teach and prepare students with the requisite legal expertise, hands-on skills, and professional identity to enjoy meaningful careers across a variety of occupations of law.

Despite the fact that the Law School begins with a clean slate, it nonetheless faces institutional pressures to conform with the standard operating procedures of legal education, especially those of the elite tier of law schools where UCI aspires to be.[2] Among those pressures, the institutionalization of a full-time professoriate that has come to enjoy both independence and a fair amount of control over academic curriculum predominates.[3] Perhaps unwittingly, this institutionalization also has contributed to the second-class status of both clinical education and the teaching of professional responsibility.[4]

[2] Other law schools have certainly attempted to develop an alternative framework for legal education including, specifically, a commitment to experiential learning. Among these schools, two are particularly noteworthy: the City University of New York (CUNY) School of Law and Northeastern School of Law. At the CUNY School of Law, first-year law students are required to take a two-semester course called a "lawyering seminar." As the Carnegie Report explains, "What is distinctive about the CUNY seminars is that they are part of the school's requirement over a three-year curriculum of lawyering whose aim is to integrate the students' learning of the skills of practice and the ethical demands of professional identity with the more typical courses in civil and criminal procedure, contracts, torts, and so forth. Each lawyering seminar is linked to a 'doctrinal' or substantive course, and both are taught by the same instructor." *Id.* at 35. Since 1968, the Northeastern School of Law has incorporated a "co-op" program into its curriculum. During the first year, students are required to complete a traditional curriculum, including Civil Procedure, Constitutional Law, Contracts, Criminal Justice, Property, Torts, and a "signature" first-year course entitled Legal Skills in Context. In the fall semester, the Legal Skills course introduces students to legal research and writing with client representation and oral skills; in the spring semester, students learn how to prepare a brief and present oral arguments while working in a law office to "execute a social justice project – an extensive real-world legal research project on behalf of a community-based or public service organization." After the first year, students alternate semesters between full-time placements in practice settings, ranging from law firms to government agencies to NGOs in the United States and abroad, and coursework on campus. By graduation, each student completes four full-time internships. Northeastern University School of Law, http://www.northeastern.edu/ law/co-op/index.html (last visited Jan. 5, 2010).

[3] Robert Stevens, Law School: Legal Education in America from the 1850s to the 1990s 38–42 (1983).

[4] On clinical education, see The Carnegie Report, *supra* note 1, at 89–91. On professional responsibility, see Russell G. Pearce, *Teaching Ethics Seriously: Legal Ethics as the Most Important Subject in*

To appreciate the integrated architecture that UCI has begun to develop, as well as the challenges it faces, this chapter proceeds as follows. In the first part, we elaborate on the institutionalization of an informal division of labor between legal education and apprenticeship. We then examine reform efforts to bring clinical education and professional responsibility under the umbrella of the law school curriculum, and briefly summarize the essential reforms outlined by the Carnegie Foundation. Next, we describe UCI's proposed pedagogy for teaching professional identity and practice skills through its Legal Profession course and clinical education requirement. We conclude by considering the challenges that UCI faces to institutionalize a new, or at least a reformed, model of legal education among its elite peers.

MODERN LEGAL EDUCATION AND THE EMERGENCE OF A FULL-TIME PROFESSORIATE OF LAW

Across a variety of worksites, sociologists have demonstrated that professional work requires both technical expertise and hands-on apprenticeship.[5] A large body of research suggests that with time in the field and specialization in an area of practice, whether antitrust or divorce, lawyers develop a tacit knowledge about how to hear clients' stories, gain their trust, and represent them effectively.[6] For the better part of the twentieth century, learning the skills of lawyering has been marked by an informal division of labor: Professional schools focus on the cultivation of analytical thinking, or what is commonly referred to as "learning to think like a lawyer," and the first years of practice focus on the acquisition of the hands-on skills of working with clients and learning the day-to-day ropes.[7] This informal division of labor plays out in different ways depending on lawyers' credentials and aspirations. For example, for young lawyers from prestigious schools who are destined for careers in large firms, elite government agencies, or corporations, mentorship often takes place at

Law School, 29 Loy. U. Chi. L.J. 719, 719–22 (1998), and Deborah L. Rhode, *Ethics by the Pervasive Method*, 42 J. Legal Educ. 31, 33–42 (1992).

5 Andrew Abbott, The System of the Professions: An Essay on the Division of Expert Labor 33–59 (1988); Eliot Friedson, Professional Powers: A Study of Institutionalization of Social Knowledge 20–41 (1986); Robert Nelson, Partners With Power: The Social Transformation of the Large Law Firm 159–89 (1988); Everett Hughes, *Dilemmas and Contradictions of Status*, 50 Am. J. Soc. Knowledge 353 (1945).

6 On lawyers in large firms, see Nelson, *supra* note 5, at 205–31. On solo and small firm attorneys, see Austin Sarat & William L.F. Felstiner, Divorce Lawyers and Their Clients: Power and Meaning in the Legal Process 26–106 (1995); Carroll Seron, The Business of Practicing Law: The Work Lives of Solo and Small Firm Attorneys 1–19 (1996).

7 David Wilkins & Mitu Gulati, *Why Are There So Few Black Lawyers in Corporate Law Firms? An Institutional Analysis*, 84 Cal. L. Rev. 493, 524–30, 537–42 (1996).

one's first job, usually at a large firm.[8] Lawyers with credentials that gear them toward a career in solo or small-firm practice are likely to acquire hands-on skills at a first job working for a small firm or a government agency such as the District Attorney's office.[9] Indeed, research across a variety of legal practice sites suggests that whatever the career trajectory, newly minted practitioners view their first job as a transitional apprenticeship. Today's formal education in the law is a three-year program of graduate study at an accredited law school in preparation for a bar examination and admission to practice, but informal professional socialization is actually longer and includes the first few years of practice.

This informal division of labor between technical and hands-on education evolved during the first half of the twentieth century in reaction to the laissez-faire environment and Jacksonian ethos of legal education in the late nineteenth century.[10] The story begins with the development of the Socratic method of teaching at Harvard Law School in the late nineteenth century during the tenure of Christopher Columbus Langdell. Harvard is important not only because it set the standard of legal education as a three-year course of graduate study in appellate case law taught by a full-time professoriate, but also because it became the model adopted by aspiring schools at both public and private universities. Substantively, Langdell's approach to legal education borrowed from the era's fascination with scientific method; in his well-known words,

[8] The classic description of mentoring in large firms during the "golden years" is captured in Erwin Smigel's classic, THE WALL STREET LAWYER: PROFESSIONAL ORGANIZATION MAN? (1969). As the profession became more diverse by way of race, ethnicity, and gender, the limitations of this mentoring process became apparent. Wilkins and Gulati present a very thoughtful analysis of the pitfalls of relying on an informal and subjective mentoring process for associates. They suggest that whether and to what extent new recruits are actually mentored depends on informal, subjective dynamics that run the risk of being systematically more effective for more "traditional" recruits, i.e., white men. *See* Wilkins and Gulati, *supra* note 8; *see also* CYNTHIA FUCHS EPSTEIN, WOMEN IN LAW (1983); MARC GALANTER & THOMAS PALAY, TOURNAMENT OF LAWYERS: THE TRANSFORMATION OF THE BIG FIRM (1991); JOHN P. HEINZ & EDWARD O. LAUMANN, CHICAGO LAWYERS: THE SOCIAL STRUCTURE OF THE BAR 137–58 (1982); JOHN P. HEINZ, ROBERT L. NELSON & REBECCA SANDEFUR, URBAN LAWYERS: THE NEW SOCIAL STRUCTURE OF THE BAR (2005); Bryant Garth & Joyce Wilkins, *Exploring the Inequality in the Corporate Law Firm Apprenticeship: Doing the Time, Finding the Love*, 22 GEO. J. LEGAL ETHICS 1361(2009) .

[9] In his classic study of solo lawyers, Jerome Carlin describes the haphazard ways in which these attorneys learn the craft of hands-on work through observation and a lot of trial and error. JEROME CARLIN, LAWYERS ON THEIR OWN 3–41 (1962). Evidence suggests that this theme persists, as suggested by more recent studies. *See* SERON, *supra* note 6; Leslie Levin, *Guardians at the Gate: The Backgrounds, Career Paths, and Professional Development of Private US Immigration Lawyers*, 34 LAW & SOC. INQUIRY 399 (2009).

[10] In his fascinating history of the American law school, Stevens demonstrates that the goal was standardization of legal education through accreditation, but its success has been less than complete, particularly when comparing elite law schools to regional and local ones. STEVENS, *supra* note 3; *see also* RANDALL COLLINS, THE CREDENTIAL SOCIETY 131–82 (1979); STEVEN J. DINER, A VERY DIFFERENT AGE: AMERICANS OF THE PROGRESSIVE ERA 183–88 (1998); MAGALI SARFATTI LARSON, THE RISE OF PROFESSIONALISM: A SOCIOLOGICAL ANALYSIS (1977).

Langdell argued that "we have also constantly inculcated the idea that the library is the proper workshop of [law] professors and students alike; that it is to us all that the laboratories of the universities are to the chemists and physicists, the museum of natural history to the zoologists, the botanical garden to the botanists."[11] Despite its criticisms and challenges, the case method, with some modification, continues to hold sway as an "unparalleled method for training students to be lawyers."[12]

In addition to its full-time teaching responsibilities, the law professoriate anchored its gatekeeping role through scholarship. Reflecting the values of the modern, research university, legal scholars again borrowed from the era's fascination with science and, consequently, eschewed concern about values, ethics, and other "soft" issues such as what it means to be a lawyer.[13] Like all professional schools housed in a university (medicine, engineering, architecture, and business), there is an inherent tension between the commitment to prepare practitioners and the demands of the research university. Beginning in the early twentieth century, the law professoriate published its research in student-managed law reviews – a convenient relationship for faculty and student editors looking to fill their issues. The legal academy, like all intellectual communities, has gone through various fads and trends in its scholarly pursuits over the course of the twentieth century.[14] But whether the fad is legal realism in the early part of the twentieth century or critical legal studies or law and economics in the later part of it, the assumptions, tone, and style of research are directed toward an audience of academic peers both within the legal academy and, to some extent, the broader disciplines. The institutionalization of a full-time professoriate housed in complex, research-oriented universities has left a strong imprint on the orientations, values, and concerns of the faculty to preserve their independence and to remain somewhat aloof from teaching the materials required of daily legal practice.

As Stevens' careful history shows, the institutionalization of legal education (including the requirement of an undergraduate degree, a three-year course of graduate study taught by a full-time professoriate,[15] accreditation of law schools by the American Bar Association (ABA), membership in the American Association of Law Schools (AALS), and bar examination by the respective states) unfolded with fits and starts, amidst debate and contestation among deans (at elite, aspiring, and

11 STEVENS, *supra* note 3, at 146.

12 *Id.* The "trump card" of the Langdellian model of legal education, as Stevens notes, is "finance," that is, the case method is "cheaper" because it assumes large classes. *Id.* at 148–149.

13 *See* Pearce, *supra* note 4, at 729; *see also* BURTON J. BLEDSTEIN, THE CULTURE OF PROFESSIONALISM: THE MIDDLE CLASS AND THE DEVELOPMENT OF HIGHER EDUCATION 84–85 (1976); DOROTHY ROSS, THE ORIGINS OF AMERICAN SOCIAL SCIENCE 390–471 (1991).

14 *See* STEVENS, *supra* note 3.

15 For a fascinating history of the efforts to maintain a full-time faculty in the early years, see Bruce A. Kimball, *The Principle, Politics, and Financing of Introducing Academic Merit as the Standard for Hiring for 'the teaching of law as a career,' 1870–1900*, 31 LAW & SOC. INQUIRY 617 (2006).

proprietary law schools), legislators, and bar leaders. For our purposes, a particularly important theme is the way in which those trained at elite institutions – first Harvard, followed by Yale and Columbia – became key stakeholders in the new professionalism as they joined the faculties of aspiring law schools such as Stanford, Michigan, Berkeley, Northwestern, or Iowa. For example, as Michigan sought to secure legitimacy as a premier institution, one easy and obvious step was to recruit faculty with the right pedigree – Harvard law graduates. The movement to hire at least a portion of faculty for full-time positions from elite law schools was critical for ensuring legitimacy and, perhaps not surprisingly, had the serendipitous effect of solidifying and homogenizing the curriculum around an analytical focus on learning law through cases. This move toward standardization began in the 1880s and was more or less in place by 1940.[16]

Beginning in the latter half of the twentieth century, we see a change in the credentials of full-time faculty: from law degrees from elite schools (often capped by service on law review and a prestigious clerkship) to law degrees and a Ph.D. in an academic discipline. The trend toward joint degrees began in the 1960s with support from the Russell Sage Foundation, which supported a number of centers around the country dedicated to the study of "law and society," including those at the University of California, Berkeley, the University of Wisconsin, Northwestern University, and the University of Denver. In addition, Russell Sage provided support for graduate students to enroll in joint degree programs in law and various social science disciplines, including sociology, psychology, anthropology, history, political science, and economics. Although joint-degree programs remain relatively small in absolute number, they have played an important, if unintended, role in further institutionalizing the orientations, interests, and concerns of full-time faculty around scholarship.[17]

THE ROLE OF PROFESSIONAL IDENTITY AND CLINICAL EDUCATION COURSES IN TWENTIETH-CENTURY LEGAL EDUCATION

The Harvardization of legal education as a self-contained experience housed in the academy did not unfold without dissent.[18] One of the ironies of this story, Stevens points out, is that the emergence of the Wall Street firm (the Cravath system) and

[16] STEVENS, *supra* note 3, at 205–16. As Stevens goes on to explain, there were still states that allowed law schools to operate without accreditation through the early years after World War II. *Id.* at 205–28.

[17] Based on data collected by Scott Cummings, as of 2009, the top 20 law schools had 183 junior ladder-track (nonclinical) faculty; among those faculty, 16 had earned a Ph.D. and 73 had earned some type of a Master's degree.

[18] Not all legal academics were comfortable with the Langdellian model. For example, Jerome Frank, in his 1933 article, *Why Not a Clinical Lawyer School?*, 81 U. PA. L. REV. 907, expressed early and eloquent dissent.

the shift in elite practice from a focus on litigation to one of advice to industrial corporations takes place just as law schools organize legal education around appellate case law.[19] Among graduates slated for practice in less august settings, where the work often involves solving relatively predictable legal problems, the focus on learning through appellate case law is perhaps even more off kilter.[20] From its inception, then, the adoption of the case method of legal education created a mismatch between legal education and legal practice – at least from the vantage point of the lawyers themselves – which generated a powerful critique (and calls for reform) from the bar that echoed across the legal profession. The central thrust of this critique is that law school does not prepare its students for the actual practice of law.

Against this backdrop, we focus on two facets of this critique from the bar and, eventually, from law students themselves: the need to inculcate students with the proper attributes of their calling through an emphasis on professional responsibility, and the importance of incorporating the actual practice of law into legal education.

The Cultivation of a Professional Identity and the Teaching of Legal Ethics

In the early twentieth century, the concept of professional ethics existed in tension with the evolving model of legal education. Even though members of the emergent, full-time professoriate did participate in the development of a canon of professional responsibility, they resisted pressures from the bar to incorporate the teaching of legal ethics into the curriculum. Part of the professoriate's resistance to teaching professional ethics may have come from a concern that such questions were "soft," but an equally compelling factor was their desire to establish themselves as the specialized gatekeepers of the curriculum, which meant holding the bar's demands in check.[21]

In the wake of the medical profession's promulgation of a revised code of professional ethics in 1903, leaders of the bar felt some pressure to follow suit and appointed committees to draft a code of professional ethics.[22] At its 1906 annual meeting, the ABA's Committee on a Code of Professional Ethics presented its report

19 Stevens, *supra* note 3, at 9; *see also* Jerold L. Auerbach, Unequal Justice: Lawyers and Social Change in Modern America (1976); C. Wright Mills, White Collar: The American Middle Class 121–29 (1953).

20 For this and other reasons, Alfred Z. Reed, in his 1921 report to The Carnegie Foundation for the Advancement of Teaching, proposed that lawyers should be trained in different ways, depending on whether they planned to practice in corporate or individual-client settings. Alfred Z. Reed, *Training for the Public Profession of Law*, Carnegie Bulletin No. 15 (1921).

21 Susan D. Carle, *Lawyers' Duty to Do Justice: A New Look at the History of the 1908 Canons*, 24 Law & Soc. Inquiry 1, 27–29 (1999). Accreditation requires that a proportion of the faculty teach on a full-time basis; law schools have long filled in the teaching ranks with part-time practitioners. Our point here is that full-time faculty are the keepers of what constitutes a "proper" education in the law.

22 *Id.* at 7.

and "stressed the need for clear, uniform rules that could be used to discipline unethical lawyers of low character who were joining the ranks at an alarming pace."[23] The ABA's adoption of the Canons of Professional Ethics in 1908 was part of the larger professionalization project at the turn of the century: Codes of ethics were designed to institutionalize the distinction between a professional calling and other occupations, and further, to legitimate the profession's authority to self-regulate and discipline its peers.[24] Before the ink was dry on the Canons, there were criticisms and calls for further revision. Criticisms ranged from claims that the Canons were unnecessarily vague to concerns that they did not provide the concrete guidance necessary to discipline lawyers. Indeed, promulgation, debate, adoption, and criticism of this and subsequent codes become a common feature of bar politics.

Three high water marks of legal ethics reform coincide with broader watersheds in American society. The Canons were codified in the Progressive Era as the profession responded with concern to an influx of immigrants and the perception that a "high calling" would be reduced to the "level of a trade."[25] During the Great Depression of the 1930s and the left-leaning politics of that era, bar leaders remained suspicious of lawyers who did not share their background and were concerned that too many lawyers were being admitted to practice without the requisite commitment to a shared code of ethics.[26]

By the late 1960s, bar leaders reached a consensus that a "'gentleman's code' enforced by the sanction of shame" was no longer adequate.[27] At least three important events focused this concern: First, there was a significant increase in the size of the profession due to the expansion of law schools;[28] second, there were incipient

[23] Paul T. Hayden, *Putting Ethics to the (National Standardized) Test: Tracing the Origins of the MPRE*, 71 Fordham L. Rev. 1299, 1307 (2002–2003).

[24] Based on her analysis of newly discovered documents, Carle, *supra* note 21, at 32, shows that there was significantly more debate about the form that the Canons of Professional Ethics should take than is often acknowledged. In her careful review of these documents and the biographies of key stakeholders in the debate, she shows that on just one issue, lawyers' duty to do justice, there was a great deal of debate about whether and to what extent lawyers have a responsibility to certify to the court, among other things, that their clients' claims are just. As she concludes, "the standard assumption that the development of our legal ethics rules proceeded in a relatively harmonious fashion until our present more contentious period thus bears reexamination." *Id.*; *see also* Abbott, *supra* note 5, at 86–115; Freidson, *supra* note 5; Larson, *supra* note 10. For our purposes, however, the point to keep in mind is that bar leaders advocated that the Canons be taught as part of a student's legal education.

[25] Hayden, *supra* note 23 at 1307.

[26] *Id.* at 1310; *see also* Carle, *supra* note 21; Rayman L. Solomon, *Five Crises or One: The Concept of Legal Professionalism, 1925–1960, in* Lawyers' Ideals/Lawyers' Practices: Transformations in the American Legal Profession 144 (Robert L. Nelson, David M. Trubek & Rayman L. Solomon, eds. 1992).

[27] Rhode, *supra* note 4; Pearce, *supra* note 4; Roger C. Cramton & Susan P. Koniak, W.M. *Keck Foundation Forum on the Teaching of Legal Ethics: Rule, Story, and Commitment in the Teaching of Legal Ethics*, 38 Wm. & Mary L. Rev. 145 (1996).

[28] In academic year 1963–1964, there were 135 accredited law schools with an enrollment of 49,552 students; by academic year 1974–1975, the number of accredited law schools had grown to 157 and

changes in the gender, racial, and ethnic composition of the profession;[29] and, third, there was a significant (albeit temporary) move leftward among young lawyers, particularly at elite institutions.[30] Together, these events – along with the protest movement against the Vietnam War – challenged the values, assumptions, and orientations of the traditional elite of the bar. This challenge crystallized around the Watergate scandal, which prompted outrage that so many of the key players were in fact lawyers. Whether Watergate "caused" the adoption of a stronger professional code, or was simply the event that tipped the scale, is not clear. Change was already underway, but accelerated in the wake of the scandal. In 1970, the ABA had adopted a new code that included "Disciplinary Rules, albeit also retaining (in the Ethical Considerations) the fraternal voice of the Canons."[31] Then, in the midst of Watergate, the ABA adopted Standard 302(1), which required that all accredited law schools provide "instruction in the duties and responsibilities of the legal profession" as well as "training in professional skills, such as counseling, the drafting of legal documents and materials, and trial and appellate advocacy."[32] Soon thereafter, the bar instituted a new standardized, multiple-choice ethics exam as part of the bar: Beginning in 1980, prospective lawyers were required to sit for the Multistate Professional Responsibility Exam (MPRE), a national exam on legal ethics, in order to qualify for the bar.

However, in their quest to modify the law-school curriculum to include courses in legal ethics (culminating in the MPRE), the leaders of the bar may have won

the enrollment of students had more than doubled to 110,713. *See* Am. Bar Ass'n, Legal Education Statistics, http://www.abanet.org/legaled/statistics/stats.html.

29 Richard L. Abel, American Lawyers 74–112 (1989); Robert L. Nelson, *The Futures of American Lawyers: A Demographic Profile of a Changing Profession in a Changing Society*, 44 Case W. Res. L. Rev. 345, 359–67 (1993–1994).

30 Stevens, *supra* note 3, at 234; *see also* Michael J. Powell, From Patrician to Professional Elite: The Transformation of the New York City Bar Association 161–65 (1988).

31 *Quoted in* Hayden, *supra* note 23, at 1311.

32 *Id.* at 1331. The current Standards in §§ 302(a) and (b)(1) substantially expand on the original language adopted, and tie professional responsibility education to clinical education:

> A law school shall require that each student receive substantial instruction in:
> (1) the substantive law generally regarded as necessary to effective and responsible participation in the legal profession;
> (2) legal analysis and reasoning, legal research, problem solving, and oral communication;
> (3) writing in legal context, including at least one rigorous writing experience in the first year and at least one additional rigorous writing experience after the first year;
> (4) other professional skills generally regarded as necessary for effective and responsible participation in the legal profession; and
> (5) the history, goals, structure, values, rules and responsibilities of the legal profession and its members.
>
> (b) A law school shall offer substantial opportunities for:
> (1) live-client or other real-life practice experiences, appropriately supervised and designed to encourage reflection by students on their experiences and on the values and responsibilities of the legal profession, and the development of one's ability to assess his or her performance and level of competence...

the battle but lost the war in the transformation of legal curriculum. Although legal ethics courses became a pervasive feature of the modern law school curriculum, they were often viewed with skepticism by faculty dubious of their intellectual content and with resentment by students forced to learn their rules.[33]

Learning the Skills of Legal Practice and the Emergence of Clinical Education

The story of clinical coursework as a feature of legal education also begins in the early twentieth century and shares with legal ethics training a similarly fraught relationship to the development of the modern law school curriculum.[34] The full-time, university-based law professoriate – committed to the case method of teaching and to the production of academic scholarship – opposed efforts by law students, practice-oriented faculty, and the ABA to incorporate clinical education into the law school. But even with such sustained and ongoing resistance, clinical education increasingly played a role in educating law students, particularly in the second half of the twentieth century.

In the early 1900s, shortly after the case method emerged as the predominant form of teaching in law schools, students at a handful of schools led the first efforts to incorporate experiential learning into legal education by creating volunteer organizations that provided legal assistance to indigent persons. Some of the organizations were affiliated with existing legal aid offices, and others served as the only free legal service provider in the community.[35] A few legal scholars, particularly legal realists, applauded these student-initiated efforts to incorporate experiential learning. They argued that clinical coursework should become an integral part of every law student's education.[36]

Am. Bar Ass'n, Section of Legal Educ. and Admissions to the Bar, Standards and Rules of Procedure for Approval of Law Schools 2009–2010, 21, 22 (2008) [hereinafter 2009 ABA Standards].

33 Cramton & Koniak, *supra* note 27; Pearce, *supra* note 4; Rhode, *supra* note 4.

34 What is appropriately termed a clinical course within a law school curriculum has long been the subject of debate both within the legal academy and among those law professors who identify courses they teach as clinical. It is beyond the scope of this paper to attempt to provide an answer to this question. For purposes of this project, we define the term "clinical course" as one in which a law student, for academic credit, performs legal tasks on behalf of an actual client or clients, and is evaluated on the basis of those activities. We use the term "experiential learning" in a broader sense, to refer to any activity, whether for academic credit or not, in which a law student performs legal tasks on behalf of a real client.

35 Margaret Martin Barry, Jon C. Dubin & Peter A. Joy, *Clinical Education for this Millennium: The Third Wave*, 7 Clinical L. Rev. 1, 6 (2000–2001); John S. Bradway, *The Nature of a Legal Aid Clinic*, 3 S. Cal. L. Rev. 173, 174, 177 (1929–1930).

36 *See* Ass'n of American Law Schools, Committee on Curriculum, The Place of Skills in Legal Education (Karl Llewellyn, Chair, 1944) *published in* 48 Colum. L. Rev. 345, 346 (1944); Bradway,

During this same period, the Carnegie Foundation for the Advancement of Teaching funded a study on legal education. The resulting report identified three components necessary to prepare students to practice law: at least two years of pre-legal college education; a theoretical knowledge of the law; and practical skills training.[37] In 1921, no state yet required attendance at law school as a condition for bar admission, proprietary schools were still prevalent, and legal apprenticeship remained the sole training for many entering the profession. In the course of the next two decades, the ABA and AALS both chose to focus their reform efforts on getting their membership to adopt standards requiring college education for admission to accredited law schools.[38] Neither organization, however, made efforts to advocate a requirement for clinical skills training.[39]

Despite the lack of bar leadership on clinical education, a small number of experiential learning courses began to appear at various law schools. By the late 1950s, thirty-five ABA-approved law schools offered some kind of experiential learning opportunity. The majority of these programs were still volunteer projects for both students and faculty.[40] Only fifteen schools offered academic credit for clinical work, and only five schools had clinical courses in which professors received teaching credit.[41] During the second half of the twentieth century, however, clinical education courses increasingly appeared in law school curricula, due to three factors: the advent of substantial outside funding for clinical education programs; student demand for social relevance in legal education; and the increasing role of the ABA in promoting clinical education.[42]

Money made a difference. Beginning in 1959 and continuing until 1978, the Ford Foundation provided funding to law schools for the development of clinical programs. From 1959 to 1965, through a program administered by William Pincus, Ford provided $500,000 to nineteen law schools in intermittent grants. In 1965, it made additional grants totaling $950,000. From 1968 to 1978, Ford granted an additional $11 million to the Council on Legal Education for Professional Responsibility (CLEPR), the final name of Pincus's program. CLEPR awarded 209 grants to 107 ABA-approved law schools, totaling approximately $7 million. In 1978, the final year of the Ford grants, the federal government stepped in to provide additional funding for law school clinics. From 1978 to 1997, the Department of Education

supra note 35; Frank, *supra* note 18; William V. Rowe, *Legal Clinics and Better Trained Lawyers – A Necessity*, 11 ILL. L. REV. 591 (1916–1917).

37 STEVENS, *supra* note 3, at 172; Barry et al., *supra* note 35, at 7–8; Reed, *supra* note 20.

38 STEVENS, *supra* note 3, at 172–180.

39 Barry et al., *supra* note 35, at 8–9.

40 *Id.* at 10.

41 *Id.*

42 *Id.* at 12–21.

awarded $87 million to at least 147 law schools. Law schools around the country began creating legal clinics, and with them, an ever-increasing number of clinical teachers became full-time employees of law schools.[43]

Law students continued to play a role in the development of clinical education during this phase. According to Stevens, "Growing student demands for relevance, and the increasing sense of boredom felt by the elite law schools' carefully selected students in their second and third years, fueled the demands for clinical studies."[44]

As a response, the ABA increasingly supported the incorporation of clinical education into law school curricula. In 1969, the ABA adopted a Model Student Practice Rule that set forth requirements that, if satisfied, allowed a law student to engage in the varied aspects of legal practice, under the close supervision of an attorney. Soon after the ABA adopted this model rule, many jurisdictions that did not already have a student practice rule adopted one.[45] In 1992, The ABA McCrate Report emphasized the importance of teaching "lawyering skills and professional values by means of well-structured clinical programs."[46] In 1996, the ABA amended its accreditation standard to require, in section 302(d), that every ABA-accredited law school "offer live-client or other real-life practice experience."[47] In August 2004, the ABA deleted Section 302(d) and amended Section 302(b) to require law schools to "offer substantial opportunities for: (1) live-client or other real-life practice experiences, appropriately supervised and designed to encourage reflection by students on their experiences and on the values and responsibilities of the legal profession, and the development of one's ability to assess his or her performance and level of competence."[48] At the same time, the ABA adopted Interpretation 302–5, clarifying that "substantial opportunities" does not mean a law school must make clinical education available to everyone: "The offering of live-client or real-life experiences may be accomplished through clinics or field placements. A law school need not offer these experiences to every student nor must a law school

[43] *Id.* at 19–20; 30–31.

[44] STEVENS, *supra* note 3, at 216. For a more recent assessment of students' experience with clinical education, see Rebecca Sandefur & Jeffrey Selbin, *"The Clinic Effect"* 16 CLINICAL L. REV. 1001 (2009).

[45] Barry et al., *supra* note 35, at 20.

[46] *Id.* at 20 (citing AM. BAR ASS'N, SECTION OF LEGAL EDUC. & ADMISSIONS TO THE BAR, LEGAL EDUCATION AND PROFESSIONAL DEVELOPMENT – AN EDUCATIONAL CONTINUUM; REPORT OF THE TASK FORCE ON LAW SCHOOLS AND THE PROFESSION: NARROWING THE GAP 234–36 & 331–32 [Robert MacCrate, chair, 1992]).

[47] Barry et al., *supra* note 35, at 20 (citing AM. BAR ASS'N, SECTION OF LEGAL EDUC. AND ADMISSIONS TO THE BAR, STANDARDS FOR APPROVAL OF LAW SCHOOLS, Standard 302(e) (1999)).

[48] Memorandum from John A. Sebert, Consultant on Legal Education, to Deans of ABA-Approved Law Schools, et al. 5–7 (Aug. 23, 2004), http://www.abanet.org/legaled/standards/archives.html (under "2004, 302 and 305 Standards") (last visited Jan. 4, 2009); *see also* 2009 ABA STANDARDS, *supra* note 32, at 21–22.

accommodate every student requesting enrollment in any particular live-client or other real-life practice experience."[49]

In the late 1970s, the ABA also began to express concern about the value, or lack thereof, that law schools were placing on the status of clinical teachers within the legal academy.[50] The Council of the ABA Section of Legal Education made several attempts to create an accreditation standard that required terms and conditions of employment for clinical teachers to be substantially equivalent to those offered to nonclinical, full-time members of the faculty. These attempts were repeatedly opposed by leadership within the AALS.[51] Nonetheless, in 1984, the ABA House of Delegates – the ultimate decision-making body of the ABA with respect to the adoption of accreditation standards – finally adopted a weak standard stating that law schools "should" provide a form of security of employment to clinical faculty that is "reasonably similar" to nonclinical faculty.[52] The Delegates also adopted an interpretation that states that a separate tenure track or long-term contracts qualify as "substantially similar."[53] In 1996, after several more years of effort on the part of ABA leadership, the House of Delegates changed the language from "should" to "shall."[54] In 2005, after the Association of Law Deans of America attempted to repeal the mandatory language, the ABA instead clarified the standard by specifying that a "'long term contract' means at least a five-year contract that is presumptively renewable or other arrangement that is sufficient to ensure academic freedom."[55] For more than thirty years, in the face of consistent AALS opposition, the ABA has demonstrated its commitment to improving the status of clinical faculty.

[49] 2009 ABA Standards, *supra* note 32, at 22.

[50] Peter A. Joy & Robert R. Kuehn, *The Evolution of ABA Standards for Clinical Faculty* 75 Tenn. L. Rev. 183, 191–95 (2007–2008).

[51] *Id.* at 195–205, n.122 (quoting Am. Bar Ass'n, Section of Legal Educ. & Admissions to the Bar, Standards for Approval of Law Schools, Standard 405(e) (1986) [hereinafter 1986 ABA Standards]).

[52] Joy & Kuehn, *supra* note 50, at 205, n.123. After these revisions, Standard 405(e) read:

> The law school should afford to full-time faculty members whose primary responsibilities are in its professional skills program a form of security of position reasonably similar to tenure and perquisites reasonably similar to those provided other full-time faculty members by Standards 401, 402(b), 403 and 405. The law school should require these faculty members to meet standards and obligations reasonably similar to those required of full-time faculty members by Standards 401, 402(b), 403 and 405. *Id.*

[53] The new interpretation read, in part, "A form of security of position reasonably similar to tenure includes a separate tenure track or a renewable long-term contract." *Id.* at 205 n.123 (quoting 1986 ABA Standards).

[54] Joy & Kuehn, *supra* note 50, at 210–13. The amended Standard, still in effect, reads "A law school shall afford to full-time clinical faculty members a form of security of position reasonably similar to tenure, and non-compensatory perquisites reasonably similar to those provided other full-time faculty members. . . ." 2009 ABA Standards, *supra* note 32, at 35.

[55] Interpretation 405–6, 2009 ABA Standards, *supra* note 32, at 36.

Although, as discussed earlier, the ABA has required every law school to offer "substantial opportunities" for clinical education or other "real-life" practice experiences,[56] at most law schools, clinical education still is not fully incorporated into the curriculum. Few schools have a requirement that each student participate in even one experiential learning course.[57] None of the law schools with such a requirement is ranked in the top twenty by *U.S. News and World Report*.[58] Despite the ABA's efforts, most clinical faculty in U.S. law schools remain marginalized.[59]

In many respects, the antipathy toward clinical education and legal ethics should come as little surprise. Just as bar leaders worked over most of the twentieth century to move their agenda, the professoriate institutionalized its commitment to a scholarly pursuit of the law and its pivotal gatekeeping role with respect to curriculum. We began by noting that professional work requires both technical expertise and tacit understandings derived from practice. The "hybrid" nature of professional work in law school is constructed through the competing interests of students (most of whom seek to be practicing lawyers), practitioners themselves (who argue that graduates need to be prepared for the "real" world of work), and academics (who enjoy relative independence to shape how law is taught while pursuing their own scholarly interests).[60] Summarizing his exhaustive and provocative history of American legal education, Stevens speculates that:

> Students will continue to reiterate the complaints about law schools that have been mouthed with remarkable regularity since the Harvard student survey of the 1930s.

[56] 2009 ABA Standards, *supra* note 32, § 302(b), at 21–22.

[57] *See* David A. Santacroce & Robert R. Kuehn, Center For the Study of Applied Legal Education, Report on the 2007–2008 Survey, *available at* http://www.csale.org/CSALE.07–08.Survey.Report.pdf (last visited Jan. 1, 2010) [hereinafter CSALE Report]. Twelve (10%) of the 145 schools that participated in the CSALE study reported requiring students to complete an experiential learning course (either an in-house, live client clinic, or field placement program) before graduating. CSALE Report, *supra*, at 10. They are CUNY, Northeastern University, St. Thomas University, Thomas M. Cooley, University of Detroit, University of Florida, University of Maryland, University of Montana, University of New Mexico, University of Puerto Rico, University of Washington, and Yeshiva University Cardozo School of Law. Email from David A. Santacroce, Clinical Professor of Law, University of Michigan Law School, to Carrie Hempel, Associate Dean of Clinical Education and Service Learning Programs, UC Irvine School of Law (August 12, 2009). Since the publication of the CSALE Report, at least one other law school, Washington and Lee University School of Law, also has adopted an experiential learning requirement for graduation as a component of the law school's new comprehensive program for all third-year students. *See* Washington and Lee University School of Law, The Third Year at a Glance, http://law.wlu.edu/thirdyear/page.asp?pageid=650 (last visited Jan. 8, 2010).

[58] *See* U.S. News & World Report, Best Law Schools Ranked in 2009, http://grad-schools.usnews. rankingsandreviews.com/best-graduate-schools/top-law-schools/rankings (last visited Jan. 8, 2010).

[59] *See* CSALE Report, *supra* note 57, at 29–32 (providing a detailed composite description of the differences in rights and privileges of the clinical and nonclinical faculty at the seventy schools responding to the Staffing Sub-Survey).

[60] The Carnegie Report, *supra* note 1, at 88–89.

> Faculty solutions will involve reforms requiring more student research in a period when students are apparently increasingly less interested in things academic, as well as require a faculty-student ratio that would be unthinkable even if universities were not in a financial crisis.[61]

So, is reform of legal education possible? Stevens suggests that there is not much room for optimism.[62] Yet reformers persist in their aims. Two events in particular have focused new attention on the possibilities for, and challenges to, transforming legal education to incorporate a deeper commitment to an ethical, practice-oriented pedagogy. The first – the release of the 2007 Carnegie Report – sets forth a blueprint for reforming legal education, whereas the second – the launch of the UCI School of Law – seeks to implement a new pedagogical vision. In particular, the Carnegie Report proposes that law schools reorganize the informal division of labor that has evolved between the teaching of legal expertise, hands-on practice, and professionalism. Beginning with a clean slate, UCI seeks to design a program that takes seriously the concerns raised by the Report. First, we provide a synopsis of the Carnegie Report recommendations, and then turn to the Law School's plan.

The Carnegie Report's Recommendations

According to the Carnegie Report, if law schools themselves received grades for their pedagogical efforts, they would be a far cry from Order of the Coif. Whereas law schools would receive an "A-" for teaching students how to "think like a lawyer," they would get only a "C" to "C+" at best for craft and ethical-social responsibility. This is hardly a surprise in light of the direction that legal education has taken. In thinking through their analysis of legal education, the authors of the Report begin with two concepts: First, they ask, what are the "signature pedagogies" of legal education, and second, what are the "apprenticeships" required of professional education? They borrow the concept of "signature pedagogies" from linguistic theory, focusing on the "surface structure," "underlying intentions," "values," and "shadow structure" of teaching law; by contrast, the concept of apprenticeship derives from the "learning sciences," which shows that "experts" in a field possess two kinds of knowledge: one derived from mastery of material, or "'schemas,' for thinking and acting," and one that is "conditioned, or related to contexts."[63] Integrating these concepts, the authors argue that professional education is best understood as three "apprenticeships": (1) intellectual/cognitive, (2) expert practice, and (3) identity and purpose. Whereas

[61] Stevens, *supra* note 3, at 278.

[62] *Id.*

[63] The Carnegie Report, *supra* note 1, at 24, 25. Of course, this theme very much echoes findings from the studies of professionals at work. *See, e.g.*, Hughes, *supra* note 5.

the intellectual/cognitive apprenticeship may be quite comfortably housed in the university, apprenticeships in practice and identity formation must draw on the settings where "competent practitioners" work.[64]

Echoing earlier reform proposals, the Carnegie Report begins with the premise that there is a "crisis of professionalism."[65] The roots of this crisis are familiar: The public lacks confidence in lawyers, who have played notable roles in scandals such as Enron. Reformers also point to a "declining morale" among lawyers, many of whom say that they would not enter the practice of law if they had it to do over again. One clear response to this "crisis" is to transform legal education by giving *equal* commitment to the three legs of the professional stool: expertise, practice, and identity. Further, it is time, the Carnegie Report argues, to take seriously the "latent" messages that the current emphasis on cognitive/intellectual education sends, particularly the cordoning off of values or ethics.

To put matters in context, today's law schools have robust clinical programs offering opportunities to learn lawyering skills in a variety of substantive areas. Further, law students take courses in professional responsibility. The problem, then, is not so much that these courses and opportunities for balanced apprenticeships are not present in law schools. Rather, the problem is twofold: First, that apprenticeships are not adequately integrated into the broader curriculum; and second, that they still lack legitimacy.[66] Thus, the Carnegie Report calls for promoting the integration of clinical education as a strategy for larger institutional reform.

THE UCI SCHOOL OF LAW

Beginning in the fall of 2008, the founding faculty of the UCI School of Law took careful steps to design the curriculum.[67] The founding faculty were already seasoned teachers and scholars in their respective fields of expertise.[68] Faculty developed a

[64] The Carnegie Report, *supra* note 1, at 28.

[65] *See id.* at 29–33; *see also* Solomon, *supra* note 26.

[66] The Carnegie Report, *supra* note 1, at 89.

[67] UCI's founding dean, Erwin Chemerinsky, has written about his vision for integration of clinical education in the Law School. Erwin Chemerinsky, *Why Not Clinical Education?*, 16 Clinical L. Rev. 35 (2009).

[68] UCI Law School's founding faculty consists of fifteen people: ten faculty who were professors at other law schools, four UCI professors who accepted joint appointments in the Law School, and one person who left a thirty-year-position as a journalist with *The Los Angeles Times*. Twelve of the fifteen faculty have a law degree. Four of the twelve with law degrees have secondary post-graduate degrees: one a Ph.D. in Urban and Regional Planning, one a Master's degree in Indo-European Linguistics and a second Master's in Library and Information Science, one a Master's degree in molecular biology, and one an LL.M. Ten out of the twelve faculty with J.D. degrees received then from a law school ranked by *U.S. News and World Report* as a top-ten law school; five out of the twelve worked as a judicial clerk after law school, and eleven out of the twelve practiced law prior to becoming a law professor. The ten founding faculty who came from other law schools were previously employed at a top twenty law

first-year curriculum cognizant of the "standard" first-year curriculum in most elite law schools, anxieties and concerns typical of first-year law students that they learn the "right" materials, and the reality that faculty themselves would likely be comfortable with reform or tinkering but uncomfortable with a radical curricular transformation. To facilitate the discussion about curricular possibilities, faculty were given reading assignments, including the Carnegie Report and the work of Shultz and Zedeck.[69] Through a series of meetings, the faculty asked themselves: What are the substantive issues, skills, analytical techniques, and professional training that are required to begin legal practice? What is the most effective order for passing on the intellectual training required for legal practice? How can the curriculum at the Law School be innovative and responsive to changes in legal practice yet build from the traditions of legal education?

The balance between innovation and tradition is struck with an emphasis on highlighting the "methods of legal analysis and skills that all lawyers constantly use. Students thus will receive an education that includes the traditional areas of legal doctrine, but in an innovative context designed to prepare them for practice in the twenty-first century."[70] The emphasis on modes of analysis required of practitioners is captured in the innovative titles of the courses. The goal is to introduce students to the multiple ways of thinking and conceptualizing problems required for effective practice.

In the fall semester, as described on the Law School's website, first-year students were enrolled in the following courses: (1) Common Law Analysis: Private Ordering (using the common law of contracts to teach a form of legal analysis in which law is derived from judicial decisions rather than statutes or the constitution); (2) Statutory Analysis (using criminal law as a basis for teaching students transubstantive methods of statutory interpretation); (3) Procedural Analysis (using civil procedure as the foundation for teaching students about procedural rules as a component of law, and how analysis and arguments proceed in such contexts); (4) Lawyering Skills I (the first semester of a two-semester course teaching practice skills such as legal research, writing and analysis, fact investigation, interviewing, counseling, negotiation, oral advocacy, and document drafting); and (5) Legal Profession (described in detail further in the chapter).

school. Of the three founding faculty who do not have J.D. degrees (each of whom is a joint appointment), one has a Ph.D. in psychology, one a Ph.D. in Social Sciences, and one a Ph.D. in Urban Studies. The faculty has an average of twenty-one years of teaching experience.

69 Marjorie Maquire Schultz & Sheldon Zedeck, *Final Report – Identification, Development and Validation of Predictors for Successful Lawyering* (Working Paper, Conference on Empirical Legal Studies 2009), *abstract available at* http://papers.ssrn.com/sol3/papers.cfm?abstract_id=1442118 (last visited Jan. 12, 2010).

70 UC Irvine School of Law, Curriculum, http://www.law.uci.edu/registrar/curriculum.html (last visited Jan. 8, 2010).

In the Spring Semester, students continue to be enrolled in the Lawyering Skills and Legal Profession courses while adding: (1) Common Law Analysis: Government Regulation (using torts as a way to further examine the common law, and how lawyers reason and develop arguments in this area); (2) Constitutional Analysis (teaching students basic areas of constitutional law such as separation of powers, federalism, and individual liberties, as well as how courts and lawyers analyze constitutional issues); and (3) International Legal Analysis (introducing students to international law and the ways in which legal analyses in this area are similar to and different from other types of legal analyses). One might argue that the curriculum at UCI has a very familiar ring; read in one way, students will be taking courses in Contracts, Civil Procedure, Criminal Law, Torts, and Constitutional Law. But the distinctiveness of the curriculum lies in the emphasis, which is placed not so much on packing in a body of knowledge, but rather on cultivating a facility with different forms of legal analysis.

For example, two UCI professors (who had in previous years taught Criminal Law at other law schools) described the restructuring of their Statutory Analysis courses as a reframing of the focus of the course into one that provides a skill set for statutory analysis in any area of substantive law. In both courses, the professors replaced their previous emphases on theories of punishment in the first few weeks of the course with materials on and discussion of the canons of statutory construction as a framing device for the discussion of reading assignments out of the criminal law casebook. The professors supplemented the casebook materials with corresponding California Penal Code provisions and jury instructions to further illustrate statutory construction and interpretation. One of the professors described the changes made as a consistent "nip and tuck process rather than open heart surgery."[71] The two Procedural Analysis professors also described the changes they made to their courses as a "reframing" of the course, in this instance to emphasize "the elements necessary for a procedural system to have legitimacy," whether the process takes place in a federal court, tribal court, or through an alternative dispute-resolution process.[72] The Common Law Analysis professor described the changes to his course as eliminating study of the Uniform Commercial Code and creating a stronger focus on the way law is made through judicial opinions.[73]

Before turning to a more in-depth examination of the innovative features of the Legal Profession course, we consider another feature of the first-year curriculum at UCI, the pedagogical space given to learning the craft of lawyering. Deference to

[71] Interview with Jennifer Chacon, Professor of Law, UC Irvine School of Law, in Irvine, Cal. (Dec. 10, 2009); Interview with Mario Barnes, Professor of Law, UC Irvine School of Law, in Irvine, Cal. (Dec. 10, 2009).

[72] Interview with Trina Jones, Professor of Law, UC Irvine School of Law, in Irvine, Cal. (Dec. 9, 2009); Stephen Lee, Acting Professor of Law, UC Irvine School of Law, in Irvine, Cal. (Dec. 9, 2009).

[73] Interview with Christopher Leslie, Professor of Law, UC Irvine School of Law, in Irvine, Cal. (Dec. 9, 2009).

craft is captured in a more expansive take on the traditional requirement to teach Legal Writing as part of the first-year curriculum. At UCI, students enrolled in the year-long six-credit course entitled "Lawyering Skills" are not only learning the craft of legal research and writing, but also are introduced to the skills of interviewing, counseling, fact investigation, negotiation, and document drafting. Building from course work, students also get their hands "dirty": In the second semester, students move out of the classroom into practice settings where they conduct intake interviews of actual clients for legal service organizations in Orange County. Additionally, each student is assigned both a junior and senior attorney mentor and is required to spend a specified number of hours observing lawyers at work. Thus, exposure to practice begins early and is systematically built into the first-year curriculum.

In the second year, students will select the clinical course they intend to take in the third year, either an in-house clinic or an externship course. Also during the second year, each student will take one or more courses designated as prerequisites for the clinical course. The Legal Profession course, Lawyering Skills course, and other prerequisite courses are designed to help lay the foundation for – to borrow the language of the Carnegie Foundation – an apprenticeship in "expert practice" as integral to legal education.

Against this backdrop, we describe in more detail the Legal Profession course and Clinical Education program at the Law School.

Legal Profession

Practical and philosophical considerations drove the decision to teach the Legal Profession course over two semesters in the first year of study. Practically, many students work in legal organizations between their first and second year and need to have a rudimentary understanding of legal ethics and professional responsibility. Faculty reached a consensus that effective practice requires more than the tools of legal analysis in its various forms: Practitioners of the twenty-first century will need to be somewhat conversant with interdisciplinary perspectives. Experience suggests that it is often hard to persuade law students to value interdisciplinary scholarship, but this essential skill may be seen as more "relevant" when taught in a context that is useful to students' professional careers. Thus, through study of sites of legal work, a goal of the course is to examine the ways in which context shapes practice and decision making. Philosophically, the founding faculty took seriously the refrain of many commission reports over the twentieth century (including the recent Carnegie Report) that law schools do not spend a sufficient amount of time cultivating students' professional "judgment." In part, this is the case because "judgment" is difficult to assess using traditional academic techniques; in part, this is the case because learning "judgment," of necessity, requires exposure to situations and challenges that cannot be gleaned from textbooks.[74] To address this concern, the Legal Profession course includes a number of simulation exercises "based on typical problems confronted in practice," as well as a speaker series, in which practitioners from various settings (solo and small firm, large firm, general counsel, government, nonprofits) introduce students to the challenges and pitfalls of various career trajectories. Finally, placing the Legal Profession course in the first year sends the very important practical and philosophical message that legal ethics and professional responsibility, as well as the cultivation of identity and judgment, matter for a meaningful career in the law.[75]

Building from these goals, the Legal Profession course begins with a consideration of the role of the lawyer and the legal profession in society, followed by discussions of an attorney's duty of confidentiality and conflicts of interest. In subsequent modules, students are exposed to interdisciplinary scholarship by reading about legal practice in "context," including research on criminal practice, the "hemispheres" of private practice demarcated by individual and small businesses on the one hand and corporate and large-scale organizations on the other, and the public interest sector (including legal aid and cause lawyers). Further exposure to interdisciplinary scholarship unfolds through a reading of the challenges practitioners face in the twenty-first century, including access to legal services, diversity (race and gender), and discipline and malpractice, among other topics. The course is grounded in both the traditional, bread-and-butter materials of legal ethics and responsibility and the more innovative, interdisciplinary research that examines lawyers at work.[76]

Summarizing the faculty's deliberations with respect to a required course on the Legal Profession, it was suggested that too often, the professional responsibility course is treated as the "driver's ed" of legal education – that is, students need to take the course and they need to pass the multiple-choice MPRE to get their license. The goal of the UCI Legal Profession course is, however, much more comprehensive: It takes seriously the School's commitment to cultivate professional craft and identity as central to legal education.

Clinical Education

The faculty's decision to require a clinical course for all UCI law students is premised on the belief that every law student should learn, as part of their formal legal training,

[74] THE CARNEGIE REPORT, *supra* note 1, at 173.

[75] Interview with Catherine Fisk, Professor of Law, UC Irvine School of Law, in Irvine, Cal. (Aug. 13, 2009); Interview with Ann Southworth, Professor of Law, UC Irvine School of Law, in Irvine, Cal. (Aug. 13, 2009).

[76] Interview with Fisk, *supra* note 75; Interview with Southworth, *supra* note 75.

what it means to be a lawyer by actually practicing law.[77] This practice should take place under the close supervision of an experienced attorney and involve opportunities for simulated practice, feedback on performance, and reflection. Each clinical course should provide the student with the opportunity to engage some of the specific skills they will use in their chosen practice, whether that choice is to become, for example, a transactional lawyer or litigator in private practice, a government trial attorney or a legal aid lawyer practicing in the area of community economic development. It should also provide the student with opportunities to consider questions of professional responsibility in the context of actual legal problems of a real client and instill the importance of regularly providing pro bono legal assistance as an essential responsibility of bar membership. Finally, each clinic should provide an opportunity for students to play an integral role in addressing broader social justice concerns through the legal problems it addresses.[78]

The development of UCI Law School's clinical curriculum is still in its initial phase. The law school intends to provide a one- or two-semester in-house clinic experience to most, if not all, of its law students. In the first several years of the program, the law school plans to provide 70 percent to 75 percent of its students an in-house clinical experience, with the remaining students satisfying the requirement through field placements with government and nonprofit legal services organizations in Southern California. To achieve the goal of enrolling most students in an in-house clinic, the law faculty has reserved ten out of the planned fifty full-time faculty positions for faculty whose primary teaching responsibility will be teaching in a live-client clinic ("Clinical Faculty"). The law school plans to hire one or two Clinical Faculty each year over the next several years until the ten Clinical Faculty positions have been filled. These faculty members will be hired into a clinical tenure track, clinical tenure, academic tenure track, or academic tenure position, depending on the individual's interest and productivity (or lack thereof) in academic scholarship. Faculty with clinical tenure enjoy the same job security as academic tenured faculty and have the right to vote on all matters with the exception of the tenure of academic faculty.[79]

[77] At least one person offered a position on the founding faculty turned down the offer in part because of the law school's planned emphasis on clinical education and the right of clinical faculty to vote on all faculty appointments. Interview with Erwin Chemerinsky, Dean, UC Irvine School of Law, in Irvine, Cal. (Oct. 7, 2009).

[78] For an interesting perspective on the ability of a clinical program to both maintain the "traditional social justice mission of clinics" and also focus on teaching practice skills, see Rachel Moran, *The President's Message: Transformation and Training in the Law: Serving Clinical Legal Education's Two Masters*, AALS NEWS, (Association of American Law Schools, Washington D.C., May 2009), *available at* http://www.aals.org/documents/newsletter/april2009newsletter.pdf.

[79] The full integration of UCI's Clinical Faculty within the law school was one of Dean Chemerinsky's top priorities in his negotiations with the university prior to accepting his position. Dean Chemerinsky

The law school plans to supplement the Clinical Faculty's teaching in its live client in-house clinics with adjunct faculty, other full-time faculty who wish to teach in the clinical program, and perhaps with fellows in some clinics. For example, two to three faculty who generally teach classroom courses intend to co-teach an appellate litigation clinic to be offered in Fall 2011.

The school is using several criteria to determine the type of clinical courses to be included in the program. A clinical course must provide each student with the opportunity to serve as the primary advocate for a client in whatever context the legal problems addressed by the clinic arise. For example, if the clinic represents clients in litigation, the student must be the legal representative who appears in court on behalf of the client.[80] Second, the clinic must provide sufficient intellectual challenges for the student, ideally both in the substantive legal issues involved and the skills being developed. Third, the substantive law and skills learned in the clinic should, to the extent possible, be those that the student will use in their chosen area of practice. Fourth, to the extent possible, the law school intends to develop clinical courses that will complement areas of expertise and scholarship of nonclinical faculty. Fifth, also when possible, the clinic should provide opportunities for students to work with professionals and graduate students in other disciplines to prepare them for the interdisciplinary nature of a twenty-first-century legal practice. Finally, the clinics must provide their services pro bono to clients who otherwise would not be able to obtain legal representation.

To address the third criterion, the law school plans to have roughly an equal number of transactional and litigation clinics. During the first year, the Law School surveyed the clinical course preferences of the first class and is using this information in planning the subject matter of the initial in-house clinics and externship offerings.

As the law school currently has two nonclinical faculty with expertise in environmental law, two with expertise in immigration law, and two with expertise in intellectual property law, the faculty appointments committee has decided that hiring clinical professors to develop environmental, immigration, and intellectual property clinics is a priority. Developing clinics in these subject matter areas will allow for potential collaboration with nonclinical faculty, ranging from providing

believes that parity among all UC Irvine law faculty, to the greatest extent possible, is necessary in order to provide a legal education of the highest quality. In particular, such parity is necessary for the development of an outstanding experiential learning program, and to send the correct signal to students and others of the importance of practice-based learning. Interview with Erwin Chemerinsky, Dean, UC Irvine School of Law, in Irvine, Cal. (Sept. 4, 2009).

80 California student practice rules permit students who have completed the first year of law school, and have successfully completed or are currently enrolled in evidence and civil procedure to become certified to appear in court and perform all other functions of a lawyer, provided the work is done in the presence of a supervising attorney. CAL. R. COURT 9.42.

expertise to some supervision of student practice. Law school deans and faculty also are currently exploring, with faculty in several other academic disciplines within the university, the potential for interdisciplinary clinics in areas such as small-business transactions, community economic development, criminal justice, environmental law, international human rights, law and medicine, and law and technology.

The law school intends to structure its clinical program in a manner that will help address some of the greatest unmet needs for legal services in Orange County. To this end, faculty and staff are meeting with numerous legal services attorneys in the Orange County community to gather information on this subject. These meetings also provide the opportunity for UCI to explore the potential for field placements and/or teaching collaborations with interested legal services attorneys. The law school intends to utilize the wide-ranging expertise in the Southern California community through the creation of advisory boards that will assist the initial Clinical Faculty in the creation and development of the various clinics. The law school prioritizes developing clinics that can both help address an unmet need for legal services and satisfy the broad pedagogical goals outlined earlier in the chapter.

The existence of a "blank slate" on which to write a blueprint for the development of the law school's clinical education program, and the commitment of substantial resources to build from that blueprint, provide a unique opportunity to create a program that focuses closely on providing experiences that will better meet the needs of all law students at UCI.

CONCLUSION

The blueprint for the UCI School of Law takes seriously a more integrated approach to legal education. As we have argued, the incorporation of coursework in professional responsibility and clinical education have a prominent role in contemporary legal education, but the commitment to making them integral to the curriculum has been somewhat haphazard and uneven. At top-tier law schools, significant resources are often devoted to creative clinical programs, but these programs and their faculty remain somewhat marginal to the central institutional focus on classroom teaching and scholarship. By making the concept of practice central to UCI's mission, there is the expectation that students' preparation for careers in the law will be more integrated and comprehensive. In its commitment to interdisciplinarity, the Law School takes seriously what decades of sociological research on legal practice has repeatedly demonstrated: Professional practice is as much about technical or cognitive expertise as it is about judgment, craft, and responsibility. Further, UCI recognizes that a more integrated legal education requires resources, including smaller classes and full-time faculty lines for clinical education. The Law School has dedicated resources for these purposes.

Despite these commitments, we close by speculating on the institutional forces that challenge UCI's creative blueprint. Even though the Law School opens with a clean slate, it nonetheless operates within a highly developed institutional field of legal education where taken-for-granted practices constitute the markers of prestige and reputation.

Resources are an obstacle to the full realization of the UCI blueprint. Because the faculty-student ratio in clinical education is, of necessity, smaller than traditional, podium-style classes, it is a relatively more expensive undertaking. Although the initial blueprint sets aside adequate resources for the scope of the undertaking, and the founding faculty support this allocation of resources, commitments may change as the school grows, new faculty are hired, and the traditional pressures of rankings, among other factors, take shape. Research on organizations poses two competing hypotheses on how this might play out: Neo-institutional theory hypothesizes that in its effort to gain legitimacy within its organizational field, the Law School will adopt strategies that conform to practices in other similarly situated schools; from this perspective, the commitment to clinical education and the resources required will act as a drag on the Law School's larger strategy to gain legitimacy; hence, UCI will, over time, conform to the practices of its peer institutions.[81] As Powell and DiMaggio point out, professionalism itself poses a particularly powerful pull toward institutional conformity, or "isomorphism," to use their language; UCI's current and likely continued governance by faculty who are, at some deep level, invested in the system that created them and that has rewarded them handsomely captures the essence of the neo-institutional challenge.[82] Challenging this perspective, organizational ecology posits that new practices established at the time of founding take hold and following that, inertia sets in such that change is hard to pull off.[83] From this perspective, the founding commitment to clinical education will be cemented at UCI and create its own inertial force over time.

Prestige poses a second and two-fold challenge. Professions, whether law or medicine, are engaged in a project to assert and maintain control over a body of knowledge that, to be effective, must be abstract yet useful. As Abbott notes, "professions expand their cognitive dominion by using abstract knowledge to annex new areas, to define them as their own proper work."[84] Among faculty, prestige is conferred on

[81] *See, e.g.*, The New Institutionalism in Organizational Analysis (Walter W. Powell & Paul J. DiMaggio eds., 1991).

[82] *Id.* at 70–74; *see also* Carroll Seron & Susan Silbey, *The Dialectic Between Expertise, Knowledge and Professional Discretion: Accreditation, Social Control and the Limits of Instrumental Logic*, 2 Engineering Stud. 101 (2009).

[83] Michael T. Hannan & John Freeman, Organizational Ecology (1989); Michael T. Hannan & John Freeman. *Population Ecology of Organizations*. 82 Am. J. Soc. 929 (1977).

[84] Abbott, *supra* note 5, at 102.

those who mine and expand the abstract and then publish their work in law reviews that are themselves ranked.[85] In this game of prestige, those who teach professional responsibility and clinical courses can rarely win: It is hard to imagine a scenario where legal ethics gets as arcane as, for example, taxation or intellectual property, and clinicians, by definition, are users of abstract knowledge. The *U.S. News & World Report* rankings both reinforce and expand the parameters of the prestige game. Ironically, these rankings do not take account of faculty publications but rely instead on a composite metric derived from reputational scoring, measures of student selectivity, resources for students (for instance, direct expenditure per student and library expenditures, among others), and placement success.[86] The rankings have been critiqued on methodological and philosophical grounds.[87] Nonetheless, they have become a powerful and all-pervasive mechanism of disciplining law schools to make policy decisions and then allocate resources to guard against losing ground.[88] With this shadow hanging over law schools, resources may very well be allocated to what is measured – for example, placement services – over what is omitted – for example, the "educational benefits of attending a certain law school" as a result of programs like clinical education.[89]

In the short term, legitimacy and prestige pose significant hurdles for the reform of legal education and specifically the niche that the UCI School of Law seeks to fill. Indeed, it would be naïve to not take these factors seriously. In the long term, however, the history of the professions demonstrates that change does occur, and that it is not always of its own making.

[85] Law faculty do publish in other outlets, including social science journals that are peer reviewed. As a general matter, however, publication in law reviews is the preferred and certainly the typical outlet.

[86] Stephen P. Klein & Laura Hamilton, The Validity of the U.S. News and World Report Rankings of ABA Law Schools (1998), *available at* http://www.aals.org/reports/validity.html (last visited Jan. 12, 2010).

[87] *Id.*

[88] Michael Sauder & Wendy Nelson Espeland, *The Discipline of Rankings: Tight Coupling and Organizational Change*, 74 Am. Soc. Rev. 63 (2009).

[89] Klein & Hamilton, *supra* note 86, at 2.

PART III

LAWYERS AND SOCIAL CHANGE: MOBILIZING LAW FOR JUSTICE

10

Without Fear, Favor, or Prejudice

Judicial Independence and the Transformation of the Judiciary in South Africa

Penelope Andrews

"While the independence of our judiciary is partly safeguarded by the institutional mechanisms contained in the Constitution, the judiciary can be said to be truly independent only if all important role players in society respect and protect the freedom of judges to do their jobs 'without fear, favour or prejudice.'"[1]

INTRODUCTION

The system of apartheid was deemed a crime against humanity by the United Nations in 1973.[2] As Martin Chanock[3] and John Dugard[4] have demonstrated in their scholarship, it was primarily the processes of law that maintained this system. Under apartheid, the system of parliamentary supremacy allowed the executive and legislature to ride roughshod over a judiciary that was not empowered to overturn laws passed by Parliament.[5] Moreover, judges – all white – appointed during the apartheid years for the most part supported the status quo and were indeed appointed largely on the basis of their commitment to white supremacy.[6] In contrast, one of the defining

I want to thank Rick Abel, Scott Cummings, Napoleon Williams, Michael Osborne, Stephen Ellmann, and Heinz Klug for helpful comments on my earlier draft.

1 *Press Statement Issued by Patric Mtshaulana SC, Chairman, GCB, Johannesburg on July 28, 2008*, ADVOCATE, Aug. 2008, at 35.

2 The International Convention on the Suppression and Punishment of Apartheid, Nov. 30, 1973, 1015 U.N.T.S. 243.

3 MARTIN CHANOCK, THE MAKING OF SOUTH AFRICAN LEGAL CULTURE, 1902–1936: FEAR, FAVOR OR PREJUDICE (2006).

4 JOHN DUGARD, HUMAN RIGHTS AND THE SOUTH AFRICAN LEGAL ORDER (1978).

5 Some legal scholars have argued that, despite these impediments, limited legal victories were possible, particularly in the dying days of apartheid. *See, e.g.*, RICHARD L. ABEL, POLITICS BY OTHER MEANS: LAW IN THE STRUGGLE AGAINST APARTHEID, 1980–1994 (1995).

6 Hugh Corder, *Seeking Social Justice? Judicial Independence and Responsiveness in a Changing South Africa, in* JUDICIAL INDEPENDENCE IN THE AGE OF DEMOCRACY: CRITICAL PERSPECTIVES FROM AROUND THE WORLD 194 (Peter H. Russell & David M. O'Brien eds., 2001). As Corder observes, "it

features of the post-apartheid constitutional democracy is the independence of an increasingly racially diverse judiciary, and the power vested in the courts, particularly the Constitutional Court, to act as a check on executive and legislative power.

Against the backdrop of the emergence from authoritarianism and apartheid to a constitutional democracy embracing human rights for all, this chapter explores two questions. The first relates to "the circumstances under which, extent to which, and way in which legality constrains state power."[7] The second question relates to whether such constraints also lead to human rights victories in the courts and whether such victories translate into change on the ground.

The first question was raised in the context of apartheid by the legal scholar, Richard Abel, and in the contemporary context by South African High Court judge and constitutional scholar, Dennis Davis.[8] Abel examines the last decade of the system of apartheid – a decade marked by some legal victories over authoritarianism and racial oppression, which were the hallmarks of apartheid. His examination, a narrative of ten "pivotal legal campaigns during the last years of apartheid,"[9] provides an evaluation of the possibilities, as well as the limitations, of strategic public interest lawyering despite the absence of a bill of rights or other constitutional guarantees of human rights and due process. Stephen Ellmann also examined these questions in the context of South Africa's state of emergency between 1985 and 1990.[10]

Exploring the synthesis of law reform and social movements, so thoughtfully theorized by Joel Handler,[11] Stuart Scheingold,[12] and others,[13] Abel examines the

is now widely acknowledged that biased judicial appointments in particular periods, selective composition of the benches to hear particular types of cases, and the dominance of an executive-minded approach … combined to produce a judicial culture closely attuned to the interests of white South Africans." *Id.* at 201. There were judges who defied this characterization and went on to serve on the Constitutional Court, including Justices Goldstone, Didcott, Kriegler, and Ackermann.

[7] ABEL, *supra* note 5, at 3. In his book, Abel explored the possibilities of attaining human rights victories in the courts despite the absence of a Bill of Rights and the ubiquity of oppressive and discriminatory laws. In other words, Abel explores the "the value and limits of legality in resisting authoritarian regimes." *Id.*

[8] As Abel ponders, "[i]s law, like war, merely politics by other means? Or can legal institutions be relatively autonomous, reaching decisions that do not simply reflect political forces and significantly constraining state power?" *Id.* at 7. Davis refers to "lawfare" as replacing "political warfare." *See* Dennis Davis, Lecture to University of Cape Town Summer School (Jan. 18, 2010), *available at* http://www.mg.co.za/uploads/2010/01/22/dennisdavis.pdf.

[9] ABEL, *supra* note 5, at 7.

[10] STEPHEN ELLMANN, IN A TIME OF TROUBLE: LAW & LIBERTY IN SOUTH AFRICA'S STATE OF EMERGENCY (1992).

[11] JOEL J. HANDLER, SOCIAL MOVEMENTS AND THE LEGAL SYSTEM: A THEORY OF LAW REFORM AND SOCIAL CHANGE (1978).

[12] STUART A. SCHEINGOLD, THE POLITICS OF RIGHTS: LAWYERS, PUBLIC POLICY, AND POLITICAL CHANGE (2007).

[13] *See, e.g.*, William N. Eskridge, Jr., *Channeling: Identity-Based Social Movements and Public Law*, 150 U. PA. L. REV. 419 (2001); Michael McCann, *Law and Social Movements: Contemporary Perspectives*, 2 ANN. REV. L. & SOC. SCI. 17 (2006).

legal victories generated by marrying the twin processes of strategic lawyering and grassroots campaigns. Abel's conclusions – namely that limited legal victories are possible despite the obstacles of parliamentary sovereignty and executive-minded judges – are almost counterintuitive if one considers them in a comparative context. For example, it is hard to imagine similar possibilities in repressive societies such as Burma/Myanmar, Iran, North Korea, or the Sudan. The explanation for the South African legal victories are to be found in the notion of a "dual state," explored by Jens Meierhenrich,[14] who posits the idea of a "normative" state (the "white" democratic legal system), and the "prerogative" state (the law relating to the majority black population). Meierhenrich argues that the normative state, although accruing to the benefit of only the white minority, sometimes had a "spill-over" effect, and that in fact its legal imperatives sometimes allowed some maneuvering for those governed by the prerogative state.[15]

My paper traces this counterintuitive proposition regarding limited legal victories under the system of apartheid by focusing on the contemporary constitutional framework. I explore both the independence of the judiciary[16] and its transformation from a system made up overwhelmingly of white males, who embraced an authoritarian and racist world view, to a multiracial judiciary formally committed to the values of justice and equity that are incorporated in the constitution. My thesis is that since the old apartheid order was characterized and shaped by unchecked executive power, the struggle in the post-apartheid state is about limiting executive and legislative power by ensuring that the doctrine of separation of powers and an independent judiciary are entrenched. In addition, the socioeconomic rights provisions in the Constitution obligate the state to positively redress the economic legacy of apartheid, and the judiciary has to ensure that the state meets that obligation.[17]

I argue that the constitution and bill of rights may provide formal protections and guarantees, but that operationalizing these may be hindered by political hostility or political indifference – and that this is one aspect of the legal struggle for social justice in South Africa today. In addition, I argue that although the transformation

[14] JENS MEIERHENRICH, THE LEGACIES OF LAW: LONG-RUN CONSEQUENCES OF LEGAL DEVELOPMENT IN SOUTH AFRICA, 1652–2000 (2008).

[15] *Id.*

[16] This focus on judicial independence validates the idea, although contested by legal scholars, that only judicial review by an independent judiciary can curb state power and create the organizing space for rights pursuits in the court. *See* Ruthann Robson, *Achieving Sexual Freedom Through Constitutional Structures: The Problem of Judicial Review, in* LAW AND RIGHTS: GLOBAL PERSPECTIVES ON CONSTITUTIONALISM AND GOVERNANCE 101 (Penelope E. Andrews & Susan Bazilli eds., 2008); *see also* Brian Flanagan, *Judicial Rights Talk: Defects in the Liberal Challenge to Judicial Review*, 22 S. AFR. J. HUM. RTS. 173 (2006); Jeremy Waldron, *The Core of the Case Against Judicial Review*, YALE L.J. 115 (2006).

[17] *See* Penelope E. Andrews, *The South African Constitution as a Mechanism for Redressing Poverty, in* REFORM IN AFRICA: ITS IMPACT ON GOVERNANCE AND POVERTY 57 (Muna Ndulo ed., 2006).

of the judiciary is vital, particularly with respect to race and gender – and to a lesser extent, sexuality and disability – this imperative may obscure the need to transform the ideological makeup of the judiciary as well, and that only a complete transformation will guarantee genuine judicial independence.[18] Although the independence of the judiciary is incorporated in the constitutional text, political considerations and struggles around the meaning and the reality of transformation of the judiciary are severely straining the ideal of an independent judiciary.[19]

In particular, the effects of racism within the legal profession, the fact that the legal profession in South Africa is still very racially segregated,[20] and the lingering suspicion of the judiciary among certain sectors of the black population have ironically resulted in a call for executive control over the judiciary through legislation.[21] These calls have emanated from members of the black legal profession as well as certain members of the ruling political alliance, who see in the struggles around transformation the attempts by "counter-revolutionaries" to maintain the apartheid status quo.[22] At the core, these tensions are about the legitimacy and the credibility of the judiciary, and the idea that only a transformed judiciary – that is, a representative one – can be truly independent and give effect to the rights embodied in the constitutional text.

In this chapter, I address the twin imperatives of the constitution regarding the judiciary: judicial independence and judicial transformation. I argue that these twin imperatives have resulted in an ongoing tension.[23] At the heart of this tension lies

[18] For example, it has been argued that transformation requires that sitting judges eschew the formalism that typifies South African legal culture. *See* Cora Hoexter, *Judicial Policy Revisited: Transformative Adjudication in Administrative Law*, 24 S. Afr. J. Hum. Rts. 281 (2008); *see also* Deeksha Bhana, *The Role of Judicial Method in the Relinquishing of Constitutional Rights Through Contract*, 24 S. Afr. J. Hum. Rts. 300 (2008).

[19] *See* Penelope Andrews, *The Judiciary in South Africa: Independence or Illusion? in* Judicial Independence in Context 466 (Adam Dodek & Lorne Sossin eds., 2010).

[20] *See* Peggy Maisel, *An Alternative Model to United States Bar Examinations: The South African Community Service Experience in Licensing Attorneys*, 20 Ga. St. U. L. Rev. 977 (2004). Maisel notes that, by 2004, Black South Africans only made up a fraction of the legal profession compared to their numbers in the overall population. *Id.* at 984.

[21] *See* Murray Wesson & Max Du Plessis, *Fifteen Years On: Central Issues Relating to the Transformation of the South African Judiciary*, 25 S. Afr. J. Hum. Rts. 187 (2008).

[22] *See* Matuma Letsoalo, Mandy Rossouw & Sello S. Alcock, *ANC Boss Accused Judges of Conspiracy against Zuma*, Mail & Guardian, July 4, 2008, *available at* http://www.mg.co.za/article/2008–07–04-anc-boss-accuses-judges-of-conspiracy-against-zuma; *see also COSATU: We Do Not Disrespect the Judiciary*, Mail & Guardian, Aug. 21, 2008, *available at* http://www.mg.co.za/article/2008–08–21-cosatu-we-do-not-disrespect-the-judiciary.

[23] The Constitution mandates the independence of the judiciary. S. Afr. Const. § 165(2) ("The courts are independent. . . ."). The language regarding transformation of the judiciary states as follows: "The need for the judiciary to reflect broadly the racial and gender composition of South Africa must be considered when judicial officers are appointed." S. Afr. Const. § 174(2). Although the text of the Constitution suggests that transformation is mandatory, it is arguable that the consideration of racial

the contested vision of the constitution, namely its transformative potential, as Karl Klare argues,[24] or its potential to deliver "a measured process of change"[25] that serves to "guarantee both the security of those threatened by the transition"[26] and the aspirations of the "democratic majority."[27] In short, the tension exists between the vision of the constitution as a liberal document, with a strong commitment to the rule of law and a commitment to neutrality, and a vision that views the constitution as driving the transformative agenda for legal, political, economic, and social change.[28] This tension has its origins in the legal struggle against apartheid, and it highlights the question of what public interest or human rights lawyering can achieve in the face of formidable legal obstacles. Conversely, this chapter focuses on law's possibilities within a constitutional framework that explicitly guarantees the achievement of rights – at least in theory.

In this chapter, I offer three criteria for assessing the constitutional mandates of judicial independence and judicial transformation, and their evolution in the post-apartheid era. First, I assess whether the judiciary has been transformed demographically and ideologically to give effect to the transformative vision encapsulated in the Constitution. Second, I examine whether the judiciary, through its judgments, has created the discursive space for rights mobilization and rights pursuits. Finally, I evaluate whether the independence of the judiciary will be sustained in the face of political pressures from within and outside the judiciary.

THE ROLE OF THE JUDICIARY: TRANSFORMATION OR ACCOMMODATION?

Law provided the veneer of credibility for the apartheid government, because the trappings of the legal system, its formal infrastructure, personnel, and processes

and gender diversity is mandatory but the outcome discretionary. This is borne out by the failure, for example, to appoint significant numbers of female judges. *See* Ruth Cowan, *Women's Representation on the Courts in the Republic of South Africa*, 6 Md. L.J. of Race, Religion, Gender & Class 291 (2006).

24 Karl Klare, *Legal Culture and Transformative Constitutionalism*, 14 S. Afr. J. Hum. Rts. 146 (1998).

25 Heinz Klug, *Constitutional Rights, Democracy and Inequality in South Africa*, 9 Int'l Rev. Const. 135 (2009).

26 *Id.*

27 *Id.*

28 I am not suggesting that judicial independence and judicial transformation are in tension, since both relate to judicial autonomy with respect to the expectations and demands of the government of the day. However, the ideals of transformation and independence may conflict if, and to the extent to which, the government imposes on the judiciary its own particular vision of what constitutes "transformation." *See* Wesson & Du Plessis, *supra* note 21. If one, for example, peruses the public attacks on the judiciary, it is arguable that at least some sectors of the ruling party view judicial independence as a liberal distraction from the imperatives of a complete transformation of every level of society.

resembled that of other democracies like the United Kingdom, India, Australia, and elsewhere. Indeed, for South African liberal scholars, this facade of legal formalism and legal autonomy was vital, and provided the yardstick by which the deviance of apartheid laws could be measured and critiqued. As the South African legal scholar Hugh Corder has noted:

> It is correct to state … that *outside of the "political sphere,"* in its widest sense, judicial development of the common law relating to crime, contracts, and family relations, for example, has been at least as good as comparable courts in the Commonwealth.[29]

In a system that was deemed a crime against humanity, as apartheid was, this location of law "outside of the political sphere" relegates apartheid laws to an aberration from its Anglo-European moorings. Moreover, this view locates law as neutral and distinct from the political system – a view that law and society and other critical scholars have challenged.[30]

But it was the structured racism of the system of apartheid that was in violation of international law, and attempts to transform the legal system in its totality, including the appointment of judges, is what is, in part, influencing the struggle for judicial independence. On the one hand, for those who insist on the primacy of judicial independence, an appointment process focused on transforming the racial and gender makeup of the bench is seen as a challenge to judicial independence.[31] On the other hand, those who argue for the racial and gender transformation of the judiciary see the insistence on judicial independence as a smokescreen to exclude blacks and, to a lesser extent, women from the judiciary.[32] This group, predominantly black, may at times fail to see judicial independence as integral to realizing the transformative potential of the Constitution, especially because this constitutional mandate emerges from the ignominious past of an apartheid executive-minded judiciary.[33]

29 Corder, *supra* note 6, at 201 (emphasis added).

30 *See* Mark Tushnet, *Following the Rules Laid Down: A Critique of Interpretivism and Neutral Principles*, 96 HARV. L. REV. 781 (1983); *see also* Cary Peller, *Neutral Principles in the 1950s*, 21 U. MICH. J.L. REFORM 561 (1988); Cedric M. Powell, *Rhetorical Neutrality: Colorblindness, Frederick Douglass, and Inverted Critical Race Theory*, 56 CLEV. ST. L. REV. 824 (2008).

31 Not all who are formally committed to the principle of judicial independence are opposed to the racial and gender transformation of the bench. But fears about the appointment of unqualified applicants, or political appointments – whether valid or not – appear to be motivating those who want to temper transformation of the bench, or at least slow the process. *See* Justice Johann Kriegler, *Can Judicial Independence Survive Transformation?*, Address to the Law Faculty of the University of the Witwatersrand (Aug. 18, 2009) (on file with the author).

32 *See Kriegler's 'Condescending Attitude' Slammed*, MAIL & GUARDIAN, Sept. 7, 2009, *available at* http://www.mg.co.za/article/2009–09–07-krieglers-condescending-attitude-slammed; *see also* Angela Quintal & Michael Morris, *'Unknown Forces' Targeting Hlophe, Say Judges*, CAPE ARGUS, Oct. 15, 2005, *available at* http://www.capeargus.co.za/index.php?fArticleId=2947624.

33 Although eradicating apartheid was uncontroversial, it has also been argued that there is a lingering suspicion among some sectors of the population regarding the origins and context of the

On August 5, 2009, the President Jacob Zuma nominated Justice Sandile Ngcobo as the fourth Chief Justice of South Africa.[34] The nomination of Justice Ngcobo, although welcomed by almost all commentators, emerged amidst some hostility by the ruling tripartite alliance – the African National Congress (ANC), the Congress of South African Trade Unions, and the South African Communist Party – directed toward certain members of the judiciary.[35] Indeed, in the last few years, commentators have argued that a disturbing tension – some would say a clandestine struggle – has been underway in South Africa between the ruling political alliance on the one hand and the leadership of the judiciary and the legal profession on the other.[36] As I will suggest, this ongoing tension has great ramifications for the future of South Africa's constitutional democracy and for the possibilities of rights mobilization. It is unclear at this juncture, however, whether we are witnessing a historical aberration or the institutionalizing of an ongoing relationship of mutual distrust and antipathy between the ruling political coalition and the judiciary.

The outcome of this apparent conflict may determine whether South Africa transitions successfully into a constitutional democracy, with the independence of the judiciary entrenched not just as a legal formality, but as part of the legal fabric and legal culture. Otherwise, the outcome may be a weaker legal and political system in which the executive and ruling political party curtail the independence of the judiciary, despite the existence of a formal constitutional mandate for such independence. In short, the question is whether South Africa follows the trend in most of postcolonial Africa, where unchecked executive power and weak judiciaries have often resulted in the failure of democracy and widespread human rights abuses.[37] Or,

constitutional framework. As Judge Dennis Davis has noted, "[a]rguments are still raised about the alleged 'Eurocentric' nature of the Constitution, in that a text borrowed to a large degree from Canada, the United States of America, the European Convention on Human Rights and the German Constitution, is not a 'truly African' Constitution." *See* Davis Lecture, *supra* note 8.

[34] *Zuma Looks to Ngcobo as New Chief Justice*, MAIL & GUARDIAN, Aug. 6, 2009, *available at* http://www.mg.co.za/article/2009–08–06-zuma-looks-to-ngcobo-as-new-chief-justice.

[35] *See* Letsoalo, Rossouw & Alcock, *supra* note 22; *see also* COSATU, *supra* note 22.

[36] *See Attacks on the Judiciary*, MAIL & GUARDIAN, Aug. 8, 2008, *avalable at* http://www.mg.co.za/article/2008–08–8-attacks-on-the-judiciary. This is not surprising and is to be expected as South Africa attempts to strike a balance between, on the one hand, an accountable and responsive legislature and executive and, on the other, an independent judiciary, which is effective at restraining legislative and executive power when appropriate. Indeed, these tensions are not confined to emerging democracies only. For example, during the New Deal, the U.S. Supreme Court thwarted some of President Roosevelt's programs. *See* WILLIAM E. LEUCHTENBURG, THE SUPREME COURT REBORN: THE CONSTITUTIONAL REVOLUTION IN THE AGE OF ROOSEVELT (1996). Similarly, the Chilean Supreme Court opposed many of President Allende's policies, leading to the crisis in that country. *See* HEDDA GARZA, SALVADOR ALLENDE (1989).

[37] Martin Chanock, *Cutting and Sewing: Goals and Means in the Constitutionalist Project in Africa*, *in* LAW AND RIGHTS, *supra* note 16, at 47. One recent example is Zimbabwe, where the Supreme Court started out as an important transformative institution in the post-independence state. However, President Robert Mugabe continues to erode the stature of the institution by appointing judges that are sympathetic to his ruling party.

alternatively, will the South African constitutional model instead provide the example of a constitutional framework, with an entrenched separation of powers and an independent, racially diverse judiciary, that gives effect to the promises encapsulated in the constitution and Bill of Rights?[38]

My focus here is on the Constitutional Court, although my comments regarding the judiciary apply to all the courts, including the regional high courts and the Supreme Court of Appeal.[39] I focus on the Constitutional Court because it was created by the Constitution, and it alone has the mandate to deliberate on the final outcome of constitutional matters. The establishment of the court, including its processes, structure, personnel, culture, and even its architecture, is emblematic of the new human rights system.[40]

The context within which the South African Constitutional Court operates raises some interesting questions. The context includes a de facto one-party state, characterized by the entrenchment of the ANC's legacy as the main "liberation movement" and the dominance of the ruling ANC over virtually all state institutions.[41] In addition, the context involves the failure of Parliament to develop itself as a power center that could review the actions of the executive, as well as its failure to be truly representative and accountable to the citizenry, as opposed to its accountability to the party.[42] And even though it has not prevented the creation of an independent judiciary, nor has it prevented the pursuit of human rights in the courts, this context has led to the situation in which courts are burdened with the mantle of transformation far beyond their institutional capability.

[38] I am not suggesting that this problem is unique to the African continent. My comparative method merely alludes to the possibilities for a vibrant constitutional democracy in Africa that the political transition in South Africa appears to promise.

[39] For a description of the structure and hierarchy of the court system, see the Department of Justice and Constitutional Development website at http://www.gov.za/justice.

[40] The Court was built on the site of the Old Fort Prison in Johannesburg and the entire structure was designed to symbolize access by ordinary South African citizens to the court. *See* LIGHT ON A HILL: BUILDING THE CONSTITUTIONAL COURT OF SOUTH AFRICA (Bronwyn Law-Viljoen ed., 2008).

[41] South Africa is not a one-party state in the traditional sense in which the dominant party uses both legal and extralegal methods to thwart any opposition. The situation is rather one in which the ruling party overwhelmingly dominates because of an ineffective opposition that has failed to attract a membership beyond the white community and a fraction of the black electorate. In addition, the ruling coalition includes a tripartite alliance of the South African Communist Party, the Congress of South African Trade Unions. and the African National Congress. These groups exert some influence over the government with respect to its policies and programs, and arguably the democratic struggles in South Africa are taking place within the ruling coalition.

[42] South Africa's electoral system is structured in a way that allows parliamentarians to be elected through the political party list. Parliamentarians are therefore elected indirectly and not directly by constituents. Their allegiance therefore runs to the political party of which they are members and not to citizens who might elect them during the ordinary course of elections. They are also not individually accountable to an electorate, but instead to their political party.

THE SOUTH AFRICAN CONSTITUTION AND THE JUDICIARY

The ANC, when it was still a party in exile, did not start out with a commitment to an independent judiciary,[43] but in the period leading to the constitutional negotiations and just before it became the governing party in South Africa, the ANC formally committed to an independent and transformed judiciary.[44] These commitments were embodied in the Harare Declaration that paved the way for the negotiations that led to the democratic transition in South Africa.[45] A section of the Harare Declaration included the principle that South Africa should have an independent and nonracial judiciary.[46] In 1991, just as negotiations were proceeding in the wake of the release of Nelson Mandela and other ANC leaders from Robben Island, the ANC adopted a set of principles encapsulated in the document, *Constitutional Principles for a Democratic South Africa*. That document provided for:

> A constitutional Court that enjoys the respect of all South Africans, that draws on the experience and talents of the whole population, that is independent and functions in the manifestly fair and objective fashion, accountable only to the principles of the Constitution, should be created.[47]

The South African Constitution and Bill of Rights gives effect to some of the principles adopted in the Harare Declaration, although the document represents the product of a process of negotiations and compromise.[48] The Constitution includes an impressive array of substantive and procedural rights,[49] provides for the independence of the judiciary, and states that all organs of state are bound by the Constitution.[50] The Constitution states clearly that, "the courts are independent and subject only to the Constitution and the law, which they must apply impartially and without fear, favour or prejudice."[51] The Constitution also provides that "no person or organ of state may interfere with the functioning of the courts,"[52] and

[43] Until the 1980s, the notion of an independent judiciary was seen by leading ANC intellectuals as a bourgeois idea. The Soviet model, in which the judiciary must serve the revolution, was dominant.

[44] For a thoughtful discussion of the negotiations and the processes that led towards democratization, see HEINZ KLUG, CONSTITUTING DEMOCRACY: LAW, GLOBALISM AND SOUTH AFRICA'S POLITICAL RECONSTRUCTION (2000); *see also* ALISTER SPARKS, TOMORROW IS ANOTHER COUNTRY: THE INSIDE STORY OF SOUTH AFRICA'S ROAD TO CHANGE (1995).

[45] Organization of African Unity (now the African Union), Harare Declaration, Dec. 14, 1989.

[46] *Id.* at cl. 16.7.

[47] AFRICAN NATIONAL CONGRESS, CONSTITUTIONAL PRINCIPLES FOR A DEMOCRATIC SOUTH AFRICA (1991).

[48] *See* THE SOUTH AFRICAN CONSTITUTIONS: REFLECTIONS ON SOUTH AFRICA'S BASIC LAW (Penelope E. Andrews & Stephen Ellmann eds., 2001); *see also* Peter N. Bouckaert, *The Negotiated Revolution: South Africa's Transition to a Multiracial Democracy*, 33 STAN. J. INT'L L.J. 375 (1997).

[49] *See* S. AFR. CONST. 1992, Chapter 2.

[50] *Id.* at § 165(3).

[51] *Id.* at § 165(2).

[52] *Id.* at § 165(3).

mandates that state authorities "must assist and protect the courts to ensure the independence, impartiality, dignity, accessibility and effectiveness of the courts."[53] As the apex court, the Constitution provides that the Constitutional Court has the sole power to determine the constitutionality of bills or acts of the national and provincial parliaments, local municipalities, and other state organs.[54]

To further the pursuit and implementation of these rights, the Constitution sets out a system that regulates judicial appointments and seeks to ensure that appointed judges are philosophically committed to the principles embodied in the Bill of Rights, and that the judiciary reflects the demographic makeup of South African society. There are varying procedures that exist for the appointment of judges that are determined by the specific court and the seniority of the positions sought. But the President, as head of the executive, officially appoints all judges, selected from a list provided by the Judicial Services Commission, after he consults with the Chief Justice and leaders of the opposition parties in Parliament.

Providing that "any appropriately qualified woman or man who is a fit and proper person" (but who must be a South African citizen) is eligible for appointment as a judge, the Constitution also states the "need for the judiciary to reflect broadly the racial and gender composition of South Africa."[55] It is this constitutional provision that appears to have generated some controversy, and which provides the backdrop for the discussion of judicial transformation.

THE JUDICIARY AND TRANSFORMATION

Transforming a judiciary that was overwhelmingly white and male to one that represents the racial and gender diversity of South Africa has been the driving force behind the judicial appointments process in South Africa – a process that, until a few years ago, occurred with relative ease, despite some rancor regarding a few

[53] *Id.* at §165(4).

[54] *Id.* at §§ 167(1) & (5) provide that:

4. Only the Constitutional Court may
    a. decide disputes between organs of state in the national and provincial sphere concerning the constitutional status, power or functions of any of those organs of state;
    b. decide on the constitutionality of any parliamentary or provincial Bill, but may do so only in the circumstances anticipated in section 79 or 121;
    c. decide applications envisaged in Section 80 or 122;
    d. decide on the constitutionality of any amendment to the Constitution;
    e. decide that Parliament or the President has failed to fulfill a constitutional obligation; or
    f. certify a provincial Constitution in terms of Section 144.
5. The Constitutional Court makes the final decisions whether an Act of Parliament, a provisional Act or conduct of the President is constitutional, and must confirm any order of invalidity made by the Supreme Court of Appeal, a High Court, or a court of similar status, before that order has any force.

[55] *Id.* at § 174(2).

appointments.[56] For example, in 1997, when President Mandela appeared to favor Justice Ismail Mahomed for the position of Chief Justice[57] – the first non-white person appointed to the post – several white senior judges tried to rally support for their candidate of choice, Justice Van Heerden, who was then a judge of the Court of Appeal, and who had been appointed by the apartheid government. The activities of the white senior judges included a public call for Justice Mahomed to withdraw his candidacy, because they believed that his experience did not match those of Justice Van Heerden.[58] President Mandela nonetheless appointed Justice Mahomed as Chief Justice, who went on to serve in this capacity with great honor.[59]

South Africans have generally accepted the proposition that the post-apartheid judiciary not only has to embrace a radical new set of values, but also that those who adjudicate on and interpret those values should reflect the demographics of the wider society. This acceptance is not predicated on political considerations and an unthinking nod to diversity, but rather the appreciation that the very legitimacy and credibility of the judiciary demands such an altered demographic profile.[60] This recognition became especially urgent in the wake of the report of the Truth and Reconciliation Commission, particularly its institutional hearings on the role of the judiciary during apartheid.[61] Moreover, the judiciary is required to unequivocally reflect the principles of equality and dignity – pre-eminent in the Bill of Rights – in its processes and membership.[62]

[56] Penelope Andrews, *The South African Judicial Appointments Process*, 44 OSGOODE HALL L.J. 565 (2006).

[57] Under the 1993 Constitution, South Africa effectively had two Chief Justices – one was head of the Court of Appeal and all lower courts and the other was President of the Constitutional Court. The situation was changed under the 1996 Constitution so that there is only one Chief Justice.

[58] *See* Media Announcement by the Judicial Service Commission: Appointment of New Chief Justice, Oct. 24, 1996, *available at* http://www.info.gov.za/speeches/1996/10250w30096.htm. Another controversy occurred the following year when several judges from KwaZulu-Natal petitioned the Judicial Services Commission to appoint a white judge over the black candidate, Judge Tshabalala, for Judge-President, claiming that Judge Tshabalala would not command the respect of other judges because of his lack of experience. *See* DIANA GORDON, TRANSFORMATION AND TROUBLE: CRIME, JUSTICE AND PARTICIPATION IN DEMOCRATIC SOUTH AFRICA 154 (2006). Similarly, when Justice Ngcobo was appointed over Edwin Cameron – now a Justice of the Constitutional Court – after the intervention of President Mbeki, the issue caused some controversy in the legal community, generating some public discourse on the issue. *See Judge Ngcobo Gets the Nod*, BUSINESS DAY, May 31, 1999, *available at* http://www.ugandaruralcommunitysupport.org/1999/05/31/judge-ngcobo-gets-the-nod-business-day-johannesburg-31-may-1999/.

[59] Tragically, his tenure was rather short because he died soon after he was appointed.

[60] Defining transformation in racial terms is all about legitimacy in the eyes of the majority of South Africans. It is in this sense a pragmatic rather than a principled matter. By contrast, ideological transformation is about principle. *See* Andrews, *supra* note 56.

[61] DAVID DYZENHAUS, JUDGING THE JUDGES, JUDGING OURSELVES (2001).

[62] Section 9 of the Constitution incorporates the principle of equality, but also states that, "[t]o promote the achievement of equality, legislative and other measures designed to protect or advance persons, or categories of persons, disadvantaged by unfair discrimination may be taken."

Between 1994 and the present, South Africa's judiciary has undergone a profound makeover with respect to its racial and gender composition.[63] Although signifying a diminished commitment to gender transformation (despite formal utterances to the contrary),[64] today the judiciary boasts a significant increase in number of black judges. This is evident when one reviews the appointment of judges to the Constitutional Court. At its founding, the Court was composed of eleven judges, three of them black and two female. Today there are two female judges and only three white judges.[65] One of the judges is an openly gay male who is HIV-positive. Under the system of apartheid, there was no expectation that judges would be independent, and indeed, as a group they were not, although some judges defied expectations and allowed some human rights legal victories.[66]

Under apartheid, the appointment of judges was at the discretion of the President on the recommendation of the Minister of Justice. No input was required of members of the legal profession or members of civil society, although no doubt the input of influential members of the bar and of the governing National Party was sought. The process was devoid of any public scrutiny, with judges appointed for the most part from the ranks of the Afrikaner elite whose political ideologies coincided with that of the ruling Afrikaner elite. In short, they were, with notable exceptions, either active supporters, apologists for, or indifferent to the system of apartheid.[67]

In addition to altering the philosophy and demographic makeup of the judiciary, the Constitution also provides for a relatively transparent process that attempts to ensure that those appointed as judges have engaged in a nominations process that allows for public scrutiny and participation. A Judicial Services Commission (JSC) is established to give effect to the constitutional values of transparency and accountability. Those members of the JSC are supposed to reflect a representative sample of the South African legal and political establishment. The membership of the JSC includes the Chief Justice, one Judge President from any of the Provincial Divisions of the High Court, the Minister of Justice, members of the legal profession and the legal academy, politicians, and members of civil society.[68]

The JSC has seen itself as shepherding the process of judicial transformation and has stated clearly its aims of diversifying the judiciary. In addition, candidates have

63 Andrews, *supra* note 56.

64 Indeed, when the two founding female justices of the Constitutional Court retired in October 2009, they were replaced by only one female justice (although a female justice had been appointed in 2005).

65 *See* Constitutional Court, http://www.concourt.org.za.

66 As Hugh Corder notes, "there have at all times been judges who have used their power to counter legislative and executive injustices." Corder, *supra* note 6, at 201.

67 *See* ALBIE SACHS, JUSTICE IN SOUTH AFRICA (1973); *see also* DYZENHAUS, *supra* note 61.

68 *See* Carmel Rickard, The South African Judicial Services Commission, *available at* http://www.law.cam.ac.uk/docs/view.php?doc=879.

to pass an "ideological litmus test" to ensure that their values comport with those outlined in the Constitution and Bill of Rights. The questionnaire that prospective judicial candidates have to complete explores not just the standard biographical information and ethical considerations, but also whether the candidate has committed him- or herself to the anti-apartheid struggles and contributed to the project of democracy in South Africa.[69]

Despite these ostensible protections regarding the transparency of the process, and the attempts to include a range of perspectives in the judicial selection process, the JSC has not been without its critics.[70] In particular, its putative narrow definition of diversity has been criticized. For example, the JSC has been chastened for not seeking diversity beyond race, gender, and other marginal identity indicators.[71] It has been urged to interrogate a judicial candidate's innovative and inspired approach to judging, an approach that recognizes the paradigmatic constitutional shift that the new Constitution demands.[72] In short, the JSC has been urged to ensure that prospective judges are imbued with "the kind of openness that will ensure that the values of the Constitution shape the way they approach" legal controversies.[73] Indeed, one of South Africa's most eminent jurists, Johann Kriegler, a retired judge of the Constitutional Court, has criticized the JSC sharply for its rigidity and hostility in evaluating the philosophical values of candidates.[74] In sum, the vision represented in the Bill of Rights regarding the appointment of judges is viewed as being transformative,[75] and those judges appointed are mandated to pursue that vision.

69 *See* Andrews, *supra* note 56. In addition to the usual personal and professional details, the questionnaire is quite extensive, including questions about the candidate's employment history and membership of legal, community, and political organizations. The forms also inquire into a candidate's financial and other proprietary interests, as well as the candidate's legal and other publications. The questionnaire is designed not just to elicit the candidate's competency and skills as a jurist, but also whether the candidate is committed to the broader justice project envisioned in the Constitution.

70 Questions have, for example, been raised about the merits of those appointed to the JSC and the political ideology of those members (particularly when they are chosen by the ruling party). Questions have also been raised about the assumptions made by members of the JSC during the interviewing of candidates, including the nature of the questions that have been asked, particularly of female candidates. Questions have also been raised about how candidates are shortlisted and whether impermissible inferences may be drawn during the selection process that may exclude certain categories of candidates, for example, women of childbearing years, or those whose political affiliations may not coincide with that of the ruling party. *See* Carmel Rickard, *Judging Women Harshly*, SUNDAY TIMES, Oct. 23, 2005, *available at* http://www.sundaytimes.co.za/Articles/TarkArticle.aspx?ID=1735237.

71 *Id.*

72 *Id.*

73 *Id.*

74 Justice Kriegler notes the experience of a white applicant who, in his opinion, was humiliated in his questioning before the JSC. *See* Kriegler, *supra* note 31; *see also Whites Shouldn't Apply to Be Judges – Ntsebeza*, POLITICSWEB, July 22, 2009, *available at* http://www.politicsweb.co.za/politicsweb/view/politicsweb/en/page71627?oid=136958&sn=Detail.

75 Although the Constitution does not mention the word "transformative," it arguably purports to be so in spirit and vision. The Preamble states that the Constitution is meant to "[h]eal the divisions of

THE RULINGS OF THE CONSTITUTIONAL COURT AND JUDICIAL INDEPENDENCE

The judgments of the Constitutional Court since its inception in 1995 indicate that its members have taken their mandate to interpret and apply the Constitution "without fear, favour or prejudice" with commitment and courage. The Court has adjudicated a range of controversial issues that include the interpretation of the socioeconomic rights provisions,[76] the separation of powers,[77] the rights of indigenous and religious minorities,[78] and race and gender equality.[79] The stature of the Court's members and the range of impressive judgments have made the South African legal establishment proud and burnished the Court's reputation in the international arena.[80] Both former Presidents Nelson Mandela and Thabo Mbeki have always been staunch supporters of the Court, even though they may not have agreed with the judgments, particularly in the area of socioeconomic rights or separation of powers. In addition, President Jacob Zuma has also stated publicly his support for a transformed and independent judiciary.[81] Moreover, the business community and the media in South Africa are great supporters and admirers of the Court, even if they too do not always agree with its holdings. It is the independence of the judges that these groups find most admirable.

The Court's jurisprudence has contributed greatly to the discourse of transformation in South Africa, and with respect to gender equality, the Court's decisions have been bold.[82] The Court's first significant judgment regarding judicial independence and judicial review arose in its decision to certify the second Constitution in 1996, in which the Court directed the government of President Mandela to bring the constitutional amendments in line with the principles outlined in the first Constitution.[83]

the past and establish a society based on democratic values, social justice and fundamental human rights." It should also: "Lay the Foundations for a democratic and open society. . . ." For a thoughtful discussion of the transformative potential of the Constitution, see Klare, *supra* note 24.

[76] *See, e.g., Government of the Republic of South Africa & Others v Grootboom & Others* 2000 (11) BCLR at 1169 (CC) (S. Afr.); *Minister of Health v Treatment Action Campaign* 2002 (5) SA at 721 (CC) (S. Afr.).

[77] *See, e.g., President of the Republic of South Africa and Others v South African Rugby Football Union and Others* 2000 (1) SA 1 (CC) (S.Afr.); *Premier of Kwazulu-Natal and Others v President of the Republic of South Africa and Others* 1995 (12) BCLR at 1561 (CC) (S.Afr.).

[78] *See, e.g., Christian Education South Africa v Minister of Education* 2000 (4) SA at 757 (CC) (S.Afr.); *Alexkor Ltd and Another v The Richtersveld Community* 2003 (12) BCLR at 1301 (CC) (S.Afr.).

[79] *Gumede (born Shange) v President of the Republic of South Africa and Others* 2009 (3) BCLR 243 (CC) (S.Afr.); *Moseneke and Others v Master of the High Court* 2001 (2) SA 18 (CC) (S.Afr.).

[80] *See* Mark Kende, Constitutional Rights in Two Worlds: South Africa and the USA (2009).

[81] *Ruling ANC of South Africa Will Respect Judiciary, Says Zuma*, Somalipress.com., http://www.somalipress.com/news/2009/apr-20/ruling-anc-south-africa-will-respect-judiciary-says-zuma.html.

[82] *See* Elsje Bonthuys, *The Personal and the Judicial: Sex, Gender and Impartiality*, 24 S. Afr. J. Hum. Rts. 239 (2008).

[83] *See* Carmel Rickard, *The Certification of the Constitution of South Africa, in* The South African Constitutions, *supra* note 48, at 224.

It was a wonderful symbolic moment in the country when the Court only allowed the second Constitution to pass constitutional muster after the amendments had been done in accordance with its constitutional guidance – a very far cry from the doctrine of parliamentary supremacy that had allowed South Africa during its dark days of apartheid to slide into authoritarianism and unfettered repression.[84]

The Court has struck down executive action deemed unconstitutional, including action that may have popular resonance. For example, although the Court could not provide relief to the complainant, the Court found the executive had acted unlawfully when it handed over a terrorist suspect to the American authorities without obtaining an undertaking that he would not be executed if found guilty.[85] In another judgment assessing the principles of representative democracy, the Court delivered a textbook illustration of the importance of the doctrine of separation of powers and, more significantly, the central role of judicial review to strengthen the doctrine. The Court rejected a bill passed by the parliament on the basis that there had not been sufficient public consultation, as required by the Constitution.[86] In an exploratory and thoughtful judgment, Justice Ngcobo, delivering the opinion for the Court, noted that South Africa's representative democracy would be rendered "meaningless without massive participation by the voters."[87] In addition, he observed that "the participation by the public on a continuous basis" is crucial to the "functioning of representative democracy."[88]

Despite its admirable record that vindicates its independence and accountability, the Court has received some criticism for its apparent failure to be more receptive to poor South Africans and for its timid response to the government with respect to the enforcement of social and economic rights.[89] These criticisms stem mostly from the narrow interpretation given by the Constitutional Court to the constitutional provision that allows citizens, in certain circumstances, to approach the Constitutional Court at first instance, or to appeal to the Court directly from

[84] As Jackie Dugard has observed, "[u]nlike today's non-racial constitutional democracy with independent judicial review, the apartheid legal order was premised on an explicitly racist Constitution and parliamentary supremacy, unencumbered by the British doctrine of the Rule of Law. The virtually all-powerful executive and legislature regard judicial review as anathema." Jackie Dugard, *Judging the Judges: Towards an Appropriate Role for the Judiciary in South Africa's Transformation*, 20 Leiden J. Int'l L. 965, 967 (2007).

[85] *Mohamed and Another v President of the Republic of South Africa and Others* 2001 (3) SA at 893 (CC).

[86] *Doctors for Life International v. Speaker of the National Assembly and Others*, 2006 (12) BCLR at 1399 (CC).

[87] *Id.* at ¶ 115.

[88] *Id.* at ¶ 116.

[89] Jackie Dugard & Theunis Roux, *The Record of the Constitutional Court in Providing an Institutional Voice for the Poor, 1995–2004, in* Courts and Social Transformation in New Democracies: An Institutional Voice for the Poor 107 (Robert Gargarella, Pilar Domingo & Theunis Roux eds., 2006); *see also* Jackie Dugard, *Court of First Instance?: Towards Pro-Poor Jurisdiction for the South African Constitutional Court*, 22 S. Afr. J. Hum. Rts. 261 (2006).

a holding by a lower court.[90] This provision was seen as one of the most progressive in the Constitution, potentially providing somewhat unfettered access to the Constitutional Court to large numbers of South Africans, especially those who are poor and marginalized.

Although there is no doubt that the Court could have taken a more intrusive and vigorous approach with respect to the enforcement of social and economic rights, arguably the Court has struck a sound balance between its mandate to interpret and enforce the rights on the one hand and its awareness of limited government resources on the other. The Court is also mindful of its institutional limitations with respect to its ability to negotiate competing claims from a broad sector of disadvantaged and marginalized South Africans, and its ability to determine how the government ought to spend and allocate resources among the neediest South Africans.[91] The record suggests that the problem lies not so much with the Court's restrained approach in this area, but rather with the government's reluctance to give effect to the Court's judgments, despite official lip service to do so.[92] It is unclear whether this reluctance stems from incompetence, hostility, or indifference, but despite the causes, this inability to give effect to the Court's judgments strains the integrity and credibility of the Court, and makes a mockery of judicial independence and judicial review. Such inability may engender disillusionment and cynicism within the populace regarding the possibility of rights pursuits in the courts.[93] This situation presents a great challenge to the rights mobilization and rights enforcement project.[94]

TRANSFORMATION OF THE BENCH: CONTROVERSY AND CONFLICT

Several controversies have occurred in the past fifteen years as attempts have been made to transform the bench, both in terms of racial and gender makeup as well as legal philosophy.[95] Although during the constitutional negotiations, the decision was made that in the interests of stability and continuity, sitting judges would be retained, the Constitution mandates that the "face" of the judiciary represent the reality of the demographics of South Africa. At the outset, therefore, the South

[90] *See* Dugard, *supra* note 89.

[91] *See* Taunya Banks, *Balancing Competing Individual Constitutional Rights*, *in* LAW AND RIGHTS, *supra* note 16, at 27; *see also* Andrews, *supra* note 17.

[92] A poignant example is the delay to grant proper housing to the applicants in the *Grootboom* case.

[93] *See* Dennis Davis, *Adjudicating the Socio-Economic Rights in the South African Constitution: Towards 'Deference Lite'?* 22 S. AFR. J. HUM. RTS. 301 (2006).

[94] Mark Heywood & Adila Hassim, *Remedying the Maladies of "Lesser Men or Women": The Personal, Political and Constitutional Imperatives for Improved Access to Justice*, 24 S. AFR. J. HUM. RTS. 263 (2008).

[95] *See* Adam Dodek, *S v Zuma: The Future of Constitutional Democracy in South Africa*, 3 J. PARLIAMENTARY & POL. L. 121 (2009).

African judiciary was faced with the challenge of giving effect to the constitutional mandates of judicial independence and judicial transformation to ensure its credibility and legitimacy.[96]

In the past few years, a series of incidents have occurred that suggest that the independence of the judiciary may be subjected to threats that are located both outside and within the judiciary. First, a threat may emerge from those outside the judiciary, who see the institution as not sufficiently "transformed." This threat became more apparent in relation to the criminal charges of corruption leveled against President Zuma, which were withdrawn a few months before he was elected to the Presidency. This withdrawal provoked widespread public criticism of the judges voiced by prominent members of the ruling African National Congress.[97] The second threat may come from within the legal establishment itself. This threat is one generated by the controversy surrounding the charges against Judge-President John Hlophe of the Cape High Court. These two threats are intertwined, as I illustrate in the discussion further in this chapter, and they suggest a looming crisis of credibility, legitimacy, and values.

The Zuma Controversy

In 2005, President Zuma's financial advisor and close friend, Schabir Shaik, was convicted of corruption and fraud. In that case, the judge noted that President Zuma had a corrupt relationship with Shaik, after finding that Schaik had disbursed to Zuma over 1 million Rand and had negotiated a bribe of over 1.5 million Rand from a French Arms manufacturer to Zuma so that Zuma would prevent further governmental investigation of its affairs.[98] In the wake of the judgment, President

[96] This task became more urgent in the wake of the Truth and Reconciliation Commission's institutional hearings on the role of the legal profession under apartheid. The judiciary's credibility was seriously challenged during the institutional hearings of the TRC, when members of the bench who had served under apartheid refused to appear before the TRC. *See* Final Report of the Truth and Reconciliation Commission (1995). That decision, though controversial, appeared to have been a strategic decision on the part of the leaders of the judiciary that, in fact, the credibility of the bench would be secured without public displays of apology. *See* Penelope E. Andrews, *A Grand Exercise in Forgiveness, or Justice Held Hostage to Truth? South Africa's Truth and Reconciliation Commission*, 24 Melbourne U. L. Rev. 236 (2000). The report on the role of the legal profession under apartheid painted, unsurprisingly, an unflattering picture of the apartheid judiciary. Final Report of the Truth and Reconciliation Commission, *supra*.

[97] *See* Letsoalo, Rossouw & Alcock, *supra* note 22; *see also* Mariette Le Roux, *Zuma Backers put SA Judges on Trial*, Mail & Guardian, Jan. 12, 2008, *available at* http://www.mg.co.za/article/2008–01–12-zuma-backers-put-sa-judges-on-trial.

[98] *S v Shaik and 11 Others*, Durban High Court (unreported decision) (S. Afr.), *available at* http://ww2.mg.co.za/contentimages/246908/Shaik_Judgment.pdf. In the words of Judge Squires: "Were they loans, as Shaik claimed was the case at Zuma's insistence, or were they non-recoverable gifts to cultivate and retain Zuma's goodwill?" *Id.* at 78.

Mbeki fired then-deputy-President Zuma, who resigned his seat in Parliament but remained as deputy-President of the ANC.[99]

A few months after Zuma's dismissal, he was charged in a highly publicized case of rape and was eventually acquitted.[100] This case highlighted what was to become a very polarizing debate about the suitability of Zuma as a future President, and the role of the judiciary in treating Zuma either fairly or harshly (in the eyes of his detractors and supporters, respectively).[101] The rhetoric by Zuma's supporters about the biased nature of the legal system abated somewhat in the face of his acquittal.[102]

It was, however, the impending corruption trial that triggered a standoff between the judiciary and the supporters of the future president, and this would lead to unprecedented attacks on the judiciary. In early 2006, the National Prosecuting Authority (NPA) filed charges of corruption and bribery against Zuma, which were subsequently dropped and then refiled in late 2006.[103] In a highly publicized and much awaited trial before a provincial court, the charges against Zuma were thrown out. The presiding judge suggested that the timing of the refiled charges against Zuma was likely politically motivated, and that there was a Kafkaesque feeling to the whole episode.[104] This decision led to the resignation of President Thabo Mbeki in 2008,[105] and an interim President was installed, with the blessing of Zuma, until elections a few months later.[106]

[99] Statement of the President of South Africa, Thabo Mbeki, at the Joint Sitting of Parliament on the Release of Hon. Jacob Zuma from His Responsibilities as Deputy President, National Assembly, June 14, 2005, *available at* http://www.info.gov.za/speeches/2005/05061415151001.htm.

[100] See discussion of the case in Penelope E. Andrews, *Learning to Love After Learning to Harm: Post-Conflict Reconstruction, Gender Equality and Cultural Values*, 15 MICH. ST. J. INT'L L. 41 (2007).

[101] During the trial, Jacob Zuma's supporters engaged in rhetoric that was subsequently carried over to the later corruption trial about him being the victim of a smear campaign. While protesting his innocence, they carried out a vicious vendetta against the complainant.

[102] Manoah Esipisu & Rebecca Harrison, *Zuma Acquitted of Rape Allegations*, NEWZIMBABWE.COM, Nov. 12, 2009, *available at* http://www.newzimbabwe.com/pages/zuma2.14120.html.

[103] *Corruption Charges Dropped Against ANC Leader Zuma*, NEWZIMBABWE.COM, Sept. 12, 2008, *available at* http://www.newzimbabwe.com/pages/zuma2.14120.html.

[104] In the words of the judge:

> The court has gained the impression that all the machinations ... form part of some great political contest or game. For years the applicant is under threat of prosecution for serious corruption and yet never brought to trial. There is a ring of the works of Kafka about this ....

Zuma v National Director of Public Prosecutions 2009 (1) SA 54 (N) at 37 (S. Afr.), *available at* http://www.saflii.org/za/cases/ZAKZHC/2008/71.rtf. The presiding judge, Chris Nicholson, is a white South African who, before his appointment, had an admirable record as a public interest lawyer. Thus the idea that lack of judicial independence is associated with judicial transformation is somewhat simplistic.

[105] Bathandwa Mbola, *Thabo Mbeki Resigns as President*, SOUTHAFRICAINFO.COM, Sept. 22, 2008, *available at* http://www.southafrica.info/about/government/mbeki-resigns.htm.

[106] Sebastian Berger, *Thabo Mbeki Resignation: Jacob Zuma Endorses Interim South African Leader*, TELEGRAPH, Sept. 22, 2008, *available at* http://www.telegraph.co.uk/news/worldnews/africaandindianocean/southafrica/3050683/Thabo-Mbeki-resignation-Jacob-Zuma-endorses-interim-South-Africa-leader.html.

The Court of Appeals, in a strong rebuke to the trial judge, overturned the latter's decision, thereby reinstating the criminal charges against Zuma.[107] The die had been cast and immense pressure began to be placed on the Constitutional Court to dismiss the charges against Zuma. While the Constitutional Court was considering the Zuma appeal, the NPA decided to drop the charges against Zuma in April 2009.[108] The prelude to this development was an unprecedented campaign by Zuma's supporters to have the charges dropped, and in the process, the attacks on the judiciary became louder and more vociferous.[109] For example, in one highly publicized speech, the Secretary-General of the ANC launched an attack on the judiciary, suggesting that it was part of "a concerted effort by counter-revolutionary forces" in a "conspiracy to undermine" Zuma.[110]

The Hlophe Affair

As these attacks were playing out very publicly in South Africa, another controversy related to the Zuma case made the headlines. The controversy involved a complaint of misconduct lodged by the Constitutional Court to the JSC against Judge Hlophe, the Judge-President of the Cape High Court and the first black person to be appointed to that position. The complaint alleged that he had attempted to influence the pending Zuma corruption and fraud proceedings in the Constitutional Court by engaging in inappropriate conversations with a junior and an acting judge of the Constitutional Court.[111] The complaint raised two specific allegations, namely that Judge Hlophe's conduct was "calculated to have an impact" on "the individual decisions of the judges" and "on the capacity of the Constitutional Court" to conduct itself in a manner that guaranteed "independence, impartiality, dignity, accessibility and effectiveness," in violation of the Constitution.[112] The complaint also alleged that Judge Hlophe's conduct was constitutionally impermissible because of its direct attempt to interfere "with the functioning" of the Court.[113]

[107] *National Director of Public Prosecutions v Zuma* 573/08 (2009), ZASCA 1 (Jan. 12, 2009), *available at* http://www.mg.co.za/uploads/zumajudgement.pdf. The Court found Judge Nicholson's finding of political chicanery "erroneous," "unwarranted," and "incomprehensible," noting, "[p]olitical meddling was not an issue that had to be determined. Nevertheless a substantial part of his judgment dealt with this question. He changed the rules of the game, he took his eyes of the ball." *Id.* at 13.

[108] NPA *Drops Corruption Charges Against Zuma*, MAIL & GUARDIAN, Apr. 6, 2009, *available at* http://www.mg.co.za/article/2009–04–06-npa-drops-corruption-charges-against-zuma.

[109] *See, e.g., Democracy Is Yesterday's Hero*, MAIL & GUARDIAN, July 11, 2008, *available at* http://www.mg.co.za/article/2008–07–11-democracy-is-yesterdays-hero. *See also ANC's Ominous Attack on Judge*, SUNDAY TIMES, Jan. 19, 2008, *available at* http://www.thetimes.co.za/PrintEdition/Insight/Article.aspx?id=686309.

[110] Letsoalo, Rossouw & Alcock, *supra* note 22.

[111] Statement in Support of Complaint to the Judicial Service Commission by the Judges of the Constitutional Court (May 30, 2008) (on file with author).

[112] S. AFR. CONST. 1996. § 165(2).

[113] *Id.* § 165(3).

Judge Hlophe defended his actions vigorously, and in response he filed a countercomplaint to the JSC against the judges of the Constitutional Court. He also approached the Johannesburg High Court seeking a declaration that the judges of the Constitutional Court had in fact violated his constitutional rights when they issued a media statement to announce the complaint against him. A divided bench of the High Court found in Judge Hlophe's favor,[114] with the majority stating that the Constitutional Court had "unreasonably and unjustifiably" violated Judge Hlophe's right to dignity and equality by not giving him a hearing before lodging the complaint with the JSC and then making the complaint public.[115] The decision was overturned by the Supreme Court of Appeal a few weeks later, and the decision was then appealed to the Constitutional Court – an interesting dilemma in light of the fact that the complainants were the Constitutional Court judges who would have to hear the appeal.[116]

In the meantime, the complaint of misconduct against Judge Hlophe by the Constitutional Court judges and his countercomplaint against them were making their way through the JSC, with several delays, amidst attempts to hold the hearings behind closed doors, away from the scrutiny of the media and the general public. Members of the media challenged this, and on July 29, 2009, a judge of the South Gauteng High Court held that a "preliminary investigation" by the JSC into the complaint and countercomplaint must be opened to the public and the media. In August 2009, the JSC decided to dismiss both the charges of the Constitutional Court against Judge Hlophe and the latter's charges against the judges of the Constitutional Court.[117] In October 2009, Judge Hlophe was interviewed by the JSC for a vacancy on the Constitutional Court, but he was not appointed.

RESPONSES TO THE CONTROVERSIES

In support of Judge Hlophe, an organization calling itself "The Justice for Hlophe Alliance" was formed to "defend and seek justice" for Judge Hlophe and "all black judges who find themselves unfairly attacked for their strong, principled and

[114] This division was a racial one: The black judges voted in favor of Judge Hlophe and the white judges voted against him.

[115] *Hlophe J v Constitutional Court of South Africa and Others* (08/22932) (2008), ZAGPHC 289 (Sept. 25, 2008) (S. Afr.), *available at* http://www.saflii.org/za/cases/ZAGPHC/2008/289.html.

[116] SCA *Upholds Appeal by Judges*, Mail & Guardian, Mar. 31, 2009, *available at* http://www.mg.co.za/article/2009–03–31-sca-upholds-appeal-by-judges-against-hlophe; *see also Hlophe to Appeal to the Constitutional Court*, Mail & Guardian, Apr. 1, 2009, *available at* http://www.mg.co.za/article/2009–04–01-hlophe-to-appeal-in-constitutional-court. At the end of the day, the appeal to the Constitutional Court was not pursued, and the issue became moot when the JSC dropped the charges.

[117] *JSC Drops Hlophe Probe*, Mail & Guardian, Aug. 28, 2009, *available at* http://www.mg.co.za/article/2009–08–28-jsc-drops-hlophe-probe.

unwavering pro-transformation stance."[118] According to the Founding Statement of the Alliance:

> Our goal is to build a public consensus behind an independent and non-racist judiciary and respect for the rights, human dignity and due process rights of the hardworking judges who form the pillar of our justice system and who are often subjected to unfair, unwarranted and politically motivated attacks. The attack on Judge Hlophe is not an isolated incident, but stands at the confluence of two different trends. First, it is the latest ad hominem, partisan attack on judges for the substance of their decisions.... Second, it is a further step in a perilous flirtation with the idea that we are better off without independent judges to ensure that the rule of law applies, not only to average citizens, but equally to those in power....[119]

The irony of the statement is the apparent conflation of the idea of an independent and transformed judiciary, and the perspective that Judge Hlophe's actions illustrate those ideals in practice. In other words, it is Judge Hlophe who is acting independently, as the representative of a transformed judiciary, whereas the judges who challenge him continue to serve the interests of the old white ruling class.[120]

The responses by the legal community to the Hlophe and Zuma controversies have been disturbingly racially polarized, although those who have been vilified by some members of the black legal establishment, including the Black Lawyers Association, are themselves black.[121] What the situation demonstrates is that parts of the legal community remain caught up in the racial divide of the apartheid era, despite enormous gains in the past fifteen years. This factor may not necessarily interfere with the independence of the judiciary. What is disturbing, however, is the inability of certain sectors of the legal community to lift themselves beyond loyalty to the ruling party. They therefore display an executive-mindedness that will surely impede judicial independence. Indeed, during the periods of vicious attacks on the judiciary, especially the judges of the Constitutional Court, the legal community has for the most part remained silent. As a former Constitutional Court Justice Kriegler laments:

> [W]hy has there been this deafening silence while politicians attack judges and courts – circumstances where the Bench is to the knowledge of the profession

[118] JFH Alliance Founding Statement (on file with author).

[119] *Id.* Indeed, there are some who have called for Judge Hlophe to be appointed the Chief Justice of South Africa.

[120] Judge Hlophe has even been quoted as referring to Chief Justice Pius Langa as a "white man." *See* Sello S. Alcock, *'I am not going to shake a white man's hand'*, MAIL & GUARDIAN, Aug. 08, 2009, *available at* http://www/mg.co.za/article/2009–08–08-i-am-not-going-to-shake-a-white-mans-hand.

[121] For example, two of the main targets have been (former) Chief Justice Pius Langa and Deputy Chief-Justice Moseneke. All of the judges of the Constitutional Court, including the black judges, signed the complaint against Judge Hlophe, illustrating that racial polarization was not complete.

> defenceless? Why has the profession left it to newspaper editors and radio commentators to step into the breach? How can we hope to preserve the independence of the judiciary if the legal profession stands by twiddling its thumbs while the moral authority of the breach is impugned?[122]

A few years earlier, when Justice Kriegler publicly called for Judge Hlophe to step down after a complaint of financial impropriety had been lodged against Judge Hlophe, Kriegler was subject to some vitriol, with a few prominent black lawyers calling for greater government regulation of judges, including the censuring of judges.[123] They interpreted Kriegler's comments as racist and appeared unwilling to engage with the merits of his arguments.[124]

To date, the general public has also for the most part held the Constitutional Court in the highest regard,[125] although the events in the past two years, and the attacks on the judges of the Court, have strained this general public acceptance. As I have suggested, the controversies around President Zuma and Judge John Hlophe may erode public confidence and trust in the Court, and this may strain judicial independence as judges may become subjected to political pressure.

CONCLUSION

At the outset of this chapter, I raised two questions: First, what are "the circumstances under which, extent to which, and way in which legality constrains state power,"[126] and second, what are the possibilities of attaining human rights victories in the courts? The analysis undertaken in this chapter of judicial independence and judicial transformation responds to those questions. Regarding the first question, the analysis reveals that the courts, especially the Constitutional Court, have in fact constrained the government in their exercise of state power, although this constraint is far from perfect. This is because – although the government often respects the courts'

[122] Kriegler, *supra* note 31. Interestingly, a few years back when the JSC decided not to pursue a complaint of financial impropriety against Judge Hlophe, black lawyers called for a contempt citation against Justice Kriegler after he wrote a newspaper opinion piece suggesting that Judge Hlophe was not fit to hold judicial office. *See Lawyers Slam Kriegler for Hlophe Judgments*, Oct. 10, 2007, http://www.iol.co.za/index.php?set_id=1&click_id=13&art_id=nw20071009220052736C482623.

[123] *See Punch-up at the Bar*, Mail & Guardian, Nov. 23, 2007, *available at* http://www.mg.co.za/article/2007–11–23-punch-up-at -the-bar.

[124] This episode demonstrates that, in addition to the idea of judicial independence, there is a need to impose standards of judicial conduct. Moreover, it is clear that any kind of criticism of the judiciary remains racially volatile.

[125] *See* James Gibson, *The Evolving Legitimacy of the South African Constitutional Court, in* Justice and Reconciliation in Post Apartheid South Africa 229 (Francois du Bois & Antje du Bois-Pedain eds., 2009).

[126] Abel, *supra* note 5, at 3.

decisions – it does not always act in the spirit of the decisions. This may be because of lack of resources, indifference, political considerations, or a combination of all.

The second question referred to the possibility of attaining human rights victories in the courts despite the absence of a Bill of Rights and the ubiquity of oppressive and discriminatory laws. Today this issue is not relevant, at one level, because the Bill of Rights expressly provides for a comprehensive range of justiciable rights. At another level, this chapter has indicated that the courts are progressing in their ability, underpinned by the Bill of Rights, to mandate the eradication of discriminatory and oppressive laws, and limiting the possibility of having an authoritarian regime in South Africa.[127] But poverty and economic inequalities remain the largest impediments to the democratic project, resulting in an enormous challenge to courts to give effect to the socioeconomic rights provisions in the Constitution. This has great implications for the institutional capability of the courts, not just with respect to their physical resources, but also their institutional role within the larger political and legal context, while raising some uncomfortable issues regarding the separation of powers.

Four new judges were appointed to the Constitutional Court in 2009 to replace the last of the founding members who had all served their time, including the Chief Justice.[128] The Constitutional Court now only has three white members – a reflection of the racial makeup of South Africa – but the only two female judges on the Constitutional Court suggest the lack of commitment to gender diversity. As South Africa evolves as a constitutional democracy, the judiciary will continue to face ongoing and fresh challenges. These include the continuing project of racial and gender transformation of the bench, ensuring that government remains committed to pursuing the rights in the Constitution, and holding the appropriate authorities accountable when they fail to do so. As this chapter has demonstrated, there is ample reason to believe that the vision of transformation encapsulated in the Constitution will continue to guide the appointment of judges as well as the jurisprudence of the Constitutional Court and lower courts. In just fifteen years, the judiciary in South Africa, and especially the judges of the Constitutional Court, have embodied the commitment to judicial independence. It is the project of racial and gender transformation that remains a central challenge.

[127] For example, in *S v Makwanyane and Another* 1995 (3) SA 391 (CC) (S. Afr.), one of the first cases heard by the Constitutional Court, the death penalty was abolished because it violated the right to life and the right to dignity. Similarly, in *Minister of Health v Treatment Action Campaign*, *supra* note 76, the Constitutional Court ordered the government to provide the medications demanded by the applicants, citing their right of access to health. But it is in the legislative arena, often without a court decision, that most of the authoritarian and discriminatory laws have been abolished.

[128] Unlike the judges of the U.S. Supreme Court, who have life tenure, the judges of the Constitutional Court ordinarily serve for a nonrenewable term of between twelve and fifteen years.

11

Lawyers in National Policymaking

Ann Southworth, Anthony Paik, and John P. Heinz

INTRODUCTION

The political influence of lawyers is a frequent topic of journalism, and Tocqueville is often quoted,[1] but systematic research on lawyers' political roles is sparse.[2] There

The authors acknowledge, with gratitude, the support of the American Bar Foundation, the University of California, Irvine School of Law, and the Institute for Policy Research, Northwestern University.

[1] *See* ALEXIS DE TOCQUEVILLE, DEMOCRACY IN AMERICA 280 (1835):

> The government of democracy is favorable to the political power of lawyers; for when the wealthy, the noble, and the prince are excluded from the government, they are sure to occupy the highest stations, in their own right, as it were, since they are the only men of information and sagacity, beyond the sphere of the people, who can be the object of the popular choice.

[2] One of the first systematic examinations of this subject is HEINZ EULAU & JOHN SPRAGUE, LAWYERS IN POLITICS, A STUDY IN PROFESSIONAL CONVERGENCE (1964). This topic represents the intersection of two broader literatures. The first is scholarship on the social networks of lawyers. *See, e.g.*, JOHN P. HEINZ & EDWARD O. LAUMANN, CHICAGO LAWYERS: THE SOCIAL STRUCTURE OF THE BAR (1982); John P. Heinz & Peter Manikas, *Networks Among Elites in a Local Criminal Justice System*, 26 LAW & SOC'Y REV. 831 (1992); John P. Heinz, Anthony Paik & Ann Southworth, *Lawyers for Conservative Causes: Clients, Ideology and Social Distance*, 37 LAW & SOC'Y REV. 5 (2005); Emmanuel Lazega & Marijtge van Duijn, *Position in Formal Structure, Personal Characteristics and Choices of Advisors in a Law Firm: A Logistic Regression Model for Dyadic Network Data*, 19 SOC. NETWORKS 375 (1997); Emmanuel Lazega & Philippa E. Pattison, *Multiplexity, Generalized Exchange and Cooperation in Organizations: A Case Study*, 21 SOC. NETWORKS 67 (1999). The second is scholarship on national political networks. *See, e.g.*, DAVID KNOKE, POLITICAL NETWORKS: THE STRUCTURAL PERSPECTIVE (1990); EDWARD O. LAUMANN & DAVID KNOKE, THE ORGANIZATIONAL STATE: A PERSPECTIVE ON NATIONAL ENERGY AND HEALTH DOMAINS (1987); Daniel P. Carpenter, Kevin M. Esterling & David M.J. Lazer, *Friends, Brokers, and Transivity: Who Informs Whom in Washington Politics*, 66 J. OF POL. 224 (2004); Robert M. Fernandez & Roger V. Gould, *A Dilemma of State Power: Brokerage and Influence in the National Health Policy Domain*, 99 AM. J. SOC. 1455 (1994); Kenneth A. Frank & Jeffrey Yasumoto, *Linking Action to Social Structure Within a System: Social Capital Within and Between Subgroups*, 104 AM. J. SOC. 642 (1998); Roger V. Gould, *Power and Social Structure in Community Elites*, 68 SOC. FORCES 531 (1989); John Higley & Gwen Moore, *Elite Integration in the United States and Australia*, 75 AM. POL. SCI. REV. 581 (1981); Charles Kadushin, *Friendship Among the French Financial Elite*, 60 AM. SOC. REV. 202 (1995); Mark S. Mizruchi, *Determinants of Political Opposition Among Large American Corporations*, 68 SOC. FORCES 1065 (1990); Gwen Moore, *The*

have, however, been some analyses of lawyers of specific types or within relatively narrow contexts. Studies have examined lawyers active as Washington lobbyists in four policy domains,[3] members of the U.S. Supreme Court bar,[4] and lawyers working for conservative and libertarian organizations in the mid-1990s.[5] The last of those pieces of research found that the networks of relationships among the lawyers and the organizations that they served were divided into segments defined by particular constituencies and that there were substantial differences in the characteristics of lawyers serving differing constituencies. Some lawyers, however, bridged the segments, serving as mediators or brokers. Organizations such as the Federalist Society and the Heritage Foundation sought to build ties within the conservative coalition, but deep cultural differences separated lawyers for social conservatives from those representing other constituencies, making cooperation difficult.[6]

In his afterword to a recent edition of *The Power Elite*, Alan Wolf observed:

> In his emphasis on politics and economics, Mills underestimated the important role that powerful symbolic and moral crusades have had in American life, including McCarthy's witch-hunt after communist influence. Had he paid more attention to McCarthyism, Mills would have been more likely to predict such events as the 1998–99 effort by Republicans to impeach President Clinton, the role played by divisive issues such as abortion, immigration, and affirmative action in American politics, and the continued importance of negative campaigning.[7]

The moral crusades of the Prohibition Era waned with the Depression, World War II, and the Cold War,[8] bringing economic and national security issues to the fore. Symbolic issues rose again in the late twentieth century and the beginning of the twenty-first, however, with political battles over abortion, gay marriage, gun control,

Structure of a National Elite Network 44 AM. SOC. REV. 673 (1979); Gwen Moore, Sarah Sobieraj, J. Allen Whitt, Olga Mayorova, & Daniel Beaulieu, *Elite Networks in Three U.S. Sectors: Nonprofit, Corporate, and Government*, 83 SOC. SCI. Q. 726 (2002); Robert Salisbury, John P. Heinz, Edward O. Laumann & Robert Nelson, *Who Works with Whom: Interest Group Alliances and Opposition*, 81 AM. POL. SCI. REV. 1217 (1987). For a review of this literature, see DAVID KNOKE, ORGANIZING FOR COLLECTIVE ACTION: THE POLITICAL ECONOMIES OF ASSOCIATIONS (1990).

3 *See* JOHN P. HEINZ, EDWARD O. LAUMANN, ROBERT L. NELSON & ROBERT H. SALISBURY, THE HOLLOW CORE: PRIVATE INTERESTS IN NATIONAL POLICYMAKING (1993); Robert Nelson, John P. Heinz, Edward O. Laumman & Robert H. Salisbury, *Lawyers and the Structure of Influence in Washington*, 22 LAW & SOC'Y REV. 237 (1988).

4 *See* KEVIN T. MCGUIRE, THE SUPREME COURT BAR: LEGAL ELITES IN THE WASHINGTON COMMUNITY (1993).

5 *See* Heinz, Paik & Southworth, *supra* note 2; Anthony Paik, Ann Southworth & John P. Heinz, *Lawyers of the Right: Networks and Organization*, 32 LAW & SOC. INQUIRY 883 (2007).

6 ANN SOUTHWORTH, LAWYERS OF THE RIGHT: PROFESSIONALIZING THE CONSERVATIVE COALITION (2008).

7 Alan Wolf, *Afterword* to C. WRIGHT MILLS, THE POWER ELITE 377 (2000).

8 *See* JOSEPH R. GUSSFIELD, SYMBOLIC CRUSADE: STATUS POLITICS AND THE AMERICAN TEMPERANCE MOVEMENT (1963).

and obscenity in broadcasting and the arts. These issues became increasingly salient with the rise of the religious right in the 1980s and 1990s and the realignment of the South into the Republican column. To some extent, of course, the change in agendas is associated with the fortunes of the two major political parties.[9]

In this chapter, we examine a set of interest groups active on a considerable range of national issues, including both moral and symbolic issues and matters of economic policy. We identify the characteristics of the groups and their advocates, and analyze the extent to which the lawyers' attributes vary systematically with the types of causes served and the organizations represented. We also examine the structure of the advocacy network and identify lines of conflict and cooperation within it.

RESEARCH DESIGN

The data considered here concern organizations and lawyers drawn from the full range of American politics – right, left, and center – and focus on a particular set of policy initiatives in 2004 and 2005. To define the relevant population of lawyers and organizations, we employed an issue events methodology, which is a strategy for delimiting the boundaries of the system under study.[10] The events examined here were classified as "legal affairs" issues by the *Congressional Quarterly Almanac* in 2004 and 2005, and dealt with abortion, gay rights, asbestos compensation, class action lawsuits, DNA testing/victims' rights, flag desecration, identity theft, medical malpractice liability, guns, bankruptcy, judicial nominations, federal court jurisdiction, eminent domain, and the Terri Schiavo case (see Appendix).

We identified interest groups that appeared in news stories about these issues in twenty newspapers and magazines (see Appendix), producing a list of more than 2,000 organizations, but we focus the analysis on the subset of 119 that appeared in at least six news accounts.[11] Those organizations, listed in Table 11.1, include businesses, trade associations, bar associations, membership organizations, religious groups, think tanks, and many of the best-known liberal, conservative, and libertarian policy organizations. Organizations were included in the sample even if they did not use lawyers in a policy advocacy role.

We then gathered publicly available data about the organizations and their advocates. We searched the LexisNexis database for records of federal litigation concerning the fourteen issues during 2004–2005. The 119 organizations litigated 136 cases

[9] *See* John W. Kingdon, Agendas, Alternatives, and Public Policies (2d ed. 1997).

[10] *See* Edward O. Laumann, Peter V. Marsden & David Prensky, *The Boundary Specification Problem in Network Analysis, in* Research Methods in Social Network Analysis (Linton C. Freeman & Douglas R. White eds., 1989).

[11] Some of the nonprofit organizations listed "related" organizations on their IRS Form 990s. We included data about those organizations in our analysis.

relating to 11 of the issues. From Westlaw's legislative database, we collected records of testimony on behalf of the organizations on the fourteen issues during the same period. They submitted testimony in forty-four Congressional hearings. We coded the positions taken by the organizations in the litigation and hearings and generated a list of advocates appearing on behalf of the organizations.

From the OpenSecrets.org database of the Center for Responsive Politics, we gathered information about the organizations' lobbying expenditures. Sixty-three of the 119 organizations had filed lobbying registration statements.[12] Reports by nonprofit organizations to the IRS and the annual reports of corporations provided information about the organizations' finances and boards of directors and advisory boards.[13] Data about foundation funding of nonprofit organizations were drawn from the Foundation Index database.[14] Sixty-six organizations received foundation grants in 2004–2005 (not surprisingly, no businesses or trade associations were among them).

We identified 1,111 lawyers who served the 119 organizations in litigation or legislative testimony on the fourteen issues, or as registered lobbyists, or as members of the organizations' boards of directors, and we then gathered information about those lawyers from the Martindale-Hubbell Law Directory and Westlaw. We were not able to identify any lawyers serving twenty-six of the organizations in those roles.

ORGANIZATIONAL CATEGORIES

For analytic purposes, we divided the organizations into eight categories: "business," "liberal activist," "liberal establishment," "conservative establishment," "religious conservative," "patriotic," "guns," and a residual "other" category (see Table 11.1).[15] The categories serve as a data reduction device – a way to avoid discussing the welter of organizations one by one, which would make it very difficult to see patterns. The categories are necessarily somewhat ill-defined at their margins; the labels are shorthand summaries that fail to capture the complexity or range of the organizations.

The "business" category includes both corporations and nonprofit groups that serve business interests. The "liberal activist" category includes groups allied with the liberal establishment but associated with its more activist elements. The "conservative establishment" category includes a variety of mainstream conservative

12 Organizations are exempt from the filing requirement if their lobbying expenses do not exceed $22,500 during a semiannual period.

13 In the few cases where 2005 Form 990s were unavailable, we used 2006 forms.

14 *See* The Foundation Center, *Foundation Directory On-Line*, http://fconline.foundationcenter.org/ (visited for research for this project in 2009).

15 Organizations assigned to the "other" category did not fit easily into any of the first seven categories. *See* Table 11.1.

TABLE 11.1. *Organizational categories*

Business
American Bankers Association
American Bankruptcy Institute
American Insurance Association
American Medical Association
America's Health Insurance Plans
Bank of America
ChoicePoint, Inc.
Citigroup
Club for Growth
Coalition for Asbestos Reform
Dupont Co.
Equitas Ltd.
Exxon Mobil Corp.
Federal Mogul Co.
Ford Motor Co.
General Electric
Georgia Hospital Association PAC
Georgia-Pacific Corp.
Halliburton
MAG Mutual Insurance Co.
Medical Mutual Liability Insurance Society of Maryland
Medical Society of the District of Columbia
National Association of Consumer Bankruptcy Attorneys
National Association of Manufacturers
National Retail Federation
Physician Insurers Association of America
Texas Medical Society
U.S. Chamber of Commerce
USG Corp.
W.R. Grace and Company
Religious Conservative
Alliance Defense Fund
Alliance for Marriage
American Center for Law and Justice
American Family Association
American Values
Arlington Group
Center for a Just Society
Christian Coalition of America
Christian Defense Coalition
Concerned Women for America
Eagle Forum
Ethics and Religious Liberty Commission of the Southern Baptist Convention

Family Foundation
Family Research Council, Inc.
Focus on the Family
Georgia Right to Life
Massachusetts Family Institute
National Association of Evangelicals
National Right to Life Committee
Operation Rescue
Traditional Values Coalition
U.S. Conference of Catholic Bishops

Liberal Establishment
AFL-CIO
Allan Guttmacher Institute
American Bar Association
Third Way
Brookings Institution
Center for Responsive Politics
Consumer Federation of America
Democratic Leadership Council
Democratic National Committee
Kaiser Family Foundation
Leadership Conference on Civil Rights
NAACP
National Consumer Law Center
Pew Research Center
RAND Corporation

Liberal Activist
Alliance for Justice
American Civil Liberties Union
Americans United for Separation of Church and State
Brady Campaign to Prevent Gun Violence
Earthjustice
Environmental Working Group
Feminist Majority Foundation
Foundation for Taxpayer and Consumer Rights
Georgia Equality
Human Rights Campaign
Innocence Project
Lambda Legal Defense and Education Fund
MoveOn
National Abortion Federation
NARAL Pro-Choice America
National Gay and Lesbian Task Force
National Organization for Women
National Women's Law Center

(*continued*)

TABLE 11.1. *(continued)*

People for the American Way
Planned Parenthood Federation of America
Public Citizen
Sierra Club
U.S. Public Interest Research Group
Conservative Establishment
American Conservative Union
American Enterprise Institute
American Tort Reform Association
Americans for Tax Reform
Cato Institute
Committee for Justice
Federalist Society
FreedomWorks
Heritage Foundation
Institute for Justice
Judicial Confirmation Network
Manhattan Institute
Progress for America
Guns
Gun Owners of America
National Rifle Association
National Shooting Sports Foundation
Patriotic
American Legion
Citizens Flag Alliance
Veterans of Foreign Wars
Other
American Association of Retired Persons
American Association for Justice
Feminists for Life
Fidelis
Foundation of the Defense of Democracies
Free Congress Foundation
Georgia Watch
Identity Theft Resource Center
Log Cabin Republicans
Trial Lawyers Association of Metropolitan Washington

TABLE 11.2. *Median founding year and median revenues*

Median founding year		Median annual revenue ($)	
Business	1907	Business	62,673,375
Patriotic	1919	Patriotic	37,752,340
Liberal establishment	1955	Guns	31,413,781
Guns	1971	Liberal establishment	7,819,349
Liberal activist	1974	Conservative establishment	7,507,175
Conservative establishment	1982	Liberal activist	6,735,030
Religious conservative	1984	Religious conservative	4,348,165

groups, many of them founded in the late 1960s and afterward with the support of conservative patrons to counter the influence of the "liberal establishment."[16] It includes libertarian groups, as well as organizations that seek to appeal to the several constituencies of the conservative coalition.[17]

Table 11.2 presents the median founding years and annual revenues for the organizational categories, and shows a rough correspondence between age and resources. The two oldest categories, business and patriotic organizations, have the most revenue, and one of the newest categories, religious conservatives, has the least.

Using information from the Foundation Center, we identified contributors to each category. Table 11.3 presents the top five. Three foundations – Ford, Pew, and the Hewlett Foundation – were among the largest funders for both the liberal activist and liberal establishment categories. Among the other organizational categories, the only major contributor found in more than one is the Scaife Foundation, which appears in both the conservative establishment and the "other" categories.

The issue agendas of the organizations differ sharply (see Table 11.4). For example, 31 percent of the organizations in the conservative establishment category and 32 percent of the religious conservative organizations were active on the

[16] SOUTHWORTH, *supra* note 6; Ann Southworth, *Conservative Lawyers and the Contest over the Meaning of "Public Interest Law"*, 52 UCLA L. REV. 1223 (2005).

[17] C. Boyden Gray founded the Committee for Justice in 2002 at the request of Karl Rove, President George W. Bush's top political strategist, to push for the confirmation of President Bush's judicial nominees. Gray enlisted the support of business organizations, which had previously resisted engaging in confirmation battles that revolved primarily around social issues rather than the economic matters that concerned their members. *See* Tom Hamburger & Peter Wallsten, *Business Lobby to Get Behind Judicial Bids: An Industry Group's Plan to Spend Millions Promoting Conservative Nominees Brings a New Dimension in the Divisive Confirmation Battles*, L.A. TIMES, Jan. 6, 2005, at A1. Gray also recruited leading lawyers for social conservative groups, including Jay Sekulow, chief counsel of the American Center for Law and Justice, to participate in confirmation battles. *See* David E. Rosenbaum & Lynette Clemetson, *In Fight to Confirm New Justice, Two Field Generals Rally Their Troops Again*, N.Y. TIMES, July 3, 2005, at A19.

TABLE 11.3. *Five largest foundation funders of each organizational category*

Business	
Starr Foundation, NY	$ 4,000,000
Johnson Foundation, Robert Wood, NJ	$ 3,626,641
AEGON Transamerica Foundation, IA	$ 2,000,000
Kauffman Foundation, Ewing Marion, MO	$ 900,000
Mott Foundation, Charles Stewart, MI	$ 450,000
Liberal activist	
Ford Foundation, NY	$ 9,191,000
Pew Charitable Trusts, PA	$ 8,570,000
Hewlett Foundation, William and Flora, CA	$ 8,075,000
Packard Foundation, David and Lucile, CA	$ 6,755,000
Open Society Institute, NY	$ 5,880,000
Liberal establishment	
Pew Charitable Trusts, PA	$ 38,242,000
Ford Foundation, NY	$ 8,116,200
Hewlett Foundation, William and Flora, CA	$ 5,618,000
Casey Foundation, Annie E., MD	$ 3,884,959
Reynolds Foundation, Donald W., NV	$ 2,327,477
Conservative establishment	
Noble Foundation, Samuel Roberts, Inc., OK	$ 5,000,000
Bradley Foundation, Lynde and Harry, Inc., WI	$ 4,900,000
Kovner Foundation, NJ	$ 2,849,301
Herrick Foundation, MI	$ 2,325,000
Scaife Foundation, Sarah, Inc., PA	$ 2,225,000
Religious conservatives	
Batten, Jr. Foundation, Aimee & Frank, VA	$ 2,000,000
God's Gift, CA	$ 1,565,000
Prince Foundation, Edgar and Elsa, MI	$ 1,108,000
DeVos Foundation, Richard and Helen, MI	$ 1,005,000
Community Foundation, Inc., MS	$ 700,000
Guns	
Sayler-Hawkins Foundation, MO	$ 215,000
San Francisco Foundation, CA	$ 25,000
Dow Foundation, Herbert H. and Barbara C., MI	$ 20,000
Anderson Family Foundation, A. Gary, CA	$ 10,000
Brook Family Foundation, ME	$ 10,000
Patriotic	
Wal-Mart Foundation, AR	$ 3,248,524
Eyman Trust, Jesse, OH	$ 6,000
Hurdus Foundation, Syde, Inc., NY	$ 1,000
Burns Foundation, Nancy and Herbert, ME	$ 1,000
Other	
Marcus Foundation, Inc., GA	$ 750,000
Abramson Family Foundation, FL	$ 485,000
Scaife Foundation, Sarah, Inc., PA	$ 400,000
Annenberg Foundation, PA	$ 275,000
Steinhardt Foundation, Judy and Michael, NY	$ 250,000

fetal protection issue, but none of the business, guns, or patriotic organizations were found there. Similarly, 68 percent of the religious conservatives were active on gay marriage and, again, none of the business, guns, or patriotic organizations were. By contrast, 43 percent of the business organizations were active on the asbestos issue, but none of the religious conservatives participated. All of the patriotic organizations were active on flag desecration; apart from them, however, we see only a few of the liberal activist, religious conservative, and conservative establishment organizations there. At the other extreme in breadth of participation, judicial nominations drew the attention of 92 percent of the conservative establishment category, 80 percent of the liberal establishment organizations, 73 percent of the religious conservatives, 65 percent of liberal activist organizations, and 50 percent of those in the "other" category, but this was the only issue that drew the participation of a broad set of the liberal organizations. Except for parental consent to abortion, on which 48 percent of the liberal activist organizations were active, and the class action issue, on which 40 percent of the liberal establishment organizations participated, relatively small percentages of the liberal organizations appeared on other issues. Because conservative Republicans controlled all three branches of the federal government in 2004–2005, they were able to dominate the issue agenda and secure active consideration of their proposals. In other periods, liberal organizations might well have broader agendas.

Using multidimensional scaling (MDS), we analyzed the extent to which the issues drew the participation of the same organizations (see Figure 11.1). In this analysis, similarity is measured by "structural equivalence" – issues that activate similar sets of organizations are close together in the figure, and those that motivate disparate sets are farther apart. Each issue is represented by a point; it is the location of those points, not of the labels identifying them, that is relevant.

We find at the upper right a rather tight cluster of issues that mobilize both liberal activists and social conservatives – judicial nominations, gay marriage, fetal protection, parental consent, and Terry Schiavo. There is a considerable gap between these issues and a much more diverse array, including bankruptcy, ID theft, medical malpractice, class actions, and asbestos, many of which are of particular concern to businesses. This pattern suggests that the agendas of conservative organizations, and the opposition of liberal activists on those issues, are a primary determinant of this structure. As noted earlier, this finding may well be historically contingent.

LAWYER CHARACTERISTICS

We tabulated the gender, type of law school attended, number of years since admission to the bar, and practice location of lawyers who served the several categories of

TABLE 11.4. *Distribution of activity of organizational categories across issue events: percent active*

Issue event	Business	Liberal activist	Liberal establishment	Conservative establishment	Religious conservative	Patriotic	Guns	Other
Fetal protection	0%	22%	20%	31%	32%	0%	0%	10%
Gay Marriage	0%	26%	33%	8%	68%	0%	0%	20%
Asbestos	43%	9%	13%	23%	0%	33%	0%	10%
Class Action	17%	9%	40%	38%	0%	0%	0%	20%
DNA / Victims	0%	9%	7%	0%	0%	0%	0%	0%
Flag Desecration	0%	13%	0%	8%	9%	100%	0%	0%
ID Theft	13%	4%	0%	0%	0%	0%	0%	10%
Medical Malpractice	33%	17%	27%	31%	18%	0%	0%	40%
Gun Liability	0%	4%	20%	23%	0%	0%	100%	0%
Bankruptcy	23%	22%	20%	8%	9%	0%	0%	0%
Nominations	23%	65%	80%	92%	73%	33%	67%	50%
Federal Courts	0%	26%	27%	8%	59%	0%	0%	20%
Eminent Domain	0%	0%	7%	8%	5%	0%	0%	0%
Parental Consent	0%	48%	20%	23%	64%	0%	0%	20%
Schiavo	3%	13%	20%	38%	59%	0%	0%	10%
Total number of orgs.	30	23	15	13	22	3	3	10

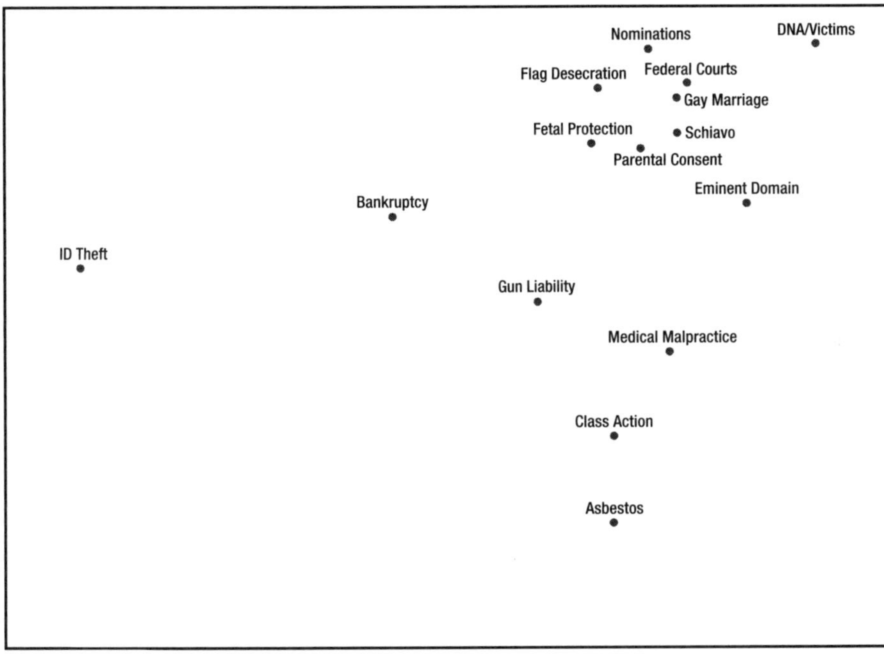

FIGURE 11.1. Relationships among issues based on organizations' patterns of activation (two-dimensional MDS; stress = .08).

organizations. There are a number of striking patterns (see Table 11.5).[18] Nearly half of the lawyers for liberal activist groups are women, but their representation among advocates for liberal establishment organizations approximates the percentage among licensed lawyers nationwide (27 percent, according to the most recent figures compiled by the American Bar Foundation).[19] Women are slightly less prevalent among business advocates (21 percent) and relatively rare among lawyers for conservative establishment organizations (11 percent) and religious conservatives (7 percent).

There are also large variations in the educational backgrounds of the lawyers. The top seven schools in the 2000 *U.S. News & World Report* rankings – Yale, Harvard, Stanford, Columbia, Chicago, Michigan, and New York University[20] – are called "elite" in Table 11.5. The "prestige" schools are those ranked from eighth to twentieth by *U.S. News*, and the "regional" category includes those ranked twenty-one

18 Lawyers who represented organizations in more than one category were counted in all of them. Therefore, to the extent that lawyers bridge categories, differentiation among the categories is reduced.

19 Clara Carson, The Lawyer Statistical Report: The U.S. Legal Profession in 2000 (2004).

20 We used the 2000 rankings to allow for comparison with other research that relies on the 2000 figures. Arguably, prestige at the time of matriculation is the more relevant variable.

TABLE 11.5. *Characteristics of lawyers in organizational categories*

Variable	Business	Liberal activists	Liberal establishment	Conservative establishment	Religious conservatives	Other	Total
Gender (%)							
Male	79	53***	76	89*	93**	84**	76
Female	21	47	24	11	7	16	24
N	479	190	132	54	56	196	1102
Law school (%)							
Elite	24***	35***	36**	22	10**	6***	24
Prestige	25	28	23	25	14	12	22
Regional	23	14	15	18	18	20	20
Local	29	24	27	35	57	62	35
N	452	177	123	55	49	177	1028
Law experience (%)							
1–20 yrs	39***	48***	12***	42	29	21***	34
21–30 yrs	39	25	34	29	51	41	36
31+ yrs	22	27	54	29	20	38	30
N	396	132	106	48	45	173	898
Location (%)							
DC	31***	31	30	27***	12***	13***	25
DC suburbs	1	1	2	14	4	2	2
Major cities	29	28	18	25	8	14	25
Elsewhere	39	40	50	34	76	72	48
N	444	163	119	44	50	184	999

Note: Significant chi-square tests are indicated for each category, † <.10; *<.05; **<.01; ***<.001.

to fifty. "Local" law schools are those ranked below fifty. Lawyers for liberal activist groups had the most prestigious credentials, with 63 percent having attended schools in the top two categories. Roughly half of the lawyers in the business, liberal establishment, and conservative establishment categories came from schools in the elite and prestige categories, but only 24 percent of lawyers serving organizations in the religious conservative category had attended such schools and more than half were educated in local schools.

Business, liberal activist, and conservative establishment groups had the youngest lawyers, and lawyers for the liberal establishment organizations were by far the oldest. Only 12 percent of the latter had been lawyers for twenty years or less, but 42 percent of those working for the conservative establishment and 48 percent of lawyers working for liberal activist organizations were in this least experienced category.

Roughly a third of the lawyers for business, liberal activist, and liberal establishment groups, and 41 percent of lawyers for conservative establishment groups, worked in the Washington, D.C. metropolitan area. All of these four organizational categories also had significant numbers of lawyers in "major cities" – defined as the ten largest U.S. cities. In contrast, only 16 percent of lawyers for religious conservative groups worked in the Washington, D.C. metropolitan area, and only 8 percent of them worked in other major cities; 76 percent of these lawyers were located outside of the major metropolitan centers.

The characteristics of the lawyers for religious conservative groups, then, set them apart from advocates in the other categories. Lawyers for the religious organizations were much more likely than those in other categories to be male, to have attended local law schools, and to work in smaller towns.

Overall, nearly half of all the lawyers we identified did not work in metropolitan Washington, D.C. or even in the ten largest cities. We had expected to find a larger number that fit the "Washington insider" stereotype. The conservative establishment category included the largest percentage of lawyers in the D.C. area and the smallest percentage working "elsewhere," suggesting that it was the most "insider" category during the George W. Bush presidency.

ORGANIZATIONAL NETWORKS

We analyzed several types of data concerning relationships among the organizations. First, we examined foundation grants received by the nonprofits. We created a matrix of funders and recipients, with each organization recorded as either receiving or not receiving a contribution from each foundation that contributed to more than one organization.[21] The pattern of foundation grants to each pair of organizations determines their proximity in Figure 11.2. We have omitted labels from some points to make the presentation easier to comprehend; the organizations we chose to omit are, for the most part, less well known. In some cases, more than one organization is represented by a single point because those organizations had identical or highly similar sets of funders.

The cluster at the left of the figure includes organizations associated with social conservatives and the religious right: American Values, The Family Research Council, Concerned Women for America, Focus on the Family, Alliance for Marriage, Alliance Defense Fund, American Family Association, and American Center for Law and Justice.

At the right is a cluster of liberal advocacy organizations. In the upper part, we see organizations associated primarily with the activist wing of the Democratic Party – groups such as the Innocence Project, Human Rights Campaign, Sierra Club, National Gay and Lesbian Task Force, People for the American Way, Earthjustice, Americans United for the Separation of Church and State, NARAL Pro-Choice

[21] We then read this similarity matrix into a multidimensional scaling algorithm, using the correlation measure.

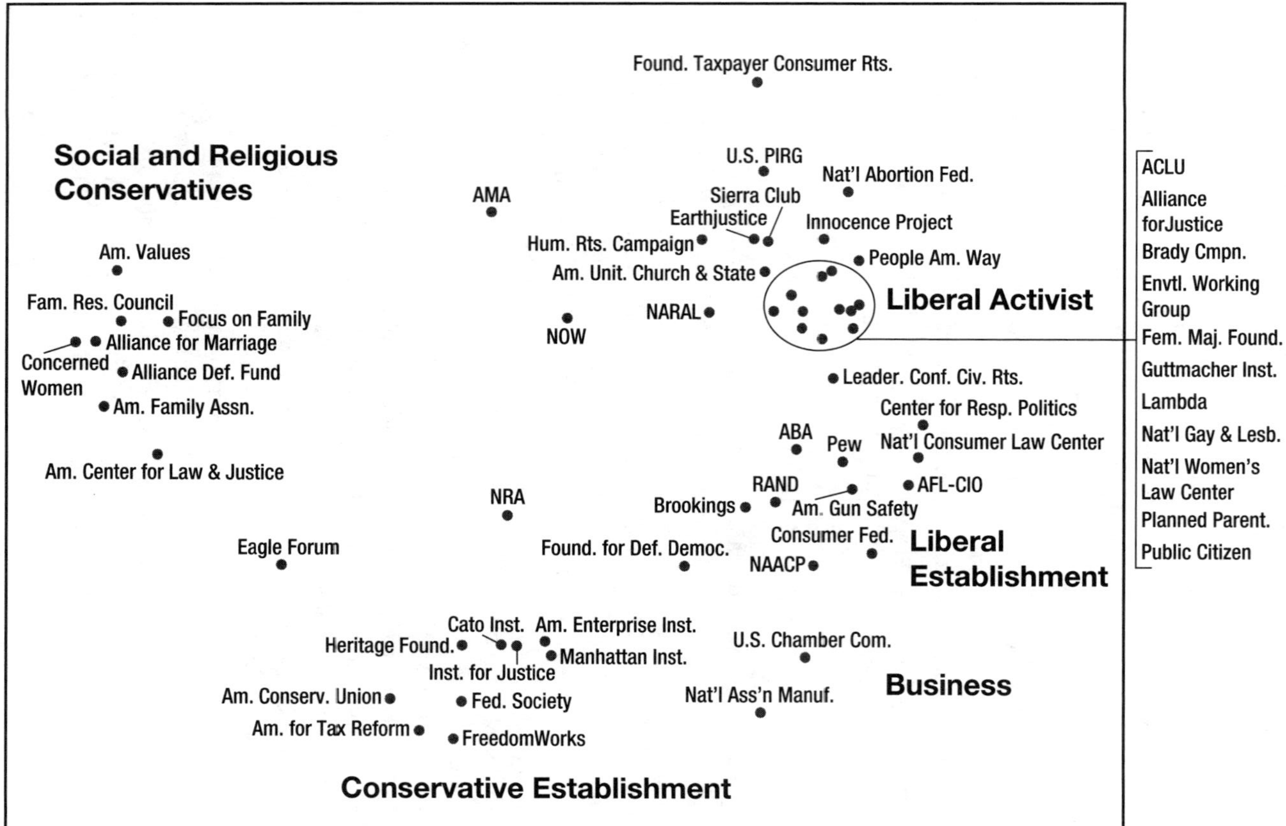

FIGURE 11.2. Relationships among nonprofit organizations based on foundation funding (two-dimensional MDS; stress = .11).

America, American Civil Liberties Union (ACLU), National Consumer Law Center, Foundation for Taxpayer and Consumer Rights (now "Consumer Watchdog"), and U.S. Public Interest Research Group. The groups in the lower section of this large cluster tend to be more established liberal organizations, such as the Consumer Federation of America, AFL-CIO, RAND Corporation, American Bar Association (ABA), Brookings Institution, Pew Research Center, and NAACP. At the lower center of the figure, we find a cluster of "conservative establishment" organizations. Just to the right of this cluster are the U.S. Chamber of Commerce and the National Association of Manufacturers, close to the conservative establishment but somewhat apart from it. As noted earlier, the foundation data do not include for-profit corporations.

We also used other measures – participation in litigation and legislative testimony, joint representation by lobbying firms, and shared board members – to assess relationships among the organizations, but the degree to which organizations share those potential sources of contact is insufficient to provide a reliable assessment of similarity on any one of these variables, considered separately. By combining data on the four variables, however, we have sufficient connections among the organizations to analyze their relationships.

Assuming that all of the organizations in the sample could, in principle, be connected, the number of possible ties among 119 organizations is 7,021. Of those, 151 ties are in fact present in the data. Thus, the density of connections is only 2 percent – a very sparsely connected network. Forty-two of the 119 organizations have no connection to any of the others on any of the four possible types of ties: overlapping directors or advisory board members, appearance in litigation on the same side of a case, legislative testimony taking the same position on an issue, or use of the same lobbying firm. Moreover, of those four kinds of ties, the shared use of a lobbying firm is the most numerous, and it is a relatively weak type of affiliation. The forty-two unconnected organizations include some prominent ones (for example, the Democratic National Committee, Eagle Forum, U.S. Conference of Catholic Bishops, Pew Research Center, and Earthjustice). The data, therefore, do not indicate a densely or tightly integrated set of Washington operatives in which the important actors are connected to a wide array of other interest groups. Rather, we found a loosely coupled system with frequent structural holes. The organizations involved in this set of issues are not characterized by extensive overlapping directorates or by frequent joint activity on litigation, legislative testimony, or lobbying.

Figure 11.3 shows the connections among the seventy-seven organizations that have ties to at least one other organization in our sample.[22] Note that some of the

[22] The analysis in Figure 11.3 uses a "spring-embedding" algorithm. The organizations, represented by points, are pulled together or apart by their varying ties to other organizations. In the algorithm, these competing forces correspond to tension exerted by springs, and the springs pull against a constant

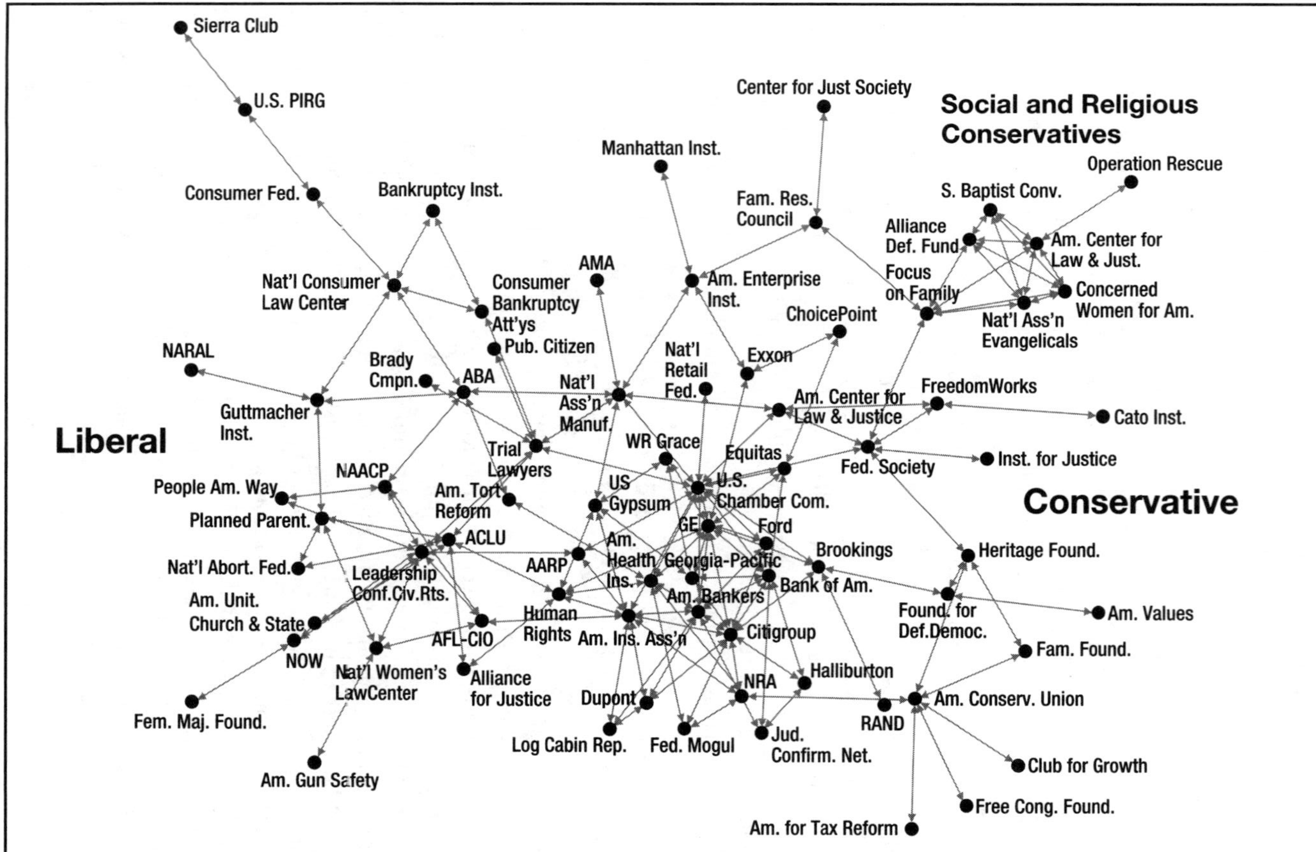

FIGURE 11.3. Affinity of active organizations based on shared board members, lobbyists, litigation participation, and legislative testimony (spring-embedding algorithm, N=77).

organizations are connected to others only through chains with single links. The Sierra Club, for example, is tied to the structure through the U.S. Public Interest Research Group, which is linked only to the Consumer Federation of America, which is in turn tied only to the National Consumer Law Center.[23]

At the upper right is a tight cluster of organizations that take conservative positions on religious and social issues. The organizations are Operation Rescue, the National Association of Evangelicals, Concerned Women for America, Ethics and Religious Liberty Commission of the Southern Baptist Convention, Alliance Defense Fund, Focus on the Family, and the American Center for Law and Justice. They work primarily on "life" issues (fetal protection, parental consent to abortion, Terry Schiavo), gay marriage, and judicial nominations, and are tied to the remainder of the structure only through Focus on the Family, which is in turn connected to the Family Research Council and the Federalist Society. The Family Research Council and the Center for a Just Society, which have policy agendas similar to those of these seven organizations, have a path to the remainder of the network through the American Enterprise Institute. Thus, the religious organizations are relatively isolated, with few channels for communication with other groups.

Lower on the right side of the space we see another cluster of conservative organizations, arrayed around the American Conservative Union (ACU). The cluster ranges from the Heritage Foundation, higher in the space, to Americans for Tax Reform, at the lower margin, and includes American Values, the Family Foundation, the Club for Growth, the Free Congress Foundation, and the Fund for Defense of Democracy, in addition to the ACU. These eight organizations are linked to others only through the Federalist Society, the Brookings Institution, and the National Rifle Association (NRA). Thus, their available channels of communication are quite limited but not as restricted as those of the religious conservatives.

At the left of the space, lower in the vertical dimension, we find a set of organizations that take liberal positions on abortion and other religious and moral issues. These groups include NARAL, the Alan Guttmacher Institute, Planned Parenthood, People for the American Way, the National Abortion Federation, the National Organization for Women, the Feminist Majority Foundation, and the National Women's Law Center. Note that the location of these organizations is diametrically opposite to that of the socially conservative groups, as far apart as it is possible for the two sets to be within the space. This is a classic oppositional structure.

In the upper left quadrant are liberal organizations that focus primarily on consumer advocacy: the U.S. Public Interest Research Group, Consumer Federation

force, pushing the organizations apart. The resulting location of each point in the solution is a product of these several forces, operating simultaneously.

23 The marginality of the Sierra Club in this analysis no doubt reflects the fact that environmental issues were present in our sample only in the asbestos compensation bill and, to a lesser extent, in the class action legislation.

of America, National Consumer Law Center, American Bankruptcy Institute, National Association of Consumer Bankruptcy Attorneys, and Public Citizen. Closer to the center of the space but still on the left side are the ABA, NAACP, Leadership Conference on Civil Rights, ACLU, AFL-CIO, and Alliance for Justice – prominent liberal organizations with broad issue agendas.

The area with the greatest density of connections is populated by businesses and trade associations. Those with especially large numbers of connections include the U.S. Chamber of Commerce, GE, Citigroup, the American Bankers Association, America's Health Insurance Plans, and the American Insurance Association. The density of connections among the business organizations is in striking contrast to the sparseness of ties in other areas of the space.

Surrounding the social and religious conservatives, there is a looser set of organizations that, in a political sense, are intermediate between those groups and business interests. These surrounding organizations, many of which are libertarian in orientation, include the Manhattan Institute, the American Enterprise Institute, FreedomWorks, and the Cato Institute. These organizations were aligned with religious and social conservatives in electoral politics and on issues such as eminent domain[24] and school choice, but they do not support the restrictions on individual liberty advocated by social conservatives, and this surely accounts for the separation of the two constituencies. The Family Research Council and the Federalist Society indirectly connect the libertarian groups to social and religious conservatives.

Overall, this appears to be a center/periphery structure. That is, organizations that have broader issue agendas (AARP, U.S. Chamber of Commerce, the National Association of Manufacturers) are more central, and those that have narrow agendas, often restricted to a single issue, are at the margins (such as NARAL, Sierra Club, Operation Rescue, and the Judicial Confirmation Network). Issue agendas motivate these relationships and may occasionally draw relatively unlikely allies together. The American Insurance Association and the AFL-CIO agreed on the wisdom of creating an asbestos compensation fund, for example, and both the ABA and the National Association of Manufacturers supported John Roberts's nomination to the U.S. Supreme Court. As a general rule, however, liberals are located near other liberals, and conservatives are close to other conservatives. Several organizations in the conservative establishment, such as the Heritage Foundation and the American Conservative Union, are peripheral to the broader structure because their role in mobilizing the conservative coalition pulls those organizations away from the center, toward other conservatives. Similarly, on the left, the AFL-CIO and NAACP are drawn toward groups advocating liberal positions on social issues. The separation

[24] The Supreme Court's decision allowing a municipality's exercise of eminent domain powers on behalf of a private developer in *Kelo v. City of New London*, 545 U. S. 469 (2005), created a firestorm among social conservatives, who feared that cities would use such powers to condemn property held by churches, which are exempt from taxes.

of the conservative establishment and the business conservatives from social and religious conservatives, however, is quite unlike the pattern on the liberal side of the space. While the liberal organizations at the left margin are loosely tied to one another, social and religious conservatives are densely clustered but have fewer links to other parts of the political network.

There are two areas of the network in which there are high levels of density within a particular cluster. The first is the cluster of social and religious conservatives at the upper right of the space, and the second and larger one is the set of businesses and trade associations at the lower middle of the figure. Unlike the social conservatives, however, the banks, insurance companies, and other large businesses are not only connected to each other but are well integrated into the overall system, with many links that provide potential for communication to other sectors.

CONCLUSION

The data indicate that the characteristics of lawyers representing the several categories of organizations vary widely (Table 11.5). Women are overrepresented among those serving liberal activist organizations, but strikingly underrepresented among those working with social and religious conservative groups. Similarly, lawyers for liberal activist groups had the most prestigious academic credentials, while those serving conservative religious organizations were much less likely to have such credentials. The lawyers working with religious conservatives were about half as likely to have attended a prestigious law school as were those serving the conservative establishment.

Moreover, analyses done at the organizational level strongly indicate that groups speaking for social and religious conservatives have few ties to other sorts of interest groups. Figures 11.2 and 11.3 suggest, respectively, that the sources of funding available to social conservatives are distinct and that there are only very limited channels of communication between them and other groups, including other conservatives.

Our previous research found that lawyers for the various constituencies of the conservative coalition are divided by class, culture, and geography, and that the two primary elements of the Republican coalition – social conservatives and business interests – occupy separate social worlds. Some individuals and organizations seek to bridge the differences and to promote cooperation across these constituencies, but dissimilarities and discord persist. The research presented here helps situate these prior findings in a broader political landscape. It suggests that socially conservative advocates and organizations stand apart not only from other conservatives but from the interconnected communities of lawyers and organizations that speak for most major players in national policy making.

During the period examined here, the Republican Party controlled all three branches of the federal government. Despite that control, which was reflected in the issue agenda, social and religious conservatives accomplished few of their major goals. Was their lack of success attributable to the fact that their lawyers were, generally, less highly credentialed and socially connected than those of other interest groups? Or was their frustration due to the constituency's own relative disadvantage – in wealth, social class, educational attainment, and political ties? Lawyers' characteristics and assets usually reflect the constituencies they represent, which makes it problematic to distinguish between the influence of lawyers and the power of the interest group base for which they speak.

APPENDIX

The Issue Events

Fetal Protection (2004): Congress passed a bill (HR 1997 – PL 108–21), which President Bush signed, giving federal legal status to a fetus. The legislation made it a separate offense to harm a fetus during the commission of a federal crime against a pregnant woman.

Gay Rights (2004): A proposed constitutional amendment to ban gay marriage failed in the House and Senate (S J Res 40, H J Res 106). Republicans hoped to prevent judges from invalidating the 1996 Defense of Marriage Act, which defined marriage as "a legal union between one man and one woman."

Asbestos Compensation (2004): Republican Senators failed to pass legislation (S 2290) to create a no-fault compensation fund for victims of asbestos exposure.

Class Action Lawsuits (2004): Failed Republican legislation (S 2062) would have limited plaintiffs' opportunities to file class action lawsuits in state courts.

DNA Testing/Victims Rights (2004): Legislation was signed into law (HR 5107 – PL 108–405) making it easier for inmates to gain access to post-conviction DNA tests while also allowing retrials for cases in which test results indicated an inmate might not be guilty.

Flag Desecration (2004): A proposed constitutional amendment to criminalize physical desecration of the American flag failed to move beyond the Senate Judiciary Committee (S J Res 4).

Identity Theft (2004): On July 15, President Bush signed into law a bill cleared by Congress (HR 1731 – PL 108–275), establishing stronger criminal penalties for identity theft.

Medical Malpractice (2004): Republicans attempted but failed to cap noneconomic damage awards in medical malpractice suits (S 2061).

Guns (2004): Due to a number of Democratic amendments, such as one renewing the 1994 ban on semiautomatic assault weapons, Republican Senators failed to pass legislation (S 1805) aimed at limiting the firearm industry's liability for gun violence. The bill would have barred civil lawsuits against manufacturers, distributors, and importers of firearms and ammunition.

Bankruptcy Overhaul (2004): Despite extensive bipartisan support for legislation aimed at making it more difficult for individuals to erase their debts by filing for bankruptcy protection, Congress was unable to clear the bill (HR 975, S1920). Nonetheless, Congress did pass legislation allowing family farmers to restructure their debts without losing their land (S 2864 – PL 108–369).

Judicial Nominations (2004): Although Democratic Senators blocked 10 of President Bush's appellate court nominees through procedural votes, Bush nonetheless filled 203 lifetime seats on federal district and appellate courts. Moreover, Republicans pushed for a Senate rules change – the "nuclear option" – requiring only a fifty-one vote majority to break filibusters of judicial nominees.

Federal Court Jurisdiction (2004): In an attempt to limit federal judges' jurisdiction over certain types of cases while also redrawing appellate court maps, the House passed three bills: HR 3313 barred federal courts from hearing cases challenging a provision of the Defense of Marriage Act; HR 2028 denied federal courts jurisdiction over challenges to the wording of the Pledge of Allegiance; and S 878 added provisions to divide the 9th Circuit into three separate appeals courts.

Judicial Nominations (2005): President Bush nominated John Roberts to succeed William Rehnquist as Chief Justice, and the Senate confirmed. The Senate also confirmed the nomination of Samuel Alito to the U.S. Supreme Court and five of seven previously filibustered lower federal court nominees.

Asbestos Compensation (2005): On May 26, the Senate Judiciary Committee approved a bill (S 852 – S Rept 109 – 97) creating a $140 billion trust fund to compensate people sickened by asbestos exposure.

Medical Malpractice (2005): In an effort to cap noneconomic damage awards in medical malpractice cases at $250,000 and to limit punitive damages to two times the economic damages or $250,000, Republicans passed a bill in the House (HR 5), but failed in the Senate.

Class Action Lawsuits (2005): On February 18, 2005, President Bush signed a measure giving federal courts jurisdiction over class action lawsuits when the total amount in dispute exceeded $5 million and the defendant and a large portion of the plaintiffs lived in different states (S 5 – PL 109–2).

Eminent Domain (2005): The House Judiciary Committee decisively approved a measure (HR 4128 – H Rept 109 – 262) limiting the effects of a controversial Supreme Court ruling, *Kelo v. City of New London*,[25] on eminent domain. The bill

[25] 545 U.S. 469 (2005).

sought to prohibit states and localities receiving federal development funds from using eminent domain to seize private property for economic development.

Guns (2005): Legislation limiting the legal liability of firearms makers and dealers was cleared and signed into law. Democrats attached several amendments, including a requirement that child safety locks be sold with all handguns.

Flag Desecration (2005): The House passed a proposed constitutional amendment (HJ Res 10 – H Rpt 109–131) to criminalize physical desecration of the American flag, but the Senate did not clear the bill.

Abortion (2005): The House passed a bill (HR 748) to expand the reach of state laws requiring parental consent or notification when a minor seeks an abortion. The measure required doctors to notify parents in person or by mail of an out-of-state minor's request for an abortion, and it gave guardians the right to sue noncompliant doctors.

Terri Schiavo Case (2005): The House and Senate passed a bill to allow the parents of Terri Schiavo to go to federal court and have their daughter's feeding tube restored. However, federal courts rebuffed Shiavo's parents' attempt to intervene.

LIST OF MEDIA FOR ISSUE EVENT SEARCHES

Wall Street Journal
New York Times
Washington Post
Los Angeles Times
Chicago Tribune
Dallas Morning News
Atlanta Journal & Constitution
Time
Newsweek
U.S. News & World Report
National Journal
Washington Monthly
Roll Call
Washington Times
National Review
The Nation
Weekly Standard
American Spectator
The New Republic
The American Prospect

12

Cause Lawyers and Other Signs of Progress

Three Thai Narratives

Frank Munger

THE ARRIVAL OF CAUSE LAWYERS

In 1973, a student-led uprising in Bangkok toppled an American-backed military dictatorship. About two decades after this turning point in modern Thai history, Benedict Anderson considered the post-uprising evolution of democratic government in a famous article, "Murder and Progress in Modern Siam."[1] The increasing number of assassinations of candidates for political office was a sign of progress, Anderson argued, because it proved that holding an elected office had become a valuable prize. Nearly a half-century later, there are more benign signs of progress, for example, the adoption of a liberal constitution in 1997[2] and laws protecting the environment,[3] women,[4] communities,[5] and human rights.[6] Western observers may

I would like to thank Amnat Wongbandit, Penny Andrews, Elizabeth Chambliss, Scott Cummings, David Engel, Jaruwan Engel, Bryant Garth, and David Schoenbrod for helpful comments. I am especially indebted to the generous and patient Thai lawyers and others who consented to be interviewed for this study. For valuable assistance I owe particular thanks to Professor Thanet Apornsuwan, Pipob Udomittipong, Somchai Homla-or, Thawilwadee Bureekul, and Professor Paisit Panitchkul. The Thai Ministry of Education and the Lawyers Council of Thailand provided essential information. Support for this research has been provided by generous funding from the Law School Admissions Council and a New York Law School Faculty Summer Research Grant.

1 Benedict Anderson, The Spectre of Comparisons: Nationalism, Southeast Asia, and the World 174–191 (1998).

2 Constitution of the Kingdom of Thailand, B.E. 2540 (1997).

3 *See* The Enhancement and Conservation of National Environmental Quality Act, B.E. 2535 (NEQA 1992), *available at* http://www.pcd.go.th/info_serv/en_reg_envi.html (last visited Aug. 30, 2009).

4 *See* Malee Pruekpongsawalee, *The Constitutions and Legal Status of Women in Family Related Laws in Thailand: A Historical Perspective*, *in* Women's Studies in Thailand: Power, Knowledge and Justice (Suwanna Satha-Anand ed., 2003). In 2007, the Thai Parliament passed a law criminalizing marital rape. *See* Isis International, http://www.isiswomen.org/index.php?option=com_content&task=view&id=758&Itemid=204 (last visited Dec. 19, 2009).

5 Thai Community Forestry Act, B.E. 2550 (2007), *available at* http://www.rightsandresources.org/blog.php?id=34 (last visited Dec. 19, 2009).

6 *See generally* Constitution of the Kingdom of Thailand, B.E. 2550, Chapter III: Rights and Liberties of the Thai People (2007).

attribute particular importance to the increasing visibility of lawyers committed to bringing these rights into play.[7]

At best, these are ambiguous signs of progress. Thailand experienced its eighteenth military coup in 2006, and although this particular coup was kinder, gentler, and shorter than in the past – and a new constitution was adopted a year later – the military reminded the politicians that it remains a strong and legitimate power broker. In 2008, demonstrators brought down the latest elected government, receiving tacit support from the police, military, and, in the view of many, the revered royal family, as well as many educated elites wary of power exercised by poor, less well educated, rural voters.[8] Mass demonstrations blockaded government buildings and seized major airports, violating laws with seeming impunity; the military and police held back.[9] Political assassinations may be down, but is the rule of law up? Do more laws protecting liberties and more social justice lawyers represent the signs of progress? In this chapter, I describe the life work of three activist lawyers in Thailand. Drawing on their career narratives and an extensive interview-based study of cause lawyers, I examine the relationship between cause lawyering and political development in this Asian society.

Cause lawyers have been described by American scholars Austin Sarat and Stuart Scheingold as lawyers who practice "with a vision of the good society."[10] They and other scholars quickly found that cause lawyers' motives are multiple, blurred, hard to measure, and influenced as much by opportunity as by idealism.[11] Cause lawyers in the United States are said to play an important political role representing marginal individuals and groups resisting exclusion or advocating social change. But this model may tell us very little about the role of cause lawyers in other societies. In outlining a comparative framework, Richard Abel identified institutions and opportunities as critical determinants of the development and success of cause lawyering.[12] Above all, cause lawyers are important because they "speak law to power" – a role,

[7] Evidence of growing public interest in the work of cause lawyers is suggested by newspaper articles appearing in the Thai and English press about the careers of several younger ("third generation") cause lawyers, including Surachai Throng-ngam, the environmental lawyer described in this article. *See* Kloykamol Siribhakdi, *The Environment and the Law*, BANGKOK POST, Jan. 15, 2008.

[8] *See* Pokpong Lawansiri, *The Continuing Crisis in Thailand*, PRACHATAI, Dec. 4, 2008 *available at* http://www.prachatai.com/english/printversin.php?id=882.

[9] *Id.*

[10] Austin Sarat & Stuart Scheingold, *Cause Lawyering and the Reproduction of Professional Authority: An Introduction*, *in* CAUSE LAWYERING: POLITICAL COMMITMENTS AND PROFESSIONAL RESPONSIBILITIES 3 (Austin Sarat & Stuart Scheingold eds., 1998).

[11] Yves Dezalay & Bryant Garth, *Constructing Law Out of Power: Investing in Human Rights as an Alternative Political Strategy*, *in* CAUSE LAWYERING AND THE STATE IN A GLOBAL ERA 354 (Austin Sarat & Stuart Scheingold eds., 2001); Stuart Scheingold & Anne Bloom, *Transgressive Cause Lawyering: Practice Sites and the Politicization of the Professional*, 5 INT'L J. OF THE LEGAL PROF. 209 (1998).

[12] Richard L. Abel, *Speaking Law to Power: Occasions for Cause Lawyering*, *in* CAUSE LAWYERING, *supra* note 10, at 69.

he argued, that can be defended by a powerful profession, especially in developed societies in the common law world. Outside the common law world, lawyers play a different role, sometimes many different ones. Abel's examination of the institutional sources of opportunity for cause lawyering worldwide suggested that liberal legal ideology is less important than the institutional and political framework of a society.[13] The United States' well-entrenched ideology of rights and relatively independent judiciary are important factors facilitating cause lawyering, but they, in turn, have developed in part *because of* the opportunities to challenge state authority created by federalism, the separation of powers, and institutional support for professional autonomy. Outside the Global North, "speaking law to power" risks more serious reprisal than in western democracies.

Underlying a growing international interest among scholars in cause lawyers is a perception that lawyers seeking social justice are important role players as agents of liberal change. In this view, cause lawyers, as agents of change modeled on American civil rights and social movement law practice, test and ultimately limit the power of private authority and public governance by invoking the rule of law. When law draws support from other power holders (and is, therefore, "legitimate" – following a well-known formulation by Arther Stinchcombe[14]), cause lawyers may limit the power of government and promote democratic, civil, or human rights. According to this view, cause lawyers are canaries in the mine: The viability of cause lawyering is a measure of the rule of law itself.[15]

Interest in cause lawyers in developing societies also reflects the dominating "rule of law" discourse in contemporary globalization.[16] Contemporary globalization emphasizes transfer of technologies for public and private governance, including constitutionalism, human rights, and other legal institutions that often mimic practices in more developed societies. Governments of economically developed societies, international agencies, and human rights advocates of nearly all ideologies have emphasized "rule of law" and related civil society capacity building as mechanisms of economic development, stability, good citizenship, democratization, equitable governance, and protection for vulnerable groups in developing societies.[17]

Reflecting his lifetime of study of the development of legal institutions in Indonesia and Malaysia, Daniel Lev concludes that many new states now face problems similar

13 *Id.*

14 Arther Stinchcombe, Constructing Social Theories 150–51 (1968).

15 *See, e.g.*, Cause Lawyering and the State in a Global Era, *supra* note 11; Fighting for Political Freedom: Comparative Studies of the Legal Complex and Political Change (Malcom Feeley, Lucien Karpik, Terrence Halliday eds., 2008).

16 Promoting the Rule of Law Abroad: In Search of Knowledge (Thomas Carothers ed., 2006).

17 The incompatibilities among these objectives reveal the symbolic politics behind such pressures, each international actor using "rule of law" language to legitimate their particular interventions. The issue is explored by Rachel Kleinfeld, *Competing Definitions of the Rule of Law*, *in* Promoting the Rule of Law Abroad: In Search of Knowledge, *supra* note 16.

to those faced a century or more ago in Europe, and influential groups have embraced a familiar solution, namely to "establish some controls over powerful governments by subjecting them to more or less autonomous legal process."[18] Nevertheless, he cautions, in new states, "pressures toward constitutionalism and more effective legal process have advantages and suffer constraints quite different from those of old Europe.... [I]deas, in Asia as in Europe or anywhere else, take hold only when they make sense domestically and are adapted to domestic purposes."[19]

In turn, making "sense" depends not only on the material interests of potential supporters, but also on the legitimacy of the legal discourse deployed to justify change. I will argue that the careers of cause lawyers are important because the lawyers' deployment of law reflects law's value not only for power seeking, but also the law's role in the wider processes of institution building and political change.[20]

To summarize the important point, drawing on the insights of Richard Abel, Pierre Bourdieu, Yves Dezalay, Bryant Garth, and Arther Stinchcombe, we should focus on the variations in institutional and political structure first, understanding that law, as a potentially important symbolic resource even where it is a relatively recent transplant, must find its support in new and unfamiliar ways. We must expect lawyers, working in any capacity, but especially in so fragile a role as cause lawyer, to be sensitive to these variations and expect cause lawyer careers to trace the limits of the symbolic power of law. To understand how law is used to broker power requires understanding first how power is created.

My interviews with Thai cause lawyers about their careers have enabled me to construct a "collective biography" of lawyer-activists over the past sixty years.[21] The narratives reveal how individuals situated themselves in relation to others in a field of power,[22] creating a map of the opportunities, institutions, resources, and intergenerational influence experienced by each generation of Thai cause lawyers. From a broader perspective, the development of several generations of cause lawyers illuminates evolution of the legal profession, legal institutions, and perhaps the broader society's taken-for-granted and unselfconscious assumptions about law or governance. Further, as Bourdieu has demonstrated, understanding the construction of a professional cohort may provide a window on the evolution of the society itself.[23]

[18] Daniel Lev, *Introduction* to TAMARA LOOS, LEGAL EVOLUTION AND POLITICAL AUTHORITY IN INDONESIA: SELECTED ESSAYS 3 (2000).

[19] *Id.* at 6.

[20] *See* Dezalay & Garth, *supra* note 11.

[21] *See* Frank Munger, *Globalization, Investing in Law, and Careers of Lawyers for Social Causes – Taking on Rights in Thailand*, 53 N.Y.L. SCH. L. REV. 745 (2008–2009).

[22] The concept of "field of power" has been used to orient career narratives of lawyers by Dezalay & Garth who draw, in turn, on the work of Pierre Bourdieu. *See* YVES DEZALAY & BRYANT GARTH, THE INTERNATIONALIZATION OF PALACE WARS: LAWYERS, ECONOMISTS, AND THE CONTEST TO TRANSFORM LATIN AMERICAN STATES (2002), and Dezalay & Garth, *supra* note 11.

[23] *See, e.g.*, PIERRE BOURDIEU & JEAN-CLAUDE PASSERON, REPRODUCTION IN EDUCATION, SOCIETY AND CULTURE (2d. ed. 1990).

THE LANDSCAPE OF THAI CAUSE LAWYERING – THREE NARRATIVES

The lives of the lawyers I have interviewed encompass Thailand's transition from absolute monarchy in 1932, through the seminal student-led uprising of 1973 during the era of American-backed military dictatorship, the era of activism by nongovernmental organizations (NGOs) beginning about 1980, liberal constitutional reform in 1997, and the reemergence of the military as a power broker in 2006.[24] These changes in the structure and institutions of government, economy, and society, which occurred over an eighty-year period, are often in the foreground of the lawyers' stories. Foregrounded or not, career choices and achievements of lawyers both reflected and contributed to the evolution of institutions and the construction of a field of power. This collective biographical and relational approach to studying advocacy, law, and social movements has suggested that there are identifiable cohorts, or generations of cause lawyers, determined by the changes that seemed most significant to the lawyers themselves to explain their distinctive career paths.[25] A first generation arose under the repressive military dictatorships prior to the 1973 uprising.[26] A second generation is comprised of law students and lawyers who participated in the student uprising of 1973 – the so-called "October generation."[27] Lawyers entering the profession a decade or more after 1973, radicalized by the legacy of the uprising, comprise a third generation. They benefitted from the establishment by October generation activists of a multilayered network of domestic NGOs, which provided apprenticeships for some.[28] A fourth generation entered the practice of law after the adoption of Thailand's historic liberal "People's Constitution" in 1997.[29]

Each of the narratives examined further in this chapter is situated in this larger generational picture. Malee Pauekpongsawale graduated from law school and became a professor of law in 1972 at Thammasat University, where the uprising began a year later. She is a member of the October generation, and she has become a leading feminist. Sutin Borommajet, in his last year of high school in 1973, was moved by the violence against the students to become a lawyer, graduating from a nonelite, open university in 1978. He is also an October generation lawyer, but, as

[24] *See* Munger, *supra* note 21.

[25] *Id.* Political and social events led to experiences that define a particular generation in Thai culture (much like World War II or the "60s" define generations in the United States). These events also radically changed the opportunities for deploying law within the society. The four generations are thus a heuristic I use to compress a more complex and complete story of law and institutional development that lies at the core of this research.

[26] *Id.* at 758–61.

[27] *Id.* at 761–63.

[28] *Id.* at 763–64.

[29] *Id.* at 764–67.

a lawyer for slum dwellers, his career has taken a very different path from Malee's. Surachai Trong-ngam graduated in 1987 from the same elite law school as Malee. He has become an important third-generation cause lawyer and litigator whose career illustrates the evolving international influence on "environmental" causes as well as the changing institutional context for litigation in Thailand.

Each narrative is also situated in a different cause or social movement – women's equality, security for slum dwellers, and resistance to development. Two of the movements have familiar counterparts in the United States and Europe, namely movements for "women's rights" and "environmental rights." The third movement, security for landless slum dwellers, is a feature of the rapidly developing Global South, which has no counterpart in contemporary western societies, has no grounding in "liberal" legal values, and, in Thailand at least, currently receives far less direct philanthropy than Thailand's environmental movement or its advocates for gender-related rights and welfare.[30] Social movements in developed societies are an important element of the narratives not only because they have influenced how a discourse of rights has been framed by international norm-setting organizations such as the World Bank or the United Nations, but also because the social construction of these issues in donor societies has influenced the rising tide of government and private "rule of law," "capacity building," and "human rights" philanthropy.[31] The domestic social movements that lawyers have embraced also reveal the influence of other important factors including social hierarchies that divide elite from non-elite, traditional beliefs and values perceived to support or conflict with movement goals, and the relative autonomy of law in relation to particular institutional changes sought by each movement.

The narratives illuminate each of these factors by showing how each lawyer perceived and responded to opportunities and limits for symbolic entrepreneurship in law.

Feminist

Malee Pauekpongsawale is the daughter of an immigrant Chinese merchant and a Thai woman. Her family farmed and maintained a shop in a small northern city.[32]

30 Slum conditions do exist in developed societies, to be sure, but large unpoliced communities of landless, illegal squatters are rare. One such rare exception has existed for decades on the Texas-Mexico border, where immigrants have formed *colonias* on illegally occupied land.

31 *See* Thomas Carothers, Aiding Democracy Abroad: The Learning Curve (1999).

32 Unless otherwise indicated, information and quotations are from interviews conducted by the author on February 28, 2008, June 24, 2008, and June 30, 2009. The role of Chinese immigrants and eventually a large number of Sino-Thai in early-twentieth-century Thai society is particularly important. The most successful Chinese merchant families became the backbone of Thailand's emerging export commercial and banking industries. By virtue of superior education, training, or entrepreneurship,

After her father's early death, an uncle educated in China and Bangkok became the head of the household and, together with a strong-willed grandmother, set Malee on her path to higher education. Malee excelled in school, and her English-speaking uncle and an American teacher gave her an early grounding in this important second language. Her grandmother shaped her consciousness in a quite different way, inadvertently helping her break away from a life of domestic chores and shop keeping:

> I had a very strong grandmother. She disciplined us, especially females. She wanted us to be in order, and so on, and she disapproved us going out and hanging around.... And at one point I was at a coffee shop of my friend and she went after me and she beat me with a stick.... I was not her favorite, and I think she was the one who taught me to understand. She was my first feminist teacher.... I ask her, I still remember, why she didn't do that to the boys? "Why? Because he's a younger brother." Or older brother! I came to a conclusion that I was treated differently because of my gender. She was my first feminist.

At age fifteen, Malee told her uncle she was not getting involved in a life of domestic work and shopkeeping, but rather wanted to become a civil servant. In 1968, she entered Thammasat University in Bangkok as a law student.[33]

Malee's plan for her life reflected an important transformation of civil society in the mid-twentieth century. In the 1960s, Thailand's economy boomed under guidance from the World Bank.[34] At the same time, American philanthropy transformed Thailand's higher education system, expanding its capacity and competence by pouring millions of dollars into programs and sending whole faculties to the United States for advanced training.[35] Malee's generation was one of the first to benefit from rapid expansion of public higher education.

Rising expectations of increasingly affluent families and their university-educated children had other consequences as well. From 1951 to 1973, Thailand was governed

Chinese in lesser circumstances made up an important part of the early middle and commercial class. While laboring under some forms of discrimination, the services of entrepreneurs and financiers paved the way to acceptance into business partnerships with the hereditary elite and intermarriage, which over time has led to reduction of de jure discrimination, if not of all social distinctions. *See* Chris Baker & Pasuk Phongpaichit, A History of Thailand 32–36,152–155 (2005).

[33] Thai "law schools" are departments or faculties within four-year undergraduate institutions, as in much of the non-North American world. Founded in 1933, the University of Moral and Political Science, later renamed Thammasat University, was Thailand's first law school open to commoners, introducing a radically democratic concept of education, especially professional education. Its founder, Pridi Banomyong, was Thailand's idealistic first Prime Minister. *See* Prasit Kovilaikool, Asean Law Ass'n, Part VI, The Legal System of Thailand 538 (1995).

[34] *See* Robert Muscat, Thailand and the United States: Development, Security, and Foreign Aid 278–279 (1990).

[35] *See id.*; Anderson, *supra* note 1, at 139–73; Gary R. Hess, *Waging the Cold War in the Third World: The Foundations and the Challenges of Development*, *in* Charity, Philanthropy, and Civility in American History (Lawrence Friedman & Mark McGarvie eds., 2003).

by brutal military dictators, backed by the Americans who were building a bulwark against communism. Long before Malee completed her undergraduate law degree and began teaching in 1972, interest in Thai society and its social problems grew among university students.[36] Their discontent and opposition to military dictatorship surfaced in massive student demonstrations in October 1973, drawing widespread popular support and toppling the dictatorship. Upward mobility and the cultural gap between the generation that remained intimately connected to the farm or the shop and the new generation of university-educated children contributed both to the rebellion's success and to the support for repression in 1976, after three years of turmoil during Thailand's first experiment in popular democracy.[37] In 1976, many student activists at Thammasat were arrested, and some were killed during the crackdown and restoration of the dictatorship. Many radicals fled to the jungle to take refuge with the communist cadres on the borders with Laos and Cambodia.[38]

Malee's membership in the October generation ripened and reinforced her commitment to gender equality and justice, learned in childhood, but the path of her career followed opportunities available to a graduate from an elite law school who spoke English, as well as opportunities created by the global politics of the women's movement.[39] Supported by American, British, and European philanthropies, many faculty members at elite universities, including Thammasat, earned advanced degrees abroad.[40] Malee studied in the Netherlands, but more importantly at Yale, which in the late 1960s and early 1970s became a gathering place for international scholars associated with the law and modernization movement, and later at New York University.

Returning to Thailand after the dictatorship established in 1976 began to give way to more moderate military leaders who restored a degree of civilian control in the late 1970s, Malee's career entered a new phase. The 1975 United Nations conference on women in Mexico City changed the emphasis of global feminism from

36 Encouraged by Thammasat's liberal rector, Puey Ungpakorn, students and faculty traveled to the countryside to observe, interact, learn, and teach the rural and urban poor. They read works of political writers and leaders from both the west and the east, and became reacquainted with radical literature suppressed by the military. BAKER & PHONGPAICHIT, *supra* note 32, at 185–189.

37 ANDERSON, *supra* note 1.

38 BAKER & PHONGPAICHIT, *supra* note 32.

39 Malee also attributes the development of her identity as a cause lawyer to other sources, including serving as an interpreter while a graduate student in the United States for Thongbai Thongpao, a famous "first generation" Thai cause lawyer who had spent many years in prison under the prior dictatorship in the 1960s and who was defending students and political prisoners against charges brought by the new dictatorship after its 1976 coup.

40 *See* MUSCAT, *supra* note 34. Much of the contemporary funding for scholarships to study abroad comes from Thai sources, including the government and Thai corporations, some of them state-owned (Siam Cement Corporation, Thailand's largest corporation, owned by the royal family's Crown Property Bureau, provides many scholarships for foreign study).

seeking legal equality to meeting the challenges for women created by poverty and unequal distribution of the benefits of development.[41] Thailand responded to the International Year of the Woman declared by the United Nations in 1975 by establishing a government working committee to report on the status of women. Malee, by now a highly credentialed member of the law faculty, was asked by her Dean to chair the committee. Soon Malee's career was proceeding on two tracks. On the one hand, she was deeply committed to supporting grassroots activism, for example, by becoming a founding board member of the Center for Protection of Child Rights, an important NGO organized by members of the October generation.[42] On the other hand, she was becoming an influential member of a group of professional women who led the movement for women's equality at a high level. Moving on from the government working group on the status of women, she became the Thailand coordinator for a Canadian-funded transnational consortium to promote improvement in the status of women.[43] Gradually, as her network of feminist faculty members, NGO leaders, and like-minded government officials solidified, she became one of a small leadership core with access to both grassroots activists and to leading officials and politicians.[44]

The influence of this network of educated feminists culminated in the formation of the Women and Constitution Network (WCN) in the mid-1990s as Thailand entered a critical period of political and economic crisis that discredited the military and its ineffective civilian surrogates and created an opening for liberal

[41] Margaret Snyder, *Unlikely Godmother: The UN and the Global Women's Movement, in* GLOBAL FEMINISM: TRANSNATIONAL WOMEN'S ACTIVISM, ORGANIZING, AND HUMAN RIGHTS (Myra Marx Ferree & Alili Mari Tripp eds., 2006).

[42] RUENGRAWEE PICHAIKUL & JAMES KLEIN, THE ASIA FOUNDATION, LEGAL LITERACY FOR SUPPORTING GOVERNANCE, LEGAL EMPOWERMENT: ADVANCING GOOD GOVERNANCE AND POVERTY REDUCTION 147 (2005); Phillipe Doneys, *Political Reform Through the Public Sphere: Women's Groups and the Fabric of Governance, in* REFORMING THAI POLITICS, 171–173 (Duncan McCargo ed., 2002).

[43] Establishment of NGOs devoted to children's and women's welfare and policy advocacy reflects not only internal consciousness raising and political openings, but also funding from foreign donors, which made larger organizations and sustained interaction with government possible. For example, DANIDA (Denmark's government development aid organization) was instrumental in funding the establishment of the NGO that Malee joined, Friends of Women and the Center for Protection of Child Rights. CIDA (Canada) supported the international working group for which Malee became the Thai coordinator. In the mid-1980s, the Ford Foundation and other foundations supported the Women's Studies Center at Chiangmai University. For other examples, see Doneys, *supra* note 42, at 170.

[44] The first NGOs concerned with women's issues were service-oriented, attempting to check abuse of power and at the same time increase the effectiveness of government agencies through direct interaction and technical assistance. As experience and frustration accumulated, NGOs turned to political solutions and building a constituency. Correspondingly, older women's advocacy groups, especially the Women's Bar Association, also shifted their approach from technical assistance to political pressure in the public sphere. *See id.* at 171–79. Malee's position as both NGO insider and elite insider made her especially valuable as the shift to politics occurred.

constitutional change.[45] The WCN brought together elite leadership, a broad NGO base, and funding from European and American philanthropies that supported constitutional reform. But even though the WCN made a determined effort to place women's equality on the agenda for constitutional reform, and achieved remarkably broad popular mobilization to support this and other liberal changes, its success was limited.[46] Although the "people's sector," of which the WCN was an important part, is sometimes credited with providing the political will for a more liberal constitution, the liberal constitution proposed in 1996 might easily have died in Parliament without the support of the business community and urban elites for more accountable, democratic, and, above all, less corrupt government.[47]

Malee has never been a confrontational grassroots cause lawyer. Drawn to feminism by experiences in her own life, she believes in finding a Thai way forward through feminism grounded in Buddhism. Asked to reflect on her advocacy as a feminist professor of law, she drew a distinction between American feminism and the Thai feminism she has helped create:

> I think that the women's movement is right there in talking about our system. They are trying to get their [standards] approved in every foreign setting.... And then my assignment was very clear. Look into the law, [see] whether there's any discriminatory provisions, and so on. And then I was trapped in the women's issue because as a woman in the process of your work you understand more about yourself. You understand about your attitude and things being forced upon you. The other influence would be Buddhism. I was very much into it. You're not so radical in your way of thinking. You look at things, trying to identify what is the root cause. I think one of the things is kindness. You don't start to accuse people and try to understand. I think that you have to take this kind of approach in our society because it's different from American society. Everyone [in America] has to protect their own right;

[45] *Id.* at 173–78.

[46] Generous interpretations have credited this women's movement, and the WCN, with adding women's voices to the political arena, an important accomplishment in a highly patriarchal society. But after intense lobbying, only six women were selected for the constitutional drafting committee of one hundred. Further, the drafting committee failed to adopt the provisions intended to correct the continuing forms of inequality that women believed were most needed to end gender discrimination in marital relationships and other important contexts. *Id.* at 173–74. The WCN could claim as its most notable success only the constitutional requirement that one-third of the commissioners of the new National Human Rights Commission be female. In spite of the talent and education of its leadership, the WCN also failed to end the glass ceiling for women in government and politics. *See* Supin Kachacupt, *Women's Equal Rights and Participation in the Thai Bureaucracy*, *in* WOMEN AND POLITICS IN THAILAND: CONTINUITY AND CHANGE 198 (Kazuki Iwanaga ed., 2008); Juree Vichit-Vadakan, WOMEN IN POLITICS AND WOMEN AND POLITICS: A SOCIO-CULTURAL ANALYSIS OF THE THAI CONTEXT, IN WOMEN AND POLITICS IN THAILAND: CONTINUITY AND CHANGE, *supra*, at 27.

[47] The timing of the 1996–1997 financial crisis was also critical, discrediting the government first for its incompetence and secondly for its inability to resist the IMF's demands for structural adjustment. Michael Connor, *Framing the "People's Constitution"*, *in* REFORMING THAI POLITICS (Duncan McCargo ed., 2002).

individualism is very strong and justifiable. But in ours, we aren't at that level yet.... I think Buddhism speaks to the roots and the cause.

Malee's preference for networking, for collaborative development of feminist consciousness in her teaching, and using her connections to other elite women to bring about change seems compatible with her Buddhist belief in understanding all points of view and all sources of difference. Her preference for a Thai feminism is well adapted to the institutional setting in which she has invested her career. In mid-career, drawn to closer involvement with NGOs working at the grassroots level and contemplating leaving the university, she was encouraged by a friend to reflect on the social and economic capital she had invested in becoming a professor of law, which would likely be lost if she gave up her position. The advice was reinforced by the continuing reality of patriarchy, because Thai women have made limited progress becoming leaders in institutional sectors outside the universities and NGOs. Malee decided not to leave the university and to remain a cause lawyer at an elite academic institution. She is an admired idealist, but her role as a leading feminist is both empowered and limited by the institutional role that legitimates her expertise.

Slum lawyer

During his final year of high school in 1973, Sutin Borommajet watched police beating student demonstrators opposing the dictatorship and demanding a more accountable political system for Thailand.[48] Sutin was on the cusp of a decision about his own future. He grew up in Sri Thammaraj, a district in Thailand's deep south. His mother was a Chinese immigrant and his father was Thai. Sutin's father died before Sutin reached the end of his secondary education, and his mother left the decision to him whether to attend university and what to study. Moved by the injustice and violence of the dictatorship, Sutin says he thought for the first time about becoming a lawyer. Other cause lawyers also said they were influenced by childhood and family encounters with the police or other government officials, although not always associated with the events of 1973.[49]

Like Malee, Sutin had opportunities to pursue a career that would not have been available to an earlier generation. After the fall of the dictatorship in 1973 and continuing expansion of the private sector, law became an increasingly popular

[48] Information and quotes not otherwise documented are from my interview with Sutin on July 2, 2008.

[49] Other unspoken influences may also have been in play in Sutin's decision. Law was, of course, a means of making a living, but a great deal of emphasis was placed by parents on becoming a prosecutor or judge, which were highly respected, secure government jobs. Sutin was not pressured by his family to consider these career choices. Nor did he mention the long history of tensions between Muslims and Buddhists in his home region, which has resulted in repeated military and police intervention.

choice among university students. The mid-1970s take-off in legal education in Thailand and increasing number of lawyers licensed for practice suggests that many students were drawn to law by the prospects for wealth from the growth in the Thai economy, whereas others (probably far fewer in number) were attracted by the ideals of a profession that seemed to provide answers to arbitrary government power.[50]

Sutin, like many poor students from the rural south, attended Ramkamhaeng University in Bangkok beginning in 1974. Founded in 1971 as Thailand's first low-cost, "open" university, Ramkamhaeng had no entrance requirements, offered a limited number of fields of study (including law and economics), and imposed no mandatory attendance or course load requirements.[51] The freedom offered by Ramkamhaeng University allowed Sutin to spend most of his time engaged in social activism, including working with slum dwellers. In 1976, Sutin was arrested along with 3,000 other students during the police and military's violent repression of protests against the government. The brief experiment in liberal democracy was coming to an end. Sutin was sent to a detention center, where his family bailed him out. Like most of the arrested students, he was never prosecuted.

Sutin's years at Ramkamhaeng created a sense of purpose but left him with few ideas about how to make a living when he graduated in 1978. By the time Sutin reached law school in 1974, the earliest NGOs had been active among the rural and urban poor for a decade. In 1965, the first Thai credit union was organized in Din Daeng, a Bangkok slum community, by Father Alfred Bonningue, a French Jesuit

[50] In 1960, there were fewer than 2,000 registered legal practitioners in Thailand. Between 1970 and 1975, the number increased by a little more than 125 attorneys a year, from 2,541 to 3,177. The number of attorneys increased to about 7,000 in 1980. Nat'l Statistical Office, Office of the Prime Minister, 28 STATISTICAL YEARBOOK THAILAND 159 (1967–1969). The Lawyers Council of Thailand listed a total of more than 19,000 registered attorneys in 1986, the year it assumed responsibility for licensing practitioners. Letter from the Office of the President of the Lawyers Council of Thailand to Frank Munger, Professor, New York Law School (July, 1, 2008) (on file with author). The current rate of increase is about 3,000 new registered attorneys each year and the total is more than 54,000 (or roughly one-fifth the per capita proportion of the United States), about 20% of whom are women. *See* Lawyers Council of Thailand, http://www.nichibenren.or.jp/en/directory/data/E07-Lawyers_Council_of_Thailand.pdf (last visited Mar. 1, 2009). Thus, the take-off in numbers began in the late 1970s, suggesting that the rise in numbers of students choosing to study law and to enter the practice of law rather than government service had less to do with the lessons of 1973 or idealism such as Sutin's, but rather coincided with the growth of opportunity in the private sector as Thailand entered a period of rapid economic growth in the 1980s. *Cf.* William Alford, *Introduction, in* RAISING THE BAR: THE EMERGING LEGAL PROFESSION IN EAST ASIA (William Alford ed., 2007).

[51] *See* Ramkhamhaeng University, History, http://www.ru.ac.th/english/english2008/about.html (last visited on Nov. 30, 2009). Graduates from Thammasat University form the largest group among my cause lawyers interviewees, but the second largest group graduated from Ramkamhaeng University. Cause lawyers who graduated from Ramkamhaeng may be numerous in part because the university is very large, and many more law students graduate each year from Ramkamhaeng than from the other universities in Bangkok combined. More significant for purposes of my research, virtually all cause lawyers from Thailand's south attended this law school.

priest, and two Thai associates, providing a self-help model that greatly influenced other Thai NGO founders.[52] In 1968, a young woman named Prateep Ungsongtham (later Prateep Hata), born in the Bangkok slum Klong Thoey, created an unofficial school for slum children, who were excluded from local schools because they lacked legal residency. The school and Prateep's subsequent conflict with the government landowner were among the earliest causes embraced by student activists in the 1970s at Thammasat University.[53] Puey Ungpakorn, Rector of Thammasat from 1969 to 1976, sided with the students. In 1969, he encouraged development of NGOs by establishing the Graduate Volunteer Service (GVS) to encourage university graduates to serve as staff members.[54]

Many of the earliest NGOs provided services to poor communities, from building schools to helping in medical clinics, but this soon changed. With encouragement from foreign funders, NGOs began to focus on community development rather than services and poverty relief – an approach that emphasized building capacity for sustained self-help rather than providing relief.[55] By the early 1980s, soon after Sutin's career began, activists returning from the jungle created a core group of coordinating and networking organizations that linked local projects to international support and funding.[56] The era of community organizing had begun and with it new opportunities for law-trained graduates.

[52] Ernst Gohlert, Power and Culture: The Struggle Against Poverty in Thailand 100 (1991).

[53] James Ockey, Making Democracy: Leadership, Class, Gender and Political Participation in Thailand 71–74 (2004); Interview with Prateep Hata (June 14, 2007).

[54] *See* Puey Ungpakorn, A Siamese for All Seasons: Collected Articles by and about Puey Ungpakorn (5th ed. 2000). Puey remained Rector from the late 1960s until the military forced him to flee in 1976. Few NGOs survived the 1976 crackdown, but GVS and Komol Keemthong Foundation were exceptions.

[55] Thai organizers were concerned less about the moral value of volunteering, which had few indigenous cultural roots, than reforming ineffective or oppressive government policies. For them, community self-help also meant empowerment, and for this work they drew not only on the traditions of the 1973 student movements and their own experiences, but also, over the next two decades, on a transnational flow of ideas about community organizing, including those from the American Saul Alinsky and the Industrial Areas Foundation and Brazilian Paolo Freire's liberation theology. Experienced organizers moved between countries carrying their philosophies, methodologies, and a new vocabulary, influencing grassroots organizers throughout Asia. As NGOs began to focus more on community development and empowerment, the value of coordinating efforts became more apparent, and a third stage of development began. A coordinating committee among foreign and Thai NGOs concerned with slums was one of the first alliances and an important step toward a national movement. *See* Gohlert, *supra* note 52.

[56] The networks included the Coordinating Group for Religion and Society (CGRS), the only human rights organization to function under the dictatorship, and the Thai Interreligious Committee on Development (TICD), founded in 1979 by a group of Thai religiously affiliated organizations, including Chulalongkorn University (Buddhist), the Catholic Council of Thailand, and the Credit Union League of Thailand (which grew out of the Din Daeng project). *Id.*

Sutin had spent little time actually studying law and he had few skills as a lawyer. Just out of law school, he considered applying to the GVS to become an NGO staff member, but because he needed a source of income he found work at a business law firm through a friend. He kept his activism alive by volunteering to work on cases with members of a group of senior, first-generation cause lawyers.[57] A number of small first-generation law firms existed, maintained by dedicated older practitioners. Though as progressives they were opposed to the dictatorship, and some were sympathetic to the Communist Party of Thailand, they carefully avoided the appearance of political affiliation in the era of virulent anticommunism by dedicating themselves to providing representation for unpopular defendants and causes and advocating for strict adherence to the rule of law. Many of these lawyers knew each other well, of course, but until the establishment of NGOs that could employ lawyers, and the enterprising use of the networking potential of the Thai practicing lawyers bar association (Lawyers Council of Thailand) in the late 1990s, there was no organized process for recruiting and training a new generation. Like Sutin, younger lawyers found their way to these mentors on their own.

Within a short time, Sutin found a home for his activism as a staff member for the Union for Civil Liberties (UCL). UCL had been created by faculty members from two leading universities after the 1973 revolution to promote human rights.[58] The English translation of the organization's name, Union for Civil Liberties, may suggest to Americans that UCL is Thailand's own American Civil Liberties Union (ACLU), but the UCL's mission has been quite different. Unlike the ACLU, which has focused on protecting freedoms under the American Bill of Rights, the UCL had no national legal charter to orient its work, nor was the concept of human rights commonly used or generally understood in Thailand. Instead, the UCL supported incipient social movements by, for example, assisting labor organizations to organize, educating workers about their rights, disseminating information about new rights, and providing criminal defense.[59] After 1976, its work frequently brought it

[57] A small group of first-generation cause lawyers organized a legal services center through Thammasat University in the wake of October 1973. Among those who worked for the center as young lawyers were the founders of some of Thailand's most important NGOs that provided lawyers and other services to needy groups. PICHAIKUL & KLEIN, *supra* note 42.

[58] The UCL was founded by a group of Western-trained faculty at Thammasat University and Chulalongkorn University. Founder Saneh Chamarik, who had received his legal training in Britain, was a professor of Political Science at Thammasat, became Thailand's most prominent human rights theorist, and later became the first chairman of the National Human Rights Commission. Cofounder Gothom Arya, a student in Paris and participant in the 1968 student movement, was a young professor of Electrical Engineering at Chulalongkorn University. A few years later, Gothom founded, with American assistance, Thailand's first human rights organization, CGRS. Interviews with Saneh Chamerick (Dec. 22, 2006) and Gothom Arya (Dec. 22, 2006). *See also* GOHLERT, *supra* note 52.

[59] Interviews with Sutin Borommajet (July 2, 2008) and Rossukon Tariya (Dec. 14, 2009).

into conflict with the government and under suspicion of communist influence. For a brief time, the UCL received significant funding from European sources,[60] but many American philanthropies, such as the Ford Foundation, avoided funding the UCL in part because the Thai government considered its leadership to be tainted by communism.

Sutin liked the UCL's ideological commitment to empowerment through support for community organizations. As a salaried staff member from the early 1980s until the early 1990s, he became a close friend of other October generation cause lawyers with a strongly progressive orientation and commitment to community-based activism.[61] While working for the UCL, he began to learn more about human rights law:

> Actually, my thinking started from the fact I wanted to see justice and equality in society. During my studies, I experienced the 6th October [19]76 event. Some of my friends died in that event. After that, some of them went to join the Thai Communist Party. I still have a relationship with them even though I didn't go into the jungle with them. But after a time, I started to think that we cannot use violence to solve social problems. The process of social development has to give law and regulation a leading role. I learned much about this when I worked with [UCL]. I had an opportunity to learn about the Universal Declaration of Human Rights. I didn't study about this directly. It came from three sources: the first one was my experience, the second from my self-study, and lastly from seminars and from exchanging ideas with specialists such as Mr. Gotom Arya [co-founder of UCL], who played a big role in developing this issue.

As an "information manager" at UCL, Sutin gathered documentation of government abuses and information needed by lawyers who defended political prisoners and alleged communists. As a lawyer, he began working on slum cases. Slum organizers, for their part, continue to place great trust in Sutin because he believes, as they do, that organizing and empowering communities is more important than winning legal cases or developing legal policy.

Sutin eventually left UCL because he saw its philosophy change:

> From my perspective, the key to solving problems is the community itself. In a former time, [UCL] mainly worked with the community and labor groups all around Bangkok and surrounding provinces. After that, their administrators changed their

[60] Funders included NOVIB (Oxfam Netherlands), Misereor (Germany), the Asia Foundation (United States), and Bread for the World (United States). All have discontinued their support, at least in part because poverty in Thailand is no longer viewed as a problem requiring international resources.

[61] Somchai Homla-or eventually made Sutin vice-chair, and likely successor chair, of the Human Rights Committee of the Lawyers Council. In 2008, the Lawyers Council chose a successor to Somchai with far less grassroots experience or commitment to activism than Sutin.

> emphasis to running campaigns [for policy development]. However, I still think that even if you have a campaign for this issue, the community itself is important because people in the community have to learn, perceive, and participate. If the people do not understand all about this, the problem cannot be solved in reality.... They should run both, but at [UCL] they focus more on campaign policy...only this policy and strategy. They do not focus on the community any more.

In 1991, Sutin left UCL to join a business law firm. He has continued to be the go-to lawyer for the Four Region Slum Network, and he is the principal coordinator for the Andaman Relief Project that helps restore land rights to villagers who lost possession of their land as a result of the devastating tsunami that struck Thailand in 2004.

Sutin, one of the most trusted lawyers for slum organizations, is no longer an NGO staff member. The back story of Sutin's career is, in part, his need for a sustaining source of income.[62] The slum movement in Thailand has been among the most militant and among the most poorly funded. Ironically, given the militancy of many slum organizers, the movement is kept alive through direct support for the network of slum organizations and a revolving affordable housing loan fund doled out by government through an umbrella agency, the Community Organization Development Institute.[63] Whereas many Thai NGOs dedicated to other causes have continued to receive support from international sources, slum organizations have received little except the small amounts that trickle down through this agency.

Environmental Litigator

Surachai Trong-ngam is a "third generation" cause lawyer who graduated from Thammasat University law school in 1987.[64] His father was a soldier and his mother a curry-rice street vendor. Surachai entered law school with no particular understanding of the October revolution and no commitment to activism, but after entering Thammasat as a student, he was greatly influenced by activists who carried on the tradition of studying social problems and visiting the countryside that had been established by students returning from the jungle in the early 1980s. Through these visits, discussions with students, and the example of a few faculty mentors

[62] A second motivating factor for Sutin's change in employment was income. For the period of time Sutin worked for UCL, until 1991, he was paid a salary of about 7000 baht per month (less than $200). Sutin's law firm does not offer particular support for pro bono, community service, or public interest law practice.

[63] *See* David Satterthwaite, *Boonyabancha 2003 and Community Organizations Development Institute*, CODI UPDATE, Issue 4, April 2004, *available at* http://www.codi.or.th/downloads/english/Paper/CODI%20in%20thailand.pdf (last visited Dec. 19, 2009).

[64] Unless otherwise indicated, information in this subsection is drawn from interviews with Surachai Trong-ngam on February 27, 2008, June 29, 2008, and June 30, 2009.

who taught about human rights, he learned about the problems of the people and about activism. Other students exposed to the same influences may have acquired an appreciation for social issues and public service, but most did not become social justice lawyers. Surachai was caught up by the ideals of the revolution and the social problems he saw on his visits to the countryside. He read voraciously in the radical literature popularized by the revolutionary generation: Marxist and socialist theory, the works of Mao, writings by the Thai Marxist Jit Phumisak, and others. He became committed to activism, but he was also pragmatic, quickly realizing that law school alone provided poor preparation for serving other people. His visits to the countryside as a student taught him about social problems, but his undergraduate legal education had provided him no knowledge about law that could be useful to villagers who were denied access to land, were abused by police, lacked government services, or had other problems experienced by the rural poor.

When law students drawn to cause lawyering, like Surachai, graduated from Thammasat University in the 1980s, they entered a field that had taken shape through the work of the October generation, especially Thammasat University's own graduates. Surachai's career provides an illustration. The handful of small law offices of first-generation social justice lawyers were unable to support many young law graduates, although willing to accept volunteers, like Sutin. Establishing a new practice with no experience would have been nearly impossible with an undergraduate legal education, and in any event, licensing required an apprenticeship. Instead, like many third-generation cause lawyers, Surachai began his career by working for an NGO, but not as a lawyer.

Within a few years, through his network of law school and NGO friends, he found a job as a litigator with the Friends of Women Foundation (FOW), one of the first and best-funded of a number of organizations founded by members of the October generation.[65] Joining FOW in the early 1990s, Surachai learned about litigation and took the first step toward becoming an accomplished litigator. His work for NGOs was a productive apprenticeship, developing his litigation skills and teaching him about the roles a cause lawyer might play in private practice. After working for the Friends of Women Foundation for a year, Surachai joined a small law firm with partners committed to working for labor organizations, slum movement groups, and other social causes.

[65] Friends of Women was founded in the early 1980s by an October generation activist influenced by first-generation cause lawyers who founded the Legal Services Center Institute at Thammasat. *See* Pichaikul & Klein, *supra* note 42. The Foundation has received funding from European philanthropies from its inception, and it has spun off related projects, including the Child Rights Protection Center, another well-known NGO. Both NGOs have provided employment for several generations of young cause lawyers and human rights activists. Interview with FOW Coordinator Chadet Chaowilai (Feb. 26, 2008).

While at FOW, Surachai's network of activists began to involve him in community development. When he entered private practice, he devoted more time to this work. For example, Surachai became involved in the work of the Alternative Energy Project for Sustainability (AEPS), an NGO that supported communities threatened with environmental, social, and economic disruption by Thailand's program for building new power plants, typically at sites selected by a private company with government cooperation but often without prior notice to the community.[66] Surachai learned more about the courts and litigation, but he also considered himself a community organizer and educator. AEPS staff, for their part, worked with communities by organizing and guiding them toward collective decision and action, but did not always share Surachai's belief in the importance of law.[67]

A few years after joining the firm, Surachai's network brought him another opportunity: an American foundation willing to fund an environmental litigation NGO in Thailand. In the late 1990s, leaders of several Thai NGOs assisting community-based organizations concluded that there was a role for the courts in enforcing Thailand's recently adopted environmental protection laws.[68] In 1999, the Blacksmith Institute in New York sent an email to international NGOs in Thailand describing its interest in funding an environmental litigation project in Thailand. Soon the directors of a number of local environmental NGOs, including AEPS, began a search for a coordinator of the new NGO to be funded by Blacksmith. Surachai's prior litigation experience and working relationship with the network of NGOs, academics, activists, and human rights lawyers made him an attractive candidate. EnLaw was created to receive Blacksmith funds and any other funding, and to direct the work of its new coordinator, Surachai. The governing board of EnLaw was comprised of long-time friends and collaborators in the network of NGOs, including some of Surachai's law school classmates and mentors as well as the directors of several important NGOs. EnLaw was thus a collaboration among mutually committed colleagues as well as a formal organization – a byproduct of the NGO network that began to take shape in the 1980s.

Cases in which Surachai was already involved through his network became the first projects handled by the new NGO. One of the earliest cases concerned improper disposal of radioactive Cobalt 60 hospital waste in the late 1990s and

[66] Interview with Watcheree Phaoleungthong, Director of AEPS (Dec. 16, 2009).

[67] Interview with Ida Aroonwong, former AEPS staff member (June 17, 2008).

[68] Thailand adopted a comprehensive environmental protection law following a United Nations world conference on the environment held in Brazil in 1992. *See* Enhancement and Conservation of National Environmental Quality Act of B.E. 2535 (1992) *available at* http://www.pcd.go.th/info_serv/en_reg_envi.html (last visited Oct. 3, 2009). Changes introduced by the Thai constitution of 1997, and the growing strength of community-based organizations, suggested to NGO leaders that the time had come to attempt to enlist the power of the courts. Interview with Sayamol Kalyoorawong (Dec. 16, 2009).

subsequent serious injury to workers who removed the waste. Thai law provided for compensatory damages from the private corporation responsible for the waste through the civil courts – a remedy seldom sought because there is no plaintiff's bar analogous to the plaintiff's bar in the United States. Thailand does not permit contingent fee tort litigation and there is no fee-shifting provision in Thailand's environmental laws. As a practical matter, litigation costs alone discourage recourse to the courts by poor communities, even if other barriers have been surmounted, such as lack of legal knowledge or problems of collective action. Surachai's litigation broke new ground in another way as well. The 1997 constitution established an administrative court system to facilitate claims against the government. Surachai's suit against the Kamol Sukosol Company, which failed to dispose of the waste in a proper manner was unprecedented – literally. The case was one of the first filed with the new court in 2001, and the judgment entered against the company in March 2004 for approximately 600,000 Baht was the first of many victories that EnLaw has achieved.[69]

Surachai's "Cobalt 60" victory is famous in Thailand. The decision by the appellate court may be understood as the beginning of a new era in environmental rights enforcement. Surachai's achievement reflects both his skill as a litigator and the development of expertise in administrative law litigation developed with the collaboration of academics at Thammasat University. Further, Surachai thinks litigation has become increasingly important for lawyers working with social movements, especially since the ratification of the 1997 constitution that incorporated extensive civil, political, and human rights protections, as well as established a new administrative court system. Surachai views the new constitution (and presumably its successor in 2007, which preserved or expanded these provisions) as an important development for movements and especially for his contribution as a lawyer:

> [T]he establishment of the Constitution in 1997 [and] the trend toward development of administrative law... make it easier for the people to oversee the state's power by creating more channels for oversight that the people's movements lack.... Until now, the legal process has been employed to limit the people's rights. Now, people have their own rights to use the legal process. The legal process is a channel for people to fight. And we think we can back them up on this part.

As a consequence of the establishment of EnLaw and its growing caseload, Surachai has become better known to the cause lawyering community and to the public at large through his cases and through publicity arranged, in part, by the Lawyers Council. He has become a go-to lawyer for communities resisting development projects that threaten their natural environment and their quality of life.

[69] *Report to New World Foundation*, EnLaw, June 2008-April 2009 1; Siribhakdi, *supra* note 7.

Surachai has been concerned about the fact that so few young public interest lawyers seem to be able to form their own firms, although his law firm has encouraged younger associates to establish practices of their own. The reasons for the slow expansion of the number of private practitioners pursuing public interest work are easy to understand and are principally financial. Most of the clients who need representation by a human rights lawyer cannot afford to pay. NGOs themselves operate on small, marginal budgets, when they have a budget. Surachai's firm was established in part to demonstrate that a social justice practice could become self-sustaining. But there are many problems with the experiment, especially the hard life they urge the next generation of public interest lawyers to accept:

> We provide opportunities to learn. Most of the people here were involved in social activities. We might not be able to fully support the next generation [of] lawyers. If they can survive here, they must have fewer financial constraints and family obligations... Many might not be able to continue to be here and will have to leave.

Surachai earns very little from his practice. His firm cobbles together income from a variety of other sources, including small grants, research work for the Thailand Social Research Institute, and from a small number of private fee-for-service cases in areas of practice that do not conflict with EnLaw's work. His firm is almost self-sustaining, but his practice may be a model that lacks broad appeal for a younger generation.

EVOLUTION OF CAUSE LAWYERING

Cause lawyers can be identified in Thailand beginning in the mid-twentieth century, when a few courageous lawyers, trained at Thailand's only public law school, confronted dictators by defending political prisoners, labor unions, and the oppressed poor. The odds against survival from political repression and poverty insured that only a few lawyers' formed small, dedicated firms that handled cases that either provided little income or were extremely unpopular with the government – and often both. Until 1973, they alone provided training for younger cause lawyers who were able to find their way to them. Their sacrifice and tolerance for insecurity was born of necessity, because no professional organization, no foreign funders, and only a handful of labor and political organizations – themselves often under attack – provided support. Their numbers have not grown much, and they now comprise an aging senior core of a network of cause lawyers.[70] In 1973, the landscape quickly

[70] In 2006, Somchai Homla-or estimated that there were perhaps eighty lawyers nationwide in his Human Rights Committee network, made up of this aging core plus a few younger lawyers like Surachai who have managed to establish self-sustaining law practices together with a later generation working mostly for NGOs. Interviews with Somchai Homla-or (Dec. 31, 2006 and June 18, 2007).

changed. During the 1970s and 1980s, the accelerated growth of lawyers from a few thousand to tens of thousands reflects not only the mushrooming number and size of universities but an awakening interest in politics and the economy. Traditionally, law as a profession was viewed as a route to prestigious government employment as a judge or prosecutor. After 1973, however, many students applying to university considered law a path to Thailand's growing private sector. Others, like Sutin, thought law could address Thailand's social problems. The great uprising shaped a generation of idealists who are still creating a legacy of NGOs and lawyer networks to train new lawyers and support efforts to promote or defend human rights.

The networks of lawyers, which helped sustain an NGO movement and embraced a human rights discourse, arose initially from a collaboration among progressive practitioners encouraged by the events of 1973 to form a Legal Services Center Institute associated with students at Thammasat University. Sutin found his way to this network early in his career. NGOs provided an ideological and practical context for cause lawyering, and as the NGO movement grew, so did opportunities for cause lawyers. Sutin found his way to one of the most important early human rights NGOs, the Union for Civil Liberties. Malee helped establish another, the Foundation for Women and the Center for Protection of Children's Rights. Surachai's career was shaped and continues to be sustained by a well-developed network of NGOs.

An October generation lawyer, Somchai Hom-la Or, who assumed the chair of the Human Rights Committee of the Lawyers Council after the adoption of the 1997 constitution, melded individual senior practitioners, younger lawyers in training, and new recruits with NGOs to form aggressive and effective teams to work on policies, projects, and important individual cases. The National Human Rights Commission created by the 1997 constitution became a second node of cause lawyering development. About a third of the commissioners were former cause lawyers or NGO activists themselves (including a student of Malee, and lawyers with long relationships with Surachai and Sutin). The commissioners used their investigative powers to gather information that could be used in litigation or to provide support for legislative reforms. They legitimated the work of many human rights lawyers by appointing them to subcommittees on particular human rights issues.

In turn, NGOs and social movements shaped the work of cause lawyers in ways that reflected the unique cultural and political context in Thailand. Many Thai NGOs, for example, have adopted "Thai-style" strategies that directly benefit women, children, sex workers, families, migrants, refugees, and other needy groups. "Thai-style"

Since speaking with Somchai, I have learned about other cause lawyers who are outside his network, in part because they are located in the provinces and linked to local NGOs or specialized causes. A few others remain apart from the Bangkok-centered network for reasons of political or regional differences that separate them from Somchai's committee members. The majority are linked in one way or another with his network.

NGOs simultaneously buffer these vulnerable groups from ineffective and authoritarian government officials and discipline the agency by asserting authority based on the NGOs' expertise, legitimacy, and insider networks. Litigation is an occasional resource, but much of their work reflects a collaborative approach with government intended to shape its policies at lower levels of administration. Not coincidentally, these methods are at once practical, given the constraints on litigation and other forms of direct confrontation, while also fitting comfortably with Malee's description of Buddhist preferences (whether or not they were inspired directly by them) for mutual understanding and collaboration with opponents. From another point of view, lawyers who work in this environment use the symbolic and moral power of the law to educate, instruct, and guide the government officials themselves, and function (among other things) as trainers of lower-level bureaucrats.[71]

Lawyers for social movements and NGOs that pursue the goal of empowerment may be influenced in other ways. The difference between the Thai Union for Civil Liberties, which emphasized organizing, and the American Civil Liberties Union, which emphasizes development of constitutional doctrine, is a good illustration. As a staff member for UCL, Sutin was involved in a wide variety of support activities intended to augment the political leverage of community-based organizations. Litigation was a strategy, but not an end in itself. Another example is the environmental organization Towards Ecological Recovery and Regional Alliance (TERRA),[72] which has drawn Surachai and other lawyers he has trained into community-led campaigns to negotiate with authorities over development projects. Lawyers are invited to assist only after the campaign has begun and on terms established by the community-based collaboration, with TERRA's assistance. Although Surachai aspires, in part, to "litigate for rules," EnLaw's governing board helps maintain the

[71] Not all observers are so generous. Thai critics suggest that "Thai style" NGOs do not advance the cause of the people for greater political space, but simply provide welfare for the people. Amara Pongsapich, *Thai Political Space for Advocacy, in* Breaking Through: Political Space for Advocacy in Southeast Asia (Joel Paredes, Marisssa de Guzman & Eltheodon Rillorta eds., 2007). Others have suggested that foreign funders moderate the influence of NGOs by selectively funding projects that (a) do not conflict with foreign policy of the funder's home nation, and (b) have a moderate, liberal, and familiar social agenda. Carothers, *supra* note 31.

[72] TERRA grew from the Project for Ecological Recovery (PER), an NGO formed by a member of the October generation after a 1984 meeting between NGOs and activists concerned about the impact of development projects in the 1970s and early 1980s. Massive projects included clearing land for export cropping and relocation of entire communities for waterway projects, such as dams. The projects displaced large numbers of people, threatening their access to land, livelihood, and the natural resources that sustained many traditional communities. PER proposed a method of conflict resolution that addressed the underlying political imbalance in representation in policy making through public demands for negotiations among stakeholders. Resistance to land grabs and development was by no means unknown in Thailand, but resistance had typically resulted in violence and brutal repression. The new approach was more sophisticated, long-term, and political. Interview with Co-Director Premrudee Daoroung (July 1, 2009).

law firm's focus on community empowerment. Surachai's use of litigation to achieve important symbolic victories is not unprecedented, but no cause lawyers before him pursued this goal systematically. His access to the courts, however, has depended on sustained NGO support, minimal but critical international funding, and institutional developments that may be the most important theme in the story of cause lawyering development (as discussed in the next section). Yet, as Surachai's law practice also illustrates, cause lawyers in private practice struggle to survive.

MOVEMENTS AND INSTITUTIONS

Movements

The narratives suggest that the three movements – women's equality, slums, and the environment – have required very different forms of cause lawyering. These variations in cause lawyering seem to reflect profound differences in the movements and the normative and political issues they raise.

Malee's elite feminist politics differ strikingly from Sutin's commitment to grassroots, community-based activism. This difference may be less a matter of their personal ideologies (Malee, after all, expressed her great attraction to grassroots politics) than the characteristics of the movements they embraced. Malee's professional capital was built on her ability to gain access to policy makers and policy making at high levels using her educational credentials, expertise, and university position. Her symbolic capital fit well with late 1970s government priorities to encourage a meaningful response to UN initiatives on behalf of women at a time when Thailand was restoring its credibility after brutal human rights abuses under prior military regimes. International educational opportunities, feminist collaborators in western nations, and funders effectively found their way to her, offering her capital and creating a role for her. As she acknowledges, elite networking – working from inside the system – suits her. Her choice of strategies is supported in several ways by the double bind of all women leaders, but especially in a patriarchal society, where women have been kept beneath a glass ceiling in government and politics, and women who assume a man's position or adopt aggressive "male" behavior are especially penalized.[73] Further, no grassroots women's movement as such exists in Thailand. Organizations such as the Women and Constitution Network and other NGOs dedicated to women's rights teach women with more limited knowledge and experience about the society and women's rights, but no broad feminist movement has emerged from this leadership.[74]

[73] *See* Vichit-Vadakan, *supra* note 46; *see also* OCKEY, *supra* note 53.

[74] Tongchai Wongchaisuwan & Amporn Tamronglak, *Political Participation of Thai Middle-Class Women*, *in* WOMEN AND POLITICS IN THAILAND, *supra* note 46, at 237.

In contrast to the women's movement, the cause of slum dwellers has had little political traction among elites in Thailand. Likewise, as illegal squatters, slum dwellers have gained little public sympathy. International funders saw Thailand's urban and rural poverty as a problem ignored by the American focus on development. In contrast to outside funding for movements challenging the authority of leftist dictators in other parts of the world, western funders (both government and private) have displayed more tolerance for stable Asian authoritarian governments and less interest in supporting grassroots challenges to these regimes.[75] Initially concerned about maintaining a bulwark against communism, since the end of the Cold War, both government and private philanthropy have tended to support "rule of law" practices that conform to western experience – constitution-based republican government, capitalism, security of property rights, and foundational civil liberties and human rights as they are understood in the West (with variations within the range of western politics). The result is that although some U.S. government funders and private foundations (such as the Asia Foundation) have supported poverty relief, economic development, community education, law-and-order initiatives, and judicial independence, they have not supported social movements or NGOs that confront government over land, housing, political liberties, or political representation.[76] As Thailand's wealth has grown, foreign funding for poverty relief has disappeared, and even though capacity building to enforce existing rights has become an important element of "rule of law" funding from major donors such as the World Bank, few established funders have been interested in movements for securing more expansive rights to housing or land redistribution. Domestically, slum organizations are now the poor sisters of the broader NGO movement. Government funding, funneled through the Community Organization Development Institute, keeps the network of slum organizations in existence and offers hope of home ownership through a government loan fund, but it does not support broader political participation or enforcement of the Convention on Economic, Social, and Cultural Rights.

Sutin has advised slum organizations for several decades, and he has defended slum dwellers in eviction suits and occasionally against charges of crime. The movement's ideologues still preach against reliance on law.[77] From the mid-1980s

[75] CAROTHERS, *supra* note 31.

[76] *Id.*

[77] Interviews with staff members of the Human Settlement Foundation (June 27, 2008); Chumchon Thai staff members Jamnong Chitnarat (June 16, 2009) and Preeda Kongpaen (July 9, 2008); and with Jeff Wong, staff member for COPA (June 27, 2008 and June 11, 2009). I have also drawn on an interview with Professor Boonlert Visetpricha, Thammasat University, (June 25, 2008), and his manuscript, "The Protest Waves of the Four Regions Slum Network, Bangkok," which the author generously shared with me.

to the mid-1990s, an American Mennonite community organizer held workshops in Bangkok that were attended by many slum organizers and their lawyers.[78] Although Sutin never attended these workshops, he was attracted to one of their most important premises, widely shared among community-based organizations and NGOs, namely community empowerment. The goals of the organizers who attended the workshops have matured through subsequent experience, but they are often still expressed in a vocabulary that would be familiar to students of Paulo Freire's theory of popular education or to graduates of the Midwest Academy. Many still believe that although gains through the legal system may be useful, law must not become the primary method for winning victories. Instead, they believe in using mass protests to force negotiations with government administrators to alter decisions and change policies. Many express reservations about lawyers, but, in the view of at least some key organizers, Sutin is an exception who can be trusted because he, too, values strengthening the community more than development of legal policy. Because slum movement members often appear far less militant, and are certainly less ideological, than the organizers, Sutin's perspective has more in common with the latter than the former.[79]

Finally, the framework of UN sponsored women's conferences and treaties – for example, the Convention on the Elimination of All Forms of Discrimination Against Women (CEDAW) – have been invaluable symbolic resources for elite feminism. Shadow CEDAW reports have been submitted along with government reports since Thailand joined the convention in 1985. There is a sharp contrast between CEDAW and the International Covenant on Economic, Social, and Cultural Rights, a subpart of which addresses housing security. This latter Covenant is both a weaker legal regime[80] and has had far less traction in the successful liberal economy of 1990s Thailand than CEDAW did in the 1970s, when Thailand was seeking to avoid being perceived as a human rights pariah.

[78] Max Ediger was an American Mennonite community worker active in Burundi between 1966 and 1968 and in Vietnam between 1971 and 1976, who later moved to Bangkok to take up the issue of human rights in Burma. In Bangkok, he assisted many fledgling NGOs and for ten years conducted seminars on community organizing that were attended by some of the slum movement's most important organizers, as well as by some of the most important Thai cause lawyers. In 2000, Ediger returned to Vietnam after being expelled from Thailand for allegedly harboring illegal Burmese immigrants. *See* Peace Signs, Max Ediger, http://peace.mennolink.org/cgi-bin/m.pl?r=20 (last visited on Dec. 21, 2009).

[79] Slum dwellers are typically poorly educated, low-wage migrant workers who left rural homes. They lack the traditional networks of family and community support shared by the poorest residents of their rural villages of origin, and their slum communities struggle to reconstitute them under the insecure conditions of slum dwelling. Interviews with slum dweller members of the Four-Regions Slum Network (June 26, 2009).

[80] Philip Alston & Girard Quinn, *The Nature and Scope of States Parties' Obligations Under the International Covenant on Economic, Social and Cultural Rights*, 9 Hum. Rts. Q. 156 (1987).

Surachai has benefited from working with much stronger grassroots movements and well-established NGOs and community-based organizations. Internationally, Thailand's grassroots social movements are synonymous with antidevelopment mobilization. Although communities face daunting barriers to collectively challenging the Thai government's development policies, a number of rural communities have mobilized effectively for resistance, some with the assistance of internationally funded NGOs, such as AEPS and TERRA, which, in turn, have called on EnLaw and Surachai to advise them about the law and to litigate on their behalf, when needed. In contrast to the absence of a grassroots feminist leadership, many of the most effective political leaders in the grassroots environmental/antidevelopment movement are women. Scholar Cambria Hamburg notes the remarkable prominence of women community leaders in movements to resist development projects.[81] Her observation is especially noteworthy because of Thailand's continuing resistance to women in positions of political leadership and bureaucratic authority. Hamburg concludes that the double bind limiting women's political involvement, which is so strong in Thai culture, actually works in women's favor when they are defending their homes and communities. Finally, environmental values promoted by Buddhism have made environmentalism a strong movement in Thailand. Environmental values include not only protection of the natural environment for the sake of the national and global commons, as in developed societies, but also defense of traditional ways of life that are dependent on local ecology. In developing countries, such conflicts involve not only local politics, but almost inevitably implicate the general redistribution of political power.

The political dimension of environmentalism is something that Surachai deeply appreciates, and no doubt his understanding has been an important factor in his success. In return, the communities he works with are often sufficiently well organized to employ multifaceted and long-term strategies that give Surachai a great deal of freedom to "play for rules" through litigation. Community organizers who have worked with rural communities are finding new legal issues for him to litigate, and well-funded Thai environmental NGOs, which also appreciate the political dimensions of the disputes, support Surachai's work without sacrificing their emphasis on political negotiation. Litigation under these circumstances much more nearly resembles the classic American civil rights model than "Thai-style" NGO correction and supplementation of bureaucratic ineptness.

Institutions

Institutional development has been, perhaps, the most important factor in the evolution of Surachai's litigation, but the institutional changes that occurred in the past

[81] Cambria Hamburg, *Prohibited Spaces: Barriers and Strategies in Women's NGO Work in Isaan, Northeastern Thailand, in* WOMEN AND POLITICS IN THAILAND, *supra* note 46, at 95.

thirty years have been so dramatic that we can learn more by asking how they have affected all three cause lawyers and their movements. The impact of the student-led overthrow of the dictatorship in 1973 has already been noted. Between 1980 and 1997, the NGO movement grew steadily in strength, partly because of foreign funding, but also because the Thai government displayed greater respect for the work of NGOs.[82] NGO strength played a role in bringing together resistance to the brief reimposition of military dictatorship in the early 1990s, which led to bloody confrontations in the streets of Bangkok and a dramatic intervention by the king to bring a halt to the confrontation and a restoration of Parliament. Thereafter, the NGO community constituted the public face of constitutional idealism in mounting pressure to draft the liberal constitution of 1997, even though it did not possess sufficient political power to press its goals within the drafting committee or to force Parliament to enact the draft constitution without the support of the business community and a fortuitous fiscal crisis. Although the NGO community did not get everything it hoped for, the remarkable "People's Constitution" marks an important departure from authoritarianism and a strong endorsement of liberal democratic government. As noted previously, the Constitution contained an extensive list of individual liberties as well as procedural innovations designed to promote access to government policy making – such as a public participation requirement for administrative policy making, an ombudsman, an initiative process for legislation and investigation of corruption, and the establishment of administrative courts to hold bureaucrats accountable. The constitution not only expanded democracy by making the upper house elected and mandating decentralization of government power, but it also established a number of independent bodies to oversee government performance, a constitutional court, a countercorruption commission, a human rights commission, and an election commission, among others. The impressive range of institutional changes emphasized accountability and popular sovereignty.

Thailand's landmark 1997 constitution, though a milestone in the articulation of liberal values and human rights protection, accomplished little directly for the

[82] *See* GOHLERT, *supra* note 52. Government support for NGOs took shape under General Prem's leadership of the government in the 1980s. Following a 1984 CIDA funded conference on rural development sponsored by the Department of Technical and Economic Cooperation, a report was issued that was highly critical of the wealth gap created by development and that acknowledged the role of NGOs in addressing the needs of those who had been marginalized. In the mid-1980s, encouraged by CIDA funding for training and networking, an NGO Coordinating Committee (NGO-COD) was created with government support to coordinate and assist the movement's growth. The 6th National Plan (1985–1991) drafting committee had at least one strong community advocate, Thammasat Political Science Professor Saneh Chamarik. Sach Zurcher, *Public Participation in Community Forest Policy in Thailand: The Influence of Academics as Brokers*, 105 GEOGRAFISK TIDSSKRIFT, DANISH JOURNAL OF GEOGRAPHY 77 (2005). NGOs were first permitted to participate in the national planning process during the drafting of the 8th National Plan (1997–2001), formally admitting them to the national economic and social planning process. BAKER & PHONGPAICHIT, *supra* note 32.

women's movement. Nor did the eventual victory in legislative battles for marital equality depend on the constitutional changes. Benefits for women's equality and greater attention to gender in the administration of government resulted from more effective channels of influence through such new institutions as the National Human Rights Commission and the elected Senate. Influence on behalf of women's rights has continued to grow to the degree that more women have been placed in influential positions within government. Likewise, the 1997 constitution offered few concrete benefits to the slum movement that won neither land distribution nor a right to shelter.[83] Few in positions of influence have taken up the cause of slum dwellers. The National Human Rights Commission has not ignored their problems, but little actual progress has been made toward a more comprehensive legislative framework, much less a position of political influence for its NGOs and other advocates.

Social movements opposing development, on the other hand, were ideally positioned to make use of Thailand's institutional evolution, both statutory and constitutional. In 1992, Thailand adopted a statutory framework for the development and enforcement of environmental policy.[84] The new statute, though often ignored by Thai bureaucrats, created government obligations to oversee and manage the environmental effects of development, rights to public participation, and a process by which environmental NGOs could seek action by bureaucrats.[85] The constitution of 1997 created a system of administrative courts, and it also incorporated a new provision protecting a right to participation in the "preservation and exploitation of natural resources and biological diversity and in the protection, promotion and preservation of the quality of the environment for usual and consistent survival in the environment which is not hazardous to his or her health and sanitary condition, welfare or quality of life. . . ."[86]

Statutory law that had previously lain dormant for lack of an adequate means of citizen enforcement now offered a ripe opportunity for litigation.[87] Surachai's

[83] The 1997 constitution granted an ambiguous right to "enjoy liberty of dwelling." CONSTITUTION OF THE KINGDOM OF THAILAND, B.E. 2540, Section 35 (1997). Many experts are of the opinion that this right will be interpreted to secure a right to occupy a dwelling undisturbed, but not to secure a right to have a dwelling.

[84] Enhancement and Conservation of National Environmental Quality Act, B.E. 2535 (NEQA 1992), *available at* http://www.pcd.go.th/info_serv/en_reg_envi.html (last visited Aug. 30, 2009).

[85] *Id.* §§ 7 & 8. Appreciation of the importance of these provisions by NGOs seems to have been critical for litigation-oriented advocacy. Interview with Sayamol Kalyoorawong (Dec. 15, 2009).

[86] CONSTITUTION OF THE KINGDOM OF THAILAND B.E. 2540, Section 56 (1997). However, the ability to bring a lawsuit to protect this right is granted only "as provided by law," rendering the provision ineffective until Parliament chose to adopt enabling legislation, which was slow in coming. A similar public participation provision in the successor constitution of 2007 removed this qualification, allowing courts to enforce this requirement, which they have proven ready to do, to the surprise of many and consternation of government officials.

[87] Interviews with former NGO staff members Pipob Udomittipong (Dec. 15, 2009) and Sayamol Kalyoorawong (Dec. 15, 2009).

"Cobalt 60" lawsuit was one of the first to be filed when the administrative courts opened in 2001, and the decision in this case was the first one issued by the court. Surachai has continued to seek opportunities to force government agencies to articulate and strengthen environmental standards, with some success. His work has helped establish causes of action against the government for neglect of statutory duties, and he has won important civil court judgments against corporations and the government for damages – successes that have encouraged other, less ideologically motivated attorneys to bring similar lawsuits.

The Thai judiciary seems quite comfortable in this collaboration, which requires no more than strict application of statutory law, rather than interpretation of open-ended rights provisions in the new Thai constitutions.[88] Thus, Surachai's successes are built on the existence of the new administrative courts, the availability of useful statutory law (which is in contrast to movements on behalf of women and slum dwellers), and the compatibility of his legal theories with a conservative judicial methodology of statutory construction.

PROGRESS

How shall we measure progress toward government accountability, respect for rights, and freedom to advocate change, consistent with a liberal interpretation of the "rule of law"? In 2004, a leading Muslim human rights lawyer, Somchai Neelapaichit, was abducted and assassinated by police. Somchai represented Muslims caught up in separatist conflict in the three southernmost Thai provinces, challenging arbitrary arrests and condemning police abuses. Unlike Benedict Anderson's cases of murdered political candidates, state violence directed against a lawyer identified with defending Muslim separatists is not a sign that law is becoming a symbolic resource of greater value. A cause lawyer's murder is not evidence of a struggle to control the institution of law, but a rejection of law altogether.

Abel's studies of lawyers' struggles against state authority show that many different types of institutional, organizational, and individual investments create opportunities for meaningful cause lawyering, and they suggest the rich potential of our examination of the three narratives for signs of progress. Cause lawyers require institutional support, but, as the narratives make clear, institutional support in Thailand is problematic. Thai courts often lack independence from other branches of government, in part because the civil law tradition on which they are largely modeled limits the power of the judiciary to act as an independent guardian against overreaching political power. By design, they are remote, bureaucratic,

88 At least one centrally placed and highly regarded Thai appellate judge was willing to acknowledge that on the whole, his colleagues do not understand human rights very well. Interview with Judge A (July 1, 2009) (on file with the author).

conservative, and relatively unresponsive to local politics. Moreover, modernization of Thailand's government has, until recently, reflected almost exclusively the will of elites – that is, modernization has extended rule *by* elites and often authoritarian rule. Many bureaucrats, and especially members of the judiciary, still serve the king and govern *for* the people. Moreover, patriarchy remains important in Thai culture, and even where Buddhism may be weakening as a system of religious practices, its hierarchical implications influence habits of political deference and patriarchy. Finally, the legal profession has not constituted itself as the guardian of the rule of law or protector of its own members.[89] There is little investment by the profession in public interest law or the defense of human rights because this work has little symbolic political value.[90]

Thus, in spite of the establishment of a network of human rights lawyers through the Lawyers Council of Thailand, a number of NGO apprenticeships for young lawyers, and increasing willingness by some NGOs to resort to the courts, Thai cause lawyers continue to struggle to sustain their work. The architect of the network of human rights lawyers, a member of the October generation, ended his term of office at the Lawyers Council in 2008 and was replaced by a far less activist lawyer. The 1997 constitution created openings within and gaps between newly empowered government institutions – a more powerful Parliament, a more independent Prime Minister, and numerous independent government agencies watching over human rights, elections, corruption, and other important public arenas. Members of the National Human Rights Commission established by the 1997 constitution became important coordinators and information gatherers for human rights defense, magnifying the work of cause lawyers. The impact of these changes was greatly moderated by the constitution drafted after the 2006 coup. For example, as reconstituted by the constitution of 2007, the commissioners of the new Human Rights Commission, now appointed by the judiciary rather than Parliament, are mostly bureaucrats with little prior involvement with the human rights community. The new constitution preserves, and indeed expands, the list of rights and liberties of citizens, and it preserves the administrative court system, among other important institutional changes carried forward from the 1997 constitution.

Yet there are also signs of progress, as Malee's access to power and Surachai's litigation successes suggest. The narratives present a textured landscape, with complex

[89] An international law firm partner interviewed for this study in 2008 said that while the assassination of Somchai is a tragedy, he and his colleagues felt little connection to Somchai because he "is a member of a different profession." A plausible explanation offered by an influential member of the local practicing bar is that local lawyers often know the perpetrator personally, if not as a friend then as a feared and violent enemy. Fear of reprisal by the powerful perpetrators of violence is a plausible deterrent. Interview with Thai Law Firm Lead Partner A (Dec. 12, 2009).

[90] This lack of interest is lamented by the current head of the practicing lawyers bar association. Interview with Dej-Udom Krairit, President, Lawyers Council of Thailand (Dec. 11, 2009).

features revealed by the careers of each of our three cause lawyers who work with different movements, cultural resources, and levels of international support, while always attempting to navigate the uneven development of the rule of law. The administrative courts (and the new Green Bench that handles environmental cases) and the still-strong network of NGOs and lawyers created by the October generation are important signs of institutional change favoring progress.

13

African Youth Mobilize against Garbage

Economic and Social Rights Advocacy and the Practice of Democracy

Lucie E. White

INTRODUCTION

In this chapter, I examine lawyers and activists using human rights to engage people in a grassroots advocacy campaign for healthy living conditions. More specifically, I map how a group of young men, organized into a Federation of Youth Clubs, worked with a nongovernmental human rights organization to challenge inadequate waste disposal in their community, a sprawling urban "slum" in the West African city of Accra, Ghana.

The chapter has four parts. In the first part, I describe their community, which is called Nima, and then sketch the tactics the youth, along with the lawyers and organizers who supported them, used in their human rights campaign.

In the second part, I examine three different framings of the issue, all of which might be consistent with an overarching human rights advocacy campaign. How did the youth and other community members understand why waste was piling up in their community and what they could do about it? What explanatory frames were the lawyers and activists pushing on them?

My own work in the community suggests that three different implicit theories – three different "namings" – were at play simultaneously. In spite of what distant analysts might believe, from a ground-level perspective no single theory seemed to drown out the others, even as wide swaths of the community used "human rights tactics" to challenge the problem. The result of these multiple framings created a messy – and "living" – campaign, for each theory pointed toward different objectives, analyses, targets, and tactics.

In the third part, I consider whether the advocacy campaign's tactics prepared participants for active roles in the reformed health and sanitation systems that the campaign sought. The campaign's legal and activist architects tried hard, and with mixed success, to bring Nima's most disadvantaged residents into the campaign's everyday activities. They chose this admittedly labor-intensive approach because of their pragmatic commitment to "strong," "grassroots" democracy in the *process* (as well as the *outcome*) of economic and social rights advocacy. Why did they make this commitment? Did the participation teach residents skills that would *prefigure* collaborative problem solving and direct democracy in the institutions, like primary health centers, designed to *maintain* the community's well-being – both its residents' and its environment's – over the longer term?

In the fourth part, I address the distribution of inclusion in the campaign's participatory advocacy projects. These projects purported to open up space where all community residents, no matter how marginal, could have their voices heard. Yet close observation of how the practices played out showed that those who entered those spaces with a greater supply of political, social, and psychological capital gained more from the supposedly neutral participation opportunities than their neighbors who entered those spaces less well endowed.

NIMA AND THE HUMAN RIGHTS CAMPAIGN

Nima from the Outside

Nima is a very-low-income area in the heart of Accra. It is located in a nation with a much more robust economy than many of its neighbors. Yet the worst off of Nima's people can expect to die before their fortieth birthdays – if they beat the odds. Their babies are dying not because they cannot afford cocktails of fancy antiviral drugs, but because they cannot afford a fifty-cent mosquito net or an oral rehydration kit. It is a place where the youth stay sick because their local district council cannot raise the cash to connect the public taps to clean water. It is a place where people take harrowing risks to get to London or New York to earn enough in a day to feed their families for weeks at a time.

Soon after World War II, the colonial authority gave the land that is now Nima to a group of elite Muslim leaders from the North, as a gesture of thanks for the service they gave to the Crown during the war. Today Nima is widely called a "city within a city." It is still substantially Muslim in a city that, though changing, has a large Christian population. Its people cycle back and forth from the destitute rural North to earn cash in the city as best they can.

Nima's cycling population mushroomed during the 1980s and 1990s, when natural disasters, political unrest, and cutbacks on agricultural subsidies forced small farmers in the North to go south to the cities during the North's "starvation time." Greater Accra now sports new skyscrapers, shopping malls, upscale beach hotels, and a Holiday Inn at the airport with a big conference room and a fancy swimming pool. Nima, which is located near the city's center, is swept up in the boom. While its migrants have long rented shelter from the "Big Men" whose families were first granted title to the land, they increasingly must rent from the real estate speculators who are rapidly buying it up.

New highways are choking Nima. Women hang their laundry along these highways' guardrails. Children gather at the interchanges at rush hour, where the smallest, boosted up by determined older sisters, tap on car door windows, trying to catch the drivers' eyes. The drivers curse at Accra's growing problem of "street kids." The children climb down from the windows and the drivers move on.

Nima from the Inside

When you look out across Nima from the second-floor balcony of the Ghana Legal Resources Centre, you see a counterpane of metal roofs spread out across the hills that drain into what's called the "Big Gutter." Families design their homes out of tarpaper, rusted metal, and discarded cargo containers from merchant ships, sealing up the cracks with black plastic bags. These families make do without clean water, electric power, wastewater drainage, rubbish pick-up, or sewage disposal. We are in the heart of the new global city. We could be anywhere in the Third World.

With no sewage treatment, a scattering of concrete bunkers housing pit toilets are open to those who can pay. Students from Harvard Law School, armed with the full battery of recommended immunizations plus plenty of Maalox and malarone, have come to help the people of Nima fight for their rights. Inside the safety of a hot conference room, the students try to listen as people have their say:

> My house is behind the public toilet. At times, the smell gets so bad that... I cannot bear to go outside.... When I use the public toilet, my skin, my hair, my clothes, they all absorb the odor, and I have to wash everything.... The toilets are not emptied regularly. Often, the hole is overflowing and the waste in the hole splashes up against me.

As they take their assigned affidavits, the students hear that some of Nima's most iron-willed young men, all leaders of the Federation of Youth Clubs have taught their bowels not to move for days at a time. The men regard this feat as an act of resistance.

At the same time that they resist it, these youth are also drawn by global culture. They wear recycled Levis, Red Sox tee shirts, and New Balance jogging shoes. They drink Guiness malt if they are Muslim or Star beer if they are not. They eat fast food from Papaya's when they have the money and cruise the city's glitzy malls when they do not. They aspire to get home loans from Barclay's Bank when they can find steady jobs. They *believe* in the neoliberal order – yet they cannot afford to use the toilets in this new Emerald City, so they relieve themselves, when they must, into black plastic bags.

How do these young men make sense of such a world? Do they lose faith in the liberal project? Do they shoot themselves up with dope, or fall, like many of their mothers,[1] into major depression? Do they pray for the world, or force their prayers on others? Do they burn down the public toilets and loot the shopping malls? Do they sign affidavits crafted by top-ranked students? Do they learn to turn planes into bombs?

The Campaign

Since 1997, the Ghana Legal Resources Centre (LRC) has been providing legal services, policy research, legislative advocacy, and organizing assistance to the people of Nima. Inspired by South Africa's Legal Resources Centre, two law students from Ghana's far North founded the LRC to serve Nima's largely Northern population. For its first few years, the Ghana LRC's office was located in a third-floor flat, upstairs from "McBonald's" fast food restaurant, on Nima's single paved road. During those years, the organization's individual legal services program focused on

[1] Allan Hill et al., *Health of Urban Ghanaian Women as Identified by the Women's Health Study of Accra*, 99 Int'l J. of Gynecology & Obstetrics 150 (2007).

landlord-tenant disputes, domestic disputes, and criminal matters. The organization received donor funding to incorporate alternative dispute resolution into its legal services program.

At the same time, the LRC had, from the start, an ambitious program of organizing Nima's people to challenge the "root causes" of the community's many forms of systemic deprivation. During those early years, this activist work had two parts. The first was for the LRC to create new organizations that it could then work with to tackle broad issues. The most successful of these LRC-created organizations was the "Gender Action Unit," which brought together Nima's elite women – professionals, elected officials, teachers and other civil servants, the wives of chiefs and other Big Men, and the like – to advocate around gender equality.

The second part of the activist work was to ally with pre-existing community organizations, most of them groups that had been independently established to do social welfare work before the LRC had arrived. The most prominent of these organizations was a network of Mothers' Clubs linked to the Red Cross and the Federation of Youth Clubs. By 2004, the Youth Clubs, with names like Nebraska and New York, were thriving. The story told in the community was that the government had established the clubs in the early 1970s to quell a rising tide of left activism among Nima's young men.

If this was indeed the origin of the Youth Clubs' elaborate formal network, the state's goal had met with mixed results. The Youth Clubs' underlying politics remained an uneasy blend of self-blame, self-help, community betterment, and Marxist-Leninist ideology, and their attitude toward the state remained both deferential and defiant. Though the Clubs organized an occasional neighborhood cleanup, most of their activities involved sports, small enterprises like chop bars, kiosks, cyber cafes, bicycle and mobile phone repair services, drug dealing, and "get out the vote" drives. The Clubs welcomed the LRC's invitation that the two groups work together and rapidly became the major community network that grounded the LRC's impressive organizing work.

In January 2002, a group of six Harvard Law School interns, paired with twelve interns from the University of Ghana Law Faculty, arrived in Accra to do good. The project emerged from discussions between one of the LRC's founders and the author of this chapter, who had met one another on the author's first visit to Ghana in the spring of 1999. The author recruited the Harvard interns from those students most committed to international human rights activism, even though this was several years before human rights clinics had become popular in U.S. law schools. Prior to launching the project, the author, with funding from a U.S. Fulbright Fellowship, had worked with the LRC to lay its foundation. The group spent their three-week January break in a seminar housed at a residential civil service training facility on the outskirts of Accra. With the help of a team of government officials, lawyers, and civil society activists, the group learned about the socioeconomic issues impacting the quality of life of Ghana's most impoverished residents and debated whether "human rights" tactics could help those people in real ways. The following summer, a smaller group of the original U.S. interns returned to make sense of what they had learned the previous winter at the Nima office of the LRC. Because of the author's wishes – and their own – the students were allowed to work "with the community" in the advocacy and organizing project of the LRC, rather than in its legal aid clinic. The students pushed hard for this role because they had taken up the mantel of "law and organizing," especially in the context of human rights advocacy, back home.

Thus, the students, with close guidance from the LRC's seasoned organizers, facilitated meetings of the community's leaders. In those gatherings, they solicited the participants' views about the community's biggest problems, like accessible healthcare, decent shelter, protection from police harassment, and income security. Each workshop ended with a brainstorming session in which students coaxed out feasible action ideas through which community members might tackle the problems they had named.

After the summer session, the group, with their teacher's passionate endorsement, decided to recruit a few more Harvard students to return to Accra the next winter term. In early fall, the group began to look for funds to return. One obvious source was an internal University program that gave small grants for groups doing work on human rights issues. Because all of the partners in the project – the interns, community leaders, and, most importantly, the LRC – had already framed their work around human rights, the decision to apply for the grant was easy. The challenge, however, was to decide which of Nima's many identified problems was the best focus for the grant application. Because healthcare had been raised in every community gathering, the decision seemed easy: For the purpose of the grant, the next winter's work was captioned a "Right to Health Campaign." Their decision meshed with the LRC's own emerging human rights focus and fundraising priority. Thus, through a serendipitous collaboration, the Nima "Right to Health Campaign," in the author's retrospective reconstruction least, was born.

The students returned the following January to find that the Youth Clubs' leaders had enthusiastically taken up the Right to Health focus and recruited their rank and file to support it. Because of the LRC organizers' long-standing ties with the Youth Clubs, neither the LRC staff nor the interns were surprised when the Federation of Youth Clubs' base followed their leaders to jump on board. The next thing that happened was a gendered division of labor. The interns worked with the Mothers' Clubs and Gender Action Unit to tackle the lack of access to health services,[2] while the Youth Clubs' men decided to take on the mountains of trash

2 Margaux J. Hall, Aziza Ahmed & Stephanie E. Swanson, *Answering the Millennium Call for the Right to Maternal Health: The Need to Eliminate User Fees*, 62 Yale Hum. Rts. & Dev. L.J. 12 (2009); Lucie

around them and the sewage clogging their uncovered drains, reframing the mess as a human rights claim.

Thus, in addition to feeling pressure from Harvard funding sources and U.S. foundations, the LRC's eventual decision to mobilize under the banner of "Health Rights" came because the LRC's organizers intuited that to name health as a justice issue would catch fire. Their faith in this frame was tentative because they could easily trace human rights ideology back to Enlightenment claims of Eurocentric Universalism. Yet they felt that in spite of this genealogical taint, core human rights values might still resonate with many people's diverse beliefs. In the organizers' calculation, this resonance seemed more like the overlap in a Venn diagram than any subjective meeting of the minds. Though they may have been too optimistic, the experiment was worth a try. And they might get a strategic advantage if indeed human rights could take hold. A "human rights" take on the problem would give the LRC organizers a blank slate on which to guide community leaders in mapping out the layers of state, "private," cultural, and familial power that worked together to legitimize the status quo and maintain de facto power distribution in the health arena.

All that said, the organizers' biggest problem was to shift peoples' *perception* and *evaluation* of their personal health situation. They had to jolt people to do a double take on the dreary stench of their everyday living conditions – the overflowing public toilets, the glutted open gutters, the unrelenting flies – and *recognize* that this sort of fundamental insult was *wrong*, according to their own moral teachings and human rights values.

Was the LRC leadership's decision to endorse the Right to Health campaign a smart one? Several Western human rights scholars, disappointed that yet another Northern discourse has penetrated the global South, would have probably said no, even on pragmatic grounds. By steeping people in traditional liberal values, such a move could draw the community even further into the grip of Northern – ostensibly "universal" – ideology and thus threaten their culture. Framing the campaign around human rights could also alienate many of Nima's activist leaders and others from confrontational politics. By stressing litigation-like procedures in official fora, a human rights frame could demobilize a nascent social movement, shifting power from community leaders' grassroots agitation to foreign lawyers' technical obsession. Yet, as emphasized earlier, the organizers sensed a resonance between the fundamental liberal values undergirding human rights – of inclusion, equality, material

E. White, *If You Don't Pay, You Die: On Death and Desire in the Postcolony*, *in* EXPLORING SOCIAL RIGHTS: BETWEEN THEORY AND PRACTICE 57 (Daphne Barak-Erez & Aeyal M. Gross eds., 2007); *see also* DYING FOR GROWTH: GLOBAL INEQUALITY AND THE HEALTH OF THE POOR (Jim Yong Kim, Joyce V. Millen, Alec Irwin & John Gershman eds., 2002); Kwadwo Konadu-Agyemang, *The Best of Times and the Worst of Times: Structural Adjustment Programs and Uneven Development in Africa: The Case of Ghana*, 52 THE PROFESSIONAL GEOGRAPHER 469, 469–83 (2000).

security, and voice – and the fundamental norms that cut across the varying faith traditions of their own peoples. Thus, in spite of the many risks, the LRC's leadership embraced the human rights frame with enthusiasm. Indeed, almost a decade later, the organization now identifies itself, proudly, as one of West Africa's leading human rights organizations.

Even though human rights *norms*, when translated into people's moral and religious values, had moral power, the organizers had to work hard before "human rights" lost its distinctly foreign sound. Among the Youth Clubs' most radical members, the competing language was that of Lenin and Mao: Some members still carried *The Little Red Book* around in their trouser pockets. With the Mothers' Clubs, it was the language of hygiene and care promulgated by the Red Cross. Theirs was the language of the nineteenth-century missionaries who strove to make the place safe for their own nations' colonial projects. Quite unlike the language of hygiene, the Gender Action Unit, most of whose members were Muslims who had come from the North, found their moral language in the Koran's teachings on wifely duties, read through a liberal lens. Interestingly, as cultural theorists have repeatedly written, none of these "indigenous" values were "pure." From left-wing communism to Victorian moral hygiene to the Koran's teachings, each of these sets of values had been transplanted and then adapted from sources as imperialistic in their origins as human rights itself.

Eventually, however, through a lot of saturation, human rights began to lose its foreign ring to Nima's leaders. They could then focus more on the choice of human rights *tactics* than the *legitimacy* of the discourse itself. Eventually the Youth Clubs' leaders decided to organize their battle against garbage and sewage around three interwoven strategic streams: (1) educating and mobilizing wider circles of Nima residents, the Ghanaian public, and global allies about the human rights dimensions of the garbage problem; (2) pressuring the government to provide the services, infrastructure, and resources needed to dispose of the sewage and to collect the garbage in an effective way; and (3) exploring entrepreneurial and cooperative approaches – such as recycling or composting – to supplement the central role that the government and donors from the Global North needed to play.

The Youth Clubs then mapped out the campaign's specific activities through a cluster of action-planning workshops. The sessions typically took place in the courtyards between dwellings, where the youth had nailed up wooden boards to tack up news about upcoming concerts and soccer games. Yet even though Nima's residents viewed garbage as a men's issue, the Federation of Youth Clubs went beyond its own membership to conduct these sessions for the Mothers' Clubs and Gender Action Unit. They also worked with "assimilated" urban traditional healers, whom community members often consulted for minor ailments or when they could not pay the up-front cash required to get in the door of the Nima Polyclinic. And with help from the interns, they worked with the chemists who dispensed medications, professional nurses, local government officials, and Nima's several dozen chiefs.

Always with backup from the LRC's in-house organizing staff, they would facilitate these sessions in the spirit of popular education, as originally fashioned by Brazilian lawyer and adult educator Paulo Freire and subsequently transplanted across the developing world.[3] Both the Youth Clubs' leaders and the LRC organizers were at home with the method and guided the facilitation with a steady hand. Some of the students, having studied the method at home, were able to take on the facilitator role with remarkable success, even given the huge cultural distance they had to bridge to do so. Through this brainstorming process, the youth devised an elaborate game plan of tactics to realize the three broad objectives outlined earlier in this chapter: educating and enabling residents, pressuring the government, and encouraging entrepreneurial and collaborative strategies for "greening" the mountains of trash.

Their tactics included the following:

First, with help from the student interns, the youth obtained the contract between the city and the for-profit garbage collection business that was paid to pick up the trash. They were then coached by the LRC's lawyers, with help from the students, to read it like lawyers, teasing out features like the rights of third-party beneficiaries, such as Nima's people, to sue for its enforcement, the available remedies, and *specific* lapses on the part of the city or garbage pickup business that might constitute "material" breaches. Although this work never produced a formal complaint, it was enough to make a plausible *threat* of litigation when subsequent negotiations with the city and garbage business faltered.

Second, starting in their first winter of work, the students helped the youth organize themselves to monitor the garbage business's performance in collecting the trash for an entire year. Thus, they would have hard evidence to use in negotiations and subsequent litigation, should that be needed. To accomplish this ambitious plan, the youth worked with the students to set up a highly structured plan that included a clear assignment of each youth's monitoring site, personalized monitoring checklists, and a small incentive payment for each completed form.

Third, the youth analyzed the results of the monitoring and then systematically brainstormed about how to use them. After compiling the data, they decided to meet with municipal authorities and the private business's owners to negotiate contract compliance. They discovered that the garbage collection business faced several obstacles in seeking to comply with the contract's terms. The community had few street lights and just one paved road. The trucks were in a perpetual state of disrepair: Their headlights seldom functioned, they frequently had flat tires and engine

[3] Paulo Freire, Pedagogy of the Oppressed (Myra Bergman Ramos trans., Continuum 2000) (1970).

trouble, drivers were not always paid, and fuel was sometimes in short supply. The company pointed to the city as the root cause of these problems: The contract amount was simply too small to enable it to do the job.

As these negotiations were going on, the youth, again with the interns' help, educated elite community members about their "legal rights" under the contract and the reasons the company gave for their many contract lapses. Did the situation counsel an adversarial battle or a broad coalition? Perhaps the World Bank and the U.K. Department for International Development were better targets because the infrastructure and funding it would take to "solve" the garbage problem clearly did not lie within the contractor's power.

With this more complex analysis of the problem's root causes, the youth sought to engage as many potential allies as possible. One part of this effort was for the LRC – again with the Federation of Youth Clubs' and interns' help – to convene a large public hearing (with about 500 in attendance), to which they invited a range of people to testify about different dimensions of the garbage problem. At the meeting, public health experts explained how the contractor's breaches jeopardized the health of Nima's residents. People affected by the garbage described how the trash piles and overflowing sewage affected their health. Nurses who worked at the Nima Polyclinic laid out how parallel issues around curative care – the illegal imposition of user fees on impoverished people seeking care at the Polyclinic, for instance – deprived health professionals like the nurses of their right to practice their vocation. And the U.S. Ambassador spoke about how Martin Luther King Jr.'s final public action was to support striking sanitation workers. The hearing was a turning point among community members. Not only did it focus the audience on the deeper causes for the glut of garbage, but it also constituted a moment when those in attendance engaged the human rights theme as their own.

By now, some of the youth leaders had become friends with the students, who were about the same age. Having placed the garbage problem on what they imagined as a world stage, the Youth Clubs, with the interns, were ready to target global, as well as local and national, players. The Youth Clubs' leaders met with local World Bank officials to seek an urban loan to improve the community's sanitation infrastructure. Such a loan would have improved drainage, upgraded roads and street lights, covered open gutters, and dredged the Big Gutter, thus making it easier for garbage trucks to service the community and reducing the risks posed by grossly inadequate sanitation.

But beyond these top-down tactics, the Youth Clubs did more. They organized a recycling cooperative among Nima residents. They worked with a network of community organizations, including the Mothers' Clubs, to do popular education workshops in the community. At one of these sessions, the Youth Clubs' members asked people how they might protect their children from malaria and waterborne diseases while becoming more active in the garbage campaign.

This pragmatic, multitactic program of human rights activism reflects a novel approach to economic and social rights promotion. The following chart illustrates how this approach contrasts with the more traditional formalistic approach that remains the norm.

Rights-Based Advocacy	
The Old Paradigm	The New Vision
➢ Targets Nation-States	➢ Traces Power
➢ Litigates	➢ Mixes Tactics
➢ Makes Enemies	➢ Creates Networks
➢ Counts Beans	➢ Builds Capacity
➢ Produces Victims	➢ Empowers Citizens
➢ A New Faith	➢ A Critical Politics

The campaign's multiple tactics worked together to catalyze several palpable effects among the participants and in the community as a whole. These included building new knowledge, skills, and confidence among community members; building new relationships, networks, and informal institutions within the community; introducing the community to new grassroots civic and political practices, such as monitoring garbage pick-up; building new ties between the community and relevant institutions, both public and private, on the municipal, national, transnational, and supranational levels, from local traditional midwives and primary care clinics on the one hand to the World Bank and World Health Organization on the other; sensitizing wider communities to the waste-removal problems in Nima and similar communities within and around Third World "global cities"; linking the problem of waste removal to its profound threat to public health; and promoting core human rights values like inclusion, equality, voice, and material security in the context of specific domains of social welfare delivery.

The campaign also engendered, among both community groups and wider publics, a new appreciation for the efficacy of human rights advocacy, when practiced in pragmatic, critical, and creative ways. Similarly, it engendered long-term hope among those residing in Nima and other distressed communities that they could take pragmatic actions to change their own social welfare services – like garbage pick-up – in specific ways. The possibility of such horizontal communication and cross-learning was not as unlikely as it sounds, when we recall that the LRC was linked to supranational funding sources, African networks of human rights and social welfare activists, and student interns from elite U.S. law schools that were starting to establish vibrant human rights programs. And on the institution-building front, the campaign schooled participants in practices of interaction among the residents of underresourced communities and between those groups of people and the state that might ground a new institutional architecture for sanitation provision and primary healthcare delivery.

THE PROBLEM'S ROOT CAUSES: THREE TAKES ON THE HUMAN RIGHTS FRAME

This section will set out three contrasting explanatory accounts that emerged in the campaign. I say "emerged" because the campaign's leaders did not self-consciously privilege any of these competing stories. Nor was a single one so much more plausible to Nima's population that it edged out the others. Rather, all three fit easily within a human rights framing of the problem at hand. All three could coexist in people's minds because they appealed to contrasting normative orientations that were often embraced by very different groups of community members, but were as easily embraced simultaneously by a single group of people.

The fact that all three stories could fit into a human rights framing of the garbage problem demonstrates that the community's belief systems are thickly plural, as is frequently the case in global cities where rapid cultural and normative changes are taking place. The compatibility of all three stories with human rights further shows how ideologically malleable rights talk can be. Even though the LRC's leaders recognized from the outset the risk that rights rhetoric could always be spun in a reactionary way, they suppressed that danger when they chose to launch a rights campaign. Yet the community members' interpretations of the rights rhetoric the campaign's organizers chose to use starkly demonstrates that it does not take right-wing agitators to give rights talk a neo-liberal spin. Rather, ordinary community members will inevitably interpret, or "domesticate," human rights talk in many different ways, only some of which will fit easily with what organizers might consider liberal or "progressive" politics.

Making sense of Nima's garbage was hard work for the residents. Most were recent migrants to the city from outlying rural areas where traditional practices of storing and preparing food produced much less concentrated waste than did urban food sources and practices. Thus, when they came to the city, many of the residents faced, for the first time, mountains of waste encroaching into their cramped living spaces. To interpret their gut fear, they drew on themes from deeply embedded cultural and moral understandings. They also consulted their own common sense about human behavior, understandings that they had acquired from living as they did in the world. Finally, they consulted the political ideologies to which they had been exposed through election campaigns, their traditional chiefs, local officials, whatever formal schooling they had, and the LRC's anti-garbage campaign. Drawing on these sources, the residents leaned toward three different explanations of why their community was swamped with waste.

The Bad Actor

The first causation story that the community considered was that "Bad Actors" had caused the problem. This was not as magical a story as it might sound. Rather it is a story of wealth maldistribution. In this story, powerful agents, motivated by prejudice, self-interest, or individual perversity, had hoarded the resources needed to provide adequate healthcare and waste-removal for Nima. Indeed, even within their own community, they have encountered plenty of people who are just plain mean. Most people in Nima have regularly experienced harassment and bias based on their poverty, ethnicity, or religion, so they are accustomed to encountering people with overt bias toward them. And looking at the vast wealth discrepancies around them has taught them that their affluent neighbors have healthcare, sewage disposal, and garbage pick-up services that work.

A more layered account about what might motivate Bad Actors to turn their heads from Nima's waste disposal problem has an ideological dimension. In that account, elite groups seek to deflect public attention from the lived experience of the people of Nima and other global "slums" because the reality that slum dwellers are human beings like themselves would undermine the plausibility of the "trickle down" theory of global development.[4] In that trickle-down account, increasing economic growth without simultaneous wealth redistribution is supposed to address inequality, albeit indirectly, because such nontargeted economic growth should increase economic opportunities across the board. The unimaginable suffering of slum dwellers in global cities debunks this theory as inadequate for the task of tackling inequality. A failure of elites to give up on this trickle-down ideology in the face of such a human catastrophe requires "disappearing" those populations with white-gloved hands.[5]

Implicit in this analysis is a progressive critique of "neoliberal" development theories. According to that critique, the redistribution of wealth in the context of sustainable growth might help in solving Nima's most critical problems.[6] In this scenario, a progressively tilted human rights analysis would promote targeting adequate resources for sanitation, healthcare, education and the like toward the

[4] *See generally* The New Law and Economic Development: A Critical Appraisal (David M. Trubek & Alvaro Santos eds., 2006).

[5] *See* Kevin Bales, Disposable People: New Slavery in the Global Economy (1999); Stones of Hope: How African Activists Reclaim Human Rights to Challenge Global Poverty (Lucie E. White & Jeremy Perelman eds., Stanford University Press, 2010); Thomas Pogge, *Why Inequality Matters*, *in* Global Inequality: Patterns and Explanations (David Held & Ayse Kaya eds., 2007).

[6] *E.g.*, Alice Amsden, The Rise of "The Rest": Challenges to the West From Late-Industrializing Economies (2001); James Ferguson, Global Shadows: Africa in the Neoliberal World Order (2006).

poorest people's needs. Such a policy emphasis – on redistribution and targeting *during* the development process – would mean that the state must recognize "disappeared" populations as *citizens* and then make adequate resources for basic material security available to them *now* rather than praying that those resources might trickle down in the future.

When the Bad Actor story is played out in this way, it points toward the tactic of broad-based mobilization within a human rights frame. This mobilization might target both global actors and the nation-state for their underlying development paradigm as well as their social welfare policies. The goal here would be nothing less than shifting political will, on the global as well as national levels. Thus, organizing within the community will be critical to this effort because it will provide a base of impassioned political agents to take a major role in "leading the charge." Yet such internal organizing will be neither easy nor enough to do the job on its own. It will not be easy because of the cleavages that divide Nima, such as those around ethnicity, religion, economic status, and access to land.[7] To overcome such divisions, the internal organizing has to unite Nima's *elites*, such as chiefs, property owners, local politicians; a *middle tier* of shopkeepers, market women, traditional healers, and others; as well as Nima's most *dispossessed*, such as the seemingly endless cycles of migrants from the severely impoverished regions and nations to the north. Here, the core human rights value of *inclusion* is critical for the organizers to emphasize. If this work can be successfully done, a sense of moral urgency and social movement, and the political agency that goes with it, will coalesce, and multiple advocacy strategies will become possible.

Because of the large gaps of power and resources among the community's intersecting schisms, however, this work of cross-class coalition building will not be easy. To give an example, consider the case of a loan that might be offered by the World Bank to enable property owners to bring piped water inside dwellings that they rent to less well-off families. Such an opportunity would generate extra income for landlords and improve the health of their tenants. But, particularly in the context of a weak state that cannot effectively enforce a rent-control measure, such upgrading might exert an upward push on rents, displacing some of those who currently reside in what had been Nima's least costly shelter.[8] Yet none but the most politicized landlords would be likely to refuse the Bank's upgrading offer.

Another perspective on organizing both within and beyond the community in response to the Bad Actor is informed by network theory. This perspective emphasizes the potential for Nima's various social groups to form networks and alliances with more privileged groups – both within Ghana and globally – whose interests

[7] *See* Mahmood Mamdani, Citizen and Subject 138–44 (1996).

[8] *See, e.g.,,* Duncan Kennedy, *The Effect of the Warranty of Habitability on Low Income Housing: "Milking" and Class Violence*, 15 Fla. St. Univ. L. Rev. 485 (1987).

or agendas overlap with theirs. Such networks might even be formed with individuals holding positions within Ghana's governmental bureaucracies charged with providing health and sanitation, as well as within multilateral or bilateral organizations. For instance, Nima's leaders might ascertain that some powerful actors have self-interested reasons to embarrass or undermine the incumbent government, or to challenge the intrusion of the World Bank and International Monetary Fund into Ghana's national sovereignty.[9] Indeed, where such overlapping interests can be identified through astute power mapping, such cross-strata coalitions might enhance the political agency of Nima's impoverished residents themselves.

"The Technical Problem"

A second perspective on the garbage issue as a human rights problem portrays it as a "Technical Problem." In this account, powerful elites are not understood to lack the *will* to fix the problem. Rather, those elites are seen to throw up their hands and claim that it is simply beyond their science to solve. The upshot from all this is *in*action. There is no question that powerful actors like Ghana's government, donors, multilaterals like the World Bank, and large corporate enterprises like the gold-mining conglomerates Anglo-Gold Ashanti might sometimes use this position as an excuse for failing to discharge their duty, however, the Technical Problem position does not reflect their point of view. Rather, the actors who fit into the Technical Problem account have good reasons to want the problem solved, but they honestly believe it to overwhelm their know-how and the resources they command.

Several reasons might motivate elites to want the problem solved if this Technical Problem were not there. For instance, they might empathize with Nima's people for religious, humanitarian, or human rights-based reasons. Or, repeating a stock argument familiar throughout colonial history, they might fear that informal communities like Nima, especially when those communities are located at the heart of global cities, pose a threat to elites themselves. Contaminated gutters will flood into neighboring areas when it rains, spreading cholera into the kitchens of fancy restaurants where the luckiest of impoverished men and women have tenuous jobs. And when mosquitoes breed in Nima, they can fly into nearby gated enclaves. A third motive for elites to take on Nima's garbage problem is professional self-interest. For just like elite lawyers who do pro bono work for their own professional enhancement, Accra's elites may want to solve Nima's garbage problem to expand the scope of their professional mastery and thus build up their stature among their peers.

9 *See* GØSTA ESPING-ANDERSEN, THE THREE WORLDS OF WELFARE CAPITALISM (1990).

Even when elites are thus *motivated* to help, however, they may believe the problem to be technically intractable and its resolution beyond the scope of their power. Surely garbage pick-up and bed net distribution could be handled with a little creativity and a reliable resource flow. Yet the longer-term issues of waste disposal and health maintenance can seem overwhelming because of the exponentially expanding populations of informal communities like Nima all over the developing world. This challenge could be abated if Nima were itself "gated," but so long as such communities keep their boundaries open, the Technical Problem caused by uncontained expansion seems to remain.[10]

Placed within a human rights frame, this account – or excuse? – might counsel creativity, collaboration, experimentation, persistence, and patience among those who feel a compulsion to help. In this account, the designated "duty bearers," as well as all other interested parties, must set aside their despair over never solving the problem for good. They must set aside their narrow interests, roll up their sleeves, and undertake a well-designed process of mutual deliberation, cross-learning, and pragmatic improvisation to address the problem at hand. Furthermore, if the process is to be "human rights sensitive," it must be conducted in a way that is insistently *inclusive* and determined to enhance the voices of those with less social power.[11]

The Act of God

A third way of understanding Nima's garbage problem is to attribute it – as well as the rapid, development-linked urbanization that underlies it – to an inevitable historical process. In this account, solving the problem is beyond the reach of those affected – both elites and impoverished people, inside and outside of Nima – *not* for a lack of political will or technical know-how, but because the problem is driven by deterministic historical processes that human agency cannot influence in significant ways. From this perspective, the twenty-first century's Great Migration is not the consequence of any particular absence of political will, wrong-headed development policy, or narrow-minded economic model.[12] Nor does it present the sort of discrete technical problems that human beings, with the appropriate commitment, can join together to solve. Rather, in this view, the flood of people to these global cities unfolds with an inexorable logic. It might as well be the Act of an inscrutable God.

One response to such an account is fundamentalist religious faith or political ideology. Indeed, evangelical sects from every faith and ideological tradition are spreading across global informal communities as quickly as those communities expand.

[10] *See* Duncan Kennedy, *Commentary on Anti-Eviction and Development in the Global South, in* STONES OF HOPE, *supra* note 5, at 41.

[11] *See infra*, "The Challenge of Exclusion."

[12] *See* JUDITH SHKLAR, THE FACES OF INJUSTICE 51–82 (1992).

Another response is denial through depression, dissociation, or drugs. A third is adaptation and escape through such moves as emigration, hard work, or absorption in the other-world of spectator culture.[13] Though all of these tactics might make sense, all mark a retreat from human agency and pragmatic politics.

How might a human rights strategy respond to this deterministic explanation for Nima's sanitation issue? One widespread response offered by traditional human rights is the practice of speaking truth to suffering. *Testimony, witness, forums for voicing truth* – all of these rituals are designed as much to make space for people to name and honor their experiences of suffering as to prosecute Bad Actors, or inch forward on solving Technical Problems, or protest an evil invisible hand. Much of the human rights advocacy around the health and sanitation conditions in Nima has had that quality. Though the discourses of blame and remedy on the one hand and innovative problem-solving on the other were the *dominant* frames for the human rights campaign, much of the passion driving the testimonial rituals such as public hearings and learning circles was to give people forums where voices that protested suffering could be clearly heard.

FROM HEALTH RIGHTS ACTIVISM TO INSTITUTIONAL REFORM?

Earlier in this chapter, I laid out several of the tactics of the Nima Right to Health campaign. I suggested that participants in the campaign learned a variety of skills and political competencies at the same time that they increased their self-confidence to play activist-citizen roles. From a normative perspective, such enhanced human potential might be viewed as a good in itself. At the same time, from an instrumental perspective – if we must dichotomize in this way – that enhanced potential might be seen to enable people to act effectively in innovative social welfare delivery institutions. For instance, the skills and confidence that youth leaders learned through the monitoring project might have taught them skills, confidence, *and* specific monitoring methods that will transfer from activist politics to ongoing health care, sanitation, or educational reform. Thus, intense participation in the *process* of economic and social rights advocacy might offer a foundation for citizen participation in state-of-the-art welfare delivery institutions and systems over the long term.[14]

This potential match between participatory advocacy tactics – most strongly demonstrated by the monitoring campaign – and innovative welfare delivery institutions was neither foreseen nor intended by the activists who shaped the campaign. For the

13 *See* Arjun Appadurai, Globalization (2001); James Ferguson, Global Shadows: Africa in the Neoliberal World Order (2006); White, *supra* note 2.

14 *See* Benjamin Barber, Strong Democracy: Participatory Politics for a New Age (1984); Peter Houtzager & Lucie E. White, *The Long Arc of Pragmatic Economic and Social Rights Advocacy, in* Stones of Hope, *supra* note 5, at 172.

focus on trash, as well as the larger Right to Health campaign of which it was a part, was aimed primarily toward *pressuring* the Ghanaian state and international donors to deliver more market-basket goods – such as garbage pick-up, sewage disposal, and basic health care – to impoverished people. It was not aimed toward *designing or realizing* those institutions directly. Yet the strongly democratic advocacy methods may have prepared people to play an active role in innovative sanitation and health delivery institutions, especially on the ground. Such institutions, in turn, might prove to be both more effective and more normatively compelling than the status quo alternatives, which are notoriously underresourced, ineffective, and exclusionary.

These speculations require further development, which is beyond the scope of this short essay. At this point, however, we can observe that some of the strikingly successful innovations in ground-level primary health and sanitation are built around the participation of patients, health providers, and a wider range of citizens in those institutions, in both governance and delivery roles.[15] One example of this potential "isomorphism" between the *process* of citizen participation in health advocacy and best practices for the design of effective and equitable primary health care delivery *institutions*,[16] over the long term, can be gleaned from the consensus principles for primary health institutions in developing nations set out in the "Alma Ata Resolution."[17]

[15] Though such best practices in health delivery bear some important similarities to experimentalist models, they also diverge from those models in significant ways. Michael Dorf and Charles Sabel define democratic experimentalism as:

> a new form of government in which power is decentralized to enable citizens and other actors to utilize their local knowledge to fit solutions to their individual circumstances, but in which regional and national coordinating bodies require actors to share their knowledge with others facing similar problems. This information pooling... both increases the efficiency of public administration by encouraging mutual learning among its parts and heightens its accountability through participation of citizens in the decisions that affect them.

Michael Dorf & Charles Sabel, *The Constitution of Democratic Experimentalism* 98 COLUM L. REV 267 (1998).

[16] *See* JENNIFER GORDON, SUBURBAN SWEATSHOPS: THE FIGHT FOR IMMIGRANT RIGHTS 237–280 (2005) (explaining that "citizens" are not just people defined as citizens by positive law, but people who live in, work in, and contribute to a particular locale).

[17] International Conference on Primary Health Care, Alma-Ata, Kazakhstan, *The Alma-Ata Declaration on Primary Health Care of 1978*, (Sept. 25, 1978). The Alma-Ata Declaration on Primary Health Care of 1978 was based on the World Health Assembly's resolution of 1977 on Health for All by the Year 2000. The Declaration was adopted during the International Conference on Primary Health Care. The Conference called for urgent and effective national and international action to develop and implement primary health care throughout the world. Governments, the World Health Organization, and other international organizations, as well as multilateral and bilateral agencies, NGOs, health workers, and the whole world community were urged to support national and international commitment to primary health care and to increase technical and financial support, especially in developing countries. The Declaration called for health to be a fundamental human right, guaranteed by the state. Furthermore, health users and providers were specified as the prime movers in shaping their health services, using and enlarging upon the capacities developed in their societies. Health services were to operate as an integral whole, with promotive, preventive, curative, and rehabilitative components.

This multilateral resolution laid out six guidelines for the architecture of such health systems – touchstones that reflect both years of evaluation research on effective institutional innovation and core human rights principles. The sort of institutions that the Resolution calls for require the active participation by those who receive treatment in primary care clinics as well as those who provide the care. People who have taken part in highly participatory human rights campaigns would, by virtue of what they learn through those experiences, be especially prepared to take on such activist health seeking or providing roles.[18]

We can bring home this convergence between advocacy processes and institutional practices by a brief review of the Alma Ata Resolution's guidelines. According to those directives, the best primary health systems evolve from the economic, sociocultural, and political characteristics of the country and its communities. They address the main health problems in the community through promotive, preventive, curative, and rehabilitative services. They include education of participants in the health system. They involve all related sectors and aspects of national and community development. They "require and promote maximum community and individual self-reliance and participation in the planning, organization, operation and control of primary health care." To do this, they make fullest use of local, national, and other available resources and to this end develop through appropriate education the ability of communities to participate. Finally, they include, among others, community workers on the health delivery team. People who come into the system with skills, competencies, and confidence honed through participatory advocacy campaigns are likely to hit the ground running as they assume their roles in every aspect of health system design and implementation that the Resolution mandates.

THE CHALLENGE OF EXCLUSION

Let us assume that the Right to Health campaign tilled the soil for the creation of robustly democratic health institutions. With this as one of the campaign's hopes, it becomes of even greater importance that, to the greatest extent possible, the campaign offer pedagogically effective participation opportunities across the entire community. This imperative will not be realized without close and ongoing scrutiny of

[18] *See id.*; *see also* TRACY KIDDER, MOUNTAINS BEYOND MOUNTAINS: THE QUEST OF DR. PAUL FARMER, A MAN WHO WOULD CURE THE WORLD (2003); Louise G. Trubek & Maya Das, *Achieving Equality: Healthcare Governance in Transition*, 29 AM. J.L. & MED. 395 (2003); William E. Forbath, *Realizing a Constitutional Social Right – Cultural Transformation, Deep Institutional Reform, and the Roles of Advocacy and Adjudication*, U. of Texas Law, Public Law Research Paper No. 143, *available at* SSRN: http://ssrn.com/abstract=1292879; Navrongo Health Research Centre, *Health for All in Sight: The Navrongo Community Health and Family Planning Project*, WHAT WORKS? WHAT FAILS? FINDINGS FROM THE NAVRONGO COMMUNITY HEALTH AND FAMILY PLANNING PROJECT (2001), *at* http://www.navrongo.org/reports/vol1/wwv1n1/ww1n1_Health4allinSight.htm.

whether the participation opportunities are tailored to reach all sectors of the community (including people from different religious and vocational backgrounds, and in different positions with respect to land and housing tenure) and – within each such sector – *both* elites and those who are more deprived. This question of de facto exclusion, despite its obvious importance, is often overlooked when scholars document participatory grassroots human rights campaigns.[19]

Participation opportunities were abundant in Nima's Right to Health campaign. Yet on close examination, it is clear that they were not distributed among community members in equitable ways. Rather, this distribution was skewed toward those of privilege. For instance, those with particular endowments – social class, education, family connections, charisma, self-confidence, interpersonal skills, and similar psychosocial qualities – were most likely to take, or be chosen for, central campaign roles. Indeed, though the Legal Resources Centre was determined to make the campaign highly participatory, its focus seemed to be the development of the community organizations' "natural leaders" into an elite corps of activists, rather than to enhance the most marginal community members' political capacities.

The monitoring project was particularly complex. To pull it off, LRC organizers had to "cream" in the way they selected the Youth Clubs' members for leadership roles. Why would the LRC want to create such a corps of "indigenous" community leaders? For one thing, emphatically demonstrating that the LRC was authentically "grassroots" was an imperative imposed by funders. For another, because of limited staff, the LRC *needed* strong community leaders to guide its campaigns. Thus, the equitable distribution of power and participation within the monitoring project became a secondary objective. To make matters worse, those with little formal education or community status would need skillful one-on-one mentoring and ongoing support to engage independently in complex tactics like the monitoring project, which required, at the very least, basic literacy and arithmetic skills.

Less socially endowed women, notably those from patriarchal cultural arrangements, were especially disadvantaged in both brainstorming sessions and women's groups' activities. Many were accustomed to taking a back seat to both their husbands and their chiefs in public interactions – if, indeed, they regularly took part in public meetings at all. Few spoke the imperial languages of Hausa, English, or Twi. Because of a maldistribution of manual labor and calories, some non-elite women tended to be noticeably smaller in stature than many men. Most had several young children. The list of socioeconomic disadvantages could go on. Furthermore, because elite women were amply represented by the Gender Action Unit's members and Mothers'

[19] *See* Development Encounters: Sites of Participation and Knowledge (Pauline E. Peters, ed. 2001). *But see* Lisa Collins, Sakisha Jackson & Jennifer MacLeod, United Nations Development Programme Case Study on Ghanaian Housing and Human Rights (2010) (unpublished J.D. case study, Harvard Law School, on file with author).

Clubs' leaders, the absence of non-elite women was rarely noticed by those who were counting gender statistics, either for the funders or for the LRC itself.

One further obstacle to inclusionary participation was the doubt among the community's rank and file that their voices would matter in critical decisions, even if they did get involved. Many believed that such skepticism was well-founded because the link between grassroots participation and state-mandated redistribution was seldom obvious, if indeed it took place at all. The most impoverished, who faced so many obstacles to active involvement, were the most likely to distrust the efficacy of participatory human rights campaigns.[20]

All of these factors created a risk that the robust *community* participation in the health campaign did *not* mean the inclusion of all sectors of the community, much less substantial representation from disadvantaged strata within any of those sectors. This gap between normative aspiration and close-up reality becomes especially unfortunate when we consider the campaign's potential to train non-elite health seekers to take active roles in state-of-the art health delivery institutions. This veiled exclusion of some from the advocacy experience will only increase their relative disadvantage in innovative primary health delivery systems over the long term.

The risks of such veiled exclusion from the opportunities the advocacy makes available can be minimized if activists come to their work with acute sensitivity to those risks. Among the questions that advocates might ask to focus their awareness include the following:

1. Which groups within the community are most likely to participate? Which are getting left out?
2. What are the "micro-obstacles" that are contributing to exclusion?
3. How do the demands of the advocacy projects themselves – the need to read and write, for example, or the need to converse in the dominant language – present obstacles to the participation of some but not others?
4. What specific strategies might lift the micro-obstacles, adapt the campaign's tactics, and affirmatively enable more equitable and widespread participation?

CONCLUSION

My final question about the campaign is whether its intensely participatory quality was, in the end, worth all of the effort that was sunk into it. Did it meaningfully

[20] This is *not* to say that the participatory activities seemed illegitimate to those who received immediate satisfaction from the performances that their leadership roles made available to them. *See, e.g.*, Archon Fung & Erik Olin Wright, Deepening Democracy: Institutional Innovations in Empowered Participatory Governance (2003); Innovations in Government: Research, Recognition, and Replication (Sandford F. Borins ed., 2008).

promote important human rights norms of inclusion, equality, voice, and material security? Did it pressure the government for redistribution and institutional innovation as effectively as other political strategies might have? Did it *really* ground health seekers' long-term participation in state-of-the-art health delivery institutions? Or, rather, did it aggravate potentially explosive divisions within the community? Because participation is an ideologically charged strategy, with some people resolutely "for it" and others opposed, these are the sorts of questions that are too often avoided when case studies of participatory activities – whether they be human rights campaigns or municipal budgeting initiatives[21] – are done. My closing hope is that this essay will invite rather than discourage such questions.

[21] *See* GIANPAOLO BAIOCCHI, MILITANTS AND CITIZENS THE POLITICS OF PARTICIPATORY DEMOCRACY IN PORTO ALEGRE (2005); David Lewit, *Porto Alegre's Budget of, by, and for the People*, YES! MAGAZINE (2004), *at* http://www.yesmagazine.org/issues/what-would-democracy-look-like/562.

14

Epilogue

Just Law?

Richard L. Abel

Can law promote justice? Or is it just law – a set of positive directives, which are obligatory if created according to Hart's secondary rules but likely to be followed only if the benefits exceed the costs?[1] What makes law distinctive as a subject of social scientific inquiry is its normative essence (a quality it shares with religion). Disregarding instructions for assembling an Ikea bookcase or installing software on your computer can lead to failure and frustration, but such behavior usually does not incur disapproval. Exceeding the speed limit or evading taxes deserves opprobrium. People do not always behave like Holmes's "bad man,"[2] or economists' profit maximizer, simply calculating the costs of noncompliance in terms of the sanctions likely to be imposed. Law is obligatory because it is just. That law is aspirational, seeking to promote justice, fundamentally shapes our research agenda. It explains why studies of the "gap" between law on the books and law in action have long been a staple of law-and-society scholarship.[3] It explains why the "hired gun" theory of legal ethics is so unsatisfactory[4] and why each new cohort of law students experiences discomfort at relinquishing moral autonomy for a career devoted to promoting the ends of clients lawyers generally do not choose.[5] It explains the persistent concern with the unequal distribution of legal services and continuing efforts to increase government spending on legal aid, expand pro bono activities, and sustain law students' commitment to public interest law. It explains the significant amounts of time many lawyers voluntarily invest in their professional associations at a time

[1] H.L.A. HART, THE CONCEPT OF LAW (1961).

[2] Oliver Wendell Holmes, Jr., *The Path of the Law*, 10 HARV. L. REV. 457 (1897).

[3] Richard L. Abel, *Law and Society: Project and Practice*, 6 ANN. REV. L. AND SOC. SCI. 1 (2010); Richard L. Abel, *Law Books and Books About Law*, 26 STAN. L. REV. 175 (1973); Richard L. Abel, *Taking Stock*, 14 LAW & SOC'Y REV. 805 (1980).

[4] David Luban, *The Adversary System Excuse*, *in* THE GOOD LAWYER: LAWYERS' ROLES AND LAWYERS' ETHICS 83 (David Luban ed., 1984).

[5] CHARLES DERBER, PROFESSIONALS AS WORKERS: MENTAL LABOR IN ADVANCED CAPITALISM (1982).

when Americans increasingly are said to prefer "bowling alone."[6] This chapter will pose three questions about the relation between lawyers and justice: the adequacy of the "professional project" as a theory of the legal profession, the commitment of lawyers to the core notion of legality, and the possibility of equal justice in unequal societies.

In 1979–1980, shortly after reviewing Larson's "The Rise of Professionalism,"[7] I commented on the 1,600-page Report of the Royal Commission on Legal Services.[8] It was one of those rare "a-ha" moments when a complex, highly abstract theory organized a mass of detailed facts. Although Larson drew on Marx, she was basically elaborating a Weberian theory of social closure.[9] That occupations professionalize by creating entry barriers and restricting internal and external competition, thereby extracting monopoly rents and enhancing status, powerfully illuminated the varied, complex, and changing trajectories of the English and American legal professions in the nineteenth and twentieth centuries.[10] My conviction certainly influenced many other contributors to the three volumes of "Lawyers in Society."[11] But the experience of trying to understand and compare diverse legal professions also exposed the Anglo-American bias of Larson's theory (she had studied only those two countries) and the profound differences between common law and civil law legal professions.[12] Nevertheless, I continue to find Larson's theory of market control and status competition the most insightful and economical explanation for the continuing saga of common law legal professions.[13]

Alan Paterson has advanced a competing "social contract" theory for understanding the legal profession;[14] but ever since Rousseau, we have known that the "social

6 Robert D. Putnam, Bowling Alone: The Collapse and Revival of American Community (2000).

7 Magali Sarfatti Larson, The Rise of Professionalism: A Sociological Analysis (1977); Richard L. Abel, *The Rise of Professionalism*, 6 Brit. J. Law & Soc'y 82 (1979).

8 Royal Commission on Legal Services, Final Report (1979) (Cmnd 7648); Richard L. Abel, *The Politics of the Market for Legal Services, in* Law in the Balance: Legal Services in the Eighties 6 (Philip A. Thomas ed., 1982); Richard L. Abel, *Toward a Politial Economy of Lawyers,* 1981 Wisc. L. Rev. 1117.

9 Richard L. Abel, American Lawyers 14–39 (1989).

10 *Id.*; Richard L. Abel, The Legal Profession in England and Wales (1988).

11 Lawyers in Society: The Civil Law World (Richard L. Abel & Philip S.C. Lewis eds., 1988); Lawyers in Society: The Common Law World (Richard L. Abel & Philip S.C. Lewis eds., 1988); Lawyers in Society: Comparative Theories (Richard L. Abel & Philip S.C. Lewis eds., 1989).

12 Richard L. Abel, *Lawyers in the Civil Law World, in* Lawyers in Society: The Civil Law World, *supra* note 11; Richard L. Abel, *Comparative Sociology of Legal Professions, in* Lawyers in Society: Comparative Theories, *supra* note 11.

13 Richard L. Abel, *Revisioning Lawyers, in* Lawyers in Society: An Overview 1 (Richard L. Abel & Philip S.C. Lewis eds., 1995).

14 Alan A. Paterson, *Professionalism and the Legal Services Market, in* Social Change and the Solicitors' Profession (Eleni Skordaki ed., 1995).

contract" is a mythic charter: a fictitious story that may serve to legitimate existing social arrangements but for which there is, and can be, no evidence. "Society" cannot make agreements. The "profession" is divided into fractions with strongly divergent, often conflicting, interests. I remain perplexed by the resistance to Larson's theory, which is most pronounced in the United Kingdom[15] (although Americans also indulge their nostalgia for a mythic professionalism).[16] Is it chauvinist resentment of American chutzpah (or its Italian equivalent)? Pragmatic English resistance to theory? English lawyers' disdain for sociology (which has relatively low status in England)? Anger at those who expose professional pretensions as mere mystifications of common "trade"? Resistance to reductionism (like the reaction against those who extend economics to explain family behavior, or Freudian interpretation of all motivation as unconscious urges)? A Burkean dislike of change? (A common English mantra is: "I'm not in favor of change for change's sake" – as though anyone is.) I suppose I should not be surprised, given the fierce hostility four decades ago to the path-breaking books by Robert Stevens and Michael Zander – both distinguished English legal academics.[17]

Let me offer three historical instances of contestations over market control and collective status. To introduce six case studies of disciplined California lawyers, I recently surveyed the history of the California State Bar, from its formation in 1927, by reading the entire run of its professional journal.[18] Much of the energy during those eight decades – especially the early ones – was devoted to: excluding competitors (unauthorized practice); apportioning turf (market-division treaties with other

[15] Michael C. Burrage, Revolution and the Making of the Contemporary Legal Profession: England, France, and the United States (2006); The Formation of Professions: Knowledge, State and Strategy (Michael C. Burrage & Rolf Torstendahl eds., 1990); Professions in Theory and History: Rethinking the Study of the Professions (Michael C. Burrage & Rolf Torstendahl eds., 1990); Michael Burrage, *Revolution as a Starting Point for the Comparative Analysis of the French, American, and English Legal Professions*, *in* Lawyers in Society: Comparative Theories *supra* note 11, at 322; Alan A. Paterson, *The Legal Profession in Scotland – An Endangered Species or a Problem Case for Market Theory?*, *in* Lawyers in Society: The Common Law World, *supra* note 11, at 76. Resistance is not limited to the common law world. *See, e.g.*, Lucien Karpik, French Lawyers: A Study in Collective Action, 1274 to 1994 (1999).

[16] Mary Ann Glendon, A Nation Under Lawyers: How the Crisis in the Legal Profession Is Transforming American Society (1994); Anthony T. Kronman, The Lost Lawyer: Failing Ideals of the Legal Profession (1993); Sol M. Linowitz, The Betrayed Profession: Lawyering at the End of the Twentieth Century (1994).

[17] Brian Abel-Smith & Robert Stevens, Lawyers and the Courts: A Sociological Study Of The English Legal System 1750–1965 (1967); Brian Abel-Smith & Robert Stevens, In Search of Justice: Society and the Legal System (1968); Michael Zander, Lawyers and the Public Interest: A Study in Restrictive Practices (1968). For reactions to Stevens, see David Sugarman, *Beyond Ignorance and Complacency: Robert Stevens' Journey through Lawyers and the Courts*, 16 Int'l J. Leg. Prof. 7 (2009).

[18] Richard L. Abel, Lawyers on Trial: Understanding Ethical Misconduct, Ch. 1 (2010).

occupations); limiting lawyer advertising and solicitation; seeking to restrict the number of unaccredited law schools; and fending off external demands for more effective regulation of misconduct and incompetence. By contrast, there was very little interest in the tasks that apologists of professionalism define as its core: ensuring that practitioners possess the necessary expertise and perform their roles with integrity.[19]

The turmoil in the English legal profession during the 1990s – widely known as the "Bar Wars" – can only be understood as a product of external demands to curtail the profession's monopoly rents (from individuals who wanted to buy and sell homes more cheaply and a state determined to control the rapidly rising legal aid budget) and internal competition between solicitors threatened with the loss of their conveyancing monopoly (who sought rights of audience in the higher courts) and barristers threatened with the loss of their advocacy monopoly (who sought direct access to clients).[20]

My third example is the refusal of lawyers to emulate doctors in making clinical training the core of professional education. Following the Flexner Report's dramatic success in transforming medical education,[21] there were various attempts and exhortations to incorporate clinical training in law school.[22] The Ford Foundation funded the Council on Legal Education in Professional Responsibility in 1968 to persuade law schools to embrace clinical education.[23] Prominent judges have harshly criticized legal education for its irrelevance to practice.[24] Yet, as Hempel and Seron describe,[25] most law schools still marginalize clinical education. The most convincing explanation is that law professors suffer from chronic status anxiety. Thorstein Veblen wrote with typical venom nearly a century ago: "the law school belongs in the modern university no more than a school of fencing or dancing."[26] Despite law's

[19] A.M. Carr-Saunders & P.A. Wilson, The Professions (1933); Talcott Parsons, *The Professions and Social Structure*, *in* Essays in Sociological Theory (1964); Talcott Parsons, *Professions*, 12 Int'l Encyc. Soc. Sci. 536 (1968).

[20] Richard L. Abel, English Lawyers between Market and State: The Politics of Professionalism (2003).

[21] Abraham Flexner, Medical Education in the United States and Canada (1910).

[22] R.D. Abrahams, *Law Offices to Serve Householders in the Lower Income Group*, 42 Dick. L. Rev. 133 (1937–38); Jerome Frank, *A Plea for Lawyer-Schools*, 52 Yale L.J. 1303 (1943).

[23] Michael Meltsner & Philip Schrag, *Report from a CLEPR Colony*, 76 Colum. L. Rev. 581 (1976).

[24] *E.g.*, Harry T. Edwards, *The Growing Disjunction between Legal Education and the Legal Profession*, 91 Mich. L. Rev. 34 (1992).

[25] Carrie Hempel & Carroll Seron, *An Innovative Approach to Legal Education: The Founding of the University of California, Irvine School of Law* (in this volume).

[26] Thorstein Veblen, The Higher Learning in America 211 (B.W. Huebsch ed. 1918). Lincoln was even more contemptuous. In 1858, he declined a request to teach someone aspiring to become a lawyer. The "cheapest, quickest, and best way" to become one was to "read[] the books for himself without an instructor." Abraham Lincoln to James T. Thornton (Dec. 2, 1858). I am grateful to Kevin Gerson for the first quotation and Gary Orfield for the second.

repeated claims to be a science, law school does not initiate novices into a discipline; it teaches students to "think like a lawyer."[27] Law professors are convinced that only by emulating their colleagues in other disciplines (who concentrate on publishing esoteric scholarship rather than teaching) can they enjoy respect within the university. It is striking that law professors have chosen to stress their identity as academics (which confers status) rather than that as practitioners (which would offer far greater material rewards). Law school embodies an inescapable tension between what William Twining called "Pericles and the Plumber," that is, skeptical questioning and craft.[28] The university is dedicated to Socrates's "examined life." First-year courses typically begin with fundamental questions: why do we punish (criminal law); what is a fair adjudicative process (civil procedure); what is property; why should people keep their promises (contracts); how should we respond to injuries (torts); how should state power be exercised (constitutional law)? Such questions rarely are posed in the other environments where lawyers operate: law practice, meetings of professional associations, legislatures, even courts. Rather than imbuing law students with the skills necessary to practice (which "social contract" theory claims is the quid pro quo for professional privilege), law school functions to rank students based on examinations that have little to do with the tasks most lawyers perform. (In this, it resembles the civil service in China and England, where rank reflected mastery of classics.) The ranking then offers a meritocratic warrant for the highly varied rewards (wealth, power, prestige) that position in the professional hierarchy confers.

Many other facets of the legal profession can be understood only through the lens of the professional project: for example, the protectionist response of national legal professions to the threat of global competition,[29] or the struggle within Japan over expanding graduate legal education as a way of increasing the number of *bengoshi*.[30] Closer to home, consider the recent *Los Angeles Times* op ed, which assailed the ABA for "continu[ing] to allow unneeded new schools to open and refus[ing] to properly regulate the schools...."[31] "[N]ew law schools continue to sprout like weeds." The author, a lawyer, argued that "the legal sector is being badly saturated with attorneys." "There is a finite number of jobs for lawyers, and this continual flood of graduates only suppresses wages. Because the ABA has repeatedly signaled its unwillingness to adapt to this changing reality, the federal government

[27] Elizabeth Mertz, The Language of Law School: Learning to "Think Like a Lawyer" (2007).

[28] W.L. Twining, Pericles and the Plumber, Inaugural Lecture, Queen's University of Belfast (1967).

[29] Richard L. Abel, *Transnational Law Practice*, 44 Case W. Res. L. Rev. 737 (1994).

[30] Tom Ginsburg, *Transforming Legal Education in Japan and Korea*, 22 Penn. St. Int'l L. Rev. 433 (2004); Takahiro Saito, *The Tragedy of Japanese Legal Education: Japanese "American" Law Schools*, 24 Wisc. Int'l L.J. 197 (2007).

[31] Mark Greenbaum, *No More Room at the Bench*, L.A. Times, Jan. 8, 2010, at A27.

should consider taking steps to stop this rapid flow of attorneys into a marketplace that cannot sustain them." "The U.S. Department of Education should strip the ABA of its accreditor status and give the authority to an organization that is free of conflicts of interest, such as the Assn. of American Law Schools...." He praised the American Dental Association for "assiduously guard[ing] the profession." "The legal profession must be saved from itself." There are unfortunate precedents. In 1932, the U.S. National Conference of Bar Examiners, noting that "the German bar threatens to become engulfed in a maelstrom of economic depression," reported (without comment) that "the German Bar Association has just adopted a resolution demanding that for the next three years there shall be no admissions to the bar...." Several months later, the National Conference observed that "forcible reduction of the number of lawyers practicing in Greece is the object of legislation now being worked out by the Minister of Justice...."[32] Plus ça change....[33]

Larson's theory exposes the many ways in which the professional project creates obstacles to justice. Entry barriers and restrictions on internal and external competition increase the cost of legal services, reducing access. Until well after World War II, both the English and the American legal professions sought to enhance their status by excluding the working class, women, and racial and ethnoreligious minorities – sometimes entirely, always from the professional apex.[34] This often explicit professional project of status enhancement reproduced and amplified social inequality, creating a white male profession, which poorly served clients who were neither. In recent decades, however, the goal of exclusivity has been replaced by representativeness, first in the United States and then in the United Kingdom.[35] That reversal (which I strongly endorse) must be reconciled with "meritocracy," the dominant contemporary warrant for inequality.[36] The difficulties of doing so are visible in terminological debates about buzz words and euphemisms: reverse discrimination, affirmative action, quotas. These efforts to correct centuries of discrimination have been the subject of litigation, legislation, referenda, and constitutional amendments at both state and federal levels. Although much attention has been devoted to law school admissions and the composition of large law firms, the real flash point has been the judiciary, especially the highest courts. George H.W. Bush claimed, with faux naiveté, that Clarence Thomas was simply "the best man" for the

[32] 2 Bar Examiner 83–84 (1933); 3 Bar Examiner 23 (1933), quoted in Richard L. Abel, *Lawyers in the Civil Law World*, *in* LAWYERS IN SOCIETY: THE CIVIL LAW WORLD, *supra* note 11, at 34.

[33] I wrote to the author of the *L.A. Times* op ed, suggesting that he read AMERICAN LAWYERS. His only response was to ask me to send him a copy.

[34] ABEL, AMERICAN LAWYERS, *supra* note 9, at 85–108; ABEL, THE LEGAL PROFESSION IN ENGLAND AND WALES, *supra* note 10, 73–85, 169–76.

[35] ABEL, ENGLISH LAWYERS BETWEEN MARKET AND STATE, *supra* note 20, at 120–58.

[36] RANDALL COLLINS, THE CREDENTIAL SOCIETY: AN HISTORICAL SOCIOLOGY OF EDUCATION AND STRATIFICATION (1979).

U.S. Supreme Court. "I don't feel he's a quota" (a typical Bushism). "I expressed my respect for the ground that Mr. Justice Marshall plowed," (another) "but I don't feel there should be a black seat on the Court or an ethnic seat on the Court."[37] Bush's son nominated his White House counsel, Harriet Miers, for the "woman's" seat after Sandra Day O'Connor retired, only to have Miers withdraw when it became glaringly obvious that she was totally unqualified (and might have skeletons in her closet that would emerge during confirmation hearings). In order to survive her own confirmation hearing, Sonya Sotomayor had to repudiate her claim that a "wise Latina" might make better decisions.[38] It was a "rhetorical flourish that fell flat." "I want to state upfront, unequivocally and without doubt, I do not believe that any ethnic, racial or gender group has an advantage in sound judging." But if background is irrelevant to judging, why are judicial appointments so hotly contested, and why has the Federalist Society sought to pack the judiciary with its members? In light of this, it is not surprising that South Africa is having difficulty deciding whether race should play any role in judicial appointments as it struggles with the heritage of apartheid.[39]

The functionalist theory of professions rested on two propositions: Only professionals could judge whether their colleagues possessed expertise, competence, and integrity; and professionals could be trusted to ensure that their colleagues did so.[40] The first claim is plausible: No one would argue that the bar exam should be written and graded by laypersons. But the second has been repeatedly falsified. There has never been any systematic effort to validate entry barriers. (While serving nearly ten years for bank robbery, Shon R. Hopwood wrote the best petition for certiorari former U.S. Solicitor General Seth P. Waxman had ever seen; it persuaded the Supreme Court to hear the case, and the brief Hopwood and Waxman wrote together secured a unanimously favorable ruling.[41]) We do not know whether the minimum standards for graduating from law school or passing the bar exam exclude the incompetent (and only them) or whether, above this threshold, performance in either of those domains is correlated with the quality of future lawyering. If these barriers are too low, the profession is endangering clients; if they are too high, the profession is overcharging and denying potential clients access to justice. Some of the *rites de passage* have no conceivable relationship to competence, such as the

[37] Maureen Dowd, *The Supreme Court*, N.Y. TIMES, July 2, 1991.

[38] Robert Barnes & Paul Kane, *Sotomayor Repudiates "Wise Latina" Comment*, WASH. POST, July 15, 2009.

[39] Penelope Andrews, *Without Fear, Favor or Prejudice: Judicial Independence and the Transformation of the Judiciary in South Africa* (in this volume).

[40] CARR-SAUNDERS & WILSON, *supra* note 19; ROYAL COMMISSION ON LEGAL SERVICES, FINAL REPORT *supra* note 8, at 28, 30; Parsons, *The Professions and Social Structure*, *supra* note 19.

[41] Adam Liptak, A *Mediocre Criminal, but an Unmatched Jailhouse Lawyer*, N.Y. TIMES, Feb. 9, 2010, at A12.

mandatory dinners in the Inns of Court (which used to degenerate into drunken food fights and humiliation of the rare woman student).[42] If the profession does a poor job of setting entry barriers correctly, it is even worse at policing lawyers during the four decades or more of their careers. My early criticisms focused on underenforcement: the dramatic attrition between complaints (almost all from clients) and formal proceedings, as well as the lenient punishments imposed on the few lawyers found guilty.[43] The usual reforms do little good: Lay participants added to existing disciplinary tribunals tend to defer to the expertise of lawyer members; additional layers of appeal or ombudsmen prolong already lengthy proceedings and handle relatively few cases. Recently, however, I have been studying cases of lawyers disciplined in New York and California. For those few who actually are punished, the sanction seems to me sufficient both to deter them from repeating (although they rarely acknowledged having been wrong and generally expressed resentment of their punishment rather than remorse) and to discourage others from engaging in similar conduct (if they learn of the outcome).[44] Indeed, for most, the process is the punishment.[45] Rather, the problem is the mismatch between the most common (and harmful) forms of lawyer misconduct and the system of professional self-regulation. Almost all complaints come from clients, who are ignorant of the rules and unable to perceive much lawyer misconduct; colleagues and judges, who have unique expertise about professional norms and observe much lawyer behavior, are reluctant to file grievances (a conspiracy of silence found in many occupational categories: doctors, police officers, soldiers). Most clients complain about cost, neglect, and quality. But disciplinary mechanisms are ill-suited to correct these problems, which primarily reflect market failure caused by information asymmetries created by specialization but aggravated by the profession's restrictive practices. Appropriate solutions would include better information, greater competition about price and quality, and more effective mechanisms for holding liable lawyers who disappoint or injure clients. But the profession has adamantly and successfully opposed mandatory malpractice insurance, disclosure of client complaints, and compensation for inadequate professional service.[46]

42 Helena Kennedy, *Women at the Bar*, *in* The Bar on Trial 148 (Robert Hazell ed., 1978).

43 Abel, American Lawyers, *supra* note 9, at 142–57; Abel, English Lawyers Between Market and State, *supra* note 20, at 354–406; Abel, The Legal Profession in England and Wales, *supra* note 10, at 126–36, 242–60; Richard L. Abel, *Why Does the ABA Promulgate Ethical Rules?*, 59 Tex. L. Rev. 639 (1981).

44 Richard L. Abel, Lawyers in the Dock: Learning from Attorney Disciplinary Proceedings (2008); Abel, Lawyers on Trial, *supra* note 18. It is important to note, however, that many lawyers are only punished *after* they have committed multiple offenses. Robert C. Fellmeth, Fifth Progress Report of the State Bar Discipline Monitor (1989).

45 Malcom M. Feeley, The Process Is the Punishment: Handling Cases in a Lower Criminal Court (1979).

46 Abel, Lawyers in the Dock, *supra* note 44, at 491–528; Abel, Lawyers on Trial, *supra* note 18, at 1–66.

If the profession is the problem, what are the solutions? Although jeremiads and exhortations have little effect,[47] professions, like all social institutions, are in constant flux.[48] As a manifestation of the division of labor, professions constantly adapt to the very market forces that gave them birth. Specialization intensifies. Internal fractions struggle for market share and status: barristers versus solicitors, outside versus in-house counsel, solo practitioners versus mass-production clinics, salaried legal aid lawyers versus court-appointed counsel. Lawyers compete with other occupations: accountants, mortgage lenders, tax preparers, real estate agents, claims agents, immigration advisers, *notarios*. Globalization opens the doors to international competition, by both mega-firms and off-shore back-office operations. The entry of women and minorities, championed by the feminist and civil rights movements and facilitated by the shift from apprenticeship to university training, has expanded the profession and transformed its composition. New sources of payment – legal aid, legal expenses insurance, conditional fees – expanded demand. Technological, social, and economic change also affected demand: The industrial revolution multiplied workplace accidents; trains and then cars cause torts; no-fault eases divorce; the criminalization of alcohol and drugs swells the prison population; easy credit must be backed by debt collection, bankruptcy, and mortgage foreclosures; the dot-com and housing bubbles created booms and busts. Government regulation increased demand for lawyers to shape the content of rules, stave off enforcement, advise on compliance (and evasion), and defend those charged with violations. The hemisphere of lawyers serving business clients has expanded relative to that serving individuals.[49] Information technology increased productivity and allowed substitution of capital for labor (both legal and lay). Subordinated occupations (such as paralegals) may seek to organize collectively (especially in the public sector) or to invade the profession's monopoly (as nurses, pharmacists, and dental hygienists have done in health services). Media exposés and populist politicians publicize scandals: indefensible monopolies (for example, conveyancing), overcharging (especially of taxpayer-funded legal aid), undisciplined misconduct (substance-abusing lawyers continuing to practice), complicity in financial scandals (the Savings & Loan industry, Enron, subprime mortgages and derivatives).

In studying lawyers, I have emphasized the professional project because most lawyers are primarily concerned with making a living. However, the very success of

[47] E.g., Glendon, *supra* note 16; Kronman, *supra* note 16; Linowitz, *supra* note 16. Rhode has many concrete, promising reform proposals. Deborah L. Rhode, *Professional Regulation and Public Service: An Unfinished Agenda* (in this volume).

[48] Rue Bucher & Anselm Strauss, *Professions in Process*, 66 Am. J. Soc. 325 (1961); *see also* Marc Galanter, *More Lawyers than People: The Global Multiplication of Legal Professionals* (in this volume).

[49] John P. Heinz & Edward O. Laumann, Chicago Lawyers: The Social Structure of the Bar, Tbl. 2.1 (1982); John P. Heinz, Robert L. Nelson, Rebecca L. Sandefur & Edward O. Laumann, Urban Lawyers: The New Social Structure of the Bar, Tbl. 2.1 (2005).

the professional project frees lawyers to pursue ideals of justice.[50] Graduating from college at the height of the civil rights movement, I chose to go to law school expecting to work in civil rights, did so in Washington and Mississippi after my second and third years, and practiced legal aid in New Haven in 1971–1972. My book on the role of law in the struggle against apartheid celebrated the dedication, skill, and surprising success of the small band of South African human rights lawyers.[51]

Since the atrocities at Abu Ghraib were exposed by journalists in spring 2004, I have been studying the defense of legality against American abuses of governmental power.[52] Although the last eight years have seen elite lawyers in positions of power construct "legal" frameworks for torture, indefinite detention without trial, secret prisons, and extraordinary rendition (John Yoo, Jay Bybee, and Stephen Bradbury in the Office of Legal Counsel, Alberto Gonzales as White House legal counsel and then Attorney General, David Addington for Vice President Dick Cheney, William J. Haynes II in the Pentagon), many lawyers have also have exhibited courage and tenacity in championing the rule of law. Leading nongovernmental organizations are dedicated to that ideal: the ACLU, Human Rights First, Human Rights Watch, Amnesty International, the Center for Constitutional Rights, Reprieve. The ABA and New York City Bar (among other professional associations) have declared their support for the rule of law.[53] Hundreds of lawyers have volunteered to represent Guantanamo detainees by bringing habeas corpus petitions and defending those charged before military commissions.[54] Career lawyers in government have resisted pressures from their political superiors: William H. Taft III (State Department

[50] TERENCE C. HALLIDAY, BEYOND MONOPOLY: LAWYERS, STATE CRISES AND PROFESSIONAL EMPOWERMENT (1987); Richard L. Abel, *Taking Professionalism Seriously*, 1989 ANN. SURVEY AM. L. 41; Richard L. Abel, *The Contradictions of Legal Professionalism*, *in* NEW DIRECTIONS IN THE STUDY OF JUSTICE, LAW AND SOCIAL CONTROL 17 (School of Justice Studies ed., 1989); Robert W. Gordon, *Are Lawyers Friends of Democracy?* (in this volume).

[51] RICHARD L. ABEL, POLITICS BY OTHER MEANS: LAW IN THE STRUGGLE AGAINST APARTHEID, 1980–1994 (1995); Richard L. Abel, *Legality Without a Constitution: South Africa in the 1980s*, *in* RECRAFTING THE RULE OF LAW: THE LIMITS OF LEGAL ORDER 66 (David Dyzenhaus ed., 1999); Richard L. Abel, *Nothing Left But Rights: Law in the Struggle Against Apartheid*, *in* IDENTITIES, POLITICS AND RIGHTS 239 (Thomas Kearns & Austin Sarat eds., 1995); Richard L. Abel, *Speaking Law to Power: Occasions for Cause Lawyering*, *in* CAUSE LAWYERS: POLITICAL COMMITMENTS AND PROFESSIONAL RESPONSIBILITIES 69 (Austin Sarat & Stuart Scheingold eds., 1998).

[52] Richard L. Abel, *Contesting Legality in the United States After September 11*, *in* FIGHTING FOR POLITICAL FREEDOM: COMPARATIVE STUDIES OF THE LEGAL COMPLEX AND POLITICAL LIBERALISM 361 (Terence C. Halliday, Lucien Karpik & Malcom Feeley eds., 2007); Richard L. Abel, *Law Under Stress: The Struggle Against Apartheid in South Africa, 1980–94 and the Defense of Legality in the United States after 9/11*, SOUTH AFRICAN J. HUMAN RIGHTS (2010); Richard L. Abel, *Professional Integrity*, *in* LAW AND ANTHROPOLOGY, 12 CURRENT LEGAL ISSUES 430 (Michael Freeman & David Napier eds., 2009).

[53] *E.g.*, Am. Bar Ass'n., Report to the House of Delegates ["Torture Resolution"] (2004).

[54] THE GUANTANAMO LAWYERS: INSIDE A PRISON, OUTSIDE THE LAW (Mark Denbeaux & Jonathan Hafetz eds., 2009).

legal adviser), Alberto Mora (General Counsel of the Navy), the JAGs of all three branches, and staff judge advocates serving as judges, prosecutors, and defenders in the military commissions. Even Attorney General John Ashcroft and his subordinates, Deputy Attorney General James Comey and Jack Goldsmith (Office of Legal Counsel), stood up to the Bush administration and refused to authorize unlawful wiretapping.[55] Federal judges appointed by Republican presidents occasionally resisted Bush. Michael Mukasey found that Jose Padilla had a right to counsel even after Rumsfeld named Padilla an enemy combatant and whisked him off to the Naval brig in South Carolina.[56] (That role influences behavior is suggested by Mukasey's subsequent actions as a private practitioner and U.S. Attorney General: calling for a national security court; demanding revision of the Office of Professional Responsibility report on Yoo and Bybee because it was too harsh; denouncing his successor, Eric Holder, for treating the suspected Christmas Day bomber just the way Mukasey had treated Padilla.) Henry Floyd, soon after being appointed by Bush to the U.S. District Court in South Carolina, went further and held that Padilla had a right to habeas corpus: "To do otherwise would not only offend the rule of law and violate this country's constitutional tradition, but it would also be a betrayal of this Nation's commitment to the separation of powers that safeguards our democratic values and individual liberties."[57] Even Judge Michael Luttig (appointed to the Fourth Circuit by Bush's father) criticized the executive for transferring Padilla from military to civilian custody:

> [The government's] actions have left not only the impression that Padilla may have been held for these years…by mistake…[but also] that the government may even have come to the belief that the principle in reliance upon which it has detained Padilla for this time…can, in the end, yield to expediency…these impressions have been left…at what may ultimately prove to be substantial cost to the government's credibility before the courts….[58]

There are numerous other examples of lawyers setting aside pecuniary motives to advocate for justice. I will discuss two. First, pro bono lawyering has grown rapidly in recent decades, primarily in the United States.[59] It is noteworthy that most of the expansion has occurred within the largest corporate firms. Is this attributable to the availability of resources, discomfort about the extraordinarily high associate salaries

[55] Barton Gellman, Angler: The Cheney Vice Presidency (2007).

[56] This and the rest of the narrative can be found in Abel, *Law Under Stress*, *supra* note 52.

[57] Padilla v. Hanft, 389 F.Supp.2d 678, 691 (D.S.C. 2005).

[58] Padilla v. Hanft, 432 F.3d 582, 587 (4th Cir. 2005).

[59] Deborah Rhode, Access to Justice (2004); Deborah Rhode, Pro Bono in Principle and in Practice: Public Service and the Profession (2005); Private Lawyers & the Public Interest: The Evolving Role of Pro Bono in the Legal Profession (Robert Granfield & Lynn Mather eds., 2009); Scott L. Cummings, *The Politics of Pro Bono*, 52 UCLA L. Rev. 1 (2004).

and partnership incomes, anxiety to demonstrate moral superiority to the personal plight hemisphere of the profession, or the influence of elite law schools? By contrast, solo and small-firm lawyers (who constitute the majority of private practitioners and arguably are better situated and equipped to render these services) often resent suggestions that pro bono should be obligatory, believing that they "gave at the office" – that their routine representation of individuals is a form of public service (especially when clients fail to pay).[60] Although I enthusiastically support pro bono, the fact that the legal representation essential to realize the ideal of equal justice under law – a foundation of the liberal state – depends on charity from the wealthiest lawyers, with all the limitations and biases this introduces, seems yet another illustration of American exceptionalism.[61] Lawyers prefer to do pro bono far removed from their paying work, substantively and often geographically, partly to avoid conflicts of interest (actual and positional)[62] and partly for the sake of novelty. (There is an awkward resemblance to religious enthusiasm for missionary activity.) The Lawyers Committee for Civil Rights Under Law (for which I worked in the summer of 1965) attracted northern corporate lawyers bent on witnessing the evils of Southern racism firsthand (rather than deal with de facto segregation at home). Young British barristers eagerly sought to represent Commonwealth death row inmates in their Privy Council appeals (rather than deal with racism in England). Although members of the "Guantanamo Bay Bar Association" (as the volunteers mockingly called themselves) were primarily motivated by outrage at injustice, many also were attracted by the novelty of the issues, the difference from their regular practice (both the law and the clients), and the bizarre remote prison site.

The alternative to pro bono, of course, would be to tax lawyers (and others) to pay salaried or private lawyers to serve the unrepresented. This is the dominant service delivery mechanism in England, Canada, Australia, the Netherlands, Germany, and Scandinavia, among other countries. It locates authority to decide who gets what services in the lawyers delivering them, subject to (the often intrusive) political constraints imposed by legislatures. It also might produce more resources than the minute fraction of lawyer effort devoted to pro bono (an average of about 1 percent in those firms with pro bono programs).

The United States is unique in relying (in whole or in part) on private action to provide a wide variety of public goods: tertiary education (and an increasing

60 Carroll Seron, The Business of Practicing Law: The Work Lives of Solo and Small-Firm Attorneys (1996); Philip R. Lochner, *The No-Fee and Low-Fee Legal Practice of Private Attorneys*, 9 Law & Soc'y Rev. 431 (1975).

61 Richard L. Abel, *State, Market, Philanthropy, and Self-Help as Legal Services Delivery Mechanisms, in* Private Lawyers and the Public Interest, *supra* note 59, at 295; Abel, *The Paradoxes of Pro Bono*, 78 Fordham L. Rev. 2443 (2010).

62 Susan P. Shapiro, Tangled Loyalties: Conflict of Interest in Legal Practice (2002).

proportion of primary and secondary), cultural activities (art, music, dance, theater, public radio, and television), and public recreation (for example, the Central Park Conservancy, land trusts).[63] This is analogous to allocating money for medical research through single-disease foundations (often funded by sufferers and their families) and big pharma (driven by profits to neglect "orphan" drugs) rather than the National Institutes of Health; or depending on Bell Laboratories or Xerox rather than the National Science Foundation for scientific research; or enhancing education by relying on parents to volunteer and raise funds rather than taxing communities to pay teachers and give them adequate resources. (Indeed, volunteerism in and for schools has become a means of evading the California Supreme Court's decision equalizing per pupil public expenditures.[64]) Universities strongly prefer unrestricted donations from alumni. Altruistic American doctors go abroad to repair cleft palates or perform eye surgery, operations that produce dramatic results, thereby attracting donations. Few Americans would donate to build sewers or ensure clean drinking water, though these might contribute far more to public health. Philanthropists can dictate cultural practices forever: the Isabella Stewart Gardner Museum in Boston cannot move a single painting; the Barnes Collection was kept in an inaccessible Philadelphia suburb for decades; Eli Broad bailed out the Los Angeles Museum of Contemporary Art on condition that it hire his candidate as director and has fought bitterly with the Los Angeles County Museum of Art over the Broad Contemporary Art Museum, whose construction he helped fund and to which he lent his collection.[65]

My second example is the idealism exhibited by so many entering law students. That may be another relatively recent, distinctively American phenomenon. (In August 1963, about to enter my second year at Columbia, I asked the law review editor for whom I was cite-checking if I could have a day off to attend the March on Washington. He hadn't heard of it and wondered why anyone would want to participate.) However, this wellspring of idealism often dries up in law school. Numerous studies have documented "public interest drift": only a tiny fraction of the many law school entrants who aspire to practice public interest law end up doing so at graduation.[66] Law school pedagogy is part of the reason, portraying social justice work

[63] Diane Cardwell, *When Parks Must Rely on Private Money*, N.Y. Times, Feb. 7, 2010, at 28 (stating that Brooklyn Bridge Park depends on luxury apartments for financing).

[64] Serrano v. Priest, 5 Cal.3d 584 (1971).

[65] Aaron Sorkin, *Wielding Iron Checkbook to Shape Cultural L.A.*, N.Y. Times, Feb. 8, 2010, at C1.

[66] Robert Granfield, Making Elite Lawyers: Visions of Law at Harvard and Beyond (1992); Debra Schleef, Managing Elites: Professional Socialization in Law and Business School (2006); Robert Stover, Making It and Breaking It: The Fate of Public Interest Commitment during Law School (1989); Howard S. Erlanger, Mia Cahill, Charles Epp & Kathleen Haines, *Law Student Idealism and Job Choice: Some New Data on an Old Question*, 30 Law & Soc'y Rev. 851

as soft and only commercial law issues as intellectually challenging. But the employment market also is responsible: the paucity of public interest jobs and the low salaries they pay compared with private practice (a difference aggravated by increasing levels of educational debt augmented by tuition, whose rise has outstripped inflation).

Just as the dominance of the professional project should not blind us to the occasions when lawyers transcend their material (and status) interests, so it is essential not to exaggerate the potential of law to promote justice. Lawyers devote the vast bulk of their work to advancing the interests of paying clients. The unequal distribution of wealth and income ensures that most lawyers will be working to reproduce or intensify that inequality.[67] The most extensive study of individual use of lawyers found a strong correlation with income and education.[68] Some lawyers may counsel reluctant clients to comply with laws, either from fear of sanctions or because it is the right thing to do. But most lawyer effort is directed toward bending, distorting, or evading the law on behalf of clients, such as minimizing taxes or finding ways around regulation.[69] It should not be surprising that lawyers who serve particular business clients for years and depend on them for a significant part of their income rarely perceive anything legally or morally objectionable in the ends those clients are pursuing.[70] Communities of legal practice can support the rule of law.[71] When Charles D. "Cully" Stimson, Assistant Secretary of Defense for Detainee Affairs, urged "corporate CEOs" to "make law firms choose between representing terrorists [by filing habeas corpus petitions pro bono for Guantanamo Bay detainees] or representing reputable firms," the outcry was so fierce (including strong criticism from the ABA president) that Stimson was forced to resign.[72] But communities of

(1996); Lewis Kornhauser & Richard Revesz, *Legal Education and Entry into the Legal Profession: The Role of Race, Gender, and Educational Debt*, 70 N.Y.U. L. Rev. 829 (1995).

67 In 2007, the top 1% of the U.S. population owned more than a third of the total wealth; the top 20% owned 85%, leaving the bottom 80% with just 15%. In 2006, the top 1% received 21.3% of income; the top 20% received 61.4%, leaving less than 40% to the bottom 80%. Edward N. Wolff, Recent Trends in Household Wealth in the United States: Rising Debt and the Middle-Class Squeeze – An Update to 2007 (Working Paper No. 589, 2009), *available at* http://www.levyinstitute.org/publications/?docid=1235.

68 Barbara A. Curran, The Legal Needs of the Public, Figs. 5.8–5.10 (1977).

69 *E.g.*, Doreen McBarnet, Crime, Compliance and Control (2004); Doreen McBarnet & Christopher Whelan, Creative Accounting and the Cross-Eyed Javelin Thrower (1999); Kenneth Mann, Defending White Collar Crime: A Portrait of Attorneys at Work (1985); Doreen McBarnet, *It's Not What You Do but the Way That You Do It: Tax Evasion, Tax Avoidance and the Boundaries of Deviance*, *in* Unravelling Criminal Justice 247 (David Downes ed. 1992).

70 Robert L. Nelson, Partners with Power: The Transformation of the Large Law Firm (1988).

71 Lynn Mather, Craig A. McEwen & Richard J. Maiman, Divorce Lawyers at Work: Varieties of Professionalism in Practice (2001); Lynn Mather, *How and Why Do Lawyers Misbehave? Lawyers, Discipline, and Collegial Control* (in this volume). The relatively small, intimate, and homogeneous groupings of English barristers into Circuits had an even stronger effect.

72 Abel, *Professional Integrity*, *supra* note 52, at 445–47.

practice also can obstruct justice. No one would argue that conformity to the modal behavior of other lawyers is always a virtue.[73] Lawyers learn unethical practice from their peers.[74] Few lawyers braved the taint of communist sympathies to defend those attacked by Senator Joseph McCarthy.[75] In the summer of 1965, the *only* lawyers who would take civil rights cases in Mississippi were the three African-American members of the state bar and the northern volunteers for the Lawyers Committee for Civil Rights Under Law. Justice advocates are far more likely to be outsiders: racial and ethnoreligious minorities, working class, and women.[76] Small-town lawyers are beholden to the local economic elite who provide most of their business.[77] Virtually *no* German lawyers stood up to Nazism, even though the very few who did suffered nothing worse than a golden handshake.[78] Aside from the Legal Resource Centre, the Centre for Applied Legal Studies, and three small professional associations (Lawyers for Human Rights, the Black Lawyers Association, and the National Association of Democratic Lawyers), the vast majority of South African lawyers enthusiastically or passively supported apartheid.[79]

I believe that the relationship of religion to the core values of political liberalism is at least as ambiguous as that of lawyers.[80] Religious minorities have often championed civil liberties – of necessity for themselves, but at the same time for others: Jehovah's Witnesses and the flag salute cases, Quakers and conscientious objection, the sanctuary movement for Central American asylum seekers. Religious beliefs have inspired opposition to the death penalty[81] and to the torture and abuse of detainees in the "war on terror."[82] But once again, it is important to put this in

[73] Sinclair Lewis, Babbitt (1922); Sinclair Lewis, Main Street (1920); David Riesman, Nathan Glazer & Reuel Denney, The Lonely Crowd (1950).

[74] Abel, Lawyers in the Dock, *supra* note 44; Abel, Lawyers on Trial, *supra* note 18; Jerome Carlin, Lawyers' Ethics (1966); Jerome Carlin, Lawyers on Their Own (1962); Leslie C. Levin, *The Ethical World of Solo and Small Law Firm Practitioners*, 41 Hous. L. Rev. 309 (2004–05).

[75] Jonathan D. Casper, The Politics of Civil Liberties (1972); Terence Halliday, Beyond Monopoly 227–37 (1987).

[76] Jack Katz, Poor People's Lawyers in Transition (1982); Abel, *Lawyers for Liberalism: Axion, Oxymoron, or Accident?* 1 Books-on-Law 9 (1998).

[77] Donald D. Landon, Country Lawyers: The Impact of Context on Professional Practice (1990); David M. Engel, *The Oven Bird's Song: Insiders, Outsiders, and Personal Injuries in an American Community*, 18 Law. & Soc'y Rev. 551 (1987).

[78] Ingo Müller, Hitler's Justice: The Courts of the Third Reich (1991).

[79] Abel, Politics by Other Means, *supra* note 51; David Dyzenhaus, Judging the Judges, Judging Ourselves: Truth, Reconciliation and the Apartheid Legal Order (1998); Stephen J. Ellmann, In a Time of Trouble: Law and Liberty in South Africa's State of Emergency (1992).

[80] *See* Terence Halliday, *"The Conscience of Society?": The Legal Complex, Religion, and the Fates of Political Liberalism* (in this volume). I believe Halliday would agree with me about the complexity of the relationship between religion and political liberalism.

[81] Helen Prejean, Dead Man Walking (1993).

[82] National Religious Campaign Against Torture, http://www.nrcat.org (last visited June 14, 2010).

perspective. Although I am no historian of religion, I can easily adduce numerous examples of religion as a force for intolerance and the suppression of civil rights and liberties: millennia of missionary activity by Christians and Muslims; the Inquisition; support for monarchies against republican movements; theological apologetics for slavery, segregation in the American South, and apartheid in South Africa; anti-Semitism over many centuries and throughout the world; the fatwas against Salman Rushdie and the Danish cartoonist; the criminalization of blasphemy and apostasy; the prohibition on Malaysian Christians referring to Allah.[83] Demands to make sharia the national law are profoundly inconsistent with political liberalism. Established churches of all denominations (Christian, Jewish, Muslim, Hindu) use state power to discriminate against nonmembers (religious symbols and ceremonies in public space, state support for religious schools, religious tests for entry to university, opposition to the construction of mosques, rules concerning dress in public). For years, the Catholic Church covered up the abuses of its priests and opposed attempts to punish the culprits or compensate the victims – not just in the United States but also in Ireland and Germany.[84] Churches committed other abuses against indigenous peoples in Canada and Australia. Churches have opposed the rights of women (marriage and divorce, inheritance, polygamy, even protection from genital mutilation) and of gays and lesbians.

Whatever the precise scorecard of religious support for or opposition to political liberalism, I believe that the two domains rest on fundamentally opposed epistemologies.[85] Religious authority is traditional or charismatic; the authority of political liberalism is based on rationality. Religion lives through ritual; political liberalism thrives on debate. Religion is static; political liberalism is dynamic. Religion uses a restricted linguistic code, political liberalism an elaborated one.[86] Religion requires dogma and faith; political liberalism constantly questions. Religion demands obedience; political liberalism assumes individual autonomy. Many religions are profoundly hierarchical; political liberalism is fundamentally

[83] I touch on some of this in my books SPEECH AND RESPECT (1994); SPEAKING RESPECT, RESPECTING SPEECH (1997). The Malaysian government has appealed a Supreme Court decision declaring unconstitutional a law banning the use of "Allah" by Christians. Aaron J. Leichman, *Malaysian Gov't to Appeal Christian 'Allah' Ruling*, CHRISTIAN POST, Jan. 3, 2010.

[84] *E.g.*, DAVID FRANCE, OUR FATHERS: THE SECRET LIFE OF THE CATHOLIC CHURCH IN AN AGE OF SCANDAL (2004); THE INVESTIGATIVE STAFF OF THE BOSTON GLOBE, BETRAYAL: THE CRISIS IN THE CATHOLIC CHURCH, (2002); *Irish Victims Write to Pope*, N.Y. TIMES, Feb. 10, 2010, at A9; Nicholas Kulish, *Accusations of Abuse Jolt Church in Germany*, N.Y. TIMES, Feb. 10, 2010, at A9.

[85] This is obviously more true of some religions than others. JAMES D. HUNTER, CULTURE WARS: THE STRUGGLE TO DEFINE AMERICA (1991).

[86] *Cf.* BASIL BERNSTEIN, CLASS, CODES AND CONTROL (1971). George Konrad and Ivan Szelenyi made a somewhat similar point about the relationship between intellectuals and the Communist Party apparatus. GEORGE KONRAD & IVAN SZELENYI, THE INTELLECTUALS ON THE ROAD TO CLASS POWER (Allen Arato & Richard E. Allen trans., 1979).

egalitarian and democratic. Religion is particularistic – only believers can be moral or enjoy salvation; political liberalism is universalistic, prohibiting distinctions based on belief or ascribed characteristics. Religion is monolithic; political liberalism is pluralist. Although I warmly welcome religious allies in the struggle for political liberalism, I have no faith that religion will always be an ally.

Law's greatest challenge is to fulfill its claim to dispense equal justice (as the pediment of the U.S. Supreme Court proclaims) in unequal societies. The professionalization of lawyers ensures that they will be distributed unequally; the more professional they are, the greater the inequality. Thirty years ago, I argued that it would be impossible to achieve equality of arms between legally opposed interests (landlords and tenants, producers and consumers, creditors and debtors, polluters and environmentalists, capitalists and workers).[87] The state would not only have to confer legal resources on the unrepresented but also expropriate them from the overrepresented – something liberal legalism would never tolerate. Even were that to be done, the overendowed would simply replace lawyers with others performing similar functions. All attempts to achieve true equality have foundered. Those with better prior endowments always benefit more from redistribution than those with worse. (Trotsky's theory of permanent revolution sought to anticipate this, Mao's Cultural Revolution to overcome it.) Cultural capital is an essential precondition to mobilizing law. People must be able to name their experience as a violation of legal rights and blame someone before they can assert a legal claim about it.[88] Equalizing these forms of legal consciousness would require enormous effort (as consciousness-raising groups discovered during the second wave of feminism).

There have been numerous utopian experiments in helping people function as their own lawyers. "Every Man His Own Lawyer" was in its ninth edition in England by 1784; variants have remained popular for the last two centuries. Law in a Free Society and street law programs educate secondary school students about their rights and duties.[89] Nolo prints legal forms and handbooks.[90] HALT champions self-help efforts.[91] Unbundling seeks to divide tasks into those laypeople can perform for themselves and those that still require lawyers.[92] But all these interventions quickly run up against the efficiencies of the division of labor, identified by Adam Smith. People simply cannot – and do not want to – master all the different kinds of expertise they want to deploy. Revolutionary societies have sought to

[87] Richard L. Abel, *Socializing the Legal Profession: Can Redistributing Lawyers' Services Achieve Social Justice?*, 1 Law & Pol'y Q. 5 (1979).

[88] William L.F. Felstiner, Richard L. Abel & Austin Sarat, *The Emergence and Transformation of Disputes: Naming, Blaming, Claiming...*, 14 Law & Soc'y Rev. 631 (1981).

[89] Law in a Free Society, A Casebook on Responsibility (1972).

[90] Nolo, Welcome to Nolo, http://www.nolo.com.

[91] HALT, http://www.halt.org.

[92] Forrest Mosten, Unbundling Legal Services (2000).

abolish the legal profession: eighteenth-century France, twentieth-century China, Tanzania, Mozambique.[93] But specialized experts have always reemerged. Legal aid schemes are chronically underfunded.[94] Although this is true of all public services, it is aggravated by the fact that legal aid typically is targeted to the poor rather than to a clientele that transcends class (like those served by highways, Social Security, or Medicare).[95] Perhaps more important, unlike education, health care, housing, food, and transportation, law is morally ambiguous. All public services must compete for scarce resources, but there is a broad consensus that providing such services enhances the common good. Law is adversarial; both sides make irreconcilable *moral* arguments; one can prevail only by defeating the other. Even if tax dollars were not at stake, there is no general agreement that society would benefit by permitting everyone to make all the claims that law allows. The ease with which the corporate disinformation campaign has convinced so many that we are suffering from a "litigation crisis" fueled by frivolous claims shows how morally tenuous legal rights seem.[96] Furthermore, different legal claims vary in their moral suasion. David Engel has shown that rural Illinois residents feel strongly that contract claims should be enforceable (indeed, by the police!) but tort claims should not.[97] Legislation caps tort damages but does not allow renegotiation of subprime mortgages.[98] Because of voter reluctance to spend tax dollars on legal aid, many have urged greater use of cheaper paralegals.[99] Although I fully acknowledge that many tasks presently performed by lawyers (because of the monopoly the profession created) could be performed just as effectively by others with less expensive educations, I am concerned that we might be entrenching inequality by relegating only the poor to paralegals.[100] We would not do this (comfortably) with education or health care. We generally do not allow people to make the trade-off between price and safety. You can "Rent a Wreck" if you don't care what your rental car looks like. But you can't "Fly a Wreck" in order to enjoy a cheap vacation. Courts have invalidated agreements not to sue[101]

[93] *Cf.* THE POLITICS OF INFORMAL JUSTICE: COMPARATIVE STUDIES (Richard L. Abel ed., 1982).

[94] Richard L. Abel, *Law Without Politics: Legal Aid under Advanced Capitalism*, 32 UCLA L. REV. 474 (1985).

[95] Richard L. Abel, *What Is the Assistance of Counsel Effective For?*, 14 N.Y.U. REV. L. & SOC. CHANGE 165 (1986).

[96] WILLIAM HALTOM & MICHAEL MCCANN, DISTORTING THE LAW: POLITICS, MEDIA, AND THE LITIGATION CRISIS (2004).

[97] Engel, *supra* note 77.

[98] I have written about the ability of tort defendants to use their legislative clout to distort the basically sound general principles of tort law. Richard L. Abel, *Questioning the Counter-Majoritarian Thesis: The Case of Torts*, 49 DEPAUL L. REV. 533 (1999).

[99] John T. Broderick, Jr. & Ronald M. George, *A Nation of Do-It-Yourself Lawyers*, N.Y. TIMES, Jan. 2, 2010, at A21 (the authors of this op ed are the Chief Justices of New Hampshire and California respectively).

[100] HAZEL GENN, UNDERSTANDING CIVIL JUSTICE (1997).

[101] Tunkl v. Regents of Univ. of Cal., 383 P.2d 441 (Cal. 1963); Dalury v. S-K-I, Ltd., 670 A.2d 795 (Vt. 1995).

and the assumption-of-risk defense[102] for precisely this reason. Should we consign the poor to second-class justice?

Cause lawyering is the latest manifestation of law's effort to realize ideals of justice. Although it originated in the United States, its rapid global proliferation is encouraging evidence of law's power to inspire idealism.[103] But cause lawyering encounters greater difficulty in other societies.[104] Unstable regimes are much less tolerant of dissent. Cause lawyers, who risk only professional marginalization in the United States, are often imprisoned or killed elsewhere.[105] Political opposition often shades into violence or guerrilla warfare. Accusations of communism or terrorism have been convenient rationalizations for suppressing dissidents, who are frequently imprisoned indefinitely without trial or "disappeared." Military coups often supplant civilian rule. Constitutions may be paper documents, which no one expects to be enforceable and which change with great rapidity. The legal profession is less supportive of cause lawyering. University legal education may be largely irrelevant to practice or hostile to social change. There are no large firms to do pro bono work. Cause lawyers often depend on the uncertain, sometimes fickle support of foreign foundations, which in turn raise government suspicions and jeopardize domestic legitimacy.[106]

Even in the United States, cause lawyering has an uncertain relationship to justice. My book on South Africa detailed the surprising success of legal challenges to apartheid during its last fifteen years. I approached my study of the defense of legality in post–9/11 America with the expectation that law would be even more effective in limiting the excesses of government power. South Africa had no written constitution, bill of rights, or tradition of judicial review; America has had them for two centuries. All South African judges had been appointed by a National Party committed to apartheid; U.S. judges have been appointed by both parties, which are roughly equally matched and periodically exchange power. The South African legal profession was

[102] Meistrich v. Casino Arena Attractions, Inc., 31 N.J. 44 (1959); McGrath v. American Cyanamid Co., 196 A.2d 238 (N.J. 1963).

[103] *E.g.*, Cause Lawyering and the State in a Global Era (Austin Sarat & Stuart Scheingold eds., 2001); Fighting for Political Freedom: Comparative Studies of the Legal Complex and Political Liberalism, *supra* note 52; Stones of Hope: How African Activists Reclaim Human Rights to Challenge Global Poverty (Lucie White & Jeremy Perelman eds., 2010); Scott L. Cummings, *The Internationalization of Public Interest Law*, 57 Duke L.J. 891 (2008); Scott L. Cummings & Louise Trubek, *Globalizing Public Interest Law*, 13 UCLA J. Int'l L. & Foreign Aff. 1 (2009) (special issue).

[104] Frank Munger, *Cause Lawyers and Other Signs of Progress: Three Thai Narratives* (in this volume).

[105] Josh Kron, *Lawyers Report Intimidation by Rwanda*, N.Y. Times, June 13, 2010, at A16; *Rwanda Charges American Over Articles*, N.Y. Times, June 6, 2010, at A14.

[106] Russia has been hostile to George Soros's Open Society Institute; Tanzania accused Americans supported by the International Legal Center's SAILER Program (Staffing African Institutions of Legal Education and Research) of being CIA agents.

virtually all white and politically disengaged; the American profession was integrated and politically engaged. The United States had created public interest law nearly a hundred years ago; by the twenty-first century, there were many well-funded institutions committed to the rule of law. South Africa excluded much of the foreign media, controlled domestic radio and television, and censored domestic newspapers; the First Amendment protected American media from government interference. Nevertheless, American law has been strikingly ineffective in resisting the excesses of executive and legislative power after 9/11. Few soldiers and almost no officers have suffered significant punishment for the abuse, torture, and killing of detainees in Afghanistan and Iraq. Detainees have languished in Guantanamo Bay for more than eight years, with minimal judicial review. The authors of the Office of Legal Counsel memoranda rationalizing the abuses have never been held to account. Damage claims against the federal government and corporations for deaths, imprisonment, torture, rendition, and wiretapping have been frustrated by claims of state secrets and sovereign immunity. (As I revise this, the Supreme Court has refused to hear an appeal from the dismissal of Maher Arar's claim for rendition to torture in Syria.)

The justice that law promises is ambiguous: Is it formal or substantive?[107] Formal justice can defeat substantive. Herbert Wechsler notoriously argued that school desegregation was inconsistent with "neutral principles" because it violated the First Amendment right of whites not to associate with African Americans.[108] The Supreme Court has used a similar rationale to limit affirmative action.[109] The Court recently insisted that the First Amendment guarantee of free speech allows corporations to spend unlimited amounts in political campaigns.[110] Courts have struck down marriage for same-sex couples and upheld statutory and constitutional bans on it in the name of formal justice. And conservative cause lawyers have thrived under the umbrella of formal justice.[111] Formal justice allows property owners to oppose condemnation under the takings clause, corporations to resist regulation in the name of due process, and right-to-life groups to oppose abortion. Formal justice exaggerates the coercion of state action and obscures constraint in the private sphere.

Let me conclude with a problem that pervades many of the examples just mentioned: the tension between law and democracy. Social justice advocates seek to empower subordinated peoples to resist their oppression. Theorists like Paulo

107 Max Weber, Law in Economy and Society (Max Rheinstein ed., 1967).

108 Herbert Wechsler, *Toward Neutral Principles of Constitutional Law*, 73 Harv. L. Rev. 1 (1959).

109 Regents of the University of California v. Bakke, 438 U.S. 265 (1978); *cf.* Gruter v. Bollinger, 539 U.S. 306 (2003).

110 Citizens United v. Federal Election Commission, 130 S. Ct. 876 (2010).

111 Ann Southworth, Lawyers of the Right: Professionalizing the Conservative Coalition (2008); Kevin R. Den Dulk, *In Legal Culture, but Not of It*, *in* Cause Lawyers and Social Movements 197 (Austin Sarat & Stuart Scheingold eds., 2006); Ann Southworth, Anthony Paik & John P. Heinz, *Lawyers in National Policymaking* (in this volume).

Freire,[112] Saul Alinsky,[113] and Ivan Illich[114] share a vision of radical democracy. Law plays an ambiguous role in realizing that ideal. On one hand, it can endow the oppressed with valuable resources: cognitive, political, economic, and social. On the other, it runs the risk of cultural imperialism, replacing one set of oppressors with another, perpetuating a cycle of dependence.[115] Derrick Bell criticized civil rights lawyers for championing school desegregation whether their black clients wanted it or not.[116] Gramsci sought to solve this problem with his theory of organic intellectuals, who embodied the interests of the proletariat without belonging to it. Cause lawyers want to be on tap, not on top.[117] They feel guilty about not sharing the suffering of those they represent, about the ease with which they can escape to the security and comfort of their bourgeois lives. (The need to identify completely with those you champion is a recurrent theme in both classical mythology and Christianity.) Anxieties about compromise, about legitimating the legal system by participating in it, lead some cause lawyers to cross the line to political action, illegality, even violence.[118]

Adversaries of cause lawyers exploit their ambiguous relationship to their clients, characterizing the lawyers as self-serving agitators, demagogues, troublemakers who exploit the poor for their own pecuniary interest. This is how most white Southerners responded to Northern civil rights lawyers. It was the justification for many of the restrictions on Legal Services Corporation lawyers. It is one basis for criticisms of class action and plaintiff's personal injury lawyers (whose fees consume a significant fraction of the recovery – sometimes all of it). It has been used to attack "fat cat" English barristers handling legal aid cases[119] and to condemn "supplier induced demand."[120]

Cultural sensitivity and political modesty undoubtedly are virtues. But cause lawyers cannot let themselves be paralyzed by self-doubt, guilt, and skepticism. I wrote at the end of my book on law in the struggle against apartheid: "Human rights lawyers,

[112] Paulo Freire, Pedagogy of the Oppressed (Myra Bergman Ramos, trans., 1970).

[113] Saul Alinsky, Rules for Radicals (1971).

[114] Ivan Illich, Deschooling Society (1971); Ivan Illich, Tools for Conviviality (1973).

[115] Much of Lucie White's work struggles with this problem, notably *Subordination, Rhetorical Survival Skills, and Sunday Shoes: Notes on the Hearing of Mrs. G.*, 38 Buff. L. Rev. 1 (1990); *see also* Lucie E. White, *African Youth Mobilize Against Garbage: Economic and Social Rights Advocacy and the Practice of Democracy* (in this volume).

[116] Derrick Bell, *Serving Two Masters: Integration Ideals and Client Interests in School Desegregation Litigation*, 85 Yale L.J. 470 (1976).

[117] For a much more nuanced account of the relationship between lawyers and clients, see Philip Lewis, *Aspects of Professionalism: Constructing the Lawyer-Client Relationship* (in this volume).

[118] William Kunstler in the Chicago Eight trial; Lynne Stewart for the blind sheikh.

[119] Abel, English Lawyers between Market and State, *supra* note 20, at 310–15.

[120] Gwyn Bevan, Tony Holland & Martin Partington, Organising Cost-Effective Access to Justice (1994).

like other progressives, too often frame the issue dichotomously: Law either makes all the difference or no difference at all." Maybe it is age – but I am a confirmed incrementalist. Any defense of the rule of law is better than capitulation to executive autarchy. Lawyers deserve praise for devoting effort to promoting justice – not criticism for failing to do more. Lawyers can trust clients – who have been schooled by suffering, tempered by tribulation – to know their own minds. Victories, even small ones, inspire further resistance, not resignation to the status quo. The struggle for justice never ends; but each chapter inspires future generations to persevere.

Index